The Savvy
Investor's
Internet
Resource

The Savvy Investor's Internet Resource

Bryan Pfaffenberger and Claire Mencke

Foreword by Beth Sawi
Executive Vice President, Electronic Brokerage
Charles Schwab & Co., Inc.

IDG BOOKS WORLDWIDE

IDG Books Worldwide, Inc.
An International Data Group Company

Foster City, CA ✦ Chicago, IL ✦ Indianapolis, IN ✦ Dallas, TX

The Savvy Investor's Internet Resource

Published by

IDG Books Worldwide, Inc.

An International Data Group Company

919 E. Hillsdale Blvd.

Suite 400

Foster City, CA 94404

Library of Congress Catalog Card No.: 96-78767

ISBN: 0-7645-3010-0

Printed in the United States of America

10 9 8 7 6 5 4 3 2 1

IB/RU/RR/ZW/FC

Distributed in the United States by IDG Books Worldwide, Inc.

Distributed by Macmillan Canada for Canada; by Computer and Technical Books for the Caribbean Basin; by Contemporantea de Ediciones for Venezuela; by Distribuidora Cuspide for Argentina; by CITFC for Brazil; by Ediciones ZETA S.C.R. Ltda. for Peru; by Editorial Limusa SA for Mexico; by Transworld Publishers Limited in the United Kingdom and Europe; by Al-Maiman Publishers & Distributors for Saudi Arabia; by Simron Pty. Ltd. for South Africa; by IDG Communications (IIK) Ltd. for Hong Kong; by Toppan Company Ltd. for Japan; by Addison Wesley Publishing Company for Korea; by Longman Singapore Publisher Ltd. for Singapore, Malaysia, Thailand, and Indonesia; by Unalis Corporation for Taiwan; by WS Computer Publishing Company, Inc. for the Philippines; by WoodsLane Enterprises Ltd. for New Zealand.

For general information on IDG Books in the U.S., including information on discounts and premiums, contact IDG Books at 800-434-3422 or 415-655-3000.

For information on where to purchase IDG Books outside the U.S., contact IDG Books International at 415-655-3021 or fax 415-655-3295.

For information on translations, contact Marc Jeffrey Mikulich, Director, Foreign and Subsidiary Rights, at IDG Books Worldwide, 415-655-3018 or fax 415-655-3295.

For sales inquiries and special prices for bulk quantities, write to the address above or call IDG Books Worldwide at 415-655-3000.

For information on using IDG Books in the classroom, or for ordering examination copies, contact Jim Kelly at 800-434-2086.

 is a trademark under exclusive license to IDG Books Worldwide, Inc., from International Data Group, Inc.

Dedication

For Suzanne, always.
Bryan Pfaffenberger

To Arul.
Claire Mencke

About the Authors

Bryan Pfaffenberger is a nationally recognized expert on the Internet. A professor in the University of Virginia's pioneering Division of Technology, Culture, and Communication, where he specializes in studying the impact of the Internet and intranets on corporations and government organizations, he is the author of numerous best-selling books on the Internet (including *The World Wide Web Bible, Internet in Plain English,* and *The Official Internet Explorer Book*). He once had numerous hobbies, but all of them — plus all his spare cash — have been swallowed whole by his beloved 34-foot sailboat *Juliana*, which plies the Rappahannock River and Chesapeake Bay, off Virginia's lovely Northern Neck. He lives in the country near Charlottesville, Virginia, with his family and a very spoiled cat.

Claire Mencke is a licensed stockbroker and an individual investor. She learned about value investing principles at *Value Line,* where she was an analyst, and about technical analysis at *Investor's Business Daily,* where she writes about markets. While on the research staff of a Wall Street investment firm, she observed how professional investors put theories of all kinds to work. She lives in upstate New York and hopes to get a private pilot's license some day.

ABOUT IDG BOOKS WORLDWIDE

Welcome to the world of IDG Books Worldwide.

IDG Books Worldwide, Inc., is a subsidiary of International Data Group, the world's largest publisher of computer-related information and the leading global provider of information services on information technology. IDG was founded more than 25 years ago and now employs more than 8,500 people worldwide. IDG publishes more than 275 computer publications in over 75 countries (see listing below). More than 60 million people read one or more IDG publications each month.

Launched in 1990, IDG Books Worldwide is today the #1 publisher of best-selling computer books in the United States. We are proud to have received eight awards from the Computer Press Association in recognition of editorial excellence and three from *Computer Currents'* First Annual Readers' Choice Awards. Our best-selling *...For Dummies*® series has more than 30 million copies in print with translations in 30 languages. IDG Books Worldwide, through a joint venture with IDG's Hi-Tech Beijing, became the first U.S. publisher to publish a computer book in the People's Republic of China. In record time, IDG Books Worldwide has become the first choice for millions of readers around the world who want to learn how to better manage their businesses.

Our mission is simple: Every one of our books is designed to bring extra value and skill-building instructions to the reader. Our books are written by experts who understand and care about our readers. The knowledge base of our editorial staff comes from years of experience in publishing, education, and journalism — experience we use to produce books for the '90s. In short, we care about books, so we attract the best people. We devote special attention to details such as audience, interior design, use of icons, and illustrations. And because we use an efficient process of authoring, editing, and desktop publishing our books electronically, we can spend more time ensuring superior content and spend less time on the technicalities of making books.

You can count on our commitment to deliver high-quality books at competitive prices on topics you want to read about. At IDG Books Worldwide, we continue in the IDG tradition of delivering quality for more than 25 years. You'll find no better book on a subject than one from IDG Books Worldwide.

John Kilcullen
President and CEO
IDG Books Worldwide, Inc.

Eighth Annual
Computer Press
Awards ≥1992

Ninth Annual
Computer Press
Awards ≥1993

Tenth Annual
Computer Press
Awards ≥1994

Eleventh Annual
Computer Press
Awards ≥1995

Foreword

There's a new player on the investing scene, and it's making headlines: the Internet.

More so than ever before, individual investors possess the tools and resources they need to make informed investing choices. By means of the Internet, you can frame investment goals, determine how to allocate your assets, obtain valuable performance data for stocks and mutual funds, and even trade stocks and funds online. What's more, the Internet enables you to perform these tasks in a fraction of the time they formerly consumed.

Thanks to the Internet, people who otherwise wouldn't have the time can plan intelligently, obtain the needed facts, and make informed investment decisions. That's nothing short of a revolution, and it's going to change the face of investing. But there's a lot out there, and not all of it is trustworthy. To find your way toward successful investing on the Internet, you need much more than a catalog of Internet sites (although you find a great one in this book's "Internet Investing Directory"). You need expert guidance as you apply Internet tools to a well-thought-out investment strategy.

And that's just what you find in *The Savvy Investor's Internet Resource*. Drawing on her considerable investment expertise as a reporter with *Investor's Business Daily,* Claire Mencke organizes this book in line with an excellent, overall investment strategy — and Internet guru Bryan Pfaffenberger shows you how to harness the Net's incredible resources as you put this strategy into play, step by step. You couldn't ask for a more capable team!

At Charles Schwab, our motto is "helping investors help themselves." And that's why we've made a major commitment to Internet investing, including online research and trading. Please be sure to visit Schwab*NOW!* (http://www.schwab.com). You find great material to get going with your own investment strategy, including interactive tools for setting your goals and allocating resources, performance data for over 1,100 mutual funds available through Schwab, and online question-and-answer forums with leading investment professionals.

Beth Sawi
Executive Vice President, Electronic Brokerage
Charles Schwab & Co., Inc.

Credits

Senior Vice President & Group Publisher
Brenda McLaughlin

Acquisitions Manager
Gregory Croy

Acquisitions Editor
Ellen L. Camm

Software Acquisitions Editor
Tracy Lehman Cramer

Marketing Manager
Melisa M. Duffy

Managing Editor
Andy Cummings

Editorial Assistant
Timothy J. Borek

Production Director
Andrew Walker

Production Associate
Christopher Pimentel

Project Coordinator
Katy German

Supervisor of Page Layout
Craig A. Harrison

Reprint Coordination
Tony Augsburger
Theresa Sánchez-Baker
Elizabeth Cardenas-Nelson

Blueline Coordination
Patricia R. Reynolds

Media/Archive Coordination
Leslie Popplewell
Melissa Stauffer
Jason Marcuson

Development Editor
Susan Pines

Copy Editor
Nate Holdread

Technical Reviewer
Adam B. Bergman
Equity Analyst
Scott & Stringfellow, Inc.

Production Staff
Mario F. Amador
Laura Carpenter
Kurt Krames
Mark Schumann
Dale Smith

Proofreader
Kathy McGuinness

Indexer
Anne Leach

Cover Design
Shurtz/Capriotti

Acknowledgments

Bryan Pfaffenberger:

The Internet opens new possibilities for empowering individual investors, and it's a genuine pleasure to help bring this important news to a wider public. Many people have joined the crusade, and contributed in many ways. I'd like particularly to thank Ellen Camm, Acquisitions Editor, whose good humor, patience, and excellent communication skills made this project enjoyable from start to finish. This book's excellent editorial team, led by Sue Pines, combed through all that follows with the reader's needs uppermost in their minds—and managed to do so with wit and diplomacy, much appreciated by beleaguered authors! Kudos to Nate Holdread and Katy German and the rest of the editorial and production team — thanks, all! This book's technical editor, Adam Bergman, brought his impressive acumen and intelligence to this project, and contributed in many substantive ways. Special thanks to John Bozeman for his adept research and assistance. Thanks to my able co author, Claire, for patience, erudition, and good humor throughout. Most of all, I'd like to thank my family for putting up with long hours at the keyboard, and the long, unrequested (and generally unappreciated) dinner table lectures about the need to start investing now instead of putting it off until you're my age!

Claire Mencke:

In addition to the editorial team of IDG Books, which got me into this project in the first place, I'd like to thank Bryan, who's worked a lot of magic in linking the technical, financial, and graphical features of the book. I'd also like to recognize the contribution of Veena Merchant, who's helped me rethink my notions about portfolios and financial advice.

(The publisher would like to give special thanks to Patrick J. McGovern, without whom this book would not have been possible.)

Contents at a Glance

Table of Contents

Chapter 18: Digging Deeper: Putting a Company into Context 301

Chapter 19: Choosing an Internet Brokerage 319

Chapter 23: Investing in Treasury Bills, Notes, and Bonds 381

Part VII: Personal Finance on the Internet 393

Chapter 24: Finding Personal Finance Resources 395

Internet Investing Directory 449

The Companion CD-ROM 529

Introduction

The Internet is many things — a rich source of entertainment, a tool for career advancement, and just plain fun. It's also the greatest single resource ever placed in the hands of the individual investor.

Why? In investing, the name of the game is information — quality, *timely* information. Say you've just been told about a great mutual fund. What's the fund's Morningstar rating? (Morningstar is an analysis firm that publishes *risk-adjusted* ratings of thousands of mutual funds. The funds with the highest ratings produce good gains — but without taking undue risk with your capital.) Without being able to put your hands on the right information, finding the right investment can seem like trying to pin the tail on the donkey.

This is where the Internet comes in. Put simply, the Internet is The Great Equalizer: It gives you the research power that was formerly restricted to investment professionals (or amateurs with lots of time on their hands). With a modicum of Internet knowledge and this book to help you, you can quickly research mutual fund, stock, and bond investment opportunities. You won't have to spend hours in a library, and you won't have to depend on a broker's possibly biased advice. You can find the facts yourself, and, what's more, you can manage your investments like a pro.

Skeptical? After reading this book, you'll know how to do the following, and much more:

◆ Use computer tools to sift through thousands of mutual funds so that you can identify the ones that best align with your investment goals.

◆ Set up a secure, private portfolio of your mutual funds on the Internet, with automatic share price updates. You'll be able to see at a glance how your investments are doing.

◆ Screen thousands of stocks for the ones that meet your investment criteria, such as a low price-earnings (P/E) ratio.

◆ Immediately access in-depth information about companies that you're thinking about investing in, including annual and quarterly reports, analysts' reports and recommendations, and news that may affect the company's future earnings.

◆ Obtain delayed or real-time stock quotes and display them throughout the day, and even set an alarm so that you're notified when a stock's price reaches a level that you've specified.

◆ Open an account with an Internet-based brokerage firm, enabling you to initiate buy and sell orders from your keyboard — at the lowest commission rates you find anywhere.

◆ Get all the information you need to buy Treasury bills, notes, and bonds without the aid of a broker.

The Savvy Investor's Internet Resource shows you how to make the Internet an ally, a powerful ally, in your quest for financial security. No matter what your investment objective may be, you want to make the maximum possible use of the Internet's immensely rich information resources.

What's even more amazing, as you'll discover, is that almost all the resources discussed in this book are *free*, after you pay your monthly bill for Internet access. The Internet is not only the greatest resource ever made available to individual investors but also the biggest bargain.

Who Should Read This Book?

Anyone who wants to get involved in mutual fund, stock, or bond investing and wants to make full and intelligent use of the Internet while doing so should read this book. It doesn't matter whether you're new to the Internet, new to investing, or — like millions of people — both.

◆ Are you somewhat experienced with investing but know little about the Internet? You find a concise, readable introduction to the Internet and Internet services, written from the investor's point of view. The first two chapters of this book provide the background and introduction that you need.

◆ Are you an Internet user but new to investing? You find readable, plain English explanations of investment concepts and strategies throughout this book, beginning with a good, solid tutorial about setting your investment objectives. (And, of course, you learn how you can put some nifty Internet tools to work for you while you're doing it.)

◆ Are you new to both the Internet and investing? We explain everything, every step of the way. New investment or Internet terms are flagged with a Key Term icon, and you find plain English definitions of all the key investment and Internet concepts that this book introduces.

What's So Special About This Book?

You find plenty of books about online or Internet investing that amount to little more than a survey of Web sites. (A *Web site* is a location on the World Wide Web where you can find information.) There's plenty of great stuff on the Web, and this book points you to hundreds of the best Web sites.

But frankly, a mere catalog of Web sites isn't worth much to you in the long run, for the simple reason that it would quickly go out of date. Thousands of new Web pages appear daily, and sometimes old pages move — or just disappear. You need something more than a catalog. You need a book that presents an *Internet strategy* for investment decision-making, one that places Internet tools within the broader context of a well- thought approach to investing. You need a book with a critical approach that highlights the dangers as well as the possibilities of Internet use. This book's CD-ROM offers helpful information and programs to enhance your research.

An Internet strategy for investment decision making

This book offers much more than a mere catalog of Web sites. It teaches a *strategy* for fully exploiting the riches of the Internet, and, what's more, it shows you how to weave the Internet's powerful tools into your overall investment plan. *The Savvy Investor's Internet Resource* doesn't so much tell you *what's* out there to help you as *how* you can use Internet tools to think through the key investment decisions you'll make.

Here's an example. Thinking about buying a stock? In this book, you learn how you can use the Internet as a superb research tool to get news about the company that issues the stock. You'll be able to answer questions such as these: What's going on in the company's industry? What external factors — such as changing interest rates or currency fluctuations — tend to affect stock prices in this industry? Is this firm involved in any high-stakes lawsuits? Are its finances in good shape?

A comprehensive strategy for intelligent investing

This book doesn't throw the Internet at you without placing it in a broader context; specifically, a comprehensive strategy for intelligent investing. *The Savvy Investor's Internet Resource* takes you step-by-step through the whole investment process, beginning with determining your investment objectives. The book continues with asset allocation and moves on to explore investing in mutual funds, stocks, bonds, and personal finance. At each step of the way, you learn how to put the Internet's most powerful tools and richest information resources to work for you.

A critical approach

Too many computer books convey the "gee-whiz" boosterism that's all too common in computer industry marketing. It's understandable, to be sure — these computer tools really are quite nifty. But this book puts your interests first. It tells you honestly where you're likely to find the best and most reliable resources, and where you'll waste your time. There's too much valuable material on the Net for you to waste your time with unreliable, untrustworthy, or poorly developed material. A case in point: This book's "Internet Investing Directory," which is the first resource to rank investment-related Internet sites using a four-star system.

While surfing the Web or engaging in Usenet discussions, you may hear about "sure-fire" investment opportunities that sound too good to be true. And they aren't true! Sad to say, scams are just as common on the Internet as they are elsewhere in life. That's why this book takes a critical approach to the Internet, stressing the good, reliable sources of information and the sound, responsible investments. You find plenty of warnings that help tip you off to something that's shady or downright criminal. In many ways, the Internet is like a big city; it's full of exciting and useful resources but a bit dangerous if you don't know what you're doing. With this book to help you, you can find your way safely.

What Doesn't This Book Cover?

According to investment professionals, the typical individual investor should allocate assets among insured savings accounts, money market funds, mutual funds, stocks, bonds, and cash and defer or avoid speculative investments, such as commodities, margin trading, "penny" stocks, and private partnerships. Although you can find Internet resources for these and other speculative investments, this book focuses on the three standbys: mutual funds, stocks, and bonds. This isn't to say that these investments aren't risky — some of them are *very* risky, particularly if you aren't able to hang on to them for several years — but they don't fall into the outright speculation category. We're talking about *investing* here, not betting the family farm on some crazy, speculative scheme that you don't fully understand.

Also not covered are the many resources available through online services, such as America Online or CompuServe. There's a simple reason for this exclusion: Most information providers are in the midst of making the move from online services to the Internet. It's cheaper for these providers to set up a Web server than it is to pay the online services' hefty fees. And it's cheaper for you, too, because most of the Web sites discussed in this book offer impressive and useful information for free. In short, the action is moving to the Internet, and you should, too. If you currently subscribe to an online service, you still can make full use of this book because all online services now provide Internet access.

How Is This Book Organized?

The Savvy Investor's Internet Resource begins by introducing the Internet and moves on to help you frame your investment objectives. Next, the book turns to mutual funds, stocks, and bonds, and it concludes with a section on personal finance. Throughout, you learn how to make Internet tools work for you, whether you're trying to figure out how much of your money to place into stocks or whether it's better to lease or buy a new car.

Part I: New Internet Tools for Individual Investors

You should start here if your new to the Internet (or want a plain English explanation of what all the excitement is about).

In Chapter 1, "Introducing the Internet," you learn what the Internet is and how it differs from online services. You find out how to get connected to the Internet. Also covered is the important issue of Internet security.

Chapter 2, "Understanding Internet Tools," introduces the powerful tools that you can use to exploit the Internet's vast information resources. These tools include electronic mail, mailing lists, Usenet, Telnet, FTP, Archie, Gopher, and the World Wide Web.

Part II: Developing Your Investment Strategy

If you're a beginning investor, or if you've never approached investing in an organized way, this part of *The Savvy Investor's Internet Resource* is a great place to start your exploration of Internet investing.

Chapter 3, "What is Investing?," introduces the basic concepts of investing, such as the risk/reward payoff, the difference between investing and just buying an investment, and strategies for intelligent investing. You learn how you can further educate yourself using some excellent Internet tutorials.

In Chapter 4, "Determining Your Investment Goals," you put the Internet to work for you as you calculate your net worth, decide what you're investing for, determine your investment objectives, assess your risk tolerance, and allocate your assets. Here's where you put together your long-term plan for achieving your investment objectives.

Part III: Getting Your Bearings on the Internet

Keeping up with the Internet is like trying to change a tire on a moving truck — thousands of new Web sites appear every day. To get the most out of the Internet as a tool for individual investing, you need to know not only where the good sites are but how to find the best new ones. Part 3 introduces a *strategy for Internet knowledge acquisition* that will serve you long after some of the discussed sites disappear into the void.

Chapter 5, "Investment-Related Starting Points," introduces the Internet's best starting points for investors. By visiting these Web pages, and revisiting them as the listed Web sites come and go, you learn how to stay on top of the Net's rich but fast-changing resources.

Internet search services are the focus of Chapter 6, "Finding the Information You Need." With more than 55 million documents available on the Web, you need powerful tools to find and display the information you're looking for; happily, they're available. However, you need to know a few good tricks, explained in this chapter, to make full use of these services.

Chapter 7, "Keeping in Touch," details the Internet's uses as a publication and communication medium. You learn how to find and read fast-breaking financial and investment news, how to set up automatic e-mail notification services so that important bulletins appear in your e-mail mailbox, and how to access Web versions of print-based publications in the finance and investment areas.

In Chapter 8, "Using Investment-Related Newsgroups," you learn about the uses and abuses of investment-related discussion groups on Usenet, a computer discussion system available on the Internet.

Part IV: Researching Mutual Funds on the Internet

In this section you find find everything you need to know to select the right mutual funds for your investment objectives — with the Internet's help, naturally!

If you're new to mutual funds, be sure to read Chapter 9, "Understanding Mutual Funds." You learn all the basics of mutual funds, and you'll understand why they're so popular.

Chapter 10, "Finding Funds that Meet Your Objectives," shows you how to put the Internet's powerful tools to work as you screen through thousands of mutual funds, looking for those that meet your investment goals.

"Assessing Mutual Fund Risks and Costs," Chapter 11, shows you how to put the Internet to work as you do some more fund screening. In this chapter, you look for funds that don't take undue risks with your money (while still producing good returns).

In Chapter 12, "Finding and Reading Fund Prospectuses," you learn how you can find and download mutual fund prospectuses from the Internet. Prospectuses are packed with information about funds in which you're thinking about investing. You also learn how to scan prospectuses for the information that you're looking for, information that gives you important clues about the fund's true investment philosophy, which may not be readily apparent in its advertising.

Chapter 13, "Managing Your Mutual Fund Portfolio," shows you how to track your funds using Internet- or PC-based tools. You can see at a glance how your funds are performing. If a fund falls below your definition of acceptable performance, you may want to consider switching to another.

Part V: Researching and Trading Stocks on the Internet

After you've gotten some experience with mutual funds, you may wish to try your hand at stocks. As you'll quickly discover, the Internet provides excellent resources for researching stocks and the companies that issue them. Part 5 is nothing less than a systematic approach to every aspect of stock investing on the Internet, from initial research to opening an Internet brokerage account and tracking your portfolio's performance.

In Chapter 14, "Getting Started with Stocks," you find a concise, readable introduction to investing in stocks, and you learn how to match stocks with your investment objectives. You exploit Internet resources that teach you several respected approaches to stock selection.

Chapter 15, "Getting Stock Quotes and Charts," shows you how to obtain free delayed stock quotes from the Internet and how to display graphs of stock performance.

Chapter 16, "Deciding Whether the Price is Right," shows you how to use the Internet to search for bargain stocks — stocks that appear to be priced below their true value.

Savvy investors know that revealing information about publicly-held companies is available in annual reports and other documents filed with the Securities and Exchange Commission (SEC). Savvy Internet users know that these documents are available online. Chapter 17, "Finding Information about Public Companies," shows you how to research companies using these indispensable resources, which are available for free, 24 hours per day.

In Chapter 18, "Digging Deeper: Putting a Company into Context," you learn how to make intelligent use of the Internet's search tools to build your own, detailed profile of a company. This profile includes what sort of industry the company is in, how it's doing in relation to other companys in the industry, whether it's involved in potentially dangerous lawsuits, and much more.

Ready to invest? In Chapter 19, "Choosing an Internet Brokerage," you learn how to place buy and sell orders for stock directly on the Internet — and get the lowest possible commission rates in the bargain. This chapter surveys other types of brokerages, as well, and provides some sound advice as you think through the broker-selection process.

Chapter 20, "Managing Your Stock Portfolio," explains how you can use Internet- or PC-based tools to keep track of your stock portfolio

Charles Schwab's e.Schwab and Schwab*NOW!* services provide the focus of Chapter 21. You learn how this leading discount brokerage is bringing its respected services to the Internet.

Part VI: Researching and Buying Bonds and Treasuries on the Internet

They aren't as sexy as mutual funds or stocks, but bonds — including U.S. Treasury bills, bonds, and notes — have a place in every investor's portfolio.

Chapter 22, "Introducing Bonds," surveys the various types of bonds available and shows you how to use the Internet to full potential as you research bond opportunities.

Chapter 23, "Investing in Treasury Bills, Notes, and Bonds," shows you how to use the Internet to track these popular Treasury investments and how to buy them directly from the Treasury, without paying a broker's commission.

Part VII: Personal Finances on the Internet

When it comes to personal finances — banking, college financing, credit cards, insurance, loans, and home mortgages — you'll find that the Internet is a useful resource. In this part of *The Savvy Investor's Internet Resource,* you learn how to track down the best loan rates, research college scholarship opportunities, get help with your taxes, and much more.

Chapter 24, "Finding Personal Finance Resources," is your guide to the best personal finance pages on the Net. These information centers keep you up to date on the latest and best Internet offerings in every area of personal finance.

In Chapter 25, "Banking on the Internet," you explore the fast-breaking new world of Internet banking. Already, you can open an Internet bank account, which offers the impressive convenience of automatic checkbook reconciliation. Most banks are planning some kind of foray into cyberspace, and this chapter helps you make an intelligent choice among the options that they're planning to give you.

Chapter 26, "Paying Your Bills on the Net," introduces electronic bill paying via the Internet and dial-up services. You learn about the benefits — and risks — of paying your bills via electronic transfers.

In Chapter 27, "Comparing and Analyzing Loans," you learn how the Internet can help you select the best loan for your needs. You make use of sophisticated, Net-based calculators that assist you in such planning tasks as lease versus buy decisions.

The Internet Investing Directory

The Internet is bulging with resources for investors, but not all of them are of high quality. In the Internet Investing Directory, this book's final section, you find reviews of hundreds of investment-related Internet resources. Based on a four-star system, this directory help you quickly identify high-quality resources for your investment needs.

Tips on Using This Book

Look for the following icons in this book's margins:

One of the best resources of its type on the entire Internet.

A valuable or noteworthy feature — don't miss this!

A term you need to know, with a plain-English definition.

A trick or some inside info that's known to the Internet cognoscente — and useful for you, too.

Something to watch out for!

A Word from the Authors

The Internet may be the investor's dream come true: It's an immensely valuable resource for selecting the right investment and managing your investments after you make them. But don't forget that mutual funds, stocks, and bonds aren't insured the way FDIC-insured savings accounts are. Share and bond prices can fall as well as rise. With this risk comes the hope of greater reward. Stocks, for example, have outperformed savings accounts by a wide margin throughout most of this century, but the gains may materialize only after some years. You shouldn't invest in mutual funds, stocks, or bonds until you've thought through your investment objectives, determined your tolerance for risk, and devoted some thought to how you should spread your money around so that risk is minimized. Please be sure to read Part II carefully.

One additional caution: Internet technology, including Java programs, enables you to keep up with minute-by-minute gyrations in the markets. In fact, you learn how you can set up your portfolio on a secure, private Web site so that you log on throughout the day to see how your stocks are doing. That's fun, but don't let this technology deter you from the long-range investment philosophy that this book recommends. Most investors should be thinking in terms of 15 years, not 15 minutes!

Please bear in mind, too, that Internet sites come and go. Some of the sites discussed in this book may have moved, or disappeared entirely, by the time this book reaches your hands. If the site has moved, you may see a link informing you of the site's new location. If not, try using a search engine, such as AltaVista or Lycos, to locate the resource you're looking for. Also, note that valuable new resources are bound to appear; be sure to keep checking this book's recommended starting points for the latest and best new additions.

I
PART

The New Internet Tools
for Individual Investors

Introducing the Internet

The Internet. You've heard about it, and now you're going to experience it. With this book as your guide, the Internet is about to become your ally in a comprehensive investment strategy.

However, first you need an overview of the Internet. That's the job of this chapter. If you're already familiar with the basic concepts of the Internet, including how it differs from online services, you may want to skip to the next chapter, which discusses specific Internet tools (including Usenet, newsgroups, and the Web) and shows how these tools can be used as part of your investment strategy.

A Brief, Nontechnical Definition of the Internet

KEY TERM

Essentially, the Internet is not a computer network, such as the one you may be using at work. Computer networks physically connect a few dozen computers by means of cables. The Internet is actually a means of *linking* computer networks — it's an *internetwork*, or internet for short — as well as individual computers, which results in a system capable of linking *millions* of computers (perhaps billions, eventually.) And, unlike the networks you've seen in offices or corporate buildings, the Internet can span enormous distances: It's a *wide-area network*, capable of linking

In This Chapter

- ◆ A brief, nontechnical introduction to the Internet
- ◆ What about online services?
- ◆ How do you connect to the Internet?
- ◆ Shopping for your Internet connection
- ◆ What's the World Wide Web?
- ◆ Is all that cool Web stuff really free?
- ◆ What about security?
- ◆ Is the Internet really useful?

computers from Timbuktu to Tucumcari. Wide-area networks (WANs) make use of high-capacity telephone lines, microwave relays, and even satellite links to convey computer data across vast distances.

There's only one Internet, with a capital *I*. However, many smaller internets are in action, including a new arrival on the scene, corporate *intranets*, which are designed to provide Internet-like services (including the Web) for internal, corporate purposes. But the Internet is the big, publicly accessible network that you've heard so much about.

By any standard, the Internet's pretty big. In use (by one estimate) by 33 million people in more than 100 countries, the Internet is an amazing outgrowth of the computer era. What's more, it's growing at an almost unbelievably fast rate — according to some estimates, roughly ten percent per *month*. According to some predictions, one in three U.S. households will have Internet connectivity by the year 2000. A host of firms are making Internet access available virtually everywhere; these firms include cable television companies, long-distance telephone companies (such as AT&T, Sprint, and MCI), local telephone companies, online services such as The Microsoft Network and America Online, and independent Internet Service Providers (ISPs).

The Internet is creating so much excitement because of the following:

◆ **The beauty of the Internet is that it can connect physically dissimilar computers.** It doesn't matter whether you're using a Macintosh, a PC, a UNIX computer, or something else — you can connect to the Internet using any system. You also can exchange rich data, including graphics and multimedia, with people who have different types of computers. If you think about what happened the last time you observed a Mac user try to give a disk to a Windows user, you'll appreciate the importance of connecting dissimilar computers.

◆ **Connecting to the Internet expands your computer's potential by an almost unbelievable factor.** Without using the Internet, you're restricted to using the files and programs on your computer. After connecting to the Internet, more than 195,000 computer programs and 35 million documents become accessible to you. The downside of this is that there's no central organization to give shape and order to this content, so getting lost is easy.

◆ **Unlike broadcast media (such as TV or radio), the Internet enables ordinary people to become *producers* as well as consumers of information.** This means that anyone, including you, can share expertise and experience with others who have similar interests. Altruistically minded individuals can share their experience and expertise, but sharing also opens the door to crooks and con artists.

◆ **The World Wide Web makes the Internet easy to use and adds the excitement of multimedia** (sound, graphics, animation, videos, and more). Many talented designers are working in the Web medium now, and the best sites have a slick, professional feel, similar to a high-quality, upscale magazine (for an example, see Figure 1-1).

◆ **Currently, more than 35 million documents are available for free on the World Wide Web.** Much is dreck, but there are diamonds, too, and this book helps you find them.

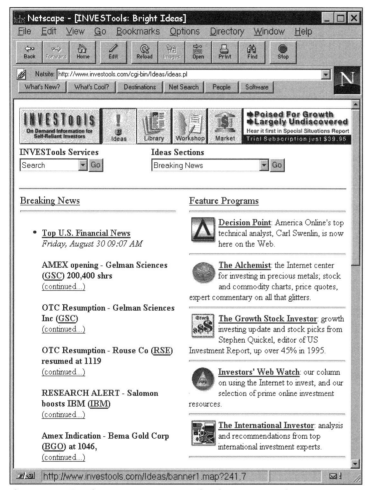

Figure 1-1: Graphics, interactivity, and rich resources characterize today's Web offerings (INVESTools).

What's the Internet about? To put it succinctly, we're witnessing the birth of a new public communications medium, comparable to the telephone network, radio, or television. But the Internet outstrips all its predecessors in offering an unbelievable wealth of information. At last count, the Lycos search engine (which prowls the Internet in search of new documents) found more than 55 million resources, including documents, programs, graphics, sounds, and videos.

What does the Internet mean for you, an investor? You have a new, powerful way to access information. Computers can sort through billions of documents in seconds, pinpointing just what you're looking for. Potentially, that means power — power for you.

Where did the Internet come from?

Whatever conclusion historians reach about the Cold War, one thing is clear — Cold War military research created many gadgets and goodies for civilians. Coming soon to an automobile near you, for example, is a homing device that automatically and instantly locates your position on a map display. Or pick up a pair of night-vision goggles and find out what your neighbors do in their backyards at night.

The Internet is another product of space-age U.S. military research. In the mid-1960s, military planners realized that computer networks would be needed to control the nation's defense systems. In those days, computer networks required one huge, centralized computer — an easy target for the enemy. So the planners put out a call for research. They wanted a *decentralized* computer system.

The Internet is the end product of this research. It began in the early 1970s as a military research network called ARPANET. (The name ARPANET is derived from the Advanced Research Projects Network [ARPA], a U.S. government agency that sponsored the Internet's early development.) Because ARPANET proved so valuable for research collaboration, the early ARPANET was split into two parts: a military research network (MILNET) and a civilian research network (NSFNET), sponsored by the National Science Foundation (NSF). Linking thousands of colleges and universities worldwide, NSFNET grew into the Internet. During most of the 1980s, the Internet's character was mainly academic and had little impact on the public. Because the network was funded by a U.S. government research agency, commercial use of the Net was sharply restricted. But privatization was not long in coming. Realizing that the Internet had enormous commercial potential, regional service providers transformed themselves from nonprofit university consortia into for-profit Internet Service Providers and built network communication lines that bypassed the government-subsidized ones. Commercial use of the Internet skyrocketed. By the mid-1990s, the Internet began its migration into the civilian sector — and that's the network we have today.

By the way, the Internet met its design goals well: It's a decentralized network that can keep functioning even if big parts of it have been blown to smithereens. That was proved during the Gulf war. Try as they might, the allied forces were never quite able to knock out Saddam Hussein's command-and-control (C&C) network. Guess why? It was based on Internet technology.

What About Online Services?

For investors thinking about going online with a modem, there's another option besides getting an Internet subscription. Online services such as Prodigy, America Online, and CompuServe offer computer users the option of subscribing to a service that provides controlled content as well as open-ended discussion groups. To make content available on an online service, a content provider must pay a fee and meet the service's quality guidelines. These services also enable you to access the Internet.

Online services have advantages

For beginning computer users, online services make good sense. In place of the Internet's decentralized anarchy, an online service gives you a single, well-organized access point. You can see at a glance what's available, and it's easy to find the resources you're looking for. Some Internet services, such as Yahoo!, try to provide a subject catalog of Internet resources, but so far they've managed to index quite a small fraction of what's available.

You find some valuable investment resources on America Online and other online services. On America Online, for example, you find NAII Online, a compendium of hundreds of articles on investing basics that's maintained by the National Association of Individual Investors. In addition to content sites, online services offer topical discussion groups that — unlike their Internet counterparts — are almost always moderated by someone who knows the topic well.

Content is migrating to the Web

Online services provide lots of great content today, but is this content going to be available in the future? Think of the economics for a minute. Content providers must pay stiff fees to keep their content available on the online service's computers. If they set up their own Internet sites, they can make the same material without paying those stiff fees. Not surprisingly, content providers are steadily moving their offerings to the Internet. For example, NAII's Internet home page (see Figure 1-2) offers the same publications that NAII Online does, although you have to join NAII to access them. In many other cases, resources that cost money on online services can be found for *free* on the Internet. Moreover, the hottest new content is appearing on the Internet — providers are bypassing online services altogether.

Continuing the economics lesson for a minute, consider what you pay. Most online services charge a fee of $9.95 per month, which includes five hours of free connect time. But serious online users typically spend 20 or more hours online, and many services you want to use charge additional fees. It's not unusual to run up bills of $30 to $100 per month when you're using an online service. In contrast, you should be able to find an Internet connection that offers *unlimited* connect time for just $19.95 per month.

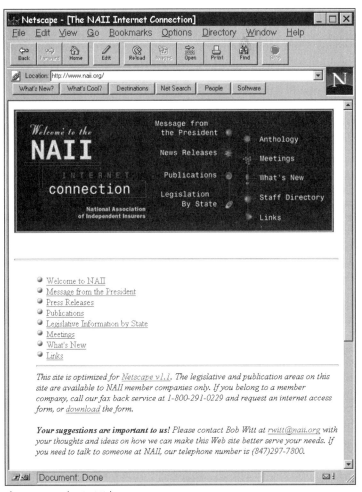

Figure 1-2: The NAII home page

Death of a proprietary online service

AT&T Interchange sounded like a great idea at the time. Developed in 1994 by Ziff-Davis and later acquired by AT&T, AT&T Interchange was to become the online service of choice for information publishers. Unlike the Internet or online services, it was designed from the start to provide business and professional information seekers with a state-of-the-art service. With a polished, professional look, AT&T

Interchange offered users full keyword searching capabilities and other advanced features. Plus, it incorporated a payment mechanism so that copyright holders could get compensated when someone downloaded their material.

By the time AT&T Interchange opened for business in mid-1995, everything had changed. Based on publicly available standards, called *open standards*, the Web quickly became the *lingua franca* for information presentation. With their proprietary technologies, online services struggled to adapt, but AT&T Interchange didn't survive. With so much compelling content available on the Web, users didn't see the need to subscribe to AT&T's pricey service. In mid-1996, AT&T laid off most of the Interchange staff and moved the service to the Web as a fee-based site (http://www.att.com). One casualty: *Washington Post's* Digital Ink subsidiary, which was to reappear on the World Wide Web (at http://www.washington-post.com, shown in Figure 1-3). (If you already have your Internet connection and your Web browser, you can access the *Post* by choosing File → Open and typing http://www.washingtonpost.com.)

Because the Internet is cheaper for content providers and users alike, most experts believe that the best content will wind up on the Internet. That's why this book emphasizes *Internet* resources for investors. The Internet is where the action is — or where it's going.

If content is moving to the Internet, what's keeping the online services in business? Simple: They're reconfiguring themselves as Internet access providers and fee-based content providers. At the same time, online services still offer all their previous advantages, including organized content and ease of access. If you're willing to pay the steeper fees, subscribing to an online service can give you the best of both worlds.

TIP

Online services are clearly superior in one area: moderated discussion groups (called *forums*) and chat rooms, which enable you to communicate *live* (or in *real time*, as computer users like to say) with other users. The Internet offers Usenet newsgroups and Internet Relay Chat (IRC), but these are seriously flawed in comparison, and they're constantly bedeviled by antisocial antics of all kinds. If communicating with other online investors ranks high on your list of priorities, consider subscribing to an online service that offers a good gateway to the Internet, such as America Online.

Figure 1-3: Business section of the *Washington Post* on the Web.

How Do You Connect to the Internet?

Most readers of this book will connect to the Internet by means of a modem and a local Internet Service Provider (ISP). To connect to the Internet this way, you need the following:

◆ **An Internet subscription from an Internet Service Provider (ISP) or an online service.** In most areas, you can find an Internet Service Provider by checking with local computer stores or looking in the Yellow Pages under Computers — Networks or Computers — Online Services. (Perhaps by the time you read this, the Yellow Pages will have a heading titled Computers — Internet Service Providers.) If you're planning to go the online service route, make sure the service offers high-speed (28.8Kbps) modem access within your local calling area. Make sure the ISP or online service can give you all the software that you need, and that this software will work on your computer.

◆ **A computer that has Internet support software.** Happily, this software is built into most recent PCs. If you're using a Macintosh, you need MacTCP. PCI Power Mac users need the most recent version of Open Transport. If you're using Windows 95, Internet support is built into the operating system. If you're using Windows 3.1, you're on your own. To connect using Windows 3.1, you have to obtain your own Internet support software. This is best done by subscribing to an online service or an independent Internet service provider that can provide the Windows 3.1 software you need.

◆ **A fast modem that's designed to work with your computer.** A *modem* is an accessory that enables your computer to send and receive data via a telephone line. Modem speeds are measured in the number of bits per second (bps) that they can transmit. For Internet connectivity, you want at least 28,800 bits per second (also written as 28.8Kbps, the "K" standing for "thousand").

◆ **A dialer program.** This program dials a local phone number and connects you to a computer that's connected to the Internet. After a brief exchange of signals, you're connected. When you subscribe to the Internet, you receive a dialer program to use.

◆ **A browser, such as Netscape Navigator or Microsoft Internet Explorer.** The browser enables you to make full use of the Internet. Both browsers are designed to access the World Wide Web and to make use of other Internet resources as well. Most Internet service providers and online services give you a browser.

Coming: Faster Ways to Connect

The modem you're thinking about buying may be obsolete in a couple years, experts say. That's because two new technologies are snaking their way towards your very own home: ISDN and Internet-friendly cable TV systems.

Critics of ISDN once said that ISDN stands for "It Still Does Nothing," but it really stands for Integrated Services Digital Network. It's becoming more widely available (especially in urban areas). In brief, ISDN is a standard for digital telephone service. With an ISDN connection to your home, you get an extremely quiet digital telephone line *and* a second line that can be used for computer data, at speeds up to 64,000 bits per second (64Kbps). That's more than twice as fast as the fastest modem.

ISDN may enjoy only a brief moment in the sun, however, because it faces some pretty stiff competition from cable TV systems. More than one million *cable modems* have already been manufactured and sold to cable TV firms, which would just love to lease them to you — it's another way to hike up that already impressive monthly bill. But you're going to get something pretty fantastic for the money. Cable modems are capable of transmitting data at speeds of up to 40 *million* bits per second. Not surprisingly, the cable modem market is currently growing at a rather impressive 92 percent annual clip, and it's just getting up steam.

Don't put off buying a modem, however. These two technologies, ISDN and cable TV, are still out in front of the market, and that means big problems for pioneer consumers — they're the "guinea pigs" who, whether they like it or not, are going to help iron out the bugs in the system. Sit back with your 28.8Kbps modem and wait until things are working smoothly.

There's more to connecting to the Internet than this brief section covers. In fact, entire books have been written on the often challenging and confusing process of getting hooked up to the Net. But there's a better way to get connected. Short of getting a B.S. in electrical engineering, your best bet is to find a good local service provider, one that offers preconfigured disks that automatically connect you to the service. Make sure that the ISP offers free, unlimited technical support in case you run into trouble.

Shopping for Your Internet Subscription

So which way should you go — online service or ISP? It's pretty simple, in my opinion. You want to be on the Web, and you want to be on the Web the cheapest way. At present, being on the Web may involve a subscription to America Online or some other online service, such as CompuServe — and that's especially true if you live in a small town or a relatively isolated area. But Internet Service Providers are making their way into every nook and cranny of settled real estate, and, generally speaking, they offer the best deal. I compare online services and ISPs in the following sections.

Online services

At the writing of this book, the major online services were charging the following monthly fees:

Service	Monthly Cost	Hourly Cost
America Online	$9.95 (5 hours free)	$2.95
CompuServe	$9.95 (5 hours free)	$2.95
Microsoft Network	$4.95 (3 hours free)	$2.50
Prodigy	$9.95 (5 hours free)	$2.95

According to a recent survey, the typical Web user spends 11 ¼ hours online per month, the time coming (mainly) from decreased TV viewing. This typical user pays $29.13 per month to access the Web via America Online, CompuServe, or Prodigy, and just $23.70 to access the Web via The Microsoft Network. Note that some of these networks have frequent user plans, which may be a good bet. For example, CompuServe charges $24.95 for 20 hours of usage per month.

When thinking about what you may pay an online service, please bear in mind that you'll run into additional charges. For example, you may have to pay a premium to access the service during business hours (rather than nights/weekends), and you may find yourself paying as much as 25 cents or more *per minute* to access fee-based services — in addition to the monthly and hourly charges.

Internet Service Providers

Most Internet users agree that Internet Service Providers give you the most cost-effective access the Internet. Generally included, along with Internet access, are Internet e-mail and Usenet newsgroups.

When you're shopping for an ISP, look for the following:

◆ **Flat-rate billing.** You pay a fixed monthly fee, as low as $19.95 per month, for *unlimited* access to the Internet. If you're currently using AT&T's long-distance service, you can sign up for AT&T's WorldNet access for a flat fee of $19.95 per month, so don't settle for a higher fee from a local provider.

◆ **Local phone access.** Make sure that the ISP's computer is accessible by means of a local phone number, or you could wind up paying hefty long-distance charges.

◆ **28.8Kbps access.** You want to access the Web using a 28,800 bps modem (also called a 28.8Kbps modem). Make sure that your ISP can handle this speed.

◆ **Point-and-click installation with automatic login.** Don't settle for less than this. The ISP should provide you with all the software you need in order to connect to their service. It should come on one or two disks, enabling you to get connected simply by starting the service provider's Setup program.

COOL SITE

If you can beg or borrow access to the Web, check out The List, which is the most comprehensive directory of Internet Service Providers that is currently available. You can find the list at the following Web address (URL): `http://thelist. iworld.comhttp://thelist.com`.

What? You want to connect *all day?*

Americans take free, unlimited local phone service more or less for granted. And, until recently, it hasn't been much of a problem for telephone companies, even when a couple of teenagers get into a six-hour marathon chat. But the Internet's causing some telephone engineers to sprout premature gray hair.

With so many ISPs offering flat-rate, unlimited Internet connectivity, there's a new pattern: The home or office computer user who remains connected 24 hours per day.

What's wrong with this? From the local phone company's perspective, plenty. When you keep your local line connected all day, you've essentially put one of your phone company's switches out of business. Phone companies typically have far fewer switches than the actual number of calls handled each day. The idea is that most calls last only a few minutes, so when somebody hangs up, the switch becomes available to handle additional calls. But what if you don't hang up? Local phone companies will have to add switching capacity as more and more users connect all day — and that's going to cost money. In some areas, you may see local phone companies trying to sneak in charges for excessive local calling.

Of course, the real challenge for local phone companies is how to make money off the Internet, which, until recently, they completely ignored. The local and regional phone companies, called the Baby Bells, were blindsided by AT&T, which recently shocked the entire telecommunications industry by offering five hours of free Internet access to its long-distance customers.

From the Baby Bells' perspective, the regulations permitting AT&T customers to have unlimited local access to AT&T's lines left an unfair "loophole," which AT&T was quick to exploit. In effect, the Baby Bells said, they have to subsidize AT&T's customer's tying up their precious switching capacity all day and get nothing in return!

What is the World Wide Web?

You can't escape the Web these days. The telltale addresses of Web pages, called *URLs* (pronounced *Earls*), are everywhere: on TV ads, billboards, magazine ads, you name it. (URL stands for Uniform Resource Locater, a standard way of providing the address of a Web resource.) What's the relation between the Web and the Internet?

Basically, the Web provides an easy, graphically-rich way to access resources on the Internet. In this way, it's like Microsoft Windows in relation to all those resources stored on your computer. Before Windows came along, you needed to type horrible commands (such as DIR *.JPG /s /b) to work with your computer files. Thanks to Windows, you can deal with files by using the mouse in a graphical, highly intuitive way.

The Web does the same for the Internet. It makes it really easy to access all those wonderful resources out there.

The Internet wouldn't be booming if it weren't for the Web, just as PCs wouldn't be racking up such huge sales gains if it weren't for Windows. Think of the Web as a Windows for the Internet, and you won't be very far off base. (There's more to it than that, but we deal with the finer points in the next chapter.)

Is All That Cool Web Stuff Really Free?

The Internet grew out of universities, where it's considered very bad form to charge people for the knowledge you create. Because the Internet was essentially a college network for so long, the preference for freebies is still part of the Net's culture. In addition, the Web grew out of an academic research center, so nobody devoted any thought to building an effective payment mechanism into the system. Internet users are accustomed to getting something for nothing, and that's what they expect. Put simply, Internet users won't access your resources unless you're willing to give away something for free. And what you give away had better be good.

That's no problem for the legions of volunteers who willingly create and publish valuable material with a community spirit. But businesses are in business to make money (obviously). How do you make money on the World Wide Web?

Internet publishers are still trying to figure this one out, but the following strategies have emerged:

◆ Give away lots of valuable freebies, and attract hundreds, thousands, or even hundreds of thousands of people to your Web pages. Prove that you're getting lots of *hits* (accesses), and sell advertising.

◆ Offer some valuable resources for free, but create a second, paying level for additional information or services. Users have to type a password to gain entry to the fee-based level.

◆ Offer a really valuable service for free for a while, get people hooked on it, and then start charging a subscription fee. Users will have to type a password to gain entry.

How much of the Web's vaunted content is really free? Quite a bit, actually, although fee-based services are clearly on the rise. The *Wall Street Journal* recently announced subscription fees of $49 per year for the Wall Street Journal Interactive Edition (see Figure 1-4)(`http://update.wsj.com`), or $29 if you also receive the printed edition. Still, plenty of free content is on the Internet.

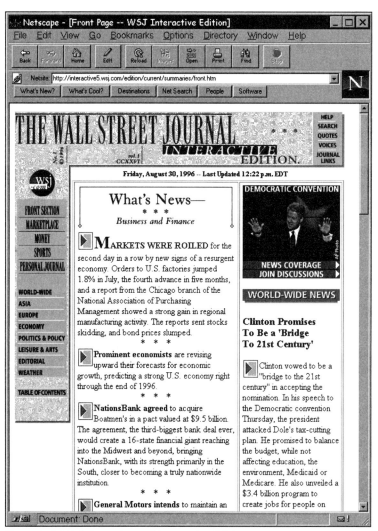

Figure 1-4: Wall Street Journal Interactive Edition.

What About Security?

We give our credit card numbers and expiration dates over the telephone all the time without thinking about it. When it comes to the Internet, however, people are very concerned about security.

Are there security problems with the Internet? It depends on what you mean by *security*. Security isn't so simple when you're talking about something as complex as the Internet. In fact, Internet experts define four different types of security:

◆ **Authentication.** This ensures, when you log on to a computer network, that you're really the person you say you are — and not some intruder bent on stealing something or causing damage.

◆ **Confidentiality.** This refers to the protection of information while it's en route to its destination. Suppose you're sending your credit card number to a Web-based investment service. Can someone intercept your message along the way, copy your credit card information, and start charging left and right? Without security measures, the answer is *yes*.

◆ **Integrity.** This refers to the exact preservation of data while it's en route so that it reaches its destination without any alteration, whether accidental or deliberate.

◆ **Anonymity.** This refers to your ability to browse Web sites or Usenet news-groups without anyone being able to tell which sites you've accessed. After all, you don't want someone tracking your movements and then targeting you for some kind of mail campaign, do you?

So how does the Internet do in the security department? Authentication is your Internet Service Provider's concern, but it's in everyone's interest to help out by changing passwords often. (Stolen passwords provide computer intruders with their chief means of entry into computer systems.)

As for confidentiality, a number of schemes are available for encrypting credit card data while you're sending it to an Internet "shopping mall," but no single scheme is in wide use — yet. Expect major developments in this area in the coming couple of years. Slow progress in this area has held back the Internet's potential for online shopping.

Integrity isn't a huge problem, although computer viruses pose a threat. Think twice before *downloading* a computer program (transferring it from an Internet site to your computer). If you do download software, you may want to run a utility program called a *virus checker* before you launch the program on your computer. (A virus checker examines program files to see if they have been altered by a known computer virus.)

Many Internet users are increasingly concerned regarding their anonymity as they use the Internet. Marketing people know that it's hard to sell advertising unless you can provide detailed demographic information about the people who see the advertisements. Not surprisingly, they're trying to collect this information. To do so, they may ask you to register and supply detailed information about yourself. There's nothing unethical about site registration — after all, you voluntarily agree to do so. What's disturbing many Internet users, however, is the growing use of technology to track your movements on the Internet. This is done so that marketers can build a profile of your interests, the better to target you with tailored advertisements. This is innocent enough, but privacy experts worry that this information could be misused. Also, tracking your movements violates a fundamental ethical rule of marketing; namely, that people shouldn't be monitored without their knowing what's going on. For now, it's wise to assume that your actions on the Internet are essentially public knowledge; don't do anything on the Internet that you wouldn't want your boss (or your mom) to know about.

C'mon. Is the Internet Really *Useful?*

You've probably heard many stories and jokes about wasting time on the Internet. Frankly, it can be a time-waster. It's all too easy to start surfing in all sorts of directions rather than concentrating on doing something productive. But you'd be making a big mistake if you dismissed the Internet out of hand, simply because it's so much fun.

In the chapters to come, you learn how to use the Internet as your ally in a savvy investing strategy. Among other things, you learn how to use Internet tools to help you define your investment goals, allocate your investment assets, and identify potential investments. You access mutual fund prospectuses instantly (instead of waiting as much as a week for them to arrive by snail mail). In the space of a few minutes, you can determine whether a "hot" stock tip is really all that hot, as measured by the company's financial performance (which you can look up online). You can even buy and sell stocks through Internet-based discount brokerages, which happen to be one of the hottest growing areas in the whole financial services industry (and for good reason, as you see). And that's just the tip of the iceberg.

Put simply, the Internet is the investor's best ally. Used wisely (and with a good dose of caution, as you'll see), the Internet can help you develop, apply, and track a sound investment strategy — a strategy that can put you on the way to achieving your dreams.

Where Is This Whole Thing *Going?*

Have you noticed that the crystal balls haven't been working too well lately? The intelligence community was completely surprised by the events leading up to the destruction of the Berlin wall, and even three years ago, no one would have predicted that the Internet would become such a big deal.

With this kind of track record, it seems intemperate, at best, to speculate on where the Internet's headed and how it's going to affect society. But maybe some of the patterns are starting to clarify.

Because the Internet enables individuals to access troves of information that were previously available only to specialists, as individuals we now can become much more proactive in making our decisions, whether it's for medical care, investing, choosing a college, financing a home, or any of a number of other challenges that in the past have driven us into the clutches of fee-charging professionals.

Potentially, this means big savings for investors. Twenty-five years ago, individuals could not easily access the information needed to select stocks, so they turned to pricey full-service brokerages. As information became more widely available and investors gained the confidence to make their own decisions, discount brokerages appeared.

Now the Internet makes it possible for just about anyone to research stocks and make their own investment choices. With the breadth of information available on the Internet comes the added plus of electronic trading, which is much cheaper than human-mediated exchanges. The Internet's fast-growing online brokerages pass the additional savings along to consumers.

To be sure, not everyone is going to feel comfortable researching his or her own investments and trading online. Discount and full-service brokerages will continue to play a valuable role. For people who do feel comfortable with the technology and know how to access the information they need, a new world of personal finance and investment empowerment can be found on the Internet.

Summary

◆ The Internet is a global network that can connect millions of computers, enabling them to exchange data that's rich in multimedia content.

◆ Connecting to the Internet expands your computer's power by an almost unbelievable factor. You'll have access to hundreds of thousands of computer programs and millions of documents.

◆ The Internet enables ordinary people to become originators as well as consumers of information. As a result, it's a much more alive, vital, and occasionally dangerous medium than the carefully controlled broadcast media.

◆ What we're witnessing is the birth of a new public medium, comparable to television or radio (but with new and different characteristics). The Internet enables ordinary people to access and synthesize information in ways that weren't possible before.

◆ Online services do a good job of grouping content for ease of access, but they're more expensive than a straight Internet connection. To remain competitive, online services offer Internet access as well as their own rather pricey content.

◆ To connect to the Internet, you need a Macintosh or Windows system, a fast modem, a dialer program, a browser (such as Netscape or Internet Explorer), and a subscription to an Internet Service Provider or an online service.

◆ The World Wide Web provides an easy-to-use interface for the Internet. With the Web, you can access just about all the Internet's many resources.

◆ Much of the content on the Internet is free, but content providers are looking for ways to make money, naturally, and sometimes advertising just won't cut it.

◆ The Internet still isn't secure enough to usher in a new age of online commerce, but the technology is almost here.

◆ A savvy investor can use the Internet to bypass the pricey services of investment professionals. For someone who's comfortable with the technology, it's the best thing to come along since discount brokerages.

From Here

◆ Learn more about Internet tools, including FTP, Usenet, and the Web, in the next chapter.

◆ Before you get started in Internet investing, make sure that you know the difference between investing and gambling. Find out in Chapter 3.

Understanding Internet Tools

I n this chapter, you learn about the many Internet *tools* you can use, including electronic mail, mailing lists, Usenet, Telnet, FTP, Gopher, and, most important of all, the World Wide Web. (You can even use the Internet as a long-distance telephone, much to the dismay of the phone companies!) As you will see, all these tools have their place in an Internet-based investment strategy.

This chapter introduces all the more important Internet tools, but investors only use three regularly: electronic mail (and its derivative, mailing lists), Usenet newsgroups, and especially the World Wide Web.

In This Chapter

◆ Electronic mail

◆ Mailing lists

◆ Usenet

◆ The big (old) four: Telnet, FTP, Archie, and Gopher

◆ The World Wide Web

Of Clients and Servers

Internet tools are designed to access a *server* of some kind. A server is a program, stored on a computer somewhere on the Internet, that makes information available on demand. When you use an e-mail program, for example, it contacts the e-mail server, which stores your mail until you're ready to receive it. By setting up a Web server (and many people are doing just that), users can make their Web documents available for others to access.

Servers are maintained by information providers. On the information consumer side, you find programs called *clients*. In networking, this word is used in a way that differs from everyday English. A client is simply a program that knows how to contact a server and get information from the server.

Most Internet users have the following clients:

◆ **An electronic mail program.** Favorites include Eudora, which is available for both the Macintosh and Microsoft Windows.

◆ **A browser.** On both Mac and Windows systems, the most popular browsers are Netscape Navigator and Microsoft Internet Explorer.

◆ **A Usenet newsreader.** A favorite among Mac users is Newswatcher, a shareware program, while Windows users like WinVN, a freeware effort. (A *shareware* program is copyrighted and requires the payment of a registration fee, while a *freeware* program — also copyrighted — is free as long as you do not use it for commercial purposes.)

Reflecting the popularity of these three clients, both Netscape Navigator and Microsoft Internet Explorer have recently added electronic mail and Usenet capabilities. With either of these programs you get Web, e-mail, and Usenet functionality in one program.

Electronic Mail

By far the most popular Internet tool, *electronic mail* (e-mail for short) enables you to send and receive messages electronically. You can exchange messages not only with people who have Internet e-mail, but also with users of online services such as America Online, CompuServe, and Prodigy.

Understanding e-mail addresses

When you sign up for Internet access, your Internet Service Provider (ISP) gives you your e-mail address. It looks something like this:

```
yourname@company.com
```

The first part of the address (yourname) is the name of your e-mail account—more than likely, it's some variation on your name or initials with some added characters. After the @ symbol (pronounced *at*), you see the Internet address of your *mail server*—the computer that handles your electronic mail.

Sending and receiving e-mail

Most Internet service providers give you a "freebie" or shareware electronic mail program, such as Eudora Light, which you can use to get started. Any Internet e-mail program can send and receive mail. With an electronic mail message, you can compose, edit, and send messages, as well as receive them. When you receive a message, you can reply, print, store, or delete the message. The better programs add attractive features, such as the capability to filter incoming mail automatically so that it goes into named folders.

To send an electronic mail message to someone, you need an e-mail address as well as your recipient's e-mail address.

Electronic mail is fast, but it isn't instantaneous. Your message probably reaches its destination in a few minutes, but your correspondent must log on to the Internet and download new mail before your message can be read. If your correspondent is out of town or doesn't log on for a while, your message sits there, unread.

The same goes for you — if you want to receive messages, you must log on to your mail server. After making the connection, your e-mail program downloads the messages you've received. In Figure 2-1, you see Netscape's e-mail window. When you select a message in the top right panel, you see the message's text in the bottom panel. You can delete, forward, save, or reply to this message.

Figure 2-1: New mail in your Inbox awaits reading.

How investors use e-mail

Investors use electronic mail in many ways:

◆ **Contacting companies for information.** When you start using the World Wide Web, you find that many Web pages have e-mail addresses, as shown in Figure 2-2. In this figure, you see the Silicon Investor home page. At the bottom of the page is a link that enables you to send comments, suggestions, or questions to the page's maintainer. You can click on this link address to activate your Web browser's mail program, enabling you to send a message to the person responsible for this Web page.

Figure 2-2: A mail link appears at bottom of this Web page.

◆ **Exchanging information with other investors.** Chances are you'll make several electronic friends as you use the Internet; you'll stay in touch with e-mail. These contacts can grow into surprisingly long-lasting and satisfying friendships, even among people who have never physically met.

◆ **Obtaining information from automated e-mail servers.** Many companies on the Internet offer the e-mail equivalent of a faxback service. You send a message to an automatic server program, which then sends back the information you requested via e-mail.

◆ **Receiving automatic updates via e-mail.** Some Web pages offer links that enable you to sign up for an automatic update service. If the page is changed, you receive automatic notification via e-mail.

◆ **Participate in investment-related mailing lists.** Mailing lists, to be discussed next, use e-mail for sending and receiving messages.

What to look for in an e-mail program

Electronic mail is easy to use, but you'll enjoy e-mail more if you get a program with some advanced features. Features to look for include the following:

◆ **Address book.** An address book enables you to store and retrieve your correspondents' e-mail addresses. This feature is a real time- and headache-saver because e-mail addresses (such as `jrl4q@atcl_furball.com`) can be the dickens to type.

◆ **Filters for incoming mail.** If you subscribe to one or more mailing lists (see the next section), you won't want to be without this wonderful feature. With filters, you can tell your e-mail program to examine incoming mail for text that you specify, such as *eINVEST,* and the program automatically places this mail in its own, separate folder. What's so great about this? Mailing lists can generate a great deal of low-priority mail and, without filters, this mail clutters up your main Inbox, making it difficult to see the really important mail you're receiving.

◆ **Signature.** Your e-mail program should enable you to create a *signature*, a mini text file that's automatically appended to every message you send. Your signature should include your name, e-mail address, and (optionally) your organizational affiliation. Many people like to include short quips, quotations, or pictures made from ASCII illustrations, but some recipients find these additions annoying!

If you're using Microsoft Windows 3.1 or Windows 95, try Pegasus Mail. It offers all the features just mentioned, plus it's free! After you get going with the Web, you can download Pegasus Mail from `http://www.cuslm.ca/pegasus/`.

E-mail: Be careful what you write!

Electronic mail is the latest happy hunting ground for lawyers. Most organizations make multiple backup copies of every e-mail message that's sent or received through their systems, and those copies sometimes stick around for years. And that's true even if you've deleted the messages. If you say something defamatory or untrue, it could come back to haunt you years later.

Don't write anything in an e-mail message (or, for that matter, in a mailing list message or a Usenet post) that you wouldn't want to wind up in the following places:

◆ Your boss's desk

◆ Your boss's boss's desk

◆ The files of attorneys of any organizations or companies you mention in your post

◆ Your mother's bulletin board

◆ Your worst enemy's hate file

◆ The front page of your hometown newspaper

We're not kidding about this. *Please* be careful!

Mailing Lists

A *mailing list* makes use of electronic mail so that one person can send a message to many. Tens of thousands of mailing lists exist, covering every conceivable subject. Some are *public mailing lists*, which allow any interested person to join. You're sure to find one or two that interest you.

How mailing lists work

Here's how mailing lists work. Someone decides to create a mailing list, obtains a mailing list program, and advertises the list to people who may be interested. A person who wants to join sends e-mail to the mailing list program; this message consists of nothing more than a SUBSCRIBE command that tells the program to add the person's e-mail address to the list. (To subscribe to the mailing list successfully, one needs to find out exactly how to type this command. This information is usually mentioned in books, Web sites, and e-mail messages that provide information about the mailing list.) Subsequently, this person receives a copy of every e-mail message that is sent to the mailing list.

To contribute a message to the mailing list, you send e-mail to the mailing list address (which isn't the same as the address of the mailing list program). Everyone on the list gets a copy of your message, so be careful what you say.

Most mailing lists are *moderated*, which is a good thing. The human moderator doesn't accept the contribution unless it's pertinent to the list's objectives and topics. This helps to ensure that the overall quality of discussion is good.

Help! I'm getting 500 messages per day!

Mailing lists are fun and often generate meaningful discussion. The problem is, you're going to get many messages — as many as several dozen per day. One way around this problem is to subscribe to the *digest* edition of the mailing list. With a digest, you receive just one message a day, in which all the contributions to the list are grouped together in one long e-mail message. The down side of digests is that they're hard to read, and it's a job to reply to just one of the messages. Digests are a good choice if you plan to read the list but don't plan to contribute very often.

Another way to solve the too-many-messages problem is to get an e-mail program that can filter incoming messages (see "What to look for in an e-mail program," earlier in this chapter).

Please don't forget to save the instructions that tell you how to unsubscribe to the mailing lists you join. To unsubscribe, send an UNSUBSCRIBE message to the mailing list program (*not* to the mailing list). You must carefully follow the instructions you were given to type this message. But most people forget this and send pathetic, pleading "Please get me off this list!" messages, which pollute the mailboxes of everyone on the list (and generate quite a lot of hate mail). Don't be one of the nebbishes that does this, please!

Mailing lists to join right now

Consider joining the following mailing lists today:

eINVEST (*Electronic Journal of Investing*). Maintained by Joseph Friedman, a professor of economics and finance at Temple University, eINVEST is a moderated discussion concerning investment and trading strategies. To subscribe to eINVEST, send

(continued)

(continued)

e-mail to LISTSERV@VM.TEMPLE.EDU and type the following in the first line of text: **SUB E_INVEST** followed by your first name and your last name. (For example: **SUB E_INVEST Jennifer Smith**.)

MONEY DAILY. From *Money* magazine comes this indispensable and interesting daily report or analysis concerning personal finance and investing. To subscribe, use your Web browser to access http://pathfinder.com/money/moneydaily/latest/, and click on the Subscribe link. Alternatively, you can send e-mail to listproc@pathfinder.com. The message should contain **subscribe money daily,** followed by your name. (For example: **subscribe money daily Jennifer Smith**.)

PERSFIN (*The Personal Finance Mailing List*). This moderated mailing list covers topics such as retirement planning, insurance, investing, mortgages, and credit cards. To subscribe to the digest version of the list, send e-mail to majordomo@shore.net and type the following in the body of the message: **SUBSCRIBE PERSFIN-DIGEST** followed by your e-mail address. (For example: **SUB-SCRIBE PERSFIN-DIGEST jsmith@flamebearer.com**.) With the digest format, you receive just one message daily. This message contains all the contributions made to the mailing list within the last 24 hours.

Usenet

Usenet is a collection of topically named *newsgroups*, which are similar to mailing lists except that they don't appear in your e-mail mailbox. To access Usenet, you use a program called a *newsreader*. (Netscape Navigator, the most popular Web browser, includes a built-in newsreader.)

How Usenet works

When you sign up for your Internet account, your service provider gives you the Internet address of your Usenet *server*, the computer that stores Usenet messages so that you can read and reply to them. After you supply this address to your newsreader program, you can access Usenet.

First, your newsreader downloads the names of all newsgroups you can access, which may take some time. Many servers enable you to access as many as 20,000 newsgroups.

After you download all the newsgroup names, decide which groups you want to subscribe to. When you subscribe to a newsgroup, its name appears in a much shorter list of only those newsgroups that you use on a regular basis. (You can still subscribe to any of the others, if you want.)

When someone posts a message (called an *article*) on a new subject, the Usenet software springs into action and distributes a copy of this message to Usenet servers worldwide. (Currently, about 200,000 Usenet servers are in action.)

Most servers don't keep articles for very long. They need to make room for the flood of new messages. Currently, Usenet participants contribute about 80,000 messages per day, enough to fill a 24-volume encyclopedia.

How newsgroups are organized

With more than 20,000 newsgroups in existence, it's obvious that some method is needed to organize and categorize them. Unfortunately, Usenet's method isn't very systematic.

Newsgroups are first categorized by the *top-level category* that they belong to. These categories are divided into two types, the *standard newsgroups* and the *alternative newsgroups*. Every Usenet server is supposed to carry the standard newsgroups, which fall into the following categories:

- ◆ **comp:** Computer-related topics
- ◆ **misc:** Miscellaneous (including investing)
- ◆ **news:** About Usenet itself
- ◆ **rec:** Recreation-related subjects
- ◆ **sci:** The sciences
- ◆ **soc:** Society and social newsgroups

The alternative newsgroups fall under the *alt* heading. Anyone with the requisite technical know-how can create an alt newsgroup, but there's no guarantee that anyone will carry it. Still, thousands of alternative newsgroups are available on most news servers. Most are very low-quality newsgroups that generate considerably more heat than light. In addition to the alternative newsgroups are hundreds of top-level local, regional, organizational, and company categories; your server probably carries some of these, too.

Within a top-level category, newsgroups are further categorized using some kind of logical scheme, such as the following:

◆ **misc.invest:** General information about investments

◆ **misc.invest.funds:** Specific information about mutual funds

◆ **misc.invest.stocks:** Specific information about stocks

Sometimes you see a reference to the *misc.invest.** newsgroups, using an asterisk. This is a shorthand way of referring to all the newsgroups under that category.

TIP

If you're hunting for specific information on Usenet, some Web search services enable you to perform key word searches through zillions of megabytes of Usenet postings. Curious to know what Usenetters are saying about Fidelity mutual funds? Try one of these search services, such as Deja News. You see a list of articles that contain the key words you type. Many people think that using these search services is much more valuable than trying to follow the hue and cry of Usenet discussions, which so easily degenerate into *flame wars* (endless, vituperative arguments over something too controversial to resolve), name-calling, and *spamming* (flooding newsgroups with unwanted advertising).

Moderated and unmoderated newsgroups

A few newsgroups are moderated, which means that contributions are examined by a human moderator to see if they fall within the newsgroup's topical (and taste) guidelines — if not, they're rejected. Needless to say, moderated newsgroups are generally much more informative and worthwhile than their unmoderated counterparts, in which anyone can post a message about anything.

The bane of unmoderated newsgroups is spamming. You can be quite sure that anything advertised this way isn't worth buying!

Unfortunately, all the investment-related newsgroups on Usenet are unmoderated. (One exception is the investment-related groups in the clari.* category, which include nothing but newswire reports from Reuters and UPI.)

Reading and posting articles

It's a good idea to read a Usenet newsgroup for a few weeks so that you see what types of topics are legitimately discussed. As you will see, people sometimes post inappropriate or unrelated material, and they find themselves on the wrong end of *flames* (angry e-mail messages). Don't let this happen to you.

When you read a Usenet newsgroup, you see a list of message subjects, as shown in Figure 2-3. This figure shows how Netscape Navigator displays Usenet news postings. Netscape, like the best newsreaders, *threads* the messages so that replies are grouped with the original posts (so that you can follow the "thread") of discussion. You then select the message you want to read.

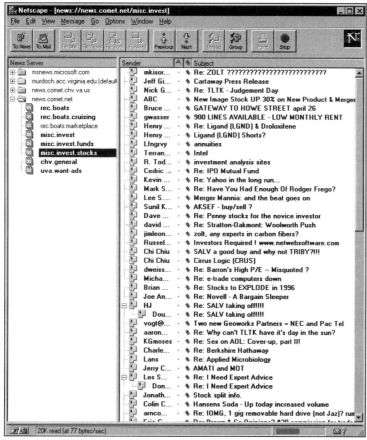

Figure 2-3: The message subjects posted in misc.invest.stocks.

To join the fray, you can post an article on a new subject or reply to an article. When you reply, you can choose to reply directly to the author via e-mail, or you can post the reply to the group (a *follow-up reply*) so that everyone can read it.

Which is the best way to reply? If your reply is of interest only to the person who posted the original article, reply by e-mail. If you think the reply would be of interest to everyone, post a follow-up reply.

Isn't Usenet just so much fluff?

Usenet has a poor reputation in some circles and frankly, it's deserved. Anyone, including ten-year-old hackers, disgruntled ex-employees, psychotic loners, and the usual assortment of hucksters, sharpsters, con artists, and pranksters, can post an article to Usenet. Worse, Usenet discussions frequently degrade into flame wars, which get increasingly nasty and personalized.

Still, Usenet has its merits. You won't find a more freewheeling discussion of investment-related topics anywhere, and reading the investment-related news-groups is certain to bring you face-to-face with fresh, new perspectives. Just don't take it too seriously.

The Big (Old) Four: Telnet, FTP, Archie, and Gopher

Before the World Wide Web came along, four services — Telnet, FTP, Archie, and Gopher — provided the most popular ways to access information on the Internet. Much data is still made available with these services, but the action is shifting to the Web. One of the wonderful things about the Web is that you now can use a Web browser program to access Telnet, FTP, Archie, and Gopher information. Sometimes, you don't even know that you're doing so because access is so seam-lessly integrated with the Web stuff.

Because these services are best accessed by means of the Web, you don't need to know much more about them than the following:

◆ **Telnet.** This service provides a means to communicate with text-only com-puters that can't directly "talk" to the Internet. These text-only computers include bulletin board systems (BBS) and old IBM mainframes. When you access a Telnet session with the Web, your browser starts a Telnet *helper application* (a program that starts automatically when you access Telnet data), and you communicate with the other computer by typing commands and receiving lines or screens of data in return.

◆ **FTP.** This service, short for *File Transfer Protocol*, enables you to receive (download) or send (upload) files via the Internet. To access the file directo-ries of most computers, you need an account and a password. But many com-puters have areas set up for *anonymous FTP*. These are public file repositories that anyone can access. You can use an FTP program for this purpose, but the easiest way to access these files is to use your Web browser, which can han-dle FTP file directories and enables you to download the files you want.

◆ **Archie.** This service enables you to search for specific filenames in anony-mous (public) FTP file archives. It's obsolete because much better services are available on the Web.

◆ **Gopher.** This service provides a menu-based means for accessing a variety of Internet resources, including files, documents, graphics, and sounds. The best way to access Gopher resources is to use your Web browser, which can access Gopher menus directly. Very little new information is appearing on Gopher now; the action is on the Web.

◆ **Veronica.** This is a crude search service that enables you to search the titles of items in Gopher menus. It's old hat now that the Web offers much more sophisticated search services.

The Web Is Where It's At

Unless you've been living on an isolated South Pacific island the past three years, you've surely heard a lot about the World Wide Web. You've even see those funny-looking Web addresses (such as `http://www.yahoo.com/`) on billboards and on TV.

What's all the fuss about? We're clearly seeing the birth of a new communications medium, akin in its potential social penetration to radio, telephones, and TV. In brief, the Web provides an easy-to-use way of accessing Internet resources; in fact, it turns the entire Internet into a seamless tapestry containing untold millions of documents. It's so easy to use that you don't even need to be aware of the location where a document physically resides — it could be in Tokyo, or Tucumcari for that matter — you just click on link after link, and you're off.

How the Web works

The Web is pretty simple, actually. Embedded in Web documents are *hyperlinks*, which appear in a distinctive color and (usually) underlining on-screen. Hidden "beneath" the hyperlink is a URL, which is short for *Uniform Resource Locator*. The URL specifies the exact location, somewhere on the Internet, of the resource that's described by the hyperlink. If you click on <u>Review of Security APL Server</u>, for example, your computer automatically goes out over the Internet, finds the computer that houses this document, downloads the document to your computer, and displays it on your screen.

Two types of programs make this wonderment possible: *Web servers* and *Web browsers*. Web servers respond to incoming requests for Web documents and dish them out. Web browsers enable Web users to obtain and read Web documents. With the proper configuration, Web browsers can also display graphics, play sounds, show movies, and run animations, making the Web a lively place indeed.

With more than 200,000 Web servers in existence and more than millions of documents available, the Web has become one of humanity's richest information resources. But what is this new medium about? Essentially, it's a new method of publication that offers distribution costs approaching zero. There's no paper, printing, ink, postage, envelope-stuffing, or snail mail delay. For this reason, thousands of individuals and small organizations are now able to get their message out without paying to physically transport the paper it's printed on.

Are print-based media going to disappear? Not anytime soon. The Web is a great way to distribute information at low cost, but there's still a role for books, newspapers, and magazines. Most people still don't like to read while sitting at the computer.

Using a Web browser

When you start a Web browser, such as Netscape Navigator or Internet Explorer, you see the *default start page*. This is a Web page housed in the corporate offices of the browser's publisher. Because you see this page every time you start the program, the publisher can go to advertisers and say, "Look, we're getting zillions of hits (accesses) per month—this is where you want to advertise."

From the default start page, you can do the following:

◆ **Search for information.** Most start pages have a Search button or link that you can click on. You see a search page, which enables you to type key words (such as **mutual funds** or **small-cap stocks**). After you click on the Submit or Search button, you see a list of documents that match the key words you typed.

◆ **Access a trailblazer page.** A trailblazer page contains many links in a given category, such as investment. You can click on these links to access high-quality sites in your area of interest. Figure 2-4 shows *Money* magazine's Top Web Sites page, with in-depth reviews of some great Web sites.

◆ **Type a URL directly.** If you find a cool URL (say, in a newspaper, a magazine, a TV ad, or this book), you can type it directly by using the Open command in your browser's File menu.

◆ **Surf mindlessly from link to link.** Surely one of the greatest time-wasters of the century, this technique is lots of fun but not very efficient as an information discovery tool.

After you find a Web page that looks interesting, you can read it, click on one of the links on it, save it, or print it. The better Web browsers enable you to *bookmark* a useful Web page. After setting the bookmark, you can choose the page from a menu within the program.

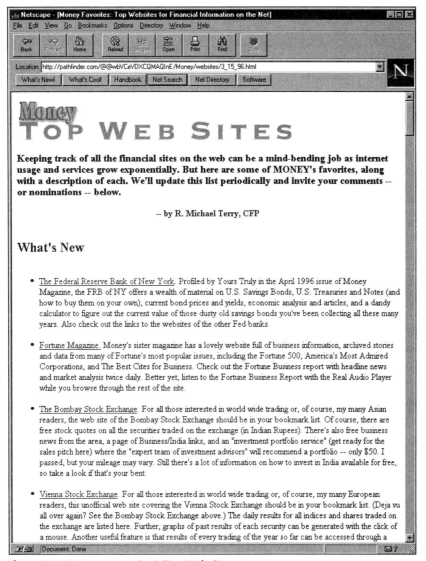

Figure 2-4: *Money* magazine's Top Web Sites page.

Navigating the Web

The Web's hyperlinks make it easy to move from page to page within the Web, but getting lost is pretty easy. Here are some tips to help you get oriented.

◆ If you're really, madly, truly lost, click on the Home button to display the default start page again.

◆ To see the page you viewed previously, click on Back.

◆ Look on your browser's menus to see the names of pages you accessed previously. In Netscape, you find these names in the Go menu.

◆ If you find a page that you want to access again, mark its location with a bookmark (Netscape Navigator) or a favorite (Internet Explorer). You can quickly return by choosing the bookmark or favorite.

◆ Don't drive yourself crazy trying to find things by surfing. See the directory section at the back of this book to locate the addresses of great investment-related trailblazer pages, and lots more.

◆ Remember that URLs are case-sensitive. You have to type the exact pattern of lowercase and capital letters in the URL or it won't work. When you're typing a URL, don't forget the colon and two slash marks after the *http* part (http://).

◆ When you access a Web page, you'll probably find that the page's author has included some helpful navigation aids. Use them to get around the several pages that are available.

One of the smartest things you can do for yourself, Web-wise, is to learn how to use the Web's search tools, such as Infoseek, Yahoo!, and AltaVista. These tools enable you to pinpoint the information you're looking for. For more information on searching the Web, see Chapter 6.

How investors use the Web

As you see in the coming chapters, the Web is packed with useful information and services for investors. Here's just a sampler, to whet your appetite:

◆ Home pages of mutual funds and mutual fund families, offering downloadable prospectuses and performance data

◆ The latest business and investment news, updated hourly

◆ Performance charts and graphs for popular stocks and mutual funds

◆ Detailed financial information on thousands of publicly held companies, including balance sheets and annual reports

In the chapters to come, you learn how to exploit the Web fully, as well as the other Internet tools, as you create an Internet strategy for investing and personal finance.

Summary

- ◆ The most popular Internet tools are electronic mail, mailing lists, Usenet newsgroups, and the World Wide Web.

- ◆ Electronic mail (e-mail) is an indispensable part of any Internet investor's war chest. You use it to contact companies, schmooze with other online investors, participate in mailing lists, and obtain information from automated servers.

- ◆ Mailing lists provide high-quality (usually moderated) discussion of investment-related topics. The quality is much better than the free-for-all of Usenet, but the messages can really clutter up your mailbox—unless you have an e-mail program that has filters (hint, hint).

- ◆ Usenet is the computer equivalent of the Wild West. Use it, but with a healthy dose of skepticism. Think of Usenet as a means of broadening your perspectives. Don't buy ANY stock just because you saw it mentioned or recommended on Usenet.

- ◆ In the past, you needed a whole slew of different tools to access Telnet, FTP, Archie, and Gopher. Nowadays, a properly configured Web browser can access these.

- ◆ The Web makes the Internet easy to use. To access a resource stored somewhere on the Internet, you just click on an underlined word or phrase, and your Web browser does the rest.

- ◆ To use the Web effectively, you need to learn how to search for information efficiently. Use search services (such as Infoseek or Yahoo!) and trailblazer pages.

- ◆ You can access hot Web sites directly by typing the URL, but remember to match the exact pattern of lowercase and uppercase letters.

From Here

- ◆ Begin planning your Internet investment strategy by learning the basics of sound investment (see Chapter 3).

- ◆ Use the Web to determine your investment goals (see Chapter 4).

- ◆ Explore starting points pages to get a better idea of what's out there for investors (see Chapter 5).

- ◆ Use the Web's search engines to find information on the Internet (see Chapter 6).

- ◆ Keep up with the latest business news using mailing lists, e-mail notification services, and Web-based newspapers and magazines (see Chapter 7).

- ◆ Learn about the perils and pitfalls of Usenet (see Chapter 8).

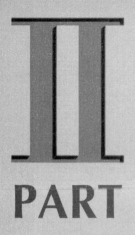

II
PART

Developing Your Investment Strategy

What Is Investing?

You're going to become an investor, and you're going to use the Internet as an information discovery tool. But what is investing? This chapter reviews some of the basics of sound investing — and for good reasons. It isn't wise to jump onto the Internet looking for investment advice until you've thought through your investment objectives, given some thought to asset allocation, and fully understand the risks involved in various types of investments. If you're already conversant with these investment fundamentals, you can skip this chapter — but a quick skim wouldn't hurt.

Some people follow the investment advice of people they don't know, about investments they don't really understand. They may "take a flyer" on the stock of a new technology company with little or no operating history.

This is isn't necessarily bad. But it's not investing. It's just buying an investment. It's more akin to what people do when they spend money on lottery tickets each week. As long as you don't spend the grocery money on it, it can be an enjoyable bit of gambling. But it's not investing — any more than buying lotto tickets is.

Hold on, you may say. I put some money in my company's 401(k) plan last year — in a growth stock mutual fund — and it went up 35 percent. That's not small potatoes. It's part of my savings, but I can't tell you what's in that fund.

In This Chapter

◆ The risk/reward tradeoff

◆ Top ten tips for intelligent investing

◆ Where the Internet comes in

Yes, it is possible to get some outsized returns on your money, even if you don't know much about the markets. In 1995, for instance, the Dow Jones Industrial Average of 30 representative blue chip stocks was up 33 percent, and the Standard & Poor's 500 Index, which includes a cross-section of stocks to mimic the activity of the whole U.S. economy, was up 34 percent. In fact, many stocks rose quite a bit in 1995.

So what's investing? It isn't just taking a flying leap into something you don't understand. *Investing* is a planned and timed strategy of wealth-building. Investing involves the acceptance of a certain amount of risk in the hope of getting a better return and uses diversification so that you don't put all your eggs in the same basket. This chapter explains the risks, shows you how to get started on your planning, and suggests some strategies for linking your investments to your life goals.

The Risk/Reward Tradeoff

The investments that hold the biggest payoff potential don't come with guarantees. Many are sold in markets. They're auctions — literally. Stocks, bonds, options, futures, currencies, and many other investments are sold to the highest bidder. The gains investors received for them in the past are no guide to what they will yield in the future. The future is uncertain.

Investments have varying levels of risk. The higher the risk investors take, the bigger the reward they expect for taking it. Table 3-1 categorizes various investment options in terms of risk. In general, the higher the risk, the greater the potential reward (or loss!). With some exceptions, investments in companies are riskier than investments in state and local governments, which are in turn riskier than putting your money in the federal government.

Table 3-1: The risk/reward tradeoff	
Risk	**Investment options**
Very high	Futures
	Options
	Penny stocks
	Stocks of new companies
	Junk bonds

Risk	Investment options
High	Value stocks
	Growth stocks
	Blue chip stocks
	Income stocks
Moderate	Preferred stocks
	Corporate bonds
	Municipal bonds
	Long-and intermediate-term U.S. Treasury notes and bonds
	Agency bonds
Limited	U.S. Treasury bills
	Money market funds
	Certificates of deposit (CDs)
	Insured savings accounts

Where do *mutual funds* fit into this table? Mutual funds enable investors to pool their money, which is invested in various ways by the fund's manager. Some funds specialize in a given type of investment, such as growth stocks. The risk of these funds is close, therefore, to growth stocks in general, except that — unlike most individual investors — a growth stock mutual fund invests in dozens or hundreds of stocks, which tends to reduce the overall risk. Other, riskier funds invest in junk bonds. Still other funds spread their investments all over the map, making it somewhat difficult to assess their risk level.

You learn more about mutual funds, and their varying levels of risk, later in this book. For now, take a closer look at the risk levels of futures, options, stocks, bonds, and savings accounts — the raw materials of any investment strategy.

Very high-risk investments

Only those investors with nerves of steel — and plenty of money in less risky investments — should consider a high-risk investment. An example of high-risk investments is *futures* or *options*, which enable you to gamble on what something will cost in the future.

Most futures or options speculators leverage their investment, meaning that they pay a small amount of money for a futures or options contract that's worth much more. If you bet correctly on the future price, you could make big money — but you could also lose big because you may be responsible for a much larger loss if the price doesn't go the way you thought it would.

Penny stocks (stocks with a value of less than $5) sometimes produce big payoffs, but many of these companies won't ever turn a profit, and some won't survive. (You also hear about *small-cap stocks*, but these are a different breed of horse: They're the shares of firms of all whose stock is worth less than $100 million. Many of these stocks fit into the growth and value stock categories.)

The stocks of new companies are made available in *initial public offerings* (IPOs). If you're lucky enough to buy the initial offering of a company that later turns out to be a hotshot, you can make big profits. But the company may not live up to expectations.

Junk bonds, the bonds issued by companies with poor (or no) credit ratings, offer high rates of interest. However, the company may default on its debt, leaving you with a fraction of your investment.

High-risk investments

Coming down the risk ladder a bit from the high-risk investments just described, you find many people's favorite investment — *common stocks*. They're risky because they're nothing but a piece of paper that says you own a piece (a *share*) of the company, which is why common stocks are also called *equities*. (When you own one or more shares, you own some of the company's equity — part of its net worth.) If the company makes a profit, the value of your share may grow. If the company goes out of business, that's the end of your claim.

The key words here are "the value *may* grow." There's no guarantee that it will — and that's true even if the company turns a profit! Why? There are many ways to value a stock, and they don't all agree. The price of a stock depends on what buyers are willing to pay and what sellers are willing to accept — and these are determined by many factors (including the firm's financial picture, the actions of its competitors, favorable or adverse news about the company, changing levels of interest rates, the flow of money into the stock market, and many other factors, including whether the stock is the darling of Wall Street). As time passes, many stocks turn out to be *overvalued* (priced too high), while some are *undervalued* (priced too low).

You can make money with common stocks in two ways:

◆ **You sell the stock for more than you paid.** If the company's financial situation, profits, and prospects improve, if the wider market environment is favorable, *and* if Wall Street likes the stock, the stock's price may go up —

sometimes dramatically. The difference between what you get for a stock when you sell it and what it cost you is called *capital gain* (or capital loss, if you get less than you paid).

◆ **The company may pay dividends.** A company making money has the option of distributing part of the profits to shareholders by means of payments called *dividends*.

There are many different kinds of common stocks. *Growth stocks* are the stocks of companies whose earnings are rising faster than average or faster than the economy in general. Many technology stocks (such as Microsoft and Netscape) fall into this cateogry because they're in industries expanding everal times faster than the rest of the economy. They may have varying degrees of risk — sometimes quite high. Usually, they reinvest all or most of their profits in an effort to grow relative to other companies in their industries. Growth stocks generally pay little or no dividends, but people buy them anyway in the hope that the stock's price will go up. Somewhat less risky are the *blue-chip stocks* of large, respected, and well-established companies, such as Bristol-Myers Squibb, Xerox, or General Electric. *Income stocks* (such as utilities stocks) pay high dividends but usually don't rack up the kind of stock price gains that growth stocks sometimes do.

Moderate-risk investments

KEY TERM

Lower in risk, but with less potential for gain, are preferred stocks and bonds.

Often overlooked, *preferred stocks* combine some qualities of both stocks and bonds, although they're truly stocks, which give you no legal claim if the company goes under. Their dividends are higher than those on common stocks most of the time. This gives them some of the advantages of bonds (a steady income). However, preferred stocks trade like stocks, giving them some of a stock's appreciation possibilities. The high dividends set a kind of floor for the stock price, supporting it when other stocks may slump. But there's a trade-off here. Preferred stock often has what's known as a *call* or *redemption* feature — meaning the company can buy it back from you at a predetermined price at certain times. That takes away your source of income and usually gives you back your purchase price with a small bonus for your time and trouble. And don't forget, because preferred stocks are stocks, they can decline as well as gain in price.

Also in the moderate-risk category are fixed-income investments, called *bonds*. When you buy a bond, you're making a loan to the company or government agency that issued the bond. Buying a *corporate bond* enables you to loan a company money. Even though bonds give you a legal claim if the company goes under, there's no guarantee that the company is going to pay the money back if it gets into serious financial trouble, so there's risk. How much risk depends on the company's financial strength. If you buy bonds from a well-established company that's doing pretty well, the risk is limited.

Your risk also depends on how long you're willing to hold on to the bond. If you hold the bond until its *maturity*, the date on which you can cash in the bond, you get your capital back. If you wish to sell the bond before its maturity, you may find that the price of the bond in the market has risen or fallen due to interest rate fluctuations. Suppose a similar, new bond is paying 7.5 percent, but you have a bond that pays 8.5 percent. Buyers will be willing to pay more to get your bond. But if your bond pays 6.5 percent, they won't buy your bond unless you come down on the price.

Think about this point again, because it sometimes seems to run counter to common sense. You may think that bond prices would go up when interest rates go up. But the bonds that have already been issued (including *yours*) have lower rates, which means that they're worth less money to investors. Conversely, when interest rates go down, the bonds that have already been issued may have higher rates, which means that investors are willing to pay more for them.

There are many kinds of bonds, including *municipal bonds* (offered by local and state governments), *U.S. Treasury bonds* (offered by the U.S. federal government), and *agency bonds* (offered by government and government-sponsored agencies).

U.S. government bonds are generally considered less risky than other bonds because they're backed by the full faith and credit of the U.S. government. You lose your money only in the case of some unbelievable catastrophe, such as the financial or political collapse of the U.S. government (and if that happened, we'll have plenty of other things to worry about besides your Treasury bills). But they're still not guaranteed. Also, long-term and intermediate-term bonds of any kind are more subject than short-term bonds to price fluctuations due to changing interest rates; the risk here is that if you buy a bond only to find that interest rates are going up, you're stuck holding the bond to maturity or selling it for a lower price.

Limited-risk investments

This section is titled "Limited-risk investments" because there's no such thing as a "risk-free" investment. In this category are *short-term U.S. Treasury bills* and *money market funds* (which generally invest in short-term securities such as Treasury bills). Treasury bills and money market funds generally pay slightly higher rates than bank certificates of deposit (CD), but they're not insured. A money market fund is essentially a short-term bond fund that tries to maintain a *net asset value (NAV)*, or share price, of exactly $1.00. There's no guarantee that the fund will be able to do this, but (to date) no money market fund has ever failed in this aim; although, in the late 1980s, a few came close. On the positive side, short-term Treasuries and money market funds have one big advantage over CDs: They're *liquid*, meaning that it's easy to get your money if you need it. (Many money market funds, for example, give you a checkbook, which you can use just like an interest-bearing checking account.) CDs force you to lock up your money for a given period (usually six months to five years), during which you can't get your money back without paying a hefty interest penalty.

Is a CD really risk-free?

Certificates of deposit in banks insured by the U.S. FDIC are insured up to $100,000. This means that you can get your money back if the bank goes belly-up. But is a CD really risk-free?

Not if you consider how inflation affects your investment. Inflation has been running at about a two percent clip, alhough it has been much higher in the past. If you're earning five percent on your certificate of deposit, after subtracting inflation and taxes on the interest you've earned, you may find that you're making very little money on your investment — if you're making any at all.

The moral: There's no such thing as zero risk. With a low-risk investment, you minimize the risk of losing your capital in a big, cataclysmic bust, but inflation is going to eat away at your earnings over time. If you buy nothing but short-term U.S. Treasury bills, you probably won't make much after taking inflation and taxes into account.

On the low end of the risk scale, you find CDs, which are insured up to $100,000 by the Federal Deposit Insurance Corporation (FDIC) or the Federal Savings & Loan Insurance Corporation (FSLIC). Note, however, that some banks do not offer either form of insurance; don't assume that a CD is automatically insured. With CDs, however, you have to tie up your money for a fixed period, and you incur severe interest penalties if you withdraw your money early.

And the rewards?

The more risk, the greater the potential reward. To see why, take a look at the last half century.

For the last half century, the average return on stocks each year has been 13 percent, a figure that includes capital gains due to share price appreciation as well as dividends. This compares to an average of 5 percent for long-term bonds, and 4.5 percent for Treasury bills, which mature in less than a year. An equal mixture of stocks, bonds, and Treasury bills would give you an average return of 7.5 percent. Meanwhile, inflation has been running at an average 3.1 percent clip annually.

Having some money in stocks enables you not only to keep up with inflation, but actually to increase your capital. That's why people buy stocks — as long as they're willing to hold on to them long enough to ride out the ups and downs along the way.

Learning about investing: beginner's sites on the Web

You find excellent introductions to investing at the following Web sites:

Building Your Portfolio (http://www.vanguard.com/educ/module2/univ_m2.html). Created by the Vanguard fund family, this tutorial features step-by-step instruction, replete with quizzes and recommended readings. Highly recommended! Part of the extensive table of contents is shown in the accompanying figure.

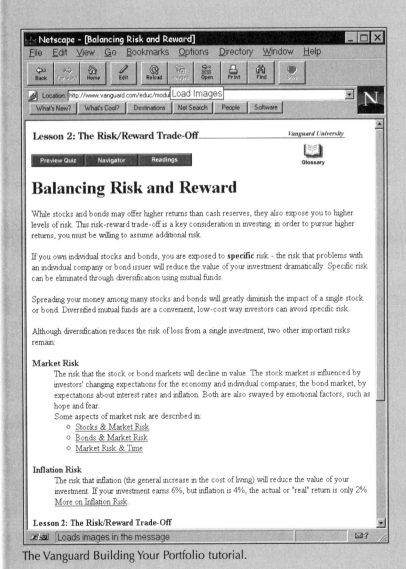

The Vanguard Building Your Portfolio tutorial.

Quotable Quotes (http://www.moneypages.com/syndicate/stocks/qquotes. html). Douglas Gerlach's fun collection of investment-related quotations from the likes of Benjamin Franklin, Peter Lynch, and Mark Twain. My favorite: "The first rule is not to lose. The second rule is not to forget the first rule." (Warren Buffet)

101 Questions To Ask Before Investing (http://mosl.sos.state.mo.us./ sos-sec/101que.html). Don't even think about investing your money without reading this.

Frequently Asked Questions About Investing (http://www.fid-inv.com/ investors/faqs/faqs.html). Focusing on mutual funds (but of interest to all investors), this well-organized list of common questions (and answers) is produced by Fidelity Investments, the nation's largest mutual fund family.

Top Ten Tips for Intelligent Investing

Is all this confusing? Let's sum up everything with ten solid rules.

1. **Figure out what you're investing for and how much time you need.** What are you investing for? Are you saving for a down payment on a house? For your kids' college educations? For retirement? In general, the longer the time horizon, the more likely the market's up-and-down gyrations will even out, giving you a healthy average annual increase. If you don't need the money for 20 or 30 years or more, you should put a good chunk of it — as much as 50 to 70 percent — into stocks. If you're saving for a down payment six months away, however, buying stocks is a riskier idea; a temporary downward plunge could wipe out part of your money. Put it into short-term bonds or six-month CD.

2. **Determine your risk tolerance.** You have to be comfortable with an investment plan to stick with it long term. New investors often want to start with low-risk investments. This is a good idea. But when your total investment is small, it's hard to diversify away what risk is there. Eventually, you may want to take on more risk to increase your rewards for doing so. The key is to keep learning all you can about investing. Knowledge about what you're doing takes some risk away. Knowing more also helps you avoid situations in which you can't win. All the while, the best way to deal with risk while you're building up your investments may be to avoid taking too much of it head on.

3. **Start small, and start liquid.** You don't have to wait until you have ten grand socked away. Even kids invest now. Find, say, a mutual fund with a small account minimum, and keep putting a little bit into it regularly.

4. **Make investing part of your budget.** If you can't do it right away, look at the more discretionary items in your budget, like clothing, and see if you can squeeze a few bucks out of them every month.

5. **Invest regularly.** The earlier you start, the more money you accumulate. Time is the one big side of the compounding of return equation. Here's a good example. Two investors both can get a 10 percent return on their money each year. One invests $2,000 for eight years and then stops. The other doesn't invest for those eight years, then socks away $2,000 for 32 years. How much do they each have at the end of the whole 40 years? The first, with just a $16,000 total investment, has $515,188. The second, who put in $64,000, has $378,496 in the end.

6. **Start out with a good mutual fund, but don't overlook stocks.** A broadly based mutual fund, such as Vanguard's Institutional Index Fund, gives you diversification automatically; a big fund such as this one invests in hundreds of stocks. But don't overlook individual stocks, even though they take time to research and you must pay commissions when you buy and sell. Using your personal knowledge and experience, you may be able to select stocks that will perform very well.

7. **Diversify.** One of the biggest mistakes beginning investors make is to put all their eggs into one basket (for example, buying a bunch of growth stocks concentrated in only one or two industries). If these investments go up, great. If they go down, you lose — big. What most beginners don't realize is that when some investments go down, others go up. For example, income stocks may go up when growth stocks decline. Health sector stocks may soar when technology stocks go bust. For stocks, you should try to pick stocks in different industries, with different degrees of risk, of different sizes, and bring in some fixed-income securities. Diversified mutual funds give you diversification automatically, and you don't have to pay broker's commissions.

8. **Hold on to your investments.** Don't react to temporary market downswings by selling out — you miss out on the appreciation when the market comes back up. Buying and holding stock you've researched well is a better starting-point strategy than trying to time the market, which gives even the pros a difficult time. On the other hand, there's no point in holding a stock that's not performing up to your expectations. Track your investments, but don't react to temporary market swings.

9. **Stick to your plan and be patient.** One of the worst mistakes beginning investors make is to buy at the top of the market, usually after a big upswing when everyone's talking about how "hot" the market is. Having bought at the top, these investors panic when the market drops and sell at the bottom. That's why people lose their money in the stock market — it's a psychological thing.

10. **Remember that past performance doesn't guarantee future yields.** Another big mistake made by beginning investors is to chase after "hot" mutual funds — you know, the ones that racked up those 53 percent gains last year. But those results could be a fluke. Perhaps the fund invested big in technolo-

gy stocks, which were really hot in 1995. But they could go down big time in the future, dragging the fund down with it. In 1993, for example, emerging markets funds produced big gains, and investors poured money into them. These investors got a nasty surprise when Mexico defaulted on its loan payments and many emerging-market funds suffered 20 percent losses.

Where Does the Internet Come In?

Whether you're trying to get control over your spending, determining your optimum asset allocation, or spending or tracking down fast-growing companies, the Internet is a splendid tool for knowledge acquisition. In the chapters to come, you find out what the Internet is all about, and you become acquainted with the most valuable Internet tools. You learn how to pinpoint the information you need as part of your overall investment strategy.

Summary

◆ Investing is a planned and timed strategy of wealth-building. It involves accepting a certain amount of risk in the hope of getting a better return. It uses diversification to help protect your capital from market gyrations.

◆ You can rank investments on a risk continuum, ranging from very high to limited (but there's no such thing as a "no risk" investment). At the very risky end are futures, options, penny stocks, stocks of new companies, and junk bonds. In the high-risk category are growth stocks, most stock mutual funds, and blue chip stocks. Moderately risky are preferred stocks, corporate bonds, municipal bonds, long- and intermediate-term U.S. Treasury notes and bonds, and U.S. governmental agency bonds. Limited-risk investments include short-term U.S. Treasury bills, money market funds, insured savings accounts, and bank certificates of deposit (CDs).

◆ Over long periods of time, stocks produce the biggest gains. During the past 50 years, stocks have gained an average of 13 percent per year, compared to 5 percent for long-term bonds, and 4.5 percent for Treasury bills. You need to make more than inflation, which can take several points of your return.

◆ Intelligent investing involves starting early, making investments part of your budget, figuring out what you're investing for and how long you need to hold your investments, diversifying your investments, determining your risk tolerance, sticking to your plans, and avoiding chasing hot past performers.

From Here

◆ Your next step: Determine your investment goals. Get Internet help in Chapter 4.

◆ Begin your exploration of Internet investment resources by exploring starting point pages, the subject of Chapter 5.

◆ Learn how to search the Net for investment-related information (see Chapter 6).

Determining Your Investment Goals

In This Chapter

◆ Calculating your net worth

◆ What are you investing for?

◆ How much will you need?

◆ Assessing your risk tolerance

◆ Allocating your assets

As you learned in Chapter 3, the difference between investing and gambling is a solid plan. You have to think about where you are financially, what your goals are, how much you need to have to meet your goals, how much risk you can tolerate, and how you should allocate your assets to achieve your goals. As you learn in this chapter, the Internet can help.

On the World Wide Web, you find many online calculators that take full advantage of the Web's forms capabilities, which enable you to type text or numbers into response fields directly on the page that you're viewing. When you click on the page's Submit button, this data is uploaded to the Web server, where it's channeled to a computer program for analysis. The result of the analysis is a new Web page, generated in response to your input, which presents the results in a readable way.

Don't rely on the Web alone to make fundamental decisions about your retirement plan — it's just a useful resource for getting started. Also, be aware that there's no single, standard, agreed-upon way of computing any of these figures, such as how much you need to save for college. Each of the online calculators you use has its own built-in assumptions, and there's a good chance that underlying assumptions may differ (in ways that aren't obvious or even discoverable). As with everything else on the Internet, be aware that the pages you access may not stem from wholly altruistic motives.

Calculating Your Net Worth

What are you worth? It's amazing how many people don't know how to answer this question. But it's the starting point for your investment planning. You need to know where you are right now financially — only then will you know how much you need to accumulate. Your goal is to increase your net worth, so you need to know where you stand right now.

The Web can help you figure your net worth, as long as you're willing to do a little legwork in gathering the needed information. To determine your net worth, you need the following information:

◆ **Your assets.** This includes everything you own, such as your house, any other real estate you may own, your cars, a boat or RV, furnishings, jewelry, savings accounts, money you've already contributed to IRAs or retirement plans — anything of value. It doesn't matter if you still owe money on it. You also can include money that's owed to you by someone.

◆ **Your liabilities.** This is what you owe, in the form of car loans, home equity loans, credit card debt, the unpaid balance on your mortgage, and that money you borrowed from your sister-in-law.

To determine your net worth, access one of the net worth calculators described in the sidebar ("Net worth calculators") and plug in the numbers. Figure 4-1 shows the Huntington Webbank Net Worth Calculator. When you click on the Calculate button, you see a new Web page that tells you your net worth. (This isn't rocket science: Your net worth equals your assets minus your liabilities.)

Are you using Netscape or Internet Explorer? To access a Web page by typing the URL directly, simply select the URL that's in the URL box and start typing the new URL. Please type carefully, watching for capitalization errors. When you finish typing the URL and you're sure it's correct, press Enter.

Calculate your net worth periodically. It's really satisfying to see it grow, which helps motivate you to stick to your investment goals.

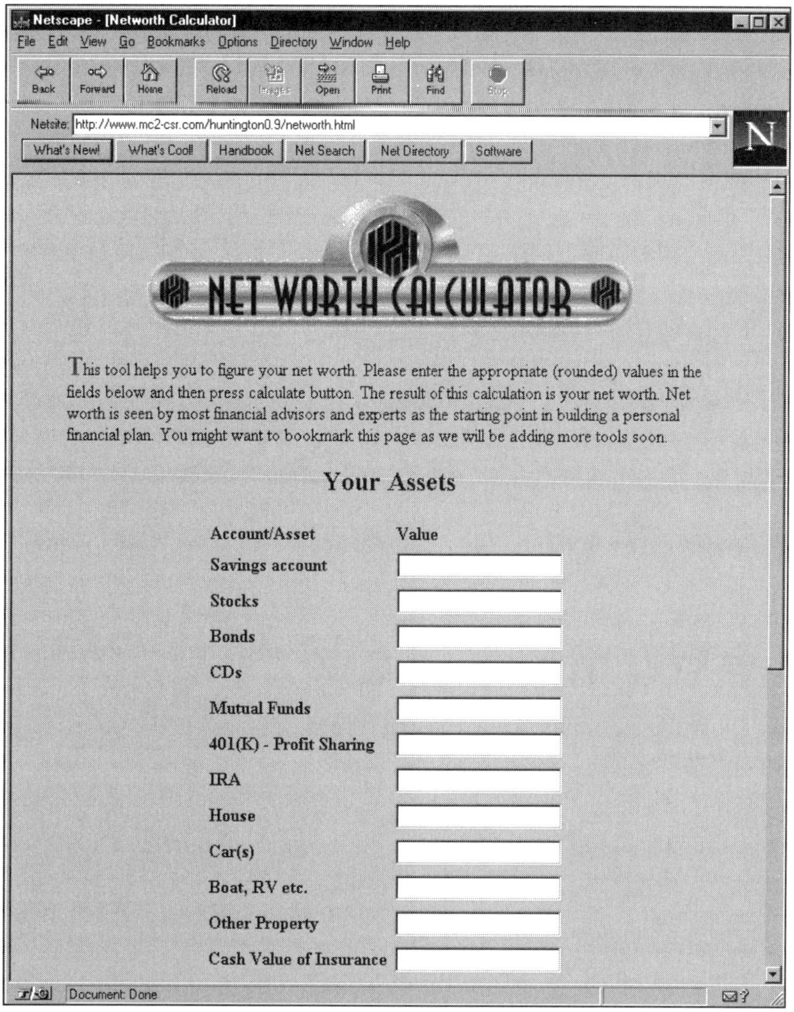

Figure 4-1: The Huntington Webbank Net Worth Calculator.

Net worth calculators

Figuring Your Net Worth (http://www.e-analytics.com/fpa1.htm). This isn't an online calculator; it's a worksheet that you can print out and use. It does a great job of breaking down assets and liabilities into categories. You may want to print

(continued)

(continued)

out this worksheet and use it to organize your information and then use one of the online calculators to total the items and compute your net worth.

Huntington Webbank Net Worth Calculator (`http://www.huntington.com/tools.html`). This calculator, accessible from the Huntingon Webbank Tools page, is easy to use and has a nice graphic design (see Figure 4-1 for a portion of this calculator).

Merrill-Lynch Net Worth Statement (`http://www.merrill-lynch.ml.com/investor/worthform.html`). This statement has plenty of room for listing investment assets, including money market funds, checking accounts, stocks, municipal bonds, government securities, and more, but it's short on space for personal assets. There's not much room for liabilities, either. This statement seems to be focused on people who have already done some investing.

What Are You Investing For?

Most people answer this question by saying, "To make money." Of course! The real question is, for *what*?

KEY TERM

The "for what" part is very, very important, because the answer to this question tells you your time frame. This time frame — the length of time you hold your investement — is called the *holding period*. There are three holding periods:

- ◆ **Short term.** One year or less.
- ◆ **Intermediate-to-long term.** Two to five years.
- ◆ **Long term.** Five years or more.

Now, what are you investing for? Here are some of the things people save for:

- ◆ **Down payment on a home.** Are you saving for a down payment for a first home or for that vacation dream house? You probably want the money fast. This is probably a short-term investment.

- ◆ **College.** Suppose your children are 11 and 8 right now. You'll start needing college funds for your oldest child seven years from now. With children of these ages, you're looking at an intermediate-term investment.

- ◆ **Retirement.** If you're saving for retirement, you need to pick a retirement age. 55 is nice to think about. However, if you take money out of retirement plans before you're 59 ½, you may have to pay a penalty. (Thanks, Uncle Sam.) Still hoping to retire early? You need savings to tide you over until the retirement checks start coming. Unless you're in late middle age, you're looking at a long-term investment here.

◆ **Starting your own business.** Fed up with the boss, huh? That's a good sign, incidentally — it gives you the motivation that small business people need in order to succeed. How far away is your startup date? This could vary a lot, depending on the kind of business you want to start.

◆ **Reduce your dependence on employment income.** With all the downsizing going on, this isn't a bad idea. At what age do you think you'll need this protection the most? You're not looking at a short-term investment here, probably, because this is an income investment for the long haul.

Do you have more than one investment goal? For example, are you saving for college and retirement at the same time? Because these investments probably have differing holding periods, you should think of them as separate investments. Saving for college three years down the road is an intermediate-term investment. Saving for retirement fifteen years from now is a long-term investment. As you see later in this chapter when we discuss asset allocation, these investments require differing investment strategies.

How Much Will You Need?

After you decide what you're investing for, you need to estimate how much you need. If you're saving for college or retirement, you'd better sit down for this one.

Investing for college

The cost of a college education has risen dramatically in recent years. Right now, the pricier private schools will set you back $120,000 for tuition, room, and board. Faced with deep cutbacks in state funding, the state schools have raised tuition, too; you'll spend about $50,000 to send your child to a good public school. And it's going to get worse: College costs are still rising at about twice the rate of general inflation. By the time today's newborns are ready to start their freshman year, the bill for four years at a public college could reach $115,000, while four years at a private school could cost more than $287,000.

Is it worth the money? For your children, college is still a good bet; in fact, it's probably the only way to prepare to earn a decent living. College graduates can expect to earn $1.421 million over their working lives, after inflation, while high school graduates will earn only $820,000.

To estimate how much money you'll need for college, you need to take into account the age of your children, the number of years until they start college, the rate of college cost inflation (which is higher than the overall rate of inflation), and other factors. Several calculators on the Web can help you determine how much you'll need for college costs.

You find many college cost calculators on the Internet. One of the best is the Prudential Education Calculator (http://www.prudential.com/educate.html), shown in Figure 4-2. This worksheet enables you to specify your income tax bracket, the college location, and residency (an important factor in tuition costs).

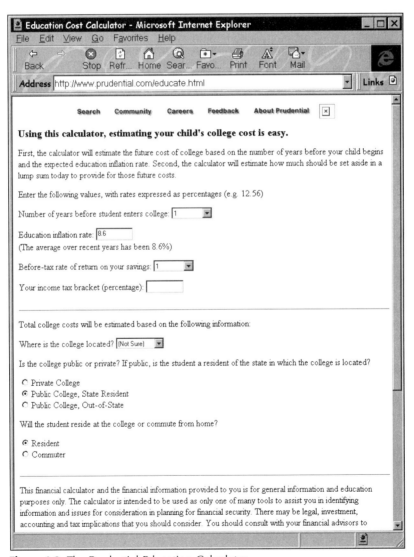

Figure 4-2: The Prudential Education Calculator.

College savings calculators

College Savings Bank College Cost Calculator (http://www.collegesavings.com/create1.html). Linked to CSB's innovative college savings CD, which links its interest rate to the rate of college cost inflation, this calculator enables you to determine how much you need to invest to meet your projected college expenses with the CollegeSure CD.

Douglas County Bank & Trust (DCB&T) College Savings Planner (http://www.dcbt.com/FinCalc/College.html). This is a simple and easy-to-use worksheet.

New England Funds: Your College Planning Worksheet (http://www.mutualfunds.com/basic/wrksheet.html). This is cumbersome to use, but you can precisely control the inflation and investment return factors.

When you're using a Web-based calculator of any kind, make sure you understand the assumptions that it's making. For example, the Prudential Education Calculator assumes college costs for public or private schools using average figures supplied by the College Entrance Examination Board (CEEB); the college you actually choose may cost more or less. Other calculators may assume fixed (and inaccurate) rates for college inflation (currently running at about six percent) or may overstate the amount you're likely to earn on your investments. These calculators may also fail to take inflation into account.

Investing for retirement

How much do you need to invest for your retirement? You need more than Social Security. Currently, the average annual social security retirement payment for a couple is less than $15,000.

When you predict your retirement income needs, you'd better take inflation into account. The Online Inflation Adjustment Calculator (http://www.hetherman.com/fnic/inflatnc.html), offered by the Financial Network Investment Corporation (FNIC), helps you do just that. It's simple. You type in the retirement income you want to receive in today's dollars, as well as the expected annual inflation rate. Then you supply the number of years before the income is received — and you get the rather depressing results. Do you want $50,000 a year in today's dollars? If you're retiring 25 years from now, you'll need $104,688!

You need the following figures before you calculate your retirement income needs:

◆ The total amount you've saved to date for your retirement.

◆ The amount you're currently contributing annually to your retirement fund.

◆ The number of years you have left to save before your retirement.

◆ The number of years your retirement savings must last you. You can start with 20 years; increase this figure if you intend to retire early (or if your parents are especially long-lived).

The Web's retirement calculators use different methods. Some start with the contributions you're making right now to your retirement fund and tell you how much you'll receive per year when you retire. Other calculators start with the income you want to receive upon retirement and calculate how much you need to save per month to achieve that goal.

COOL SITE

Let's start with the first method, figuring out your retirement income based on your current retirement savings and planned future contributions. Visit the Online Retirement Income Calculator (http://www.hetherman.com/tools/rcalfni2.html), maintained by Financial Network Investment Corporation. Type in the data and click on Calculate Your Retirement Now! You see a new screen informing you what your annual retirement income will be, but please bear in mind that this figure hasn't been adjusted for inflation.

Retirement calculators

Gabelli Retirement Savings Calculator (http://www.gabel;li.com/Gab_phtm/mfund/saving3.html). From the Gabelli Funds site, this calculator uses the projections of the USA Today/CNN/Gallup Poll regarding the amount of assets needed for retirement. It also assumes a life expectancy of 85 years. You find out whether you're contributing enough to meet this goal and, if not, how much more you need to save per month.

Retirement Savings Calculator (http://www.1sttech.com/calc/ret-calc/html). Created by First Technology Federal Credit Union, this simple calculator takes your tax bracket and inflation into account, but it doesn't enable you to state how much you've already saved.

Retirement Funding Calculator (http://www.waddell.com/fun_ill.html). Offered by Waddell & Reed, this calculator is easy to use, but it doesn't take continuing contributions into account.

You find many more retirement calculators on the Internet, but please be aware that most are too simplistic to forecast your retirement income needs. A good retirement calculator should take into account your current retirement savings and contributions; otherwise, the calculator may overestimate the amount you need to save. Don't let a simplistic retirement calculator frighten you into apathy or inaction.

Assessing Your Risk Tolerance

Investing isn't only about rationally choosing the right investment and (hopefully) getting a return. It's also about emotions — specifically, fear.

High-risk investments aren't for the faint of heart. The higher the possible return over the long haul, the more *volatile* the investment is likely to be in the short haul. A volatile investment undergoes big swings in value — up and down. Aggressive growth funds, for example, experience the biggest gains when the market is going up and the biggest losses when it's going down.

Here's the problem with volatile investments. If your risk tolerance is low, then you may panic and sell when the market plummets. In most cases, that's a bad move. You lose out on the appreciation when the market comes back. Remember, the stock market has historically produced an average ten percent gain; sometimes it gains more, and sometimes it loses. If you're in the market for the long haul — ten to fifteen years — you should see a market downturn as an opportunity to buy more stock at lower prices, not an occasion for panic selling.

To be sure, it's not all a matter of psychology. There are some good, rational reasons for low risk tolerance. Ponder these questions:

◆ **How old are you?** In general, young people are looking at longer-term investments (and the risk that goes with it).

◆ **How secure is your job?** If you're afraid that you're going to be laid off sometime in the near future, you may need to convert your investments to cash for living expenses.

◆ **What's your net worth?** After you've laid a solid financial foundation, you can set aside some money for high-risk investments.

◆ **Have you saved enough to meet your living expenses for three to six months?** You shouldn't contemplate a risky investment unless you have at least this much cash.

◆ **When do you need the money?** If you're investing on a short time frame (for example, a down payment or college starting in a year), you should be thinking about preserving your capital. You don't have the time to wait out a market downturn. In general, if you need the money in five years or less, you should choose less volatile investments.

◆ **How's your health?** If you're currently healthy and aren't looking at adverse health situations in your family, you can take on more risk than someone who has to deal with high, recurrent health care costs.

Now for some online help with risk tolerance. The Vanguard Investment Personality Profile (http://www.vanguard.com/tools/risk.html), shown in Figure 4-3, enables you to fill out an on-screen questionnaire. When you click on the Calculate button, you see a new page that fits you into one of three investment personality profiles:

◆ **Conservative.** Your main concern is capital preservation. You can't handle short-term financial setbacks. In addition, you may need your money in less than five years. You're willing to put little or none of your savings in high-risk investments, such as growth stocks.

◆ **Moderate.** You're concerned with steady growth and you're willing to sit through moderate downturns, but your ability to tolerate short-term financial setbacks is limited. About half your savings is in stocks.

◆ **Aggressive.** You're investing for the long haul, and you're willing to accept short-term setbacks. You have a secure job, a solid emergency fund, and the nerve to weather market downturns. You'll put most of your savings in stocks.

Don't rely on just one test; they're all different. For additional risk tolerance tests and worksheets on the Web, see the sidebar "Risk tolerance resources on the Web."

The effect of fear on your investment style was mentioned earlier. Another emotion that affects investors is greed. You're trying to build your wealth by investing, but doing this isn't a contest where you have to out-do all other investors. You're picking investments that will help you meet your financial goals and should satisfy your needs. That implies taking a certain amount of risk. But there's no reason to take risks that are excessive for what you need to accomplish and can afford.

Risk tolerance resources on the Web

Ameristock: Risk Tolerance Test (http://www.ameristock.com/test.htm). A good quiz, but you have to compute the totals yourself.

Fidelity Investor Profile Questionnaire (http://wps1.fid-inv.com/int.invprof.htm). Focuses on retirement investments.

MacKenzie Financial's Client Investor Profile (http://www.io.org/~nobid/star.html). An extensive and well-thought-out questionnaire.

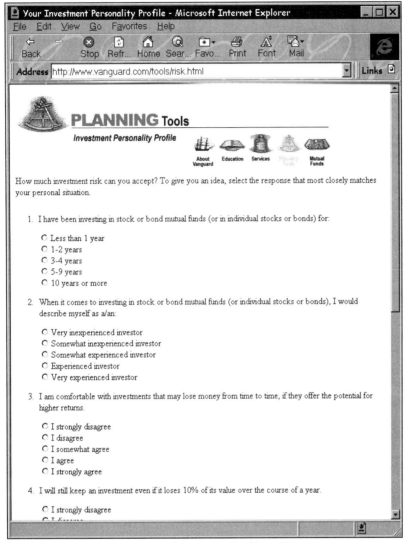

Figure 4-3: Vanguard Investment Personality Profile online questionnaire.

Allocating Your Assets

By now, thanks to the Web, you have a pretty good idea of the following:

◆ The holding period for each investment goal you've defined.

◆ Your risk tolerance.

◆ The amount of money you need.

It's time to think about how to allocate your assets to achieve your objectives. Here's where you think about diversification — not putting all your eggs in one basket. What percentage of your assets do you want to put into stocks? Into bonds? Into limited-risk money market funds and CDs?

Bank of America's Personal Investment Profile (http://www.bofa.com/tools/sri_assetall.html) quizzes you with 12 very intelligent questions and produces an asset-allocation pie chart (divided among stocks, bonds, and cash).

Financial advisors don't agree about asset allocation; some would tell you to put 50 percent of your money in stocks for a given investment profile, while others would put the figure at 75 percent. That's not surprising because no two person's investment profiles and needs are quite alike. The same goes for Web pages. Each relies on a set of assumptions that reflects the interests and biases of the page's operators. You have to decide for yourself whether these assumptions are right for you. Work through as many of these pages as you can find and, in the end, make your own decision.

Asset allocation resources on the Web

Fleet's Investment Allocation Analyzer (http://www.fleet.com/calculators_temp/retirement-invest-calculat.html). You work through a good risk tolerance questionnaire, and you see a recommended allocation among stocks, bonds, and cash as a result.

Massachusetts Mutual Risk Tolerance Quiz (http://www.massmutual.com/retire/risk1.html). This is a clever quiz with many graphics and fun questions. The result is an asset allocation model that's tailored for your risk tolerance and holding period.

Summary

◆ Begin your financial planning by determining your net worth. You find several handy net worth questionnaires and calculators on the Web.

◆ Determine your investment goal. What do you want the money for, and when do you need the money?

◆ To figure out how much money you need, use one of the college or retirement calculators that you find on the Web, but be careful about their built-in assumptions.

◆ Now that you know how much you need, figure out how much risk you can handle. This involves not only your investment psychology but also your time frame. Short-term investments should be more conservative than long-term ones.

◆ Financial advisors vary when asked to suggest asset allocations, and the Web's asset allocation calculators reflect this variation. Use several calculators to get differing opinions of how you should distribute your money among stocks, bonds, and cash. In the end, you have to decide for yourself.

From Here

◆ Begin exploring investment-related resources on the Internet by using starting points pages (see Chapter 5).

◆ Learn how to search the Internet for additional resources (see Chapter 6).

◆ Keep up with fast-breaking investment and business news (see Chapter 7).

PART III

Getting Your Bearings on the Internet

Investment-Related Starting Points

With millions of documents already available on the Web and thousands more appearing daily, finding investment-related information presents a challenge. Surfing — going from Web site to Web site by clicking on links — just doesn't cut it. Happily, some people devote time to tracking down the best investment-related sites. By accessing the pages they create, you can quickly find high-quality information.

Web pages that attempt to group a number of high-quality Web resources are often called *metapages* (pages about pages) or *trailblazer pages*. The folks at Yahoo — one of the best subject catalogs of Web sites (http://www.yahoo.com) — call them *indices*, while others call them *general guides* or *all-in-one sites*. We refer to them as *starting points*.

In this chapter, you find many pages that you'll want to visit again and again, so be sure to bookmark them. When you bookmark a page, you can return to the page easily by choosing its name from the bookmark menu. With Netscape Navigator, you can bookmark a page by displaying it and choosing Add Bookmark from the Bookmarks menu.

In This Chapter

♦ Beginner's starting points

♦ Comprehensive starting points

♦ Specialized starting points pages

Who creates starting points pages? Sometimes they're created by individuals with professional or avocational interests in an area. As these pages start to get hundreds or even thousands of hits per day, they can attract advertising, and more than a few of them have become successful business ventures. Others are created by brokerage firms, Internet Service Providers, or business service firms, mainly as a marketing tool.

With several dozen investment starting points pages on the Web, these would-be solutions become a problem. Which is the right one to use? This chapter suggests that you explore them in order, beginning with Mathew Ingram's excellent High-Tech Investor, and explore additional pages as you refine and sharpen your interests.

Beginner's Starting Points

When you're getting started with the Internet, the last thing you want is to be overwhelmed with thousands of sites. The following starting points cut down the complexity of the Web, showing you only a few good sites in each category (such as stocks, bonds, and so on). Try them in the recommended order.

The High-Tech Investor

An investment and markets reporter with the Toronto *Globe and Mail,* Mathew Ingram offers this excellent starting point for beginning Internet users. Essentially, it's a readable survey of Internet resources for investors, stressing the best and most useful sites. Rather than assembling thousands of links, Ingram prefers to introduce a few good ones and fully explain how you can use them. You can access The High-Tech Investor at `http://www.want2know.com/invest/invest.htm`.

As you can see in Figure 5-1, Ingram's site is organized like a well-written magazine article — which it is, sort of, except that it's loaded with hyperlinks. Overall, this is a nice example of thoughtful Web design.

Ingram's readable prose isn't the only reason for recommending The High-Tech Investor as a starting point: It's also his conservative, watch-out-for-scams approach. One reviewer termed Ingram's site "a rogue's gallery" of unsavory investment schemes. While emphasizing that Internet-mediated investing has its risks, Ingram is convinced that it's here to stay, and he offers sound advice for finding your way safely through the maze.

You find links in the following categories at The High Tech Investor:

◆ **Electronic stock-trading sites.** A good collection of online brokerages, which enable you to buy and sell stocks via the Internet.

◆ **General guides and all-in-one sites.** A thorough survey of starting points sites, including those that have not-so-obvious inclinations towards the speculative.

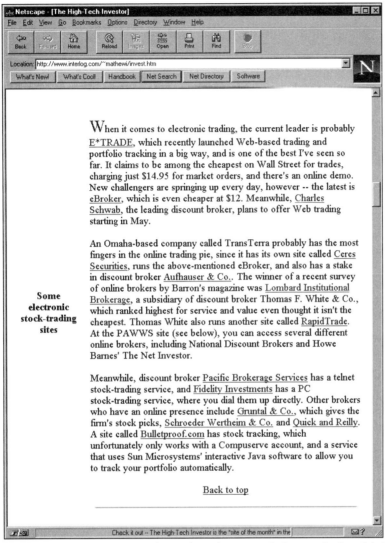

Figure 5-1: Mathew Ingram's The High-Tech Investor helps you find useful sites.

- ◆ **Brokerages with online presences.** Links to brokerage pages, including some with useful information (such as "Investing for the Perplexed").

- ◆ **Canadian sites.** A great collection of Canada-specific sites for Canadian investors or those interested in investing in Canada.

- ◆ **Quote servers.** A good collection of free, 15-minute-delayed stock quote servers.

- ◆ **Stock exchanges.** Links to Canadian, U.S., and international exchanges.

◆ **Magazines and newspapers.** A few good links to Internet versions of financial publications, including *Money* and *Bloomberg Business News.*

GNN Personal Finance Center

A division of America Online, the Global Network Navigator (GNN) offers an excellent subject catalog of high-quality Web sites, each with its own, in-depth review. By no means as comprehensive as go-for-the-big numbers sites (such as Invest-O-Rama, to be discussed later in this chapter), GNN's Personal Finance Center (see Figure 5-2) gives you a few good links in each category. Like Ingram's The High-Tech Investor, it's a great place to start if you're worried about getting overwhelmed by thousands of links.

While emphasizing personal finance subjects such as mortgages, GNN's Personal Finance page (`http://nearnet.gnn.com/gnn/wic/wics/persfin.new.html`) offers the following categories of interest to investors:

◆ **Bonds & Treasuries.** A few interesting links, including a savings bond calculator, bond investment pamphlets, and inflation/interest data.

◆ **Brokers.** A list of active online brokerages, which enable you to buy and sell stocks via the Internet.

◆ **Exchanges.** Links to the home pages of U.S. and international stock exchanges.

◆ **Financial Planning.** Thorough list of links on debt counseling, legal self-help resources, and consumer information.

◆ **International Investment.** Links and information related to international investing and foreign stock exchanges.

◆ **Investors' Reference.** Probably the most valuable resource in GNN's Personal Finance Center. Lists company reports, general research sources, information about investment fraud, and additional starting points pages.

◆ **Mutual Funds.** A first-rate collection of links, including daily net asset values (NAV), home pages of fund families, online magazines, mutual fund ratings and rankings, and investment advice.

◆ **News & Magazines.** A good survey of online newspapers and magazines with a focus on investment or finance.

◆ **Options & Futures.** A few resources, including the home pages of the Chicago Board of Trade and the Chicago Mercantile Exchange.

◆ **Stock Quotes & Market Data.** A useful list of fifteen-minute-delayed services and end-of-day summaries.

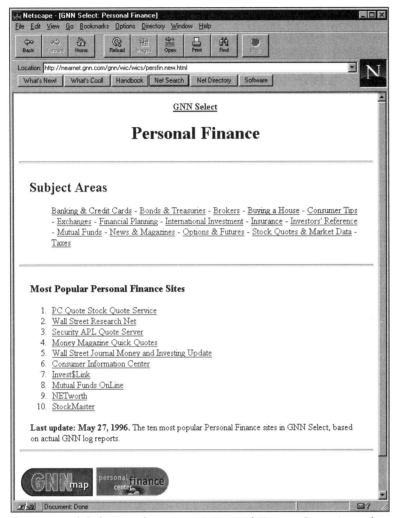

Figure 5-2: Global Network Navigator's Personal Finance Center is another great place to start.

GNN's top ten

One of the most interesting resources in GNN's Personal Finance Center is the list of GNN's top ten personal finance sites, based on the number of times these sites are accessed through GNN. Here's the rank as of this writing:

1. **PC Quote Stock Quote Service** (http://www.pcquote.com). Free stock quotes, delayed 20 minutes.

2. **Wall Street Research Net** (http://www.wsrn.com/home/index.html). Focused on stock research, this site boasts an amazing 65,000 links to company information, the economy, the market's current events, stock market publications, mutual fund indexes, corporate yellow pages, and more.

3. **Security APL Quote Server** (http://www.secapl.com/). A fifteen-minute-delayed service that offers a ticker symbol lookup service.

4. **Money Magazine Quick Quotes** (http://quote.pathfinder.com). Delayed quotes feature current price, change, daily and 52-week highs and lows, price/earnings ratio, and dividend per share.

5. **Wall Street Journal Interactive Edition** (http://update.wsj.com). The online, interactive edition of the *Wall Street Journal.*

6. **Consumer Information Center** (http://www.pueblo.gsa.gov/). An outstanding resource. Most of the consumer information pamphlets and booklets published by the U.S. Government's consumer information service are available here for free downloading or reading on-screen. A search engine enables you to search for key words. You find tons of information here on investments, including annuities, stocks, mutual funds, the Investor's Bill of Rights, and much more. Don't miss "How to Spot a Con Artist"!

7. **Invest$Link** (http://www.imfnet.com/pitbull/links1.html). One of the better investment-related starting points pages, discussed later in this chapter.

8. **Mutual Funds Online** (http://www.mfmag.com). Excellent online version of the monthly magazine.

9. **NETWorth** (http://networth.galt.com/). One of the best Internet resources for information on mutual funds — more than 5,000 of them!

10. **StockMaster** (http://www.stockmaster.com). Comprehensive stock quotes and charts for more than 300 U.S. stocks and mutual funds.

The Starting Point (Investing)

Are you looking for a site more comprehensive than The High-Tech Investor or GNN Personal Finance Center, a site that better indicates the type of resources you find on the Internet but doesn't overwhelm you with thousands of links? A good place to begin a more thorough exploration is The Starting Point's Investing page (`http://www.stpt.com/invest.html`). This well-organized page, shown in Figure 5-3, offers a good selection of high-quality sites. The brief annotations are informative and right on the money, from a critical standpoint. It's an excellent site!

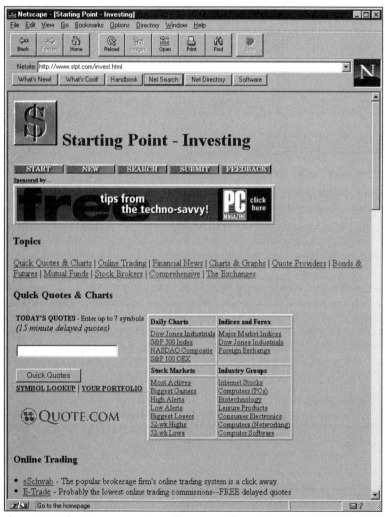

Figure 5-3: The Starting Point's well-organized Investing page.

You find the following categories of links in the Starting Point's Investing page:

◆ **Quick Quotes & Charts.** You can enter a ticker symbol into this page directly. Also available are daily charts of the Dow Jones Industrials, S&P 500 Index, NASDAQ Composite, S&P 100 Index, Most Actives, Biggest Gainers, High Alerts, Low Alerts, Biggest Losers, 52-week highs, 52-week lows, major market indices, foreign exchanges, and charts by sector (Internet, computers, biotechnology, leisure products, consumer electronics, networking hardware, and computer software). These charts don't require a Master's degree in finance to interpret. You see what the major market indexes are doing, and you find out which stocks have been the biggest gainers and biggest losers. Other charts tell which stocks have hit all time highs (and lows), and there's lots more. Don't miss these charts!

◆ **Online Trading.** A good list of links to Internet-based brokerages.

◆ **Financial News.** A few good reports, including CNNfn (CNN's financial news), Barron's, the Holt Report, and Money Daily.

◆ **Bonds & Futures.** A few links to help you get started in these areas.

◆ **Mutual Funds.** About one-half dozen links to some of the best mutual funds sites, including Mutual Funds Magazine Online.

◆ **Stock Brokers.** Links to brokerages with an online presence.

◆ **Comprehensive.** A list of additional investment-related starting points pages and other resources; it's concisely but informatively annotated.

◆ **Exchanges.** Links to U.S. stock and commodity exchanges' home pages.

Comprehensive Starting Points

After you have a feel for the resources that are out there, you'll want more — and these sites tell you where to find more resources. Unlike the sites just mentioned, which show you a few good sites in each category, these pages try to be as comprehensive as possible. Some of them offer more than two thousand links.

Invest-O-Rama

Here's an investment-related starting point that's hip to the Fifties *cachet* that you find at the Web's top sites, such as the Internet Underground Music Archive (IUMA). Maybe style matters for something on the Web, because this site is one of the best starting points (for a taste of the cool graphics, see Figure 5-4). Here you find nearly 2,000 investment-related links, sorted conveniently into 24 categories. You also find a good deal of conservative, common-sense advice for beginning investors. To access Invest-O-Rama, use `http://www.investorama.com/`.

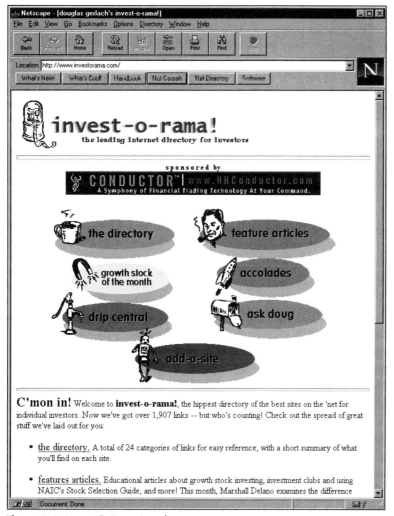

Figure 5-4: Invest-O-Rama's welcome page.

Here's what's offered at Invest-O-Rama at this writing:

◆ **The Directory.** This is Invest-O-Rama's top-level table of contents, where you find links to bonds, brokerages, dividend reinvestment plans, futures, government stuff, international investing, market letters and advisory services, mutual funds, investment clubs, quantitative analysis, quote servers, real estate, stock markets, software, taxes, and venture capital. A real plus: Each site is listed along with a short summary, which enables you to determine whether it's really of interest to you.

◆ **Feature Articles.** Well worth a visit is this collection of articles and commentary. Featured at this writing were reviews of online brokerages, a look at the gloomy predictions for investors in 1996, the difference between investing and gambling, an overview of investing resources on the Internet, and a variety of educational resources for people planning an investment club.

◆ **DRIP Central.** This is the best starting point for anyone interested in dividend reinvestment plans (DRIPs), which enable you to buy stocks directly from certain corporations instead of going through a broker.

◆ **Growth Stock to Watch.** Very much worth a monthly visit is this page, which presents Invest-O-Rama's pick of the month. It's no mystery how the stock is picked: Douglas Gerlach, the page's maintainer, simply applies the formula recommended by the National Association of Investors Corporation (NAIC).

◆ **Ask Doug.** You can address questions to the site's maintainer, Douglas Gerlach, and you can also browse previous questions and answers. Don't look for stock picks here, but you do find a great deal of solid, common sense (especially for beginning investors).

Want to learn the NAIC method for picking growth stocks? Check out the Stock Selection Guide Tutorial at Invest-O-Rama (`http://www.investorama.com/ features/ssg_00.html`). Also, don't miss the Quick Tips for Balance Sheet Analysis (`http://www.investorama.com/ features/balance.shtml`). You quickly learn how to compute a stock's book value, common stock ratio, current ratio, inventory turnover, plant turnover, preferred stock ratio, and working capital, all from publicly available figures (which you can find on the Internet). These figures help you decide whether a stock's correctly valued (for more information, see Chapter 16).

The Syndicate

One of the better starting points is The Syndicate (`http://www.moneypages. com/syndicate/`), which, despite the Mafia-sounding name, is quite a friendly place. The well-organized welcome page, shown in Figure 5-5, features Syndicate Navigator, the site's table of contents. You also find links to this month's features.

Figure 5-5: The Syndicate's welcome page is a friendly place.

You find the following groups of links at The Syndicate:

◆ **Stocks.** A brief list of high-quality sites, including many that will interest beginning investors. You learn about the Dow Jones Industrial Average, dividend reinvestment programs, and initial public offerings, or IPOs. Also included is an analysis of market performance by presidential term. You also find links to pages about investment gurus (including Warren Buffet's top holdings), foreign stocks, and options.

◆ **Finance Pages.** More than 1,600 links (at this writing) to banks, bonds, books, brokerage firms, charts, commodities, economics, insurance, mutual funds, newsletters, newspapers and magazines, personal finance, software, and more. An extremely welcome feature is a star rating system (look for four- and five-starred sites).

◆ **Broker's Corner.** Information for brokers — and investors, too. One of the most interesting links: How brokers themselves rate brokerage firms.

◆ **Bonds.** Well worth a visit for a beginner hoping to learn more about bonds. You find an explanation of how bonds are traded, historical graphs of three-month Treasury bill rates, links to other bond sites, an explanation of Moody's bond ratings, and a glossary of bond terminology.

◆ **misc.invest.funds FAQ.** The Syndicate is the official home page of the Usenet newsgroup `misc.invest.funds`, and it features the group's FAQ (a compendium of answers to frequently asked questions). Useful features include a list of mutual fund phone numbers and dozens of links to mutual fund-related sites.

Invest$Link

Gathering hundreds of links of interest to investors, Invest$Link (`http://www.imfnet.com/pitbull/links1.html`) is worth a visit, even though it's not as comprehensive as Invest-O-Rama. The site's value is enhanced by the brief but informative site descriptions, which enable you to tell at a glance whether the link is really worth a visit. Also, you can request delayed stock quotes by typing ticker symbols into the provided boxes (see Figure 5-6). On the down side, the annotations are often rather sparse, and the lengthy lists of links aren't organized in any obvious way.

How to change your default start page (Netscape)

Every time you start Netscape, you see the Netscape Communications home page. That's fine for Netscape — the more hits (accesses) they can prove, the more advertising they can sell. Why not change the default start page, the page you see when you start the program? You can change it to something that's more useful for your purposes, such as Starting Point's Investments page. You can always access Netscape's home page by choosing Home from the browser's Directory menu.

To change the default start page, open the Options menu, choose General Preferences, and click on the Appearance tab. In the Starts With dialog box, type the URL of the page you want to see when you start Netscape. To start with Starting Point's Investment page, for example, you type **http://www.stpt.com/invest.html**. To confirm your choice, click on OK.

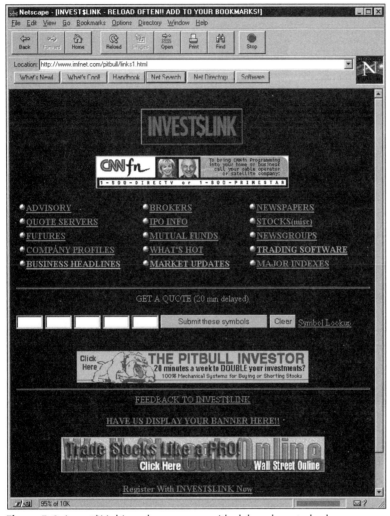

Figure 5-6: Invest$Link's welcome page with delayed quote lookup.

You find the following categories at Invest$Link:

◆ **Advisory Services.** A fairly long list of Web-accessible newsletters and stock selection advisors, without much guidance as to their value.

◆ **Brokers.** A good survey of online brokerages, but there aren't many annotations to help you distinguish among the many services mentioned.

◆ **Business Headlines.** A comprehensive but sparsely annotated list of Web-accessible newspapers and magazines with a business or investment focus.

◆ **Company Profiles.** This is a list of profilers of public companies.

◆ **Futures.** A comprehensive list of futures related links — Putbull's forte.

◆ **Major Indexes.** Links to the major U.S. and foreign stock and commodity exchanges.

◆ **Mutual Funds.** A list of mutual fund lists, focusing on fund family home pages. Not well-organized.

◆ **Newsgroups.** Links to some investment-related Usenet newsgroups, but not annotated.

◆ **Quote Servers.** A fairly comprehensive list of quote servers, including some that you won't find on stock-only lists (including currency contract quotes, commodities prices, treasury bond data, futures, and more).

◆ **Stocks (Misc).** Miscellaneous is right — it's a lengthy and disorganized list of stock-related links — but worth a visit.

Wall Street Directory, Inc.

The Wall Street Directory (`http://www.wsdinc.com/`) offers more than 2,500 links for "computerized traders and investors," using a well-organized table format (see Figure 5-7). You can also access the site's many resources alphabetically.

Not all the resources in the Wall Street Directory are Web sites or other Internet-accessible services; some are accessible only through online services, such as America Online, or through noncomputer means. Still others are resources for sale by Wall Street Directory. Nonetheless, this is an extremely comprehensive and valuable service.

Hunting for Internet resources on Wall Street Directory? Look for the [Web Link] note after the resource's name.

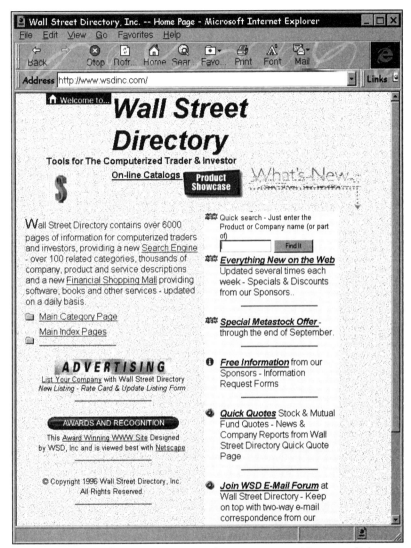

Figure 5-7: The Wall Street Directory welcome page provides many links.

One of the Wall Street Directory's best features is its extensive, specific subject categories, which organize the links into the following categories:

◆ **Advisory services.** Fax and hotline services, general investment advisory services, and newsletters.

◆ **Analysis tools.** A wonderful compendium of Internet-accessible analytical tools and strategies, spanning the gamut from astrology and Fibonacci numbers to serious fundamental and technical analysis. Fascinating stuff, but not for the beginning investor.

◆ **Associations and clubs.** A brief list of links to investment associations and clubs.

◆ **Banking services.** A good collection of banks that have established an Internet presence. Can online banking be far away?

◆ **Bookstore.** A wide selection of investment-related titles that you can order directly. Excellent, in-depth descriptions of each title.

◆ **Brokerage services.** A collection of links concerning arbitration, brokers, discount brokers, introductions to brokerage services, electronic trading, and simulated trading.

◆ **Calendar section.** This section isn't well developed; you find a few listings for investors' and brokers' associations.

◆ **Commodity services.** Links to Internet resources concerning commodities, futures, energy, fuels, and mining. Please be aware that these are high-risk investments and not for beginners!

◆ **Contests — games and challenges.** Cool survey of Internet and online-accessible investment games.

◆ **Currency rates and programs.** An extensive list of currency-related sites and services.

◆ **Data services.** The place to look if you're curious about real-time stock data services, but be forewarned: They're pricey. (It's free to check out their Web pages, though.)

◆ **Educational tools.** Listed are audios, videos, and software, as well as glossaries of investment-related terms and a collection of seminars, conferences, and workshops.

◆ **E-mail and list forums.** A useful survey of mailing lists, newsgroups, and e-mail notification services.

◆ **Fixed income.** Some useful Internet resources on bonds, mixed with lots of commercial services and for-sale items, such as bond-tracking software.

◆ **Government.** A comprehensive and useful list of free U.S. government services and resources.

◆ **Market reports.** A comprehensive survey of market wrap-up services.

◆ **Metals-coins, etc.** Probably the best collection on the Web of sites and links related to these investments.

◆ **Mutual fund services.** An excellent and comprehensive survey of mutual funds resources on and off the Internet.

◆ **News services.** A good but not terribly up-to-date survey of investment and finance-related news links.

◆ **Option services and programs.** The place to look if you're interested in derivatives and options.

◆ **Personal finance services.** An impressive collection of personal finance links and resources, covering asset allocation, bookkeeping, calculators, insurance, mortgages, pension plans, real estate, and retirement planning.

◆ **Public companies and IPOs.** Listed here are search services that enable you to perform research on publicly held companies and initial public offerings (IPOs).

◆ **Publications.** More investment-related books, which you can order from this site.

◆ **Quote services.** A good list of quote services, including freebie (delayed) and costly (real-time) services.

◆ **Software demos and trials.** One of the Wall Street Directory's best areas. You find many links to shareware and demo versions of portfolio management software, analytical tools, and lots more. You also find direct download links and reviews.

Specialized Starting Points Pages

You find more starting points collections on the Web, often with a slant toward a particular kind of investing. Here's a sample of the best of the rest:

◆ **Conscious Investing Home Page** (http://www.investing.com). This page focuses on links related to socially and environmentally responsible investing.

◆ **FINWeb** (http://www.riskweb.com). FINWeb specializes in financial economics. There's much stuff of great interest to professionals working in this area.

◆ **Hot Links for Traders!** (http://www.io.com/~gibbonsb/wahoo.html). Compiled by Gibbons Burke, the author of "The Computerized Trader" (a monthly column in *Futures Magazine*), this starting points page focuses on commodities and futures, with a nod toward stocks and bonds. If you're new to futures, there's an excellent section entitled "Reference & Learning" that has several informative links. For example, you can find out just what a pork belly is, if you're curious to know. Remember that these are high-risk investments; they're not for beginners.

◆ **NETWorth** (`http://networth.galt.com/www/home/networth.htm`). This is probably the Web's premier starting point for mutual funds and stock investors.

Summary

◆ Starting points pages (also called metapages, collections, indices, and trailblazer pages) collect a variety of links focused on a particular subject. You find dozens of these efforts on the Web.

◆ When you're getting started, work with a beginner's starting points page, one that doesn't try to throw thousands of links at you. After you explore and feel more confident, tackle one of the more comprehensive pages.

◆ Besides the pages that try to be comprehensive, there are dozens more that focus on specific aspects of investing, such as socially responsible investing, investment research, or mutual funds. As your interests and needs clarify, one of these pages may become useful to you.

From Here

◆ Now that you've learned how to use starting points pages, round out your skills by learning how to search the Internet for additional sites (see Chapter 6).

◆ Keep up with fast-breaking investment and business news with Web-based newspapers and magazines (see Chapter 7).

◆ Want to give Usenet newsgroups a try? Learn the perils, pitfalls, and possible benefits (see Chapter 8).

Finding the Information You Need

In This Chapter

◆ Introducing search services

◆ Comparing search services

◆ Searching for stocks on the Web

Starting points pages, discussed in Chapter 5, list only a tiny fraction of the millions of documents available on the Internet. Somewhere out there, you *know* a Web page or some other Internet resource contains just the information you want. But how do you find it?

Late at night, automated programs called *spiders* roam the Web, looking for new Web sites and new Web documents. One of the best spiders — Lycos — has located more than 50 million documents (the number will probably top 60 or 70 million by the time you read this). The spider's discoveries go into a database, which you can search using a *search service* (also called a *search engine,* because database programs are called search engines in an apparent effort to make them sound more muscular than they really are).

A search service enables you to specify keywords that match your interests. After you type these words, the search service hunts through its database of Web documents. The result is a list of documents that may match your needs. Positioned at the top of the list are those documents with the highest probable relevance to your interests. To see one of these documents, you just click on its title.

Knowing how to use a search service well is an essential skill for an Internet-based investment strategy. In this chapter, you learn the basics of searching with the Web's top search services. You can try searching yourself, using the extended, step-by-step tutorial that you find later in this chapter.

Don't expect miracles from the Web's search services. They work by matching words. However, language is ambiguous. If you search for *hot funds*, you may find a site that lists hot mutual funds — and you also may get a page published by the Libertarian Party's leader, Harry Browne, explaining why he won't accept federal election funds. As you learn more about search services, you can cut down the number of irrelevant documents (but you can't completely eliminate them).

Introducing Search Services

It would be nice to say that a perfect search service exists, but it doesn't. Instead, you find several search services — more than a dozen, at last count. Each uses its own proprietary database of Web documents, some larger than others. Each embodies its own particular search philosophy. Choosing the right search service is important. And sometimes it makes good sense to use more than one.

Take a look at one of the better search services, Infoseek Guide. Although this service doesn't have the largest database (that distinction is AltaVista's), it does the best job of pinpointing documents that are relevant to your interests. What's more, it has a dandy subject guide that's loaded with investing and personal finance links.

If you're near your computer, access Infoseek's home page at `http://guide.infoseek.com/`.

As this book was going to press, Infoseek was in the process of releasing UltraSeek, which is going to combine Infoseek's great qualities with a *huge* database. It's going to be a winner. Check out `http://ultra.infoseek.com/` to see what's up.

Infoseek's home page

When you access Infoseek Guide, you see a page similar to the one shown in Figure 6-1. (Chances are they've made some changes since this illustration was created.)

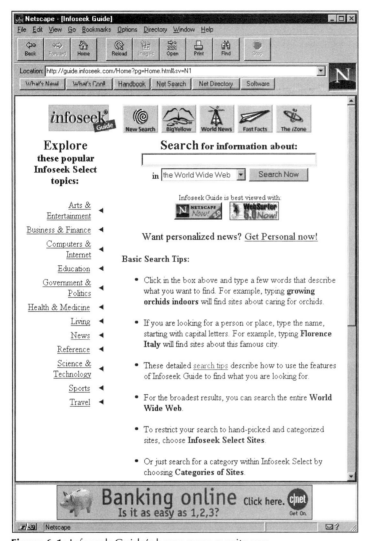

Figure 6-1: Infoseek Guide's home page awaits you.

Here's what you do to use Infoseek (it's pretty simple, actually):

1. **Type your key terms.** In the text box on-screen, you type your keywords, such as *Fidelity Investments* or *hot mutual funds*.

2. **Choose where to search.** You can search the Web, Usenet, or e-mail addresses.

KEY TERM

3. **Click on the search button.** Doing so initiates the search. The result is a new Web page showing the search results. See Figure 6-2 for the results of the *hot mutual funds* search.

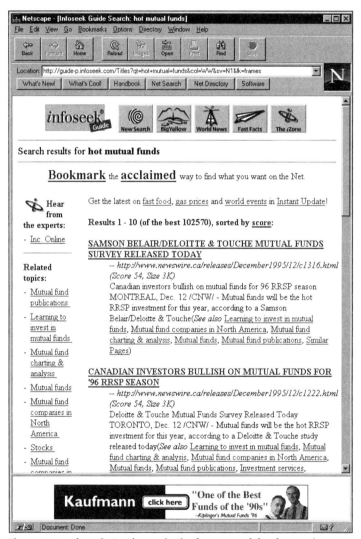

Figure 6-2: Infoseek Guide results for **hot mutual funds** search.

Scrolling down the *hot mutual funds* results list in Figure 6-2, you find a *hit* — a document that's at the heart of your interests. Click on the hit for the page shown in Figure 6-3.

Figure 6-3: A hit!

Why is Infoseek so cool? Because it offers the following:

◆ **Automatic subject category detection.** The search software has matched your keywords to subject headings in the Guide's catalog of useful Web sites. Take a look at the left column in Figure 6-2; you see *Mutual fund publications, Learning to invest in mutual funds,* and much more. If you don't find any hot documents in the list of retrieved documents, you can click on one of these subject headings to see some quality stuff.

◆ **Documents retrieved with links and abstracts.** For each document retrieved, you see a brief summary that enables you to decide whether it's relevant to your needs. There's also a list of subject categories for each document; you can click on one of these, or on the link titled *Similar Pages*, to see additional documents that match your search terms.

◆ **High precision.** In database searching, *precision* is a rough-and-ready measurement of the number of retrieved documents that actually match your interests. Infoseek is far and away the most precise search service on the Web.

Remember, just because you found it on the Web doesn't mean that it's true. Don't ever forget to ask the three *W* questions: *Who* put this page up? *What* have they to gain? *Where* are they coming from?

Help! My search didn't work

You're looking through a huge, lengthy retrieval list, and there's nothing but *false drops* — documents that have nothing to do with your interests. If you see a lot of false drops at the top of the list, don't bother going through more than two or three pages of results. All the Web's search services start the retrieval list with the documents most likely to be relevant. After two or three pages of duds, the list is just going to get worse.

Instead, check for mistakes and rethink your strategy. To make sure that you get good results, look over this list of hints and suggestions:

◆ **Check your spelling.** Search services can't handle typos. If you try searching for *mutial fends*, you get results (but very *weird* results, including "Diane's World and Welcome To It," "The Harry Crews Page," and "Ultra Poly Presents 'Hard Knocks'").

◆ **Be more specific.** To get pinpointed results, type many terms. If you type **mutual funds**, you get tons of pages. Limit the list by focusing more on what you want (for example, *mutual funds expenses 12-1(b) fees management cost no-load*).

◆ **Think of synonyms.** Don't just search for *Treasury bonds*; include the word *bills* as well.

◆ **Use truncation.** With many search services, you can type a word root (such as **invest***), followed by an asterisk, to retrieve additional forms of the word (investing, investor, investors, investment).

◆ **Learn how to use inclusion and exclusion operators.** Many of the search services on the Web enable you to specify a word that *must* be included for a document to be retrieved, as well as a word that must *not* be present.

Usually, you indicate inclusion by preceding the word with a + (plus) sign. You indicate exclusion by preceding the word with a - (minus) sign. Suppose you're searching for *treasury bonds bills* and you get many documents about the Buffalo Bills. You can exclude the poor Bills by typing **-buffalo.**

◆ **Use phrase searching.** The better search services enable you to search for a complete phrase, such as "Treasury bonds." Usually, you enclose the phrase in quotes. What's so great about phrase searching? It excludes documents that mention both words, but not together in a phrase. So you won't get "A James Bond Treasury"!

Comparing Search Services

Infoseek is a great service, but there are others. Following is a list of other search services:

◆ **AltaVista** (http://altavista.digital.com). Currently, the Web's largest database, but watch out for the low precision. AltaVista is a good choice when you're looking for something really obscure and can't find it anywhere else.

◆ **Excite** (http://www.excite.com). A smallish database, but it's easy to use and includes a big subject catalog of high-quality Web sites.

◆ **Lycos** (http://www.lycos.com). One of the first search engines, and it's getting a bit long in the tooth: It doesn't index the full text of documents, so you can't retrieve a document if the term you're searching for doesn't occur in the first 20 lines or so.

◆ **Magellan Internet Guide** (http://www.mckinley.com). A so-so search engine is coupled with thousands of site reviews. This is a good place to search for sites with substantive reviews.

◆ **Yahoo!** (http://www.yahoo.com). With Yahoo!, you search only the sites that Yahoo! has manually indexed and classified. It's similar to a subject catalog for the Internet. When you search Yahoo!, you get a list of high-quality sites. It's a great place to start your search.

Use Yahoo! to start your search — you'll find high-quality sites. To make sure that you've found everything, use AltaVista or Infoseek's new service, Ultraseek.

See Table 6-1 for a feature-by-feature comparison of Web search services.

Web search service features

Database size. AltaVista and Lycos offer the largest databases; Infoseek's and Excite's contain only (roughly) ten percent of the documents retrieved by AltaVista. In short: If you want to search the entire Web, use AltaVista or Lycos.

Phrase searching. This convenient feature enables you to search for phrases, such as *zero-coupon bonds* or *Treasury bills*. The search doesn't retrieve documents unless the exact phrase occurs. (In other words, you won't get a story in which a character named Zero Bonds says, "Hand me that coupon, OK?")

Case-sensitive searching. This feature enables you to specify a capitalization pattern when searching. For example, you can search for Fidelity Investments, and you won't get pages about the investment you make in your marriage through the simple practice of fidelity.

Subject guide to the Web. Some search engines offer a subject classification guide to the better documents on the Web. Because the classification has to be done manually, don't expect to find more than a few thousand documents in these guides. Still, they're very useful, as you see later in this chapter.

Automatic subject detection. Your search results include subject categories as well as Web documents. If you see a subject category that looks relevant, you can click on it to see more documents.

Site reviews. Of the search services that offer subject guides, some include reviews such as Magellan, with its four-star system.

Usenet, FTP sites, or Gopher sites included. All search services index Web documents. A few include FTP and Gopher sites and enable you to search Usenet newsgroups. If you're looking for a Gopher or FTP site, make sure that the search engine you're using includes these sites (along with those zillions of Web sites!).

Recall. A rough-and-ready measurement of the service's ability to retrieve all the documents that are relevant to your interests. Because of the ambiguities of language and the fact that people word the same concepts differently, no search service can ever achieve perfect recall.

Precision. The number of documents in the retrieval list that are relevant to your interests (as opposed to *false drops*, the documents that aren't relevant). For example, suppose you're searching for *CDs*, by which you mean the bank kind. As you quickly discover, you get tons of links to record stores.

Exclusion/inclusion operator. This is a very handy feature. It enables you to specify that you don't want articles that mention one word in particular, but you DO want documents that mention some other word. You can dramatically increase precision using these. For example, you can say, in effect, "I want documents about CDs. These documents must mention *bank* and they should not mention *record store*."

Table 6-1: The Web's Search Engines Compared

Feature	AltaVista	Excite	Infoseek Guide	Magellan	Lycos	Yahoo!
Database size	Huge	Small	Small	Small	Medium	Very small (searches Yahoo! listings only)
Phrase searching	Yes	No	Yes	No	No	Yes
Case-sensitive searching	Yes	No	Yes	No	No	No
Subject guide to the Web?	No	Yes	Yes	No	Yes	Yes
Site reviews?	No	Yes	Yes	Yes	Yes (in Point database)	Yes, but very brief (in Yahoo!)
Automatic subject detection?	No	No	Yes	No	No	Yes
Usenet newsgroups searched?	Yes	Yes	Yes	Yes	No	Yes
FTP sites searched?	No	No	No	Yes	Yes	Yes
Gopher sites included?	No	No	No	Yes	Yes	Yes
Portion of document indexed	All	All	All	All	20 lines or 20% of document	All

(continued)

Table 6-1 (continued)

Feature	AltaVista	Excite	Infoseek Guide	Magellan	Lycos	Yahoo!
Recall	High	Low	Low	Low	Low	Low
Precision	Low	Moderate	High	Moderate	Low	Moderate
Exclusion/ inclusion operator	Yes	Yes	Yes	Exclusion only	No	
Special features	Fast retrieval	Searchable collection of 50,000 Web site reviews	Fast Facts feature offers quick access to yellow pages information (including stock quotes)	More than 50,000 site reviews using four-star system. *Green light* sites are safe for kids	Extensive and well-thought-out subject classification system	

In Search of Stocks on the Web

As millions of investors have learned, you don't have to be a stockbroker to pick a stock that appears to meet your investment objectives. You can do the research on your own. Can the Internet help?

In this section, you work through a sample search. Here, you go from which button to press — the particulars of using a search engine — to a *conceptual* strategy for researching stocks on the Web.

Getting started

With several thousand stocks trading on three major exchanges and nearly a dozen smaller ones in the U.S., and even more thousands of stock mutual funds, what do you need to know to figure out what to buy? You want to pick winners, but what do they look like?

Start with some simple stuff. Assume that how well a company is doing is linked to how well its stock is doing. (Later, you may notice that this link isn't always strictly the case. But most of the time, it's a safe assumption.)

Looking for leaders

Strong companies and stocks usually are leaders. They're the biggest, or the best, or the fastest growing. They have the biggest market share, are the lowest cost producer, or are the most profitable. Sometimes, they're several (or even all) of these things.

However they lead, these companies have an advantage over the rest of the competition. This advantage makes their operations and their stock worth more.

You need data on the company or companies that you think you want to invest in. But you need to have more than that. You also want to look at the industry the company is in, how well the industry is doing, and how the company sizes up to other companies.

From the top — or the bottom

You can scope out investments in two basic ways. One is from the *top down* — looking at the whole economy, then at sectors and industries in it, and then at individual stocks in these areas.

You also can use the *bottom up* approach. Here, you look at features of individual stocks, screening them for different kinds of investment appeal. Ideally, you want to keep an eye on both ends, because they don't operate in isolation from each other.

The way in

On the Internet, you can find many sources of good raw data that can be used for either the top-down or bottom-up approach. The data can come from companies' legally required filings with the Securities and Exchange Commission (SEC), from government statistics, from industry trade groups, or from broad-based financial information or market research sources. These information sources contain really useful stuff, even though many times it's lengthy and unfiltered.

There has to be a way to get into the data! Actually, there are many ways. The trick is to start with something you know.

Start close

Just for practice, look at the industry you work in. Who's your best customer? Your biggest supplier? Your favorite product?

If the company is public, treat it like an investment and start looking it up on the Net, using a search service such as Infoseek Guide or AltaVista.

How about a steak?

Say you want to search on a favorite product. You want to know if a public company makes or sells the product so that you can put some of your money in this company. Using Yahoo!, which is easy to use for Internet beginners, you type in **steak.**

The search engine pumps out several pages of URLs (see Figure 6-4), mostly companies in the meat and poultry business (with a few jerky firms thrown in). It lists many companies that deal with steak in some way. Some companies will send steaks to you in the mail. Others serve them in restaurants. You pass up all the steak recipes — or maybe print some of them out for future reference.

How do you know which of these companies also sells stock? You can check each site that catches your eye for an investor information page. This page is a standard feature of many public companies' sites. Often, checking the information page is the fastest and easiest way to pop up a year's or so worth of company press releases and longer documents that these companies are required to file with regulators.

This plan, however, isn't an effective way to find information about steak companies. After you search through several files, you find no trace of any way to invest in these companies. Give up? Don't — at least not yet. There's another way to tackle this, as explained in the next section.

Go public (introducing EDGAR)

All public companies report to the Securities and Exchange Commission, right? So, go back to the Yahoo! search page and type **SEC EDGAR**. Near the top of the search results, you find that Yahoo! has an entire category devoted to EDGAR: "Business and Economy:Markets and Investments:EDGAR Databases."

What's EDGAR? Sponsored by the U.S. Securities and Exchange Commission (SEC), EDGAR — short for *Electronic Data Gathering, Analysis, and Retrieval System* — is an online database containing public securities information, the type that companies are required to file if they trade their shares publicly. This information used to be tedious, difficult, and often expensive to obtain. Thanks to EDGAR, it's available almost instantly, and it's free!

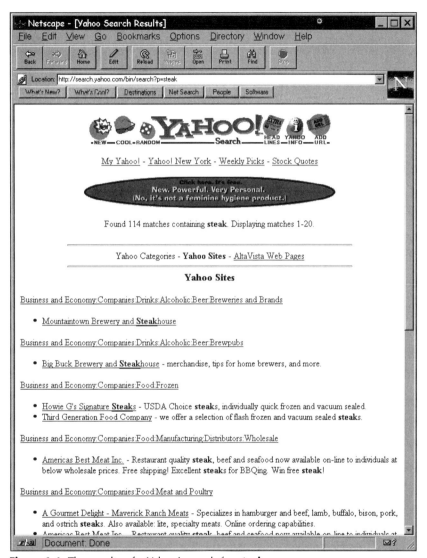

Figure 6-4: The results of a Yahoo! search for **steak.**

In the Yahoo! list of EDGAR services, you see "Search SEC EDGAR Archives." Click on this item, and you see the EDGAR search page, as shown in Figure 6-5.

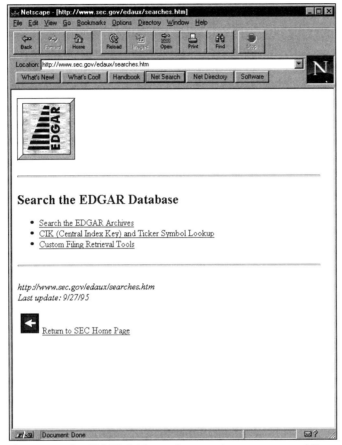

Figure 6-5: The SEC EDGAR search page gives access to public securities information.

You type in your favorite word again, with one small change. Put an asterisk after **steak**, making it **steak***. This should bring up files with "steaks" and ""steak-house". Aha! Quite a few steak and steakhouse companies' shares are publicly traded, and there's lots of information here. You find complete financial statements, including balance sheets, earnings, management's discussions and analyses of the firms' financial position, and more.

Look for the *10-Q forms*. They contain the up-to-date goodies you're looking for, including the most recent financial statements and management analyses. For more in-depth information, look for the annual 10-K reports.

Working up

You started working from the bottom up. Do you want to continue? To step up to the industry level, try looking for some trade and industry associations. Here, a good idea is to tweak your search words a bit. Type in **restaurant**. The thought here is that you want to know where steakhouses fit into the broader picture of the restaurant industry. Are firms that specialize in steakhouses growing faster than other types of restaurant companies? There *must* be some kind of national restaurant association in the U.S., and maybe it offers some data you can use.

For variety, try switching search engines, too. Use AltaVista for a change. Type in the following, *including* the quotation marks:

"restaurant association" national american

You're doing a phrase search ("restaurant association") coupled with two key-words that may bring up an association at the national level (excluding regional and state associations, of which there are many). After looking at the retrieval list, you find a hit: A pocket factbook page from the National Restaurant Association (`http://www.restaurant.org`).

When you find a Web site that looks interesting, you often enter through the back door and find yourself on some page buried within the site's depths. Look for a list of links or navigation aids, and click on the link to *Home* or *Welcome* to go to the top-level page.

After finding the NRA's top-level page, shown in Figure 6-6, you can see that it's loaded with useful information.

Don't miss the NRA's industry forecast — it's interesting reading. But you're after news about steak. The NRA's site has so many documents that it's tough to get through all of them manually. Some large sites maintain their own search engines, enabling you to search through the documents they make available. NRA doesn't, but that doesn't mean you can't search their site.

Go back to AltaVista and type the following:

"National Restaurant Association" +steakhouses +growth

This search includes a phrase ("National Restaurant Association") and a couple of *inclusion operators* (the plus sign), which say, in effect, "Don't show me anything unless it includes *steakhouse* and *growth*."

Bingo! As this book was written, NRA offered a press release (dated December 1995) titled "Steakhouses Hit the Bull's-Eye." The article is interesting. Despite the fact that U.S. per capita beef consumption has fallen to a low of 6.16 pounds (the

1993 figure), steak sales in restaurants — particularly upscale restaurants — are up significantly. Upscale steakhouses reported an increase in sales of more than 24 percent. What's the reason? Here's one, revealed with a wink of the eye by a savvy restaurant manager: Quite a few self-professed vegetarians sneak into steakhouses for a regular break from their regime!

Figure 6-6: The home page of the National Restaurant Association contains useful information.

Reaching out

With all that good news in the steakhouse industry, does anyone anywhere think that steakhouse stocks might be a good bet? To find out, go back to AltaVista and type the following:

steakhouse* + stock pick tip hot

Hmm, the list in Figure 6-7 is interesting.

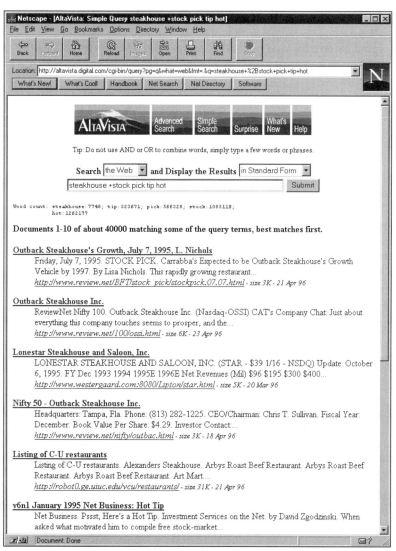

Figure 6-7: The AltaVista retrieval list of steakhouse stock tips.

Be skeptical of any investment advice that you find on the Net. Who's responsible for putting this page up? Do they have an interest in your buying the stock? What are their credentials?

A recent pick from REVIEW.NET, a Florida Web-based journal of business, technology, and commercial real estate news, has nice things to say about Outback steakhouses (Nasdaq: OSSI). Who are these REVIEW.NET folks?

Published by Warfield Media, REVIEW.NET looks like a reasonably disinterested and reliable source — at least, it's probably not a couple of college undergraduates with too much time on their hands or, worse, someone trying to pump up a stock for his or her own gain. As you browse around the site, you find that REVIEW.NET has won an award at the 1996 Interactive Newspapers conference for the best regional news service published on the Web. What's REVIEW.NET's brief on Outback? The company is based in Tampa, and REVIEW.NET keeps close tabs on Florida companies.

So, is this tip reliable? Maybe. But remember that REVIEW.NET is committed to finding and highlighting the hottest companies in Florida. What if the top 50 companies in Florida are actually pretty pathetic when compared to the top 50 companies in Kentucky? You won't find out from this site. Keep your guard up!

AltaVista can search Usenet, too. It's fun to find out what people are saying about Outback Steakhouses, so give it a try. When we performed the search, AltaVista turned up many posts on rec.food.cooking concerning Outback — most of them trying to figure out how in the heck Outback manages to cook such *delicious* steaks.

Don't run out and buy 1,000 shares of Outback, please — the research on which this tutorial is based will be out of date by the time you get this book into your hot little hands. Who knows what's up with Outback now?

The purpose here is to illustrate that the Internet can be very, very useful for research purposes, not to recommend Outback. But you may want to find out for yourself why so many people think Outback steaks are so delicious and visit one of their restaurants. Hey, it's about lunchtime, isn't it?

Summary

◆ Because millions of documents are on the Web, surfing doesn't cut it. You need search services such as Infoseek, AltaVista, and Yahoo!.

◆ Infoseek is easy to use and produces excellent results (high precision), but it doesn't have a very large database of Web pages. By the time you read this, Infoseek's new service, Ultraseek, will be available — and it's expected to have the largest Web database of all.

◆ Yahoo! is a good place to start your search. A Yahoo! search retrieves only those Web sites that have been reviewed and placed in the Yahoo! subject catalog. It contains no student home pages!

◆ AltaVista currently has the largest Web database. Search AltaVista when you want to make sure that you've found *everything* on a subject, or if you're looking for something obscure.

◆ If your search doesn't work, check your spelling, be more specific, think of synonyms, use truncation, try a phrase search, or use inclusion/exclusion operators.

◆ To perform investment research on the Web, begin by looking for leaders. You can do this from the top down — beginning with fast-growing sectors in the economy. You can also do it from the bottom up, looking at individual stocks that you've heard about. Start with an industry with which you're familiar.

◆ Be skeptical of stock picks. Always ask who's recommending the stock, and try to figure out why.

From Here

◆ Keep in touch with fast-breaking investment and business news (see Chapter 8).

◆ Try your hand at Usenet — but don't get burned! (see Chapter 8).

◆ Get started in mutual funds (see Chapter 9).

Keeping in Touch

As an informed investor, you have a fighting chance to become a successful investor; otherwise, you need pure, unadulterated luck. Surely you'd prefer to be informed. But there's a problem.

The problem is called *information overload*, which happens when you're inundated with too much information at too rapid a pace. There's so much information available on investing, whether in printed media or on the Net, that you quickly can go crazy trying to assimilate just a tiny fraction of it. The challenge you face in keeping up with business and investment news is not finding enough information — the challenge lies in *filtering* the information down to a manageable level.

This chapter shows you how to harness the power of the Internet to pare down the influx of information to a digestible level. Of the dozens of news resources discussed in this book's reference pages, this chapter highlights the ones that are just about indispensable for day-to-day reading. You take full advantage of mailing lists and business news summary services. You access national and business news summaries that enable you to assimilate a day's worth of news at a glance. If you want, you even can subscribe to an e-mail service that sends you several e-mail reports per day highlighting market trends, including economic and political analysis and commentary.

In This Chapter

- ◆ Getting a quick overview of today's news

- ◆ Scanning for fast-breaking business and investment news

- ◆ Getting updates and news by e-mail

- ◆ Going deeper: Internet resources for reading and research

Looking for information on a company or stock? In addition to searching the Web, as described in Chapter 6, be sure to search some of the news services discussed in this chapter. Often, the documents housed on these services' computers aren't detected or indexed by the Web's search engines. Look for the Cool Site icons, which (in this chapter) flag sites that enable you to perform searches on their archives.

Getting a Quick Overview of Today's News

If you're like many people, you scarcely have time to read the newspaper fully. You're sure to appreciate the following services, which provide daily-updated summaries of top news stories. (For similar services that focus on business and investment news, see the next section.)

 ◆ ***The New York Times*** (`http://www.nytimes.com/`). This excellent Internet version of the major national newspaper (see Figure 7-1) offers Quick Read summaries. You can click on the links to see the full text of articles that interest you. This is an excellent place to search for in-depth analyses of companies that you're researching.

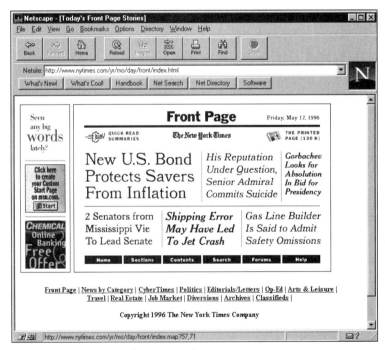

Figure 7-1: *The New York Times* on the Internet.

◆ **Pathfinder News Now** (http://pathfinder.com/News/news.html). This is an excellent place to get a quick overview of today's top news stories (see Figure 7-2). A huge plus: If you find something that interests you, perform a search of Pathfinder's huge database (including current and past issues of *Time, Money, People, Tech, Fortune*, and other Time-Warner magazines) using a search engine.

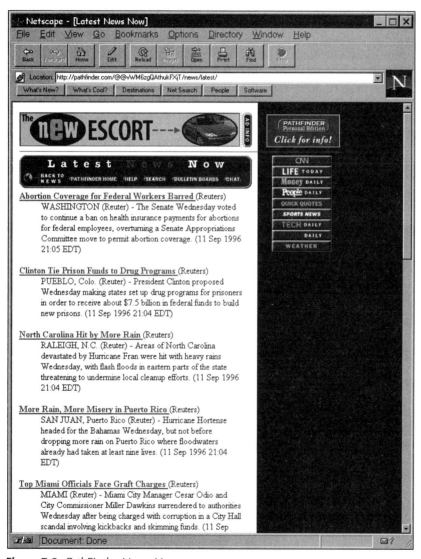

Figure 7-2: *PathFinder News Now.*

◆ **Time Daily** (`http://pathfinder.com/Time/daily/`). Make this page a part of your daily Internet usage. (See Figure 7-3.) You find intelligent summaries of top news stories, coupled with insightful analysis by Time's reporting staff. If you find a story that interests you, a search box at the end of the story is already configured to search Pathfinder's huge database for more stories pertinent to this topic. Links take you to the full text of the current edition of *Time,* which is fully searchable using Pathfinder's excellent search engine.

Figure 7-3: *Time Daily.*

Scanning Fast-Breaking Business and Investment News

Focusing on investment, personal finance, business, and economic news, these services offer news summaries that can keep you abreast of what's happening. You wouldn't want to access all of these every day, so visit them to find out which ones meet your needs.

◆ **CNN Financial Network** (`http://www.cnnfn.com/`). This is a well-designed financial and investment service (see Figure 7-4), updated daily, with the latest business news, market reports (including U.S. and world stock markets, currencies, interest rates, and commodities), personal finance articles, small business management reports, CNN show profiles, the "grapevine" (opinion and commentary — very interesting), and financial resources. A search page enables you to search the voluminous files. A search for *steakhouse* netted a story about a Florida steakhouse that's been hit with a racial discrimination lawsuit.

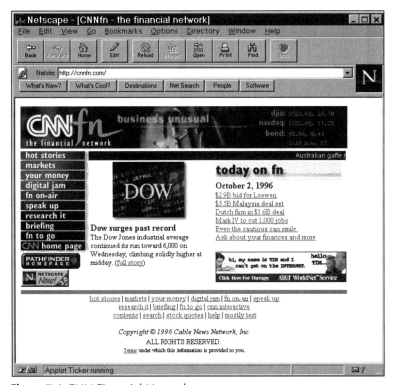

Figure 7-4: *CNN Financial Network.*

COOL SITE

◆ **USA Today Money** (`http://www.usatoday.com/money/mfront.htm`).
Here's the "Money" section from the popular national newspaper, done up in
a well-conceived Web version. As shown in Figure 7-5, you can see everything
at a glance. You find stock quotes, the latest news, commentary and opinion,
and market analyses. A plus is a search page that enables you to search for
keywords. A search for *steakhouse* retrieved a story about Outback's advertising agency.

Figure 7-5: USA Today Money is a Web version of the paper's "Money" section.

◆ **Kiplinger Online News of the Day** (http://kiplinger.com/dailynews/dailyn.html). Updated each business day, this newsletter features an in-depth article as well as brief business updates. You can access the voluminous and valuable archives from this site. You also find a link to the online version of the popular *Kiplinger's Personal Finance Magazine,* with selected articles from the current issue. You can use a search engine — a good one — to look through back issues of the magazine.

◆ **Newspage** (http://www.newspage.com). This is an excellent source of industry-specific news from a huge variety of sources, including industry-specific newspapers, magazines, and PR releases. An added benefit: You can search the huge database of articles for information on a company (or any other subject).

◆ **Eye On Banking: News Headlines** (http://www.cybertechnic.com/eye-on/newspage.html). This is an incredible compilation of headlines from more than one dozen leading news services: *Business Week,* ClariNet, CNN Financial Network, *The Economist, Hong Kong Standard, Irish Times, Knight-Ridder Financial News, Korea Herald,* Reuters business newswires, *San Francisco Chronicle, USA Today's* Money page, and *The Wall Street Journal* headlines.

◆ **Yahoo! Business Summary** (http://www.yahoo.com/headlines/current/business/summary.html). This is today's top Reuters business news stories, formatted in an easy-to-read Web page. It's not searchable, however.

◆ **Bloomberg Personal** (http://www.bloomberg.com). Bloomberg is the distributor of the Bloomberg Terminal, a dedicated system that provides stock quotes and business news to subscribers — who pay a hefty fee. This site, called Bloomberg Personal (see Figure 7-6) is free, so it's no wonder that you get only a taste of what Bloomberg offers on its pricey service. High points are the summaries of top business news stories and reports of interest to individual investors. It's worth a look, but there's no search engine.

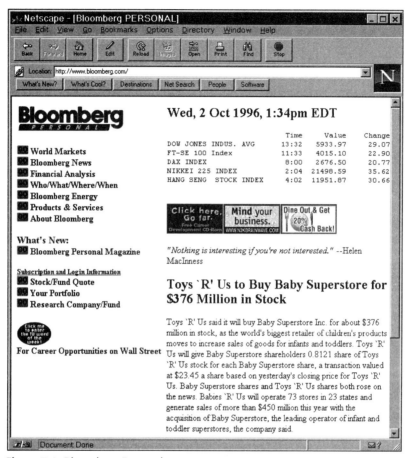

Figure 7-6: Bloomberg Personal.

Getting News and Updates by E-mail

Mailing lists are a boon, but they quickly can become a burden if you subscribe to too many of them. The following online newsletters are strongly recommended; each gives you only one, information-packed message per business day. Also strongly recommended is *Mutual Funds Magazine's* free weekly mutual funds newsletter.

◆ **The Holt Report** (`http://207.67.198.21/holt/index.html`). A daily market summary of 29 market indexes and averages that lists the most actively traded stocks, high-momentum stocks, and stocks with new highs and lows. Also included are currency and gold quotes as well as interest rates.

◆ **Money Daily** (`http://pathfinder.com/money/moneydaily/`). From the staff of the popular monthly magazine, this is a daily article on investment, finance, and personal money management. At the Money Daily Web site (Figure 7-7, you can join the mailing list and browse through recent issues of the newsletter. You also can perform a keyword search on Money Daily or articles from previous issues of *Money Magazine*.

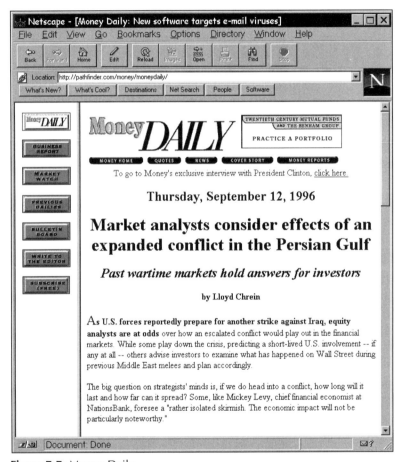

Figure 7-7: Money Daily.

◆ **Mutual Funds Online Weekly** (`http://www.mfmag.com/`). Mutual Funds Online Weekly is a free weekly newsletter that you can obtain by registering with Mutual Funds Online, the Web site of the popular monthly magazine (see Figure 7-8). Registration for both services — the Web site and the weekly newsletter — is currently free.

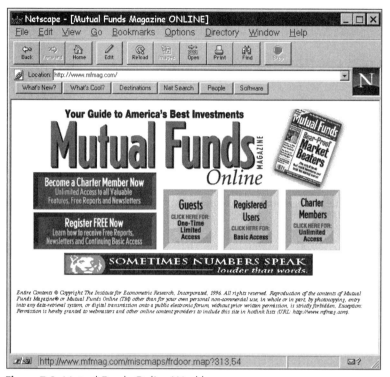

Figure 7-8: Mutual Funds Online Weekly.

◆ **Personal Finance Electronic Magazine.** A moderated personal finance mailing list. To subscribe, send e-mail to majordomo@shore.net and type **subscribe persfin-digest** followed by your e-mail address. For more information on this excellent mailing list, see http://www.tiac.net/users/ikrakow/.

If you don't mind getting mail more often than once per day, subscribe to Briefing.com's Live Market Insight, a free service that's similar to proprietary terminal-based service such as Bloomberg. You receive stock, bond, and dollar quotes throughout the day, as well as daily political, market, and economic forecasts and briefs. For more information, see http://www.briefing.com/.

Going Deeper: Resources for In-Depth Reading and Research

Even if you don't like reading lengthy articles on-screen, there's reason aplenty to visit the sites discussed here. Each of them offers the full text of current and past issues of leading investment and personal finance magazines and newspapers and, what's more, a search interface enables you to scan the site's archives. In short, these are indispensable research resources, and you find lots of stuff that's worth a closer look.

- ◆ **Fortune** (`http://www.pathfinder.com/fortune/`). Here's the full text from current and previous issues of *Fortune Magazine*, including (at this writing) a downloadable database version of the Fortune 500! Coupled with Pathfinder's outstanding search engine, this is an indispensable site.

- ◆ **Money** (`http://www.pathfinder.com/money/`). One of the best personal finance sites on the Net, Money magazine's Web site (Figure 7-9) offers the full text of the most recent and past issues, coupled with a dandy search engine.

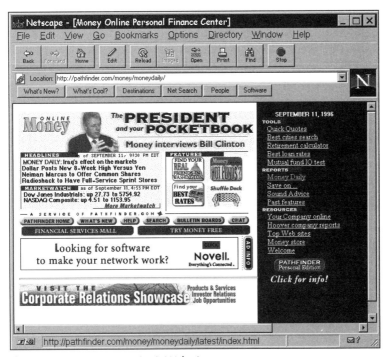

Figure 7-9: Money Magazine's Web site.

- ◆ **Mutual Funds Magazine Online** (`http://www.mfmag.com/`). *Mutual Funds Online* is available in two versions: a free version (which requires registration) and a $4.99/month version, which gives you additional privileges. The free membership is attractive; you can read the full text of current and past issues. You also can search the magazine's archives. This is an absolutely indispensable resource for mutual fund investors.

◆ **The Wall Street Journal Interactive Edition** (`http://update.wsj.com`). A fee-based service, this online version of *The Wall Street Journal* (see Figure 7-10) costs only $29 per year if you already subscribe to the *Journal* ($49 if you don't). A subscription is strongly recommended, not so much for the probing news and commentary, which are easier to read in the printed version, but for the search capabilities. Currently, you can search the past two weeks of the Interactive Edition.

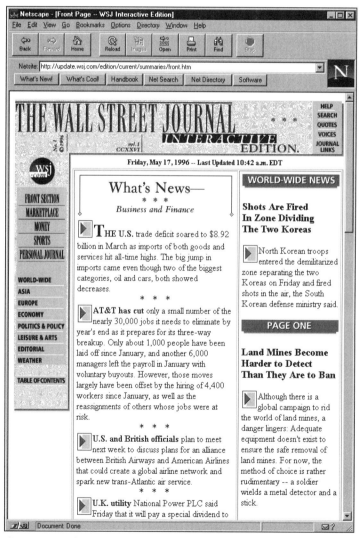

Figure 7-10: *The Wall Street Journal* Interactive Edition.

You can create your own newspaper on the Web. To do so, access Crayon (`http://crayon.net/`). Short for *Create Your Own Newspaper,* this amazing free service enables you to construct your own daily newspaper. You can draw from a huge variety of national, regional, and local news services, including *The New York Times*, *USA Today*, NPR newscasts, *The Christian Science Monitor*, and CNN. Just about every business news service on the Web is available, too. After creating your newspaper — yes, you can even include cartoons — you click on a button to "publish" it. The result is a new HTML file that contains links to the news services you've selected. Save this newspaper to your hard disk, and you can access it daily.

Summary

◆ You can use the Internet to keep yourself well informed about fast-breaking business, economic, investment, and personal finance news, as well as the broader political and economic environment that affects investments.

◆ The information-gathering strategy recommended in this chapter makes full and intelligent use of the Internet, including the Web and e-mail newsletters, to keep you well-informed without drowning you in information.

◆ The Web's several excellent news summary services enable you to scan the day's top stories quickly. Should you wish to read the full text of the story, it's a click away.

◆ A variety of business, economic, personal finance, and investment news summary services place fast-breaking business news at your fingertips. You can visit the best of these sites daily to see what's up.

◆ This chapter recommends four e-mail newsletters that you don't want to do without, including *Money Magazine's* excellent Money Daily. After you subscribe, you receive these free newsletters daily in your e-mail mailbox.

◆ Researching a company, product, or any other investment-related topic? You find the *full text* of the country's best business and investment magazines on the Web — and you can search their archives for free.

From Here

◆ Learn how to participate in Usenet newsgroups—and how to protect yourself from on-line scams—in Chapter 8.

◆ Get started in mutual funds (see Chapter 9).

◆ Learn how to find mutual funds that match your investment objectives; it's all explained in Chapter 10.

Using Investment-Related Newsgroups

According to investment guru Peter Lynch, the best source of investment information is people who have personal knowledge of companies. By participating in Usenet newsgroups, you have a chance of coming into contact with people who have just that kind of knowledge.

Unfortunately, you also have a chance — a good chance — of coming into contact with stock peddlers, brokers hunting for commissions, get-rich-quick scams, and a variety of erroneous postings, ranging from misinformation to disinformation. You find plenty of "buy" recommendations on Usenet (coming, no doubt, from interested parties), but precious few say "sell."

Usenet is the least useful of all the Internet resources this book discusses — and, in fact, it's downright dangerous unless it's approached with great caution.

For example, posting on Usenet places your e-mail address in the hands of aggressive brokers and con men; if you hint that you have some money to invest, you're certain to receive the e-mail equivalent of the broker's cold call. (If you unthinkingly include your phone number in your post, you're really going to be in for it.) For most readers, Usenet is best left alone, unless you're careful. Better yet, if you want to know whether a particular stock or mutual fund has been discussed on Usenet, use one of the Usenet search engines discussed at the end of this chapter.

To be sure, Usenet isn't all bad. Many Usenet newsgroups offer helpful and entertaining discussions of subjects such as cats, sailboats, and backpacking. The problem is, Usenet's "anything goes" philosophy and investing just aren't a good mix.

Introducing Investment-Related Newsgroups

This section gives you a brief rundown on the investment-related newsgroups and newsgroup-related resources that you find on Usenet.

Usenet newsgroups are named in a way that enables the use of a wildcard (*) to speak of a whole group of newsgroups. You'll frequently run across the expression *misc.invest.** to refer (collectively) to misc.invest, misc.invest.canada, misc.invest.funds, misc.invest.futures, misc.invest.real-estate, misc.invest.stocks, and misc.invest.technical.

Common investment-related newsgroups

You find the following newsgroups on most Usenet servers:

◆ **alt.invest.penny-stocks.** Beginning investors should stay away from this wild and often biased discussion of these high-risk stocks. The discussion is unmoderated — and dangerous. This newsgroup is a hunting ground for hucksters, who try to pump up a worthless stock so that you will buy it — then they dump it, leaving you with stock that isn't worth the paper the certificates are printed on. Not recommended.

◆ **misc.invest.** Unmoderated discussion of every investment instrument in existence, including stocks, mutual funds, bonds, Treasury bills, options, and life insurance. The group's topic is too diffuse for focused discussion, but it's often interesting and rewarding to read. Recommended with caution.

◆ **misc.invest.canada.** Unmoderated discussion of Canadian investments, emphasizing stocks and mutual funds. Recommended for Canadian readers or anyone interested in Canadian investments.

- **misc.invest.funds.** Unmoderated discussion, often informative and interesting, concerning mutual funds, mutual fund managers, and retirement investments. Recommended.

- **misc.invest.futures.** Unmoderated discussion of highly speculative futures and options. Not recommended.

- **misc.invest.real-estate.** Unmoderated discussion of real estate investments; many ads for dubious offerings. Not recommended.

- **misc.invest.stocks.** Unmoderated discussion of individual stocks and companies. Although there's some useful information here, don't buy a stock after reading a "hot tip" here — and don't respond to brokers' ads. Not recommended.

- **misc.invest.technical.** Unmoderated discussion of technical investment strategies. Not recommended for beginning investors.

ClariNet

In addition to the newsgroups just mentioned, your news server may also carry some of the ClariNet newsgroups. (Not all servers carry these newsgroups, because a fee must be paid.) These newsgroups carry wire service reports and don't allow posting. The information in these newsgroups is much more reliable than anything you find in the alt.* or misc.* groups.

The Hot Stocks Review

George Chelekis, sometimes described in Usenet posts as an "Internet investment guru," is the author of Hot Stocks Review (http://www.hot-stocks.com), a free online newsletter that discusses "high risk, speculative small cap stocks." Mr. Chelekis does not attempt to disguise the fact that he is a paid publicist. According to an informative full disclosure document that is prominently linked on the welcome page of Hot Stocks Review, companies pay a fee to be mentioned in Hot Stocks Review. Mr. Chelekis notes that he is not a licensed financial advisor and that one should consult a licensed investment professional before investing in any of the stocks he discusses.

So what's the problem? The problem is Usenet. You'll run across many posts in investment newsgroups, particularly on alt.invest.penny-stocks, in which people discuss the "buy" recommendations of Hot Stock Review without mentioning Mr. Chelekis' business relationships. Perhaps these individuals have an interest in seeing additional demand for the stock — or perhaps they're just misinformed. In either case, *caveat emptor.*

- ◆ **clari.biz.earnings.** Earnings reports from hundreds of U.S. and international firms.

- ◆ **clari.biz.economy.usa.** Newswire reports on the U.S. economy.

- ◆ **clari.biz.industry.*** More than 50 newsgroups containing newswire reports on a huge range of industries, including agriculture, aviation, energy, insurance, food, health, and many more.

- ◆ **clari.biz.market.commodities.** Newswire reports on the commodities markets.

- ◆ **clari.biz.stocks.corporate_news.** Newswire reports about companies.

- ◆ **clari.biz.stocks.dividend.releases.** Newswire reports about dividend announcements.

- ◆ **clari.biz.stocks.report.*** Newswire reports on stocks with a regional organization, featuring seven newsgroups covering Asia, Europe, USA, and other world regions. Check out clari.biz.stocks.report.top for the hottest news.

Using a Newsreader

A variety of good newsreader programs are available for Windows and Macintosh computers, but the trend is for browsers to include them. The popular Netscape Navigator browser, for example, has a News window, which is nicely integrated with the program's Web and electronic mail capabilities.

A good newsreader program should enable you to do the following:

- ◆ **Download the full list of newsgroups from your news server.** You get anywhere from 12,000 to 25,000 newsgroups, the vast majority of which won't be of any interest to you.

- ◆ *Subscribe* **to the newsgroups that you want to read on a regular basis.** Obviously, you don't want to go through a list of 25,000 newsgroups to find the ones you want to read. This feature enables you to identify a few newsgroups, which appear in a Subscribed Newsgroups window. Note that your "subscription" isn't registered anywhere except on your computer. In Figure 8-1, you see a short list of subscribed newsgroups in the upper left corner. The current newsgroup is selected.

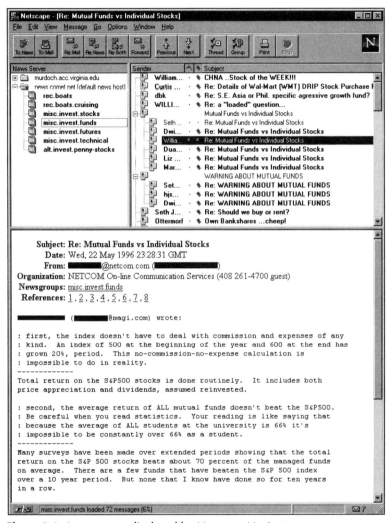

Figure 8-1: A newgroup displayed by Netscape Navigator.

◆ **Scan the current list of articles.** On a given day, you see anywhere from a few dozen to a few hundred articles. The best newsreaders are *threaded*, which means that they're able to group an article with all the replies that have been submitted. Without threading, you have to hunt manually or search for the replies, which is quite a hassle. In Figure 8-1, you see the list of articles in the upper right window. The currently displayed article is selected.

◆ **Read the articles that you find interesting.** Generally, you double-click on the article title of the article you want to read, and it appears in a new window on-screen. After you read the article, the newsreader marks it as "read," and it won't appear in the article list again. In Figure 8-1, you see an article appearing in the bottom window.

◆ **Reply to the article by e-mail.** Unless you really feel that your reply should be seen by everyone, it's best to mail your reply to only the author.

◆ **Post a follow-up article.** A *follow-up article* is a posted reply to a message that's already appeared. A good newsreader enables you to *quote* the text of the article that you're discussing so that others don't have to go back and re-read the original.

◆ **Post an article on a new subject.** You shouldn't do this until you fully understand what types of subjects are permissible for discussion in this newsgroup.

Dos and don'ts for investment newsgroups

DON'T post anything in anger. If you see an article that makes you mad, sleep on it. Chances are it won't seem like such a big deal in the morning.

DO contribute knowledge about strategies and approaches that you've found useful. If you've found the newsgroup to be useful, give something back!

DON'T badmouth a stock, a brokerage firm, or a mutual fund unless you're prepared to back up your allegations with incontrovertible evidence. You could find yourself on the wrong end of a defamation lawsuit.

DO consider other peoples' feelings. The Golden Rule provides good guidance: Post concerning others as you would like others to post about you.

DON'T pay any attention whatsoever to stock tips appearing in these newsgroups.

DO bear in mind that you don't know anything about the people posting messages. They could be saints — or crooks. Possibly they're knowledgeable — and just as possibly, they're crackpots.

DON'T take as factual anything you read on Usenet unless you're able to corroborate it with a more reliable source. Hoaxes and disinformation abound.

DO disguise your identity and personal information, as much as possible, when you post in an investment-related newsgroup. If you normally use a *signature file*, a text file that automatically appends personal information such as your phone number and address to each post you make, disable this feature when you're using these newsgroups.

DON'T post a message stating that you just received a large sum of money and you're not sure what to do with it — unless you really enjoy attracting con artists.

Watching Out for Scams

As you'll discover while reading the misc.invest.* newsgroups, they're plagued with advertisements and disguised advertisements, most of which try to snare you into some kind of (probably bogus) investment scheme. You won't be far off the mark if you simply ignore any and all advertisements or investment solicitations, equating them with a broker's "cold call" (to which you should *never* respond).

Warning flags

If you find yourself reading one of these solicitations, *please* keep the following scam-detection clues in mind. Every one of them is a warning flag:

◆ **Unsubstantiated claims of sky-high earnings potential.** "Double your money in just 50 days — guaranteed." "The upside potential is incredible! Some investors have made a 30,000 percent profit!" Demand proof.

◆ **Claiming inside knowledge.** "We can't say just who, but an inside source tipped us off about a big deal in Argentina." If they can't say just who, it probably isn't true.

◆ **Downplaying the risks.** "Your principal is guaranteed — no loss is possible." The only limited-risk investment is an FDIC-insured savings account.

◆ **Insisting that the investor act now.** "You must make a choice — within 24 hours — to be part of the greatest investment opportunity that the U.S. small investor has ever seen, or be left behind." If it's a good opportunity today, it will still be good six months from now.

◆ **Using hype titles, capital letters, and dollar signs.** "Make $$$ FAST," "HOT," "INCREDIBLE OPPORTUNITY." The use of capital letters infringes a long-standing Usenet rule of netiquette — it comes across as shouting — and may indicate that the person responsible for the post is a newcomer to the Internet (possibly a con man who's moving to new territory).

◆ **Promoting exotic investments.** "Make big money in ostrich farming," "Be part of the exploding wireless cable TV market!" You need to carefully research a topic that's unfamiliar to most people before getting involved.

◆ **Promising big returns for little or no work.** "Many people make $50,000 working 40 hours per week, but very few make that much working only five hours per week." You don't get something for nothing in this world, sad to say.

◆ **Asserting that a product has been approved by a Federal commission or a major research university.** "Approved by the FDA and recommended by a Harvard University professor!" Chances are that neither have heard of it.

◆ **Promoting unproved concepts.** "This herbal product is guaranteed to lower blood alcohol levels to below a detectable level — no matter how many drinks you've had!" If it sounds too good to be true, it isn't true. Watch out for words such as *breakthrough, secret formula,* and *miraculous results.* The only thing that's likely to be miraculous about such offers is how fast your money leaves your pocket.

◆ **Overstating product effectiveness.** "Cures or improves 27 different conditions, including hypertension, some forms of cancer, age spots, and ulcers." "Lose 50 pounds in two weeks." This is wishful thinking at work.

◆ **Failure to indicate that most of your investment goes for sales commissions and fees.** You'll find out later, however, if you try to get your money back. It's too late!

Profile of a con man

On the outside, con artists are well dressed, smooth talkers and seem to be respectable members of their communities. Inside, however, they're predators. Their prey? People who ought to know better: educated, bright, informed people. People who think that they would never become a con man's victim.

Con men work by wearing you down. They win your confidence by seeming genuinely altruistic. Each time a warning flag comes up, they have a ready explanation. In the end, you sign over your assets — your savings, your home, your retirement — and then there's a double disappearance: your "friend" and your money.

What's inside the con man's heart? A pathologically twisted moral code, in which con men see themselves as avenging angels. In the con man's view, his victims are so stupid that they *deserve* to lose their money. The con man has no sympathy for his victims, no remorse for his crimes, and — not surprisingly — very little potential for rehabilitation.

Old scams resurface online

When law enforcement turns up the heat in one area, crooks move elsewhere. Right now, crooks are moving from telemarketing to the Net. But these folks aren't too creative — they're trying the same old scams on the Internet that they pulled on the telephone. Watch out for Usenet and e-mail versions of these telemarketing scams:

◆ **Credit repair.** You're promised a new credit file that will erase past credit problems. The problem here is that this practice not only is deceptive, but could subject the consumer to possible criminal liability. If you have mistakes in your credit file, you can correct them yourself for free.

◆ **Living trusts.** In this scam, consumers are pressured to buy living trust kits to avoid probate. In return for hundreds or thousands of dollars in fees, you get shabbily photocopied form documents that may have no standing in court.

◆ **900 number "information provider" partnerships.** You're pressured to get involved in a limited or general partnership instead of owning a 900 number service outright. What you're not told is that the partnership bears the full responsibility for leasing the telephone lines, paying for promotion, and paying promoters. You're not likely to make the 250 percent profit that's promised.

◆ **Pager licenses.** A salesman offers to secure an FCC license for a paging frequency in a major U.S. city. You're asked to pay around $1,000 for the license, and you receive promises that you can reap huge profits on the resale or lease of the license. What you're not told is that the FCC bars the purchase of licenses for speculative purposes. Worse, pager frequencies aren't in short supply. No pager company has ever paid to use a pager frequency used by someone else. Because nobody needs your license, it's practically worthless.

◆ **Pyramid schemes.** A pyramid scheme is an illegal means of making money that depends on a hypothetically endless stream of entrants, each of which pays a fee to those already enrolled in the scheme. For example, a recruit pays $10 to join the scheme and then enrolls ten new recruits, who each pay him $10, for an ostensible 1000 percent profit.

◆ **Scholarship services.** For a hefty "application fee," you're promised an "excellent chance" for a college scholarship. The organization sounds like an official or even a government agency (*National Science Federation*). You're asked to submit all kinds of confidential information, including credit card numbers. You get time pressure, too. You're probably going to lose your money and get nothing in return, and you could lose big from divulging your credit card numbers. Watch out for spelling mistakes, home or apartment addresses, lack of a telephone number, and excessive hype.

Just the FAQs, Ma'am

The quality of discussion on Usenet newsgroups has a wide range; adjectives such as *brilliant, insipid, biting, egregious,* and *over-the-top* are likely to come to mind in the space of just one Usenet session. But there's at least some solid gold that comes out of Usenet: documents called FAQs (short for *Frequently Asked Questions*).

What are FAQs? Because newsgroup veterans get tired of answering the same questions over and over, such as "What is a mutual fund," or "What does net asset value (NAV) mean," they prepare these documents so that these questions do not have to be constantly addressed. They're definitely worth reading.

Be aware that most people who contributed to investment-related FAQs may not be investment professionals, and these documents shouldn't be considered authoritative. FAQs make for interesting and often enlightening reading, but don't make investment decisions based on anything you read in them.

misc.invest FAQ

This FAQ covers general investment topics. Although the coverage is uneven, some gems can be found here, and it's well worth reading. Divided into seven parts, this is a fairly weighty work, as FAQs go.

You find coverage of the following subjects in the misc.invest FAQ:

- ◆ **Advice.** Advice and aphorisms for beginning investors, one-line wisdom (quotes).

- ◆ **Analysis.** Annual reports, beta, book-to-bill ratio, goodwill, P/E ratio, same-store sales, and technical data.

- ◆ **Bonds.** Moody's bond ratings, municipal bond terminology, Treasury instruments, and zero-coupon bills.

- ◆ **Exchanges.** Circuit breakers for program trading on the NYSE, phone numbers of exchanges, and ticker tape terminology.

- ◆ **Information sources.** Books, dial-up and subscription services, freebies, Internet, and investment associations.

- ◆ **Miscellaneous.** Computing the rate of return on your investments, computing compound return, derivatives, future and present value of money, hedging, insider trading, investment jargon, life insurance, real estate investment trusts (REITs), and renting versus buying a home.

- ◆ **Options.** Introduction, how to order, and symbols.

◆ **Regulation.** Money supply measures, the Federal Reserve, the Securities and Exchange Commission (SEC), SEC Rule 144, and how to survive a bankrupt broker.

◆ **Stocks.** Basics, cyclicals, dividends, dramatic price changes, types of indexes, the Dow Jones Industrial Average, other indexes, initial public offerings (IPOs), shorting, splits, and warrants.

◆ **Software.** Investment-related programs and portfolio managers.

◆ **Tax code.** Short-term and long-term gains, tax swaps, the Uniform Gifts to Minors Act (UGMA), and the wash sale rule.

◆ **Trading.** Discount brokers, dollar cost and value averaging, direct investing and DRIPS, electronic trading, trading via the Internet, cash and margin accounts, NASD public disclosure hotline, NASD licenses, the NASDAQ, buying and selling without a broker, pink sheet stocks, and round lots.

◆ **Trivia.** Bull and bear lore, dollar bill presidents, getting rich quickly, and one-letter ticker symbols.

◆ **Warning.** Advertisements in the misc.invest.* groups, as well as famous online scams (such as the Dave Rhodes pyramid scheme).

misc.invest.funds FAQ

This FAQ discusses some of the basic concepts of mutual funds. Unlike the seven-part misc.invest FAQ, this one is much more concise; there's only one file to read. Actually, this FAQ is pretty sparse. It's worth reading, but it doesn't discuss many key points concerning mutual funds.

Here's what this FAQ covers:

◆ **Introduction.** What is a mutual fund? Why do people use mutual funds? Are there any disadvantages to a mutual fund? Can mutual fund performance be guaranteed? How does buying funds directly compare with buying through a broker? How do I put mutual funds in an IRA?

◆ **Definitions.** What is a closed-end fund versus an open-end fund? What is net asset value? Is a fund that is closed the same as a closed-end fund? What is the difference between yield and return? What are the various forms of mutual fund account registration?

◆ **Expenses.** What are the expenses for a mutual fund?

◆ **Prospectus.** What is a prospectus? What is a statement of additional information?

◆ **Redemption and gains.** What is a signature guarantee? What are capital gain distributions? What else should be known about distributions?

◆ **Fund Types.** What do mutual funds invest in? What is a socially responsible fund?

◆ **Information Sources.** Where can I get comparative information on mutual funds? A survey of printed sources.

◆ **Taxes.** What are the tax implications of mutual funds for individuals?

misc.invest.futures FAQ

If you're interested in these high-risk investments, the misc.invest.futures FAQ is a good place to start.

◆ **Introduction.** What are commodities? What are derivatives? How do derivatives and shares differ? How are derivatives used? What is the attraction of derivatives? Are derivatives complex? Are they risky? How do I invest in derivatives?

◆ **Order entry and types of orders.** Market orders, limit orders, "or better" orders, market if touched (MIT), stop orders, stop limit orders, stop close only orders, market on opening, market on close (MOC), fill or kill (FOK), one cancels the other (OCO), spread, open orders, discretion orders (DRT), and other kinds of orders.

◆ **Margin and margin policy.** Initial margin requirements, maintenance margin requirements, margin call policy, day trades, delivery month margins, securities for margin.

◆ **Option expiration and exercise.** Exercising of options, option assignments, deliveries, special offsets.

◆ **Exchange information.** Australia, Austria, Belgium, Brazil, Canada, Chile, China, Denmark, France, Germany, Hong Kong, Hungary, Ireland, Japan, Malaysia, Netherlands, Philippines, Singapore, South Africa, Spain, Sweden, Switzerland, U.K., United States.

◆ **Technical analysis and spread trading.** Stochastics (fancy statistics), spreads.

◆ **Information sources.** Commodity futures Web site links; futures markets; U.S. brokerages; futures brokers; news, magazines, and advisories; charts and quotes; futures information; general investment information; technical analysis; education and home study.

Finding the FAQs

Try the following URLs to locate the misc.invest.* FAQs on the Web:

misc.invest

```
http://www.cis.ohio-state.edu/hypertext/faq/usenet/
investment-faq/general/top.html

http://www.smartpages.com/faqs/investment-faq/general/
top.html
```

misc.invest.funds

```
http://www.cis.ohio-state.edu/hypertext/faq/usenet/
investment-faq/mutual-funds/faq.html
```

misc.invest.futures

```
http://www.ilhawaii.net/~heinsite/FAQs/futuresfaq.html
```

Searching Newsgroups

Rather than reading newsgroups — an exercise that is sure to generate more heat than light — many Internet users prefer to search for keywords in which they're interested. Several of the Internet's search services (including AltaVista, Infoseek, and Deja News) offer Usenet searches. A Usenet search results in a list of Usenet articles, honed down to only the topics that interest you.

To use these services, you type in keywords, as you would do with a Web search. The resulting list of Usenet articles (from thousands of newsgroups) contains the keywords you typed. In Figure 8-2, for example, you see the results of an AltaVista search for CCUR, the ticker symbol of the company Concurrent Technologies. If you click on any of the article titles, you see the full text of the article.

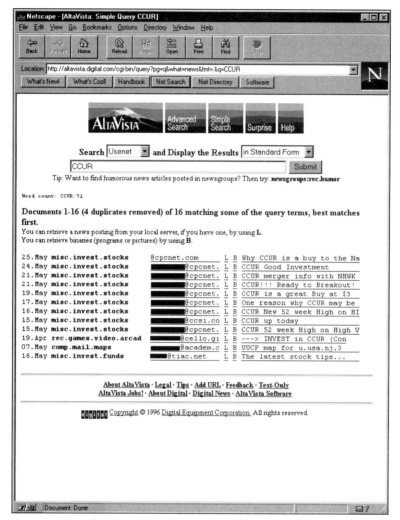

Figure 8-2: Result of an AltaVista search of Usenet.

Summary

◆ Usenet can be dangerous for investors. Posting on Usenet may put your e-mail address in the hands of con men, and you'll find all kinds of bogus investment "tips" — most of them self-serving.

◆ You find several investment-related newsgroups on Usenet, including two that focus on general investing (misc.invest) and mutual funds (misc.invest.funds).

◆ A newsreader enables you to read Usenet messages and contribute your own, if you know the basic rules of netiquette.

◆ Scams abound on Usenet. Watch out for pie-in-the-sky earnings claims, down-playing the risks of shady investments, hype, unproved concepts, and other exaggerated claims. If it sounds too good to be true, it isn't true.

◆ Usenet FAQs contain much useful information. Unlike most of the posting to newsgroups, they're actually worth reading.

◆ A quick way to find out what Usenetters are saying about a subject is to per-form a Usenet search, using services such as AltaVista or Deja News.

From Here

◆ Begin your exploration of mutual funds in Chapter 9.

◆ In Chapter 10, find mutual funds that meet your investment objectives.

◆ Chapter 11 shows you how to assess mutual fund risks and costs.

◆ In Chapter 12, you learn how to obtain mutual fund prospectuses on the Internet and how to read them so that you know what you're getting into.

◆ Chapter 13 shows you how to use online and shareware programs to manage your mutual fund portfolio.

IV

PART

Researching Mutual Funds on the Internet

Understanding Mutual Funds

9

F or most investors, mutual funds provide the best way to start investing. In this chapter, you learn all the mutual fund fundamentals, and you also learn how to use the Internet to increase your understanding of mutual fund investing.

Why Are Mutual Funds So Popular?

Currently, investors are pouring about $20 billion *per month* into mutual funds — and that's true even though the stock market dropped quite a bit during the summer of 1996. What's so great about mutual funds?

We need to backtrack a bit. Because most investments have uncertain outcomes, which involves risk, you learned earlier that you need to spread this risk over more than one kind of holding. Even if all your investments are making you money, some may not be doing as well as others at any given time. This is one more reason to diversify — to have several different types of investments.

In This Chapter

- ◆ Why are mutual funds so popular?

- ◆ What it's worth: Net Asset Value (NAV)

- ◆ What's your objective?

- ◆ The all-important prospectus

- ◆ Buying shares in a mutual fund

But when you're just starting to invest, can you diversify, or do you have to build up to it? One of the big selling points of mutual funds is their built-in diversification.

Diversity from the word "go"

Although your savings may be small, mutual funds can be a good way to avoid putting all your eggs in one basket. The funds are really companies that manage collections of investments, in which they sell you shares. Mutual funds give you the advantage of spreading your risk over a variety of holdings when you buy shares in one fund.

What else do mutual funds do for you?

Another plus the funds have going for them is professional management. When you own funds, you don't have to worry about the day-to-day management of all your investments by yourself.

The management of a mutual fund pools your money with that of other mutual fund holders to buy stocks and/or bonds in bigger quantities and varieties than individuals could buy. A benefit of buying larger quantities is that it lowers the costs of buying and selling the investments that go into the fund — the *transaction costs.* The larger the number of shares or other investment units bought, the better a deal the fund gets on the transaction cost. The fund pays much less commission when it buys and sells large quantities of shares than you would for a much smaller number of shares.

Mutual funds generally are less risky than individual stocks or bonds. But the funds also have traits in common with the stocks or bonds they comprise. By owning, for example, a growth stock mutual fund, you can learn much about growth stocks and the market and other conditions in which they operate — without some of the risk of owning the individual stocks.

Mutual Funds Are Not Risk-Free Investments

Mutual funds are many good things. But some things they are not. These funds are not insured or guaranteed either by the government or by banks — even if you buy them through a bank, and even if they have the bank's name.

You can lose on a mutual fund investment. Although their diverse holdings take away some risk, it does not remove all risk. Also, funds vary widely in their risk. Biotechnology stock sector funds are much riskier than money market mutual funds; like other investments, the riskier they are, the higher their potential reward. Before you invest, you'll be wise to learn as much as you can about mutual funds — and the Internet is a good place to start. The sidebar, "Learning about mutual funds on the Internet," suggests some good places to start, such as Funds 101 (shown in Figure 9-1).

Figure 9-1: Funds 101.

Learning about mutual funds on the Internet

You can learn more about mutual funds by accessing the following excellent free services:

◆ A readable (even fun) introduction to mutual funds for total beginners is **Funds 101** (http://www.brill.com/newbie.html).

◆ After you master the basics, check out **Understanding Mutual Funds** (http://www.farquest.com/mutual.htm). This readable and authoritative guide was created by a California estate planner and mutual fund enthusiast.

◆ To get quick definitions of key mutual funds terms, such as *net asset value, signature guarantee,* or *capital gains distribution,* check out **Frequently Asked Questions about Mutual Funds** (http://www.fundmaster.com).

◆ Somewhat more technical, but useful after you learn the basics, is the **misc.invest.funds Frequently Asked Questions** (FAQ). You can access this FAQ at http://www.cis.ohio-state.edu/hypertext/faq/usenet/investment-faq/mutual-funds/faq.html.

What It's Worth: Net Asset Value (NAV)

When you buy shares of mutual funds, you write a check for a certain amount of money. If you're a first-time investor, and the minimum investment in the fund you want is $2,500, you write a check for that amount.

KEY TERM

The fund is priced by its *net asset value* (NAV) per share. This is what the holdings in the fund actually are worth in their markets (stock and bond markets), divided by the number of shares owned by holders of the fund.

If the NAV of the fund you want is $25 a share on the day you pay for it, then you bought 100 shares. If, in a year, the NAV rises to $50 a share, then you still have 100 shares, but your investment amount has doubled to $5,000.

The NAV rises and falls with the movement of the stocks and bonds in it. It doesn't increase or decrease because fund investors buy and sell it. For this reason, this type of mutual fund is often called an *open-end fund.* What this means is that the fund can sell as many shares as it likes, and it can do so without affecting the value of existing shares. (Some *closed-end funds* work like the shares of an individual company — the value of the shares is determined by the marketplace; that is, what people are willing to pay for the shares.)

Is all this terminology driving you crazy? To look up an investment term quickly, check out the INVESCO Glossary of Investment Terms (`http://www.invesco.com/text/nvc53.html`).

What's Your Objective?

Buying a mutual fund doesn't free you from the obligation to think through asset allocation issues (see Chapter 4). Some funds emphasize growth stocks, while others focus on income stocks, and still others invest globally. Some funds focus on particular sectors, such as technology or health. Other funds invest in bonds and money market investments. Which kind of mutual fund is right for you? This section helps you think through the answer.

Although a given fund may be described as a *growth fund* (or an *aggressive growth fund*), fund managers may possess the latitude to invest in other kinds of stocks or even in bonds or cash. To find out how much freedom the manager has to change the fund's investment focus, you need to read the *prospectus*, a document that explains the fund's investment philosophy and details the risks you take when you invest in the fund.

Aggressive growth and growth funds

Aggressive growth funds, for instance, try to get the biggest possible return for you from increases in the prices of stocks in the fund — from capital gains. These funds usually invest all or most of fund purchasers' money in stocks, leaving little in cash. These funds are unlikely to pay dividends. They may also focus on one or two sectors of the market that are doing particularly well or are expected to show strong improvement in the near future. They may not be as diversified as some funds, which makes them riskier than average. But they are more diversified and thus safer than owning one or a few high-growth stocks.

Aggressive growth funds are a poor choice for short-term investments because they're *volatile*. This means that they may experience a huge NAV increase in one year and an equally huge drop in the next. Over an extended period of time, however, these funds offer the brightest hope of solid capital appreciation.

To learn more about aggressive growth and the other types of funds discussed in this section, try typing the fund type (such as "aggressive growth") into the query box of a search engine, such as AltaVista. Youll find the home pages of numerous funds in each category, such as the one shown in Figure 9-2.

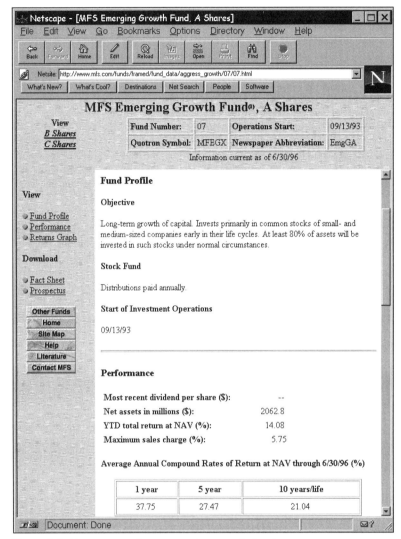

Figure 9-2: Home page of an aggressive growth fund.

Growth funds — growth funds that don't bill themselves as *aggressive* — have similar goals but often with a broader-based, somewhat less risky mix of stocks. Managers may throw in some bonds and cash investments to further spread the risk. Growth funds aren't as volatile as aggressive growth funds, but they're best bought by investors with medium- to long-range investment goals.

Growth and income funds

Growth and income funds try to balance good capital gains with dividend income. An investment that does this is said to have a good total return. These funds include stocks with dividends (such as electric utility stocks) and without dividends and may include some interest-producing bonds that are convertible to stocks as well. Growth and income funds offer much more diversity than do growth funds. Stock prices do fluctuate, however, so they're not a good choice for investors with short time frames (less than a year or two).

Balanced funds are more conservative versions of growth and income funds. They usually have a bigger helping of convertible and bond holdings in them, making them that much less risky than the growth and income funds. On the other hand, having these holdings also ensures that the payoffs won't be as spectacular if the stock market zooms upward.

Bond funds

Bonds usually are safer investments than stocks. However, bonds often have to be bought in big denominations, or can be harder to trade, or have just one maturity date that may be too many years off. Bond funds can help solve all these problems. They come in the short-term, intermediate-term, and long-term varieties. Although buying bonds can involve paying out $5,000, $10,000, or more for only a few of one kind of bond, a bond fund enables you to invest in several kinds of bonds for half or a quarter as much money.

Because federal government, municipal, and corporate bonds are taxed differently, bond funds often are organized into separate mutual funds. The income from tax-exempt bond funds is federal tax-exempt. Some funds also are set up so that their income is exempt from taxes in particular states. General funds combine bonds from the federal government, mortgage agencies such as Ginnie Mae, and corporations.

 Think long and hard before investing in a bond fund. They're riskier than you may think. When you buy a bond, you have the option of holding it to maturity — which you may be well advised to do should interest rates rise, reducing the bond's value on the open market. With bond mutual funds, you don't have the option of holding the bonds to maturity. The fund's NAV is determined solely by the market price of the bonds that the fund holds. The NAV can swing down as well as up, depending on how interest rates change.

International funds

Mutual funds offer one of the easiest ways to invest outside the U.S. Sure, there are many opportunities in foreign markets, and sometimes these markets are doing well when U.S. markets aren't. However, try to find a broker in a foreign country who will take your dollars and confirm your trade the same day! And that's before you try to figure out the taxes on your overseas investment.

International funds have a mix of stocks and bonds of other nations and governments. Funds can include a mix from several regions, one region or continent, just one country, or a type of fund — growth stocks or bonds — in any of these.

Again, because they're funds, international funds are less risky than individual investments in a stock or bond, and the more broadly they're based, the more this is true. International investments come with their own risks, too. The currency of the fund's base country or countries may change versus the U.S. dollar — for better or worse. Also, the country's government or investment policies toward foreigners can change either way. So-called global funds can spread these risks somewhat because they can include U.S. investments as well as foreign ones.

The All-Important Prospectus

A fund's name often is a pretty good first indication of whether it's one you may want to own. But before you put down your money, the fund's management company is required to send you its offering document — or *prospectus*. This booklet gives you chapter and verse on the fund, how it's organized, who manages it, which investments it includes, and what kinds of investments it's authorized to buy and hold. You must have a prospectus before you buy shares in a fund.

You can find the 800 numbers of many funds in NETWorth's Fund Family Directory (`http://networth.galt.com`). If you register with NETWorth (which is free), then you can download fund prospectuses from this site, too. The SEC's EDGAR (`http://www.sec.gov`) also has a mutual fund prospectus search service that brings the files to your screen. Chapter 12 shows you how to retrieve prospectuses from the Internet.

After you buy shares in a mutual fund, you should get more prospectuses sent to you from time to time because most mutual funds are open-ended. This means that the funds continually offer new shares as more and more investors want them, so the funds continually have to give out new prospectuses. Actually, they are required to update prospectuses only once every 14 months.

Read the cover

You can't tell a book by its cover. But a mutual fund prospectus cover can tell you whether or not you should read any further. It tells you what the fund's objective is, for one thing, and it sums up the fund's fees and charges.

If the fees and charges seem high, start shopping around for other similar funds. There are thousands of mutual funds. Many have very similar objectives — and fees vary a lot. In some cases, if they are up in the two-and-a-half or three percent range, fees can make a big difference to your yearly return from a fund. If your return is 10 percent, fees take down your return a quarter to a third. Fees and other charges can be the biggest factor in determining whether you get a great return or a not-so-great one — and for a number of years. Fees are a big discussion point for mutual funds, which usually run a fair amount of fee information on their prospectuses' front covers.

Watch out for fees

You'll hear talk about *no-load funds* — funds that don't assess sales charges — but there's no such thing as a mutual fund without fees. Here's what to watch out for:

- ◆ **Sales loads.** Sales loads and transactions fees reflect the commission that the fund pays to brokers who sell you a fund. A *front-end load* reduces the amount of your initial investment when you buy shares in the fund, because the fees are subtracted before the investment is made. A *back-end load* reduces your payout by deducting a percentage when you sell your shares. Back-end loads may be reduced over time, perhaps to zero after six or seven years, to encourage you to hold on to the fund.

- ◆ **No-load funds.** A *no-load* fund eliminates loads by eliminating the broker. A fund with a sales load must perform much better than a no-load fund to stay even with the no-load fund — and most do not. Contrary to what you may be told, there's no relationship between sales load and performance. Some of the best funds are no-load funds.

- ◆ **Ongoing expenses.** Every fund assesses a fee, usually based on a percentage of the fund's share price (such as $1^3/_4$ or $2^1/_2$ percent), for management expenses. The lower the expenses, the better the chance that you'll make money.

- ◆ **Rule 12b-1 expenses.** Some funds also charge as much as one percent a year as part of their so-called *Rule 12b-1* plans. These charges are allowed to let the funds' advisors pay for the costs of "distributing" the fund — sending out prospectuses, annual reports, ads, and the like. Some no-load funds sneak in loads through the back door by charging hefty 12b-1 fees, come out of your account balance.

For the lowdown on the benefits of no-load funds, see "Facts and Fallacies about 100% No-Load Mutual Funds" at `http://networth.galt.com/www/home/mutual/100/100ffbro.htm`.

Now, read the rest

Okay, you know that funds can give you diversification that you really can't afford on your own right now — or more diversification than you can get on your own. But what about fund management? Can these people give you an edge, too?

It depends. The popularity of mutual funds has created great opportunities for many talented fund managers. Make no mistake: Some managers are very good at what they do. The fund prospectus section on "Expenses and Performance" gives a detailed picture of just how much investment in the fund has returned each year over its life. This change in the fund's net asset value is reflected directly in the change in the fund's price per unit over the years.

But, as mentioned earlier, this (past) performance doesn't mean that the fund's management can repeat it. To find out if this "professional management" is worth it, you have to look at what you're paying for it.

In the prospectus section called "Selected Per Share Data and Ratios" is a line for expense ratios. This is the portion of the fund's value that mainly goes to management and transaction fees. If the management of your fund likes to trade the fund's holdings often, then this "active management" will cost something. The highest-cost-to manage funds are aggressive growth stock and international funds, which have expenses that average $1\frac{1}{2}$ percent of net asset value. A fund with an expense ratio higher than that is expensive.

High-cost versus low-cost plans

Any mutual fund with an active management philosophy will cost more than a "passive management" plan — such as "buy all the stocks in the Standard & Poor's 500 Index and hold them." A computer can carry out this plan for much less money. In fact, this is the way most *index* funds are managed — passively — and their low expenses show it.

Here's the real rub, however. These computers often do better at managing mutual fund holders' money than the highly paid "active" fund managers. In addition, the low-cost index funds are a good alternative to higher-cost (though higher-profile), actively managed funds. Why? The less you pay in expenses, the more you gain if the fund's share price appreciates. And not many mutual funds outperform the indexes, even the actively managed ones!

Avoid these mutual fund investing mistakes

◆ **Don't rush out and buy shares in the first mutual fund that looks good.** You need to fully understand the differences among the various types of funds, such as growth, income, and bond funds, and you need to pick the type of fund that's right for your overall portfolio.

◆ **Don't chase after yesterday's hot funds.** You see advertisements everywhere proclaiming a fund's spectacular past performance ("Up 53 percent in the last 12 months!"). Past performance is no guarantee of future performance. A fund may have been hot recently because of a lucky investment in a sector that went up unexpectedly, such as technology stocks. The fund's managers may not be so lucky in the next twelve months. Look for funds that have been steady performers over the long haul; for example, those that have averaged 15 percent gains per year for a decade.

◆ **Don't pay a broker or bank to purchase no-load mutual fund shares for you.** It's easy to purchase the shares yourself, directly from the fund.

◆ **Watch out for management changes.** A fund's stellar performance may have been attributable to an unusually talented manager. Is he or she still managing the fund?

◆ **Watch out for loads and fees.** Sales loads and 12b-1 fees can eat into your profits. With so many excellent no-load funds around, there's no need to invest in funds with sales loads or hidden sales loads in the form of 12b-1 fees.

◆ **Don't think that a mutual fund is FDIC insured if it's sold by a bank.** Banks are getting into all kinds of services, including selling mutual funds. But these funds aren't insured by the FDIC, as savings accounts and CDs are.

Checking the fund's total return

KEY TERM

The prospectus contains another jewel of information: the fund's *total return*. The total return measures increases and decreases in the NAV *after* deducting expenses. This is the only figure you should use to compare mutual funds, because it's the only figure that takes expenses into account.

When you're reading about the fund's total return, check the figures over the past ten years. A fund that may have advertised a glowing performance ("Up 110% in the past ten years!") may have had one or two good years interspersed with many mediocre ones. How volatile is the fund? How did it do in declining markets as well as advancing ones? How does it compare to its nearest competitors? Has it been a consistent performer?

You're joining a family

One more thing to consider about mutual funds: Most companies that manage them have more than one. You set up a fund transaction account with the management company when you buy shares of one of its funds. Because your investment goals (and the funds' performances) may change over time, you may want to move part or all of your fund money into another fund at some point.

The management companies usually give you a break on exchanging shares of one of their funds for shares of another. When you're mulling over which of several funds with similar fees, returns, and performance histories you may buy, it's worth looking at the other members of their family, too. It helps to have a good choice of alternate investment plans. The how-to-buy and how-to-redeem sections of the prospectus give you information on exchanges that can be made among funds in families of funds.

Buying Shares in a Mutual Fund

Selecting the right fund is the hard part — but you get some Internet help in the next chapter. After you select the right fund for your objectives and risk tolerance, buying is easy.

After you get and read the prospectuses and think you've picked the winner, you must fill out the paperwork. You need to specify if your account is to be an individual, joint, or trust account. You also give tax information and specify if you want check writing privileges and direct or automatic deposits from a paycheck or other account.

Most mutual fund companies are eager to help you set up tax-deferred retirement plans, including Individual Retirement Accounts (IRAs) and plans for the self-employed (including SEP-IRAs and Keogh plans). For more information, contact the fund company.

Summary

◆ Mutual funds offer many advantages to investors, including built-in diversity, professional management, and reduced risk. But they're not risk-free.

◆ A mutual fund's share price is called *net asset value* (NAV). It reflects the sum total of all the fund's stock, bond, and cash investments, divided by the number of shares that have been issued. Unlike stock prices, the NAV isn't affected by people wanting to buy or sell the mutual fund shares.

◆ Before you begin the process of selecting a mutual fund, discussed in Chapter 10, you need to think through your investment objectives. For long-term investments, consider aggressive growth and growth funds. For long- and medium-term investments, consider growth and income funds, income funds, and balanced funds. Bond funds and global funds have their adherents, but they're tricky due to fluctuations in interest rates and currency rates.

◆ Read the prospectus carefully before you buy a fund and scrutinize the expenses. The lower the expenses, the better the chance that you see profits from your investment.

◆ Buying shares in a mutual fund is easy — you just send the company a check. If you buy a fund in a fund family, you easily can manage your portfolio by moving your money into different funds in the same family. Often, you can do this with just a phone call.

From Here

◆ Continue your exploration of mutual funds in Chapter 10.

◆ Learn the perils and promise of mutual fund investing in Chapter 11.

◆ Download mutual fund prospectuses from the Internet following the tips and tricks you'll learn in Chapter 12.

◆ Manage your mutual fund with the Internet and your computer, as explained in Chapter 13.

Finding Funds That Meet Your Objectives

In the first four months of 1996, investors poured $99 *billion* into mutual funds, a pace far outstripping 1995's record-setting mutual funds frenzy. Clearly, mutual funds have replaced savings accounts as the investment of choice, which leads to some interesting consequences. One consequence that's good news: U.S. world leadership in technology is sure to continue because so much money is available for promising small and mid-sized companies. On the down side, it's worth remembering that mutual funds aren't insured investments: That net asset value (NAV) that you learned about in Chapter 9 can go down as well as up.

Still, mutual funds provide a great way to get started in investing, as Chapter 9 explained. There is a huge problem, however, which you run into the minute you start looking at mutual funds: There are so many of them! How do you pick the right fund for your investment needs?

In This Chapter

◆ Finding funds that meet your investment objectives

◆ Accessing fund performance

◆ Searching for more information on your fund prospects

◆ Visiting mutual fund home pages

Principles of Fund Selection

The principles of fund selection are pretty simple, really. The right mutual fund

◆ **Meets your investment objectives.** You want to allocate your investments intelligently among stocks, bonds, and cash. You can do this with mutual funds because most have clearly defined investment objectives. (For example, you find funds that specialize in growth stocks and others that specialize in bonds.)

◆ **Meets your objectives for performance (return).** Ideally, you want to find a fund that outperforms competing investments (for example, Treasury bills).

◆ **Meets your comfort level on risk.** How much risk are you willing to take on? Some funds are riskier than others.

◆ **Meets your cost requirements.** All mutual funds charge management fees, and some charge sales fees, in addition. These fees range from a low of less than 0.20 percent to a whopping 9 percent. The higher the costs, the more the fund has to gain to offset these charges.

Stating these fund selection principles is easy enough. The hard part is finding one or more funds that meet those objectives. There are *thousands* of mutual funds!

How do you choose the right fund? Remember, you shouldn't invest in mutual funds by looking for the one that posted the biggest gains in the last six weeks, and you shouldn't invest by taking tips from friends in your bowling league. That's gambling, not investing. To find the right fund, you need to do some research.

What are you looking for? Although you shouldn't chase after hot short-term gains, you don't want a dog, either. What you're looking for is *consistently good performance* — preferably in falling as well as rising markets.

The Internet provides some good tools to help you select some prospective mutual funds for your portfolio. This chapter shows you how to use these tools to start finding funds that meet your investment and return objectives. At the end of this chapter, you'll have a list of funds — perhaps five to ten of them — that are starting to look pretty darned good. Chapter 11 shows you how to delve deeper into the question of the fund's risks and costs. The toad you find after using the information in this chapter may turn out to be a prince or — watch out for this one — vice versa.

Please note that you never should invest in a mutual fund without obtaining and reading the prospectus, as explained in Chapter 12. What you're doing here is a preliminary selection — choosing a half-dozen or so funds that apparently meet your investment objectives and seem to have performed consistently over a reasonably long period of time (three years or more, if the fund has been in existence that long). To make sure that appearance matches reality, you need to delve into that prospectus.

Finding Funds That (Apparently) Fit Your Investment Goals

With more than 7,000 funds actively traded, your first order of business is to whittle this number down to a short list of five to ten funds that meet your investment objectives. To do this, try to identify the funds meeting your objectives that have *consistently* performed well in recent years. Don't chase after high gains in the past six weeks — such success could prove to be a flash in the pan. You're after consistency.

Note the word "apparently" in this section's title. You cannot know for certain whether a fund really meets your investment objectives until you have closely examined the prospectus, as explained in Chapter 12. Many funds that are supposed to be *growth* funds, for example, enable managers to invest heavily in fixed-income securities, which means that they're really *growth and income* funds. That's not necessarily a bad thing — managers are trying to preserve capital, after all, and they like having the leeway to move money around when conditions change — but it means that you may be carrying a higher percentage of bonds in your portfolio than you thought.

Finding funds with NETworth

Putting together a short list of consistently good performers can be a big job using hand-collated data and trips to the library, but you can accomplish it in minutes, thanks to the best mutual fund site on the Web. It's called NETworth, and it's located at `http://networth.galt.com`. The welcome page, shown in Figure 10-1, clearly and concisely shows what's available at the site: *the Mutual Fund Market Manager* (many goodies for mutual funds investors), the *Equities Center* (a 15-minute-delayed quote serve), the *Financial Planner* (links to financial planning sites), and the *Insider* (links to investment resources on the Web). Created by Galt Technologies, Inc., a Pittsburgh, PA-based Internet content developer, NETworth is now owned by Intuit, the makers of the Quicken financial package — which explains the omnipresence of links to the Quicken Financial Network.

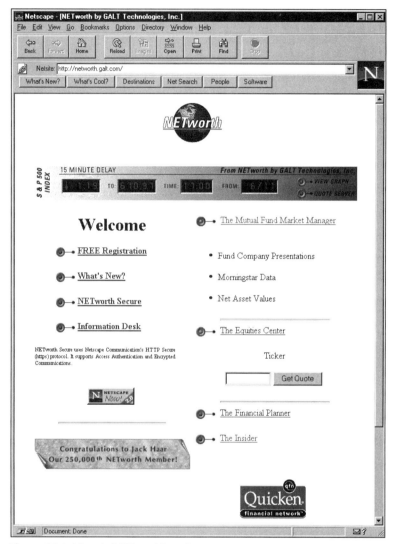

Figure 10-1: Here is NETworth's welcome page.

This site requires registration, but it's free, for now. This chapter focuses on the very impressive Mutual Fund Market Manager, which is one of the best things you find anywhere on the Web, in any information category. As you can see in Figure 10-2, you can use this page to access the home pages of mutual fund families (*Fund Atlas*), display a brief fund summary by typing the fund's ticker symbol or name (*Fund Profile*), get current share quotes (*Fund Prices*), or display the top 25 performing funds in a variety of investment objective categories.

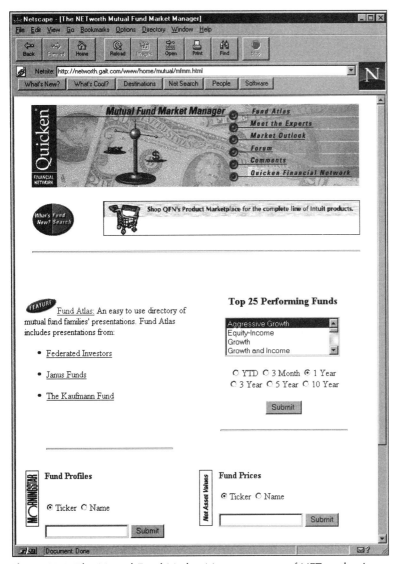

Figure 10-2: The Mutual Fund Market Manager, a part of NETworth, gives you access to many options.

The Top 25 Performing Funds is what you're after. You can use this to quickly produce a list of top-performing funds within a variety of fund categories (see the sidebar, "Classifying funds the NETworth way"). You can choose periods of time ranging from three months to ten years, including the year-to-date.

Currently, you can search NETworth's fund atlas two ways:

◆ **Simple search.** This is the least complicated search. You choose a fund category and a time interval, and NETworth shows you the top 25 performers in that category based on total return for the period you specify. This search does not currently require registration. You can access the simple search from the Mutual Funds Market Manager page.

◆ **Comprehensive search.** This search is much more sophisticated. It enables you to limit the search by risk and cost, two essential elements in fund assessment. You learn how to do a comprehensive search in Chapter 11. This search requires NETworth registration.

Performing a simple NETworth search

Try a simple search first. Your objective here is to choose a few funds to start thinking about — nothing serious yet, mind you, because you haven't taken risks and costs into account (Chapter 11 explores these aspects of fund assessment). What you're looking for here is a list of funds that

◆ Meet your investment objectives (apparently).

◆ Appear to have performed well over a good stretch of time (three to five years).

To develop a list of funds to investigate, do the following:

1. From the first list box in the Top 25 Performing Funds area, choose the type of mutual fund in which you want to invest (see the sidebar for an explanation of NETworth's fund classifications).

2. Choose a time interval. In general, the longer, the better. A fund that performs consistently well is better than one that has one good quarter against a background of average performance. Note, however, that some very good funds are relatively new and will be excluded if you choose too lengthy an interval.

3. Click on the Submit button. In Figure 10-3, you see a list of the top 25 aggressive growth funds based on returns over the past three years. From this page, you can access more information: You can view a brief fund profile and see a chart of the fund's net asset value (NAV) over the past month. If the fund's name is highlighted, you can click on the fund's name and connect directly to the fund's home page, where you can obtain additional information (including the fund's prospectus and application forms).

Figure 10-3: The top 25 aggressive growth funds for a three-year period, accessed from NETworth.

TIP

Make a note of those ticker symbols, such as KAUFX (for the Kaufmann fund). They come in handy when you're looking for price quotes.

CAUTION

NETworth's simple search is easy and fun to use, but don't take the results to heart. In many respects, it appeals to fund investors' worst instincts: Looking at hot past performance and ignoring everything else. The search you just performed does not take risk into account, and the performance figures you received may mask considerable share price volatility. Don't add any of these funds to your list of hot prospects without performing a comprehensive fund search, described in Chapter 11. As you will see, this search can take risk and costs into account — and it may change the picture considerably.

Classifying funds the NETworth way

Chapter 9 introduced a simple way of classifying funds, but you will run into more precise classifications, which are worth learning because they help you pin down the fund's investment objectives. NETworth uses the classification scheme developed by Morningstar, the respected independent mutual fund reviewer. When performing searches with NETworth, you can select from the following investment objectives:

◆ **Aggressive growth.** Seeks capital appreciation over the long haul but may be volatile, so these funds aren't suitable for short-term investments. Included within this category are funds that buy all types of growth stocks, but the funds tend to focus on smaller firms. In addition, they may use risky (but high-payoff) investment strategies, including frequent trading, selling short, and leveraging.

◆ **Asset allocation.** Allocates capital among stocks, bonds, and cash, depending on market conditions. The idea is that the fund manager can try to time the market, finding the right mix of stocks, bonds, and cash for the prevailing conditions. Asset allocation funds may do a better job of weathering market downturns, but in bull markets they generally do not perform as well as stock funds.

◆ **Balanced.** Offers a mix of growth and income stocks with bonds of various types. Within this category, investment objectives vary; read the prospectus carefully.

◆ **Convertible bond.** Invests in bonds that can be converted into the stock of the corporate issuer. Fund managers have the option of retaining the bonds if the stock market is flat or converting them into stocks if the market is rising.

◆ **Corporate bond.** Invests in corporate bonds. There are three types of corporate bond funds: *high quality* (bonds that have high or relatively high ratings from independent rating firms), *high yield* (riskier bonds, also known as *junk bonds*, issued by companies with less credit-paying ability), and *general corporate bond funds*. You need to read the prospectus carefully to determine which types of bonds the fund's managers may buy.

◆ **Diversified emerging markets.** Invests in stocks in developing countries. The risks to these funds include political instability and currency fluctuations.

◆ **Equity-income.** Focuses on stocks that pay dividends. Funds in this category invest at least 65 percent of their assets in equity securities with above-average yields.

◆ **European stock.** Invests at least 65 percent of assets in European stocks. Risks include currency fluctuations.

◆ **Foreign stock.** Purchases stocks outside the U.S. Within this category are found large-cap foreign stock funds, mid-cap foreign stock funds, small-cap foreign stock funds, and funds that specialize in a specific country or region. All foreign funds carry the risk that currency rates will fluctuate adversely. Note: Global stock funds invest in U.S. as well as foreign stocks, providing a measure of protection from currency fluctuations.

◆ **Global bond.** Invests in bonds worldwide, including the U.S. Risks include currency as well as interest fluctuations.

◆ **Global stock.** Invests in stocks worldwide, including the U.S. As with all foreign stock funds, there is a risk of currency fluctuations in addition to the usual risk factors.

◆ **Government bond.** Invests in government bonds. Distinguished are funds that invest in adjustable rate mortgages, mortgages, and Treasury bills, as well as general government bond funds. Although these funds invest in low-risk government bonds, all bond prices fluctuate as interest rates rise and fall.

◆ **Growth.** Seeks long-term capital appreciation. Although not suitable as a short-term investment, growth funds should fluctuate less than the more volatile aggressive growth funds.

◆ **Growth and income.** A mixture of growth and income fund approach; capital appreciation and current dividend income are weighted equally.

◆ **Multiasset-global.** Invests in stocks, bonds, and other investments worldwide. These are also *multi-risk* funds as well, because they may be affected by changing interest as well as currency rates.

◆ **Multi-sector bond.** Invests in bonds from more than one industrial sector. The idea here is to spread the risk through diversification. Remember that the net asset value of any bond fund fluctuates depending on interest rates.

◆ **Municipal bond.** Invests in municipal bonds. Distinguished are funds that concentrate on California, New York, and other states, as well as funds that purchase bonds from more than one state.

◆ **Pacific stock.** Invests in stocks in Pacific Rim economies, including Australia, Korea, Malasia, Singapore, and Taiwan.

◆ **Short-term world income.** Invests in short-term, fixed-income securities (mainly corporate debt) in both foreign and U.S. companies.

(continued)

(continued)

◆ **Small company.** Invests in small companies (typically, those with total capitalizations of $100 million or less).

◆ **Sector.** Eliminating some of the advantages of diversification, these funds concentrate on specific industry sectors. You can choose from Communications, Financial, Health, Natural Resources, Precious Metals, Real Estate, and Utilities funds. These funds tend to be volatile, depending on industry conditions and the state of the wider economy: This year's big gains may be nullified by next year's big losses. Generally speaking, inexperienced investors should avoid these funds.

Finding funds with Lipper Scorecards

NETworth's Mutual Funds Market Manager is a great place to start for choosing funds on the Net, but it's not the only game in town.

Appearing in *The Wall Street Journal* every day are the Lipper Analytical Service's Mutual Fund Scorecards, which list the top 15 and bottom 10 performing funds in each of 30 mutual fund categories. The entire, current set of 30 Scorecards is available on the Web via the *Wall Street Journal Interactive Edition* (`http://update.wsj.com`).

Unlike the other sites discussed here, this one is fee-based: You need to subscribe to the *Wall Street Journal Interactive Edition*, which will cost you $29 per year if you're already a subscriber to the print-based edition of the *Journal* (the fee goes to $49 if you're not).

To access the Lipper Analytical Reports, click on the Personal Resource Center button on any of the *Journal's* pages and click on the link to Mutual Fund Scorecards. You find the scorecards grouped by fund type, as shown in Figure 10-4. Click on one of the fund types to see the report. Figure 10-5 shows the scorecard for capital appreciation funds, which closely resemble Morningstar's aggressive growth funds.

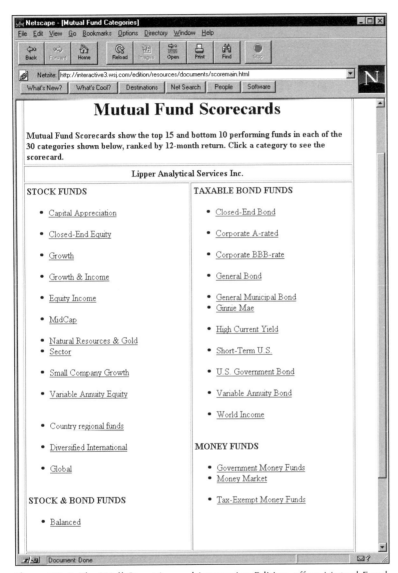

Figure 10-4: The Wall Street Journal Interactive Edition offers Mutual Fund Scorecards.

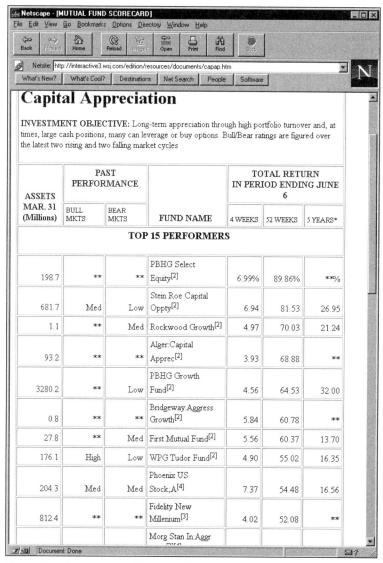

Figure 10-5: The scorecard for capital appreciation funds found in The Wall Street Journal Interactive Edition.

Assessing Fund Performance

By now, you've collected a list of a half-dozen or so funds that have performed pretty well over the past few years. But have they really? And will they continue to perform well?

Past performance is no guarantee of future performance

Many stock funds are *volatile*, which means that they experience considerable price fluctuations. A fund that goes up significantly in a three-month period may go down just as dramatically at some other time. Such a fund may be a good bet for the long haul, but you need high risk tolerance to stick with such funds during the downturns. Unfortunately, many naive mutual fund investors hear about huge short-term gains, buy the fund, and then sell off in a panic when the fund goes down. That's how many people lose money in the mutual funds market.

To establish a baseline for comparing funds, you can gain some measure of confidence by stretching out the time horizon to several years instead of several months. But even this strategy can backfire. Over three years through December, 1993, the American Heritage Fund was the top-performing mutual fund. In 1994, however, the fund lost 29.4 percent from January to July, making the fund the industry's second worst.

Do top-flyers remain at the top?

A number of mutual fund researchers point out that over a given time, the more extreme a fund's performance is relative to other funds' performance, the more likely it is that the ranking fund's performance will move closer to the average over the next period.

Vanguard Funds (http://www.vanguard.com/educ/module3/m3_5_0.html) points out that its chairman, John Bogle, a highly regarded force in the mutual funds field, has written on this in his book, *Bogle on Mutual Funds*. He noted that in a study of nearly 700 funds, the top 20 stock funds for each year between 1972 and 1982 had ranks averaging 284 in the year following one in which they ranked highly.

Should you ignore past performance completely? No. According to one study, funds that were in the top 25 percent of their category in a three-year period had a 60 percent chance of winding up in the top half of their category three years later. On the downside, this means that top-ranking funds have a 40 percent chance of winding up in the bottom half of their category by the time three years go by.

One thing to consider is the human element — namely, the fund manager. Some of the market's hottest funds didn't do as well after their manager's departure. But it isn't smart to bet on managers alone. A manager may have developed a high-risk

(continued)

(continued)

investment style that worked very well — as long as the underlying market conditions remained favorable. That same manager may crash when these conditions change.

Is anything for certain in the mutual funds business? Yes — it's that nothing is for certain. But it makes sense to avoid the rockets, preferring funds that have done a good, decent job over the long haul.

How mutual fund companies describe past performance

Funds often report returns over longer periods in three ways. One is using a *compound annual growth rate*. This is the average rate per year that the fund's return has increased (or decreased, in some cases).

A second way to show returns is with a *cumulative rate*. This is the percent increase in the return from the start of the investment period. It looks much larger than the average annual rate because it's not averaged.

The third way to measure return is to express it as the value of a certain round amount (such as $10,000) after a period of years invested in the fund.

What's wrong with all three of these measures is that they may mask risk. Suppose a fund substantially underperformed (in comparison to other funds of its type) for four years, but in one year — due to a lucky break — it shot up like a rocket. The overall five-year figure may look pretty good. In reality, you're buying a risky fund that's not a consistent performer.

To assess performance fully, you need to obtain and study the fund's prospectus, as explained in Chapter 12. In the prospectus, you find year-by-year returns. You can see whether the compounded or cumulative returns have been affected by extreme performance in one year and subpar performance everywhere else.

Remember, you're not looking for rockets. Rockets go up, but they also come down. You're looking for consistently *good* performance — which means doing better, in most years, than funds in the same category. A fund that does a bit better than average each year may be much better, in the long haul, than a fund that has one spectacular year and several losers.

Looking for average performance figures for funds in a certain category? Look no further than the Lipper Scorecards, a feature of the *Wall Street Journal Interactive Edition* (http://interactive.wsj.com/), discussed earlier in this chapter. You find average figures for each fund category. Listed are figures for the past four weeks, for the period since the beginning of the year, for the past year, and for the past five years.

What's included in those return figures, anyway?

A fund's return can be from all or any one of three sources:

◆ Yield

◆ Capital gains

◆ Change in net asset value

Yield comes from dividends or interest from the stocks or bonds the fund holds. These are usually a smaller but steadier kind of return than the other two sources because they're usually paid out at regular times in regular amounts. While you shouldn't ignore yield — especially if you're seeking income from a fund — it's not as important a measure as total return.

In fact, it's possible for a fund with a fairly high yield to have a much lower total return. This happens when the net asset value falls. Then, dividends will be larger compared to the smaller net asset value base.

Capital gains occur from the sale of securities in the fund's portfolio and are passed on to fund holders. Funds may or may not sell off parts of their portfolios over the year. Thus, capital gains can be quite large or nonexistent. They're much less predictable than dividends and interest.

The Internal Revenue Service usually requires funds to distribute net income and gains realized from its investments each year. Dividend income and realized short-term capital gains (from sales of securities the fund has held under a year) are paid out to fund holders as fund dividends. They're usually paid quarterly or monthly. Long-term gains that the fund realizes are paid out to the fund holders as capital gains distributions. These distributions are normally paid out at the end of the fund's reporting year.

Short-term and long-term gains are reported to you by funds' management each year on an IRS Form 1099. These figures should be tallied on your tax return schedule. For the official line of how the IRS wants mutual fund data handled on tax returns, get IRS Publication 564 by calling 1-800-424-3676.

Perhaps the fund may not pay out dividends or sell securities to take capital gains or losses during the year. This doesn't mean that its return has to be smaller than those of funds that do. It simply means that the fund is retaining the return — either to cover its expenses or because it hasn't sold any holdings. The gain, if any, can be noticed as an increase in the fund's net asset value — the price per unit that buyers pay for it.

In some ways, this is a better kind of gain for many fund holders. This is because it's not taxable — unless and until the fund holder sells shares.

Searching for More Information on Your Fund Prospects

Do you have your list whittled down from 7,000 to a couple dozen? Do you want to know more about the funds you're thinking of purchasing? The most important document to review is the *prospectus*, discussed in Chapter 11. For now, you may want to know what the press is saying about a mutual fund that has attracted your interest. In this section, you learn how to search several excellent mutual fund and financial magazines and newspapers for information on specific funds.

Searching *Mutual Funds*

Mutual Funds is a respected popular monthly that focuses on mutual funds. The magazine's online version (`http://www.mfmag.com/`) features free access (with registration) to the full text of current and recent articles — and what's more, the whole database is searchable.

To find articles that mention a mutual fund in which you're interested, access the Mutual Funds Online search page at `http://www.mfmag.com/srchart.htm`. Type the exact name of the fund (such as **Fidelity Asset Manager** or **Janus Worldwide**), click on the Exact Phrase button, and then click on Search. You see a list of articles that contain the words you typed.

Searching *Money*

Another popular monthly investment magazine, Time-Warner's *Money*, enables you to search the full text of current and past issues. It's another great place to hunt for news and information about prospective mutual funds.

To search *Money* for articles mentioning funds in which you're interested, access the Pathfinder search page at `http://pathfinder.com/pathfinder/search.html`. Select the option that enables you to search Pathfinder's database for keywords. You see the Pathfinder search page. In the Select a Database area, click on Money. In the Describe What You're Looking For area, type the name of the fund and press Enter to initiate the search. The result is a list of *Money* articles sorted by relevance. The higher the numerical score, the more likely it is that the document is pertinent to your interests.

Searching The Wall Street Journal Interactive Edition

The Wall Street Journal's Web edition (`http://interactive.wsj.com`), a fee-based service, offers what promises to be a valuable resource for mutual fund investors: Briefing Books, a search service that enables you to search for a fund using the ticker symbol or the fund's name. To access this service currently, you select the Table of Contents option on the front page and then select Briefing Books. Select Stock Symbol or Company Name and click on Get Briefing Book. The result is a page with five options: Background, Financial Overview, Stock Performance, News, and Press Releases. Unfortunately, this feature wasn't fully implemented at this writing, but it promises to be a useful resource — check it out.

Visiting Mutual Fund Home Pages

So far, you've been looking at independent sources. To get more information about a fund from the fund's management firm, you may wish to visit one of the several dozen mutual fund home pages you find on the Web. In Figure 10-6, for example, you see the home page of Janus Funds (`http://networth/galt.com/www/home/mutual/janus/`). Most of these home pages include descriptions of the funds, performance data, and instructions for ordering application kits (including prospectuses).

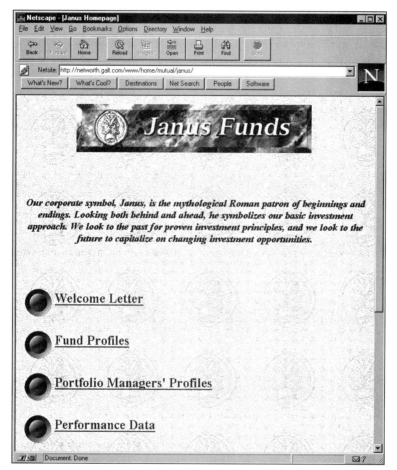

Figure 10-6: The Janus Funds home page offers profiles, performance data, and more.

A good place to start your exploration of mutual fund home pages on the Web is NETworth's Fund Family Directory, located at `http://networth.galt.com/www/ home/mutual/fund_atlas/fund_listing.html`. For more links to no-load mutual funds, check out the 100 percent No-Load Mutual Fund Council (`http:// networth.galt.com/www/home/mutual`), which lists the home pages of the council's members.

Summary

◆ Selecting the right mutual fund requires matching a given fund with your investment objectives, your return objectives, your risk comfort level, and your cost requirements.

◆ To get started selecting a fund, ignore the *hot tips* you've heard, and don't pay much attention to ads that celebrate big gains over the past three months. You're looking for funds that perform consistently, even when the market's experiencing a downturn.

◆ NETworth provides tools for developing your short list of hot sites. You can use this site to identify the 25 best-performing funds (as measured by total return) over a time period that you specify — the longer the better.

◆ Don't use compounded or cumulative total return figures all by themselves. They may mask periods of subpar performance.

◆ To learn more about your hot prospects, you can search current and back issues of *Mutual Funds* and *Money*.

◆ Some of the funds that you've selected may have home pages on the Web. Visit them to learn more about the funds, as well as to order application kits and prospectuses.

◆ You haven't finished with your initial fund assessment until you've considered risk and cost, covered in the next chapter.

From Here

◆ The next step in your search for mutual funds is to assess risks and costs. Find out how to do this — with the Internet's help, naturally — in Chapter 11.

◆ Find out whether a fund really meets your investment objectives. How? Download the prospectus from the Internet and read it carefully, as explained in Chapter 12.

Assessing Mutual Fund Risks and Costs

A s you're gathering information about funds, you may see funds' advertisements proclaiming big gains over a certain period. Naturally, a fund's advertisers want to emphasize how well the fund has performed, so they've probably chosen a favorable time period, which isn't hard to do. All you have to do is look at all of 1995, when there was a major market uptrend. Even a three-year period starting in early 1993 and ending December 1995 isn't so bad, because it smooths out all the backing and filling in the stock market during 1994 with two good years before and after. For 90 percent of mutual fund investors, big gains are all that matter. These investors don't consider risks or costs.

They should. How is your fund going to weather a market downturn? Do you have the nerve needed to ride out a period when your fund is down 38 percent in six months? Is shelling out a 2 ½ percent management fee worth it? And what's this *12b-1* fee for, anyway?

In Chapter 10, you assessed prospective funds' objectives and performance. In this chapter, you learn how to assess risk and cost — subjects that are, admittedly, not as fun as those covered in the preceding chapter. But they're just as important.

In This Chapter

- ◆ Assessing risk
- ◆ Selecting funds using Morningstar ratings
- ◆ Analyzing your prospective funds' performances in a bear market
- ◆ Assessing costs
- ◆ Looking for low-cost funds

Remember that you're still in the initial assessment mode. Before you get serious about purchasing shares in a mutual fund, you should carefully study the fund's prospectus. Prospectuses, introduced in Chapter 9, are discussed in detail in Chapter 12.

As you learn in this chapter, the Internet can be helpful when it comes to finding low-risk and low-cost funds. You can take advantage of several excellent, free services that can help you narrow down your lists of fund prospects.

The Need to Assess Risk

Too few mutual fund investors think of risk before they buy. They react to those wonderful total return figures. Risk just doesn't come up.

Investors aren't the ones who've been keen to find a better means of disclosing fund risk, but regulators are nervous about the way this information is reported now. One reason for their concern is the huge growth in investment through funds in the past few years, as baby boomers use them more and more to accumulate retirement money.

Another reason regulators think it's urgent to make changes is that individual investors have few means to anticipate some kinds of fund losses. Case in point: In 1994, when interest rates rose sharply, bond funds took big hits. Even short-term government bond funds, which many investors thought were quite safe, had large losses.

"The huge losses in bond fund (then) took a lot of individual investors by surprise," said Ronald Kahn, research director of the market and financial data and analysis firm Barra, Inc., in a mid-1995 article, "Quantitative Measures of Mutual Fund Risk: An Overview" (`http://www.barra.com/ResearchPub/BarraPub/qmfr-n.html`). "With total assets of all mutual funds now in the neighborhood of $2.5 trillion," Kahn continues, "the SEC has recognized that mutual fund investors, who are often not Wall Street experts, need more accessible information on these investments."

How risk is measured

Fund analysts use two numerical measures of fund performance that provide measures of risk. Unfortunately, neither of these measures is given in fund prospectuses.

The first measure is called *beta*. This is a number that shows how sensitive the fund's share price is to changes in the market. A beta of 1 means that this relationship is one-to-one. For each one percent rise or fall in the market, there's a one percent rise or fall in the share price — in the same direction. A beta of 1.5 means that a one percent move in the market produces a corresponding one-and-a-half percent move in the stock. A beta of -1.5 would move the investment one-and-a half percent in the opposite direction at each one percent market move. Large beta funds are extremely market-sensitive.

The second measure is called *standard deviation*. This is a measurement of how variable a fund's returns are over time — how much it varies around the average return for some period. This variability measures the *volatility* of the investment.

You never may have noticed these measures — beta and standard deviation — in any materials you've read about funds. That's because they're not there, and the funds aren't required to tell you what they are, even though their managers probably use these gauges. Funds do have some risk disclosure rules. They may describe how they hope to meet their goals, and they may describe certain means to do this that involve larger-than-average risks. But usually, no numbers are attached to the way that managers present risk.

Risk without enough return

Professional analysts measure risk using beta and standard deviation. For individual investors, though, there's another angle. Besides the risk of losing some or all of your money, there's a risk that your mutual fund investments will produce only moderate returns — returns so unspectacular that they don't justify the risk exposure you're taking when compared to other, less risky investments, such as Treasury bills. To put this point another way, your funds ought to do *much* better

Should mutual fund companies disclose risk figures?

If investors aren't doing a good job of understanding and assessing the risks they take when they buy shares of a mutual fund, perhaps it's because the mutual fund industry hasn't made risk information sufficiently available.

This situation may change. Since 1994, the Securities and Exchange Commission (SEC) has been asking for comments from many parties, including fund investors, on how to improve funds' risk disclosure. Many investors and investment managers think betas and standard deviations should be reported.

More changes may be coming soon. The SEC has been testing new, easier-to-understand prospectuses that present the basic facts about funds in plain English (rather than the dense legal language of traditional prospectuses). Investors like the new documents. Tomorrow's prospectuses may be much easier to understand.

than a competing, safer investment. If they don't, then there's no justification for exposing your capital to the higher risk that funds entail.

Selecting Funds Using Morningstar Ratings

As we've shown you, mutual fund companies don't disclose beta and standard deviation figures. But that doesn't mean you have to ignore risk when you select mutual funds. Thanks to the Internet, you can take advantage of risk assessments created by Morningstar, a for-profit fund analysis firm. This section shows you how.

Understanding Morningstar ratings

Morningstar, Inc., is an independent fund analysis service that rates mutual funds and variable annuities using a five-star system (see the sidebar, "Morningstar ratings explained"). What's of key interest here is that Morningstar takes risk into account: The funds' rankings include a risk factor that penalizes funds for periods in which the fund underperformed a competing, low-risk investment (such as Treasury bills).

Here's the point: Funds with high Morningstar ratings have *consistently* given higher returns, *adjusted for risk,* than other funds in the same category. A high Morningstar rating is no guarantee that a fund will perform well in the future, but it's a better bet than buying funds without taking risk into account. After all, you're looking for consistently good performers.

Bear in mind that historical risk assessments may not give an accurate picture of the fund's *current* risk exposure (see the sidebar, "Historical risk data may be of limited use, analyst says"). You can only fully understand a fund's current risk exposure by studying the fund's current holdings, which are given in the fund's annual report. Realistically, though, most people do not have the time or the skill to perform such an analysis.

Including Morningstar ratings in a NETworth search

NETworth's Comprehensive Fund Search enables you to bring the respected Morningstar ratings into your search. Try repeating your simple search from the last chapter — the one in which you started selecting funds that meet your investment objectives — but this time search for funds with high Morningstar ratings.

Morningstar ratings explained

Morningstar ratings use a five-star system. Note that these ratings are adjusted for risk; the philosophy here is that a risky fund should produce higher returns than a less risky fund, or it doesn't justify the risk that you take when you invest in it. Funds that rate four or five stars have produced above average or substantially above average returns, after adjusting these returns for risk. Of course, there's no guarantee that they'll continue to do so.

★★★★★   Produced substantially above-average returns (within the top 10 percent)

★★★★   Produced above-average returns

★★★   Produced average returns

★★   Produced below-average returns

★   Produced substantially below-average returns (within the bottom 10 percent)

If you have more specific search criteria, try searching for worthwhile funds using NETworth's comprehensive search. Requiring registration, this search enables you to choose specific search guidelines.

To perform a comprehensive NETworth search, do the following:

1. Access NETWorth (http://networth.galt.com), and display the Fund Atlas page.

2. From the Fund Atlas page, click on the Comprehensive Fund Search link.

3. On the Comprehensive Fund Search page, shown in Figure 11-1, choose an objective.

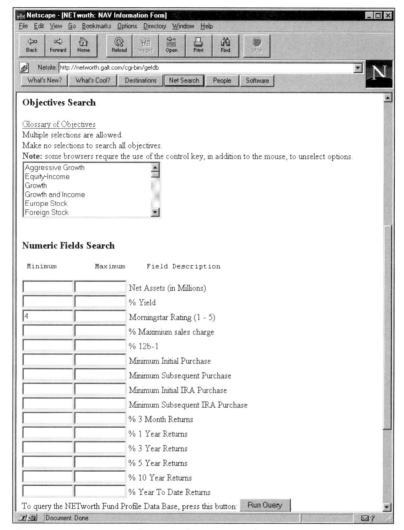

Figure 11-1: The NETworth comprehensive search page gives you many fields for data.

4. Under Numeric Fields Search, type **4** in the Minimum field (see Figure 11-1).

5. Click on Run Query. You see a new page listing the funds that match the criteria you've specified. Cool!

A Morningstar search can help you quickly develop a list of good fund prospects. Figure 11-2 shows the results of a search for balanced funds with a minimum Morningstar rating of 4. Note that the result of this query is an alphabetized list; no ranking is here, except that funds with NETworth pages are listed at the top (in bold).

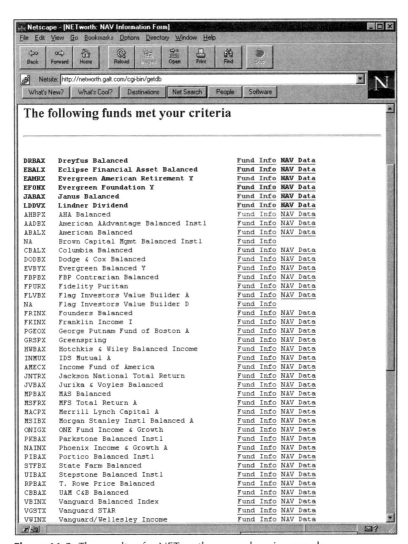

Figure 11-2: The results of a NETworth comprehensive search.

Historical risk data may be of limited use, analyst says

Consider a fund that has performed poorly the past few years. It has a low beta, however. Suddenly, the fund hires a hot-shot new manager, who changes a number of the fund's investments, making it riskier overall. The current beta may rise, but investors are still basing their decision based on historical beta data.

Ronald Kahn, research director for financial data firm Barra Inc. (http://www.barra.com), says that any risk measures should be based on the holdings currently in the fund, not on their past performance and portfolios.

"When you analyze a fund's historical results, it's like looking in a rearview mirror," he says, in "Quantitative Measures of Mutual Fund Risk: An Overview" (cited earlier in this chapter). "You can see where the fund has been in the past, but you can't tell where it is now. And there can be a big difference.

"By basing risk analysis on a fund's current portfolio of securities, it is possible to provide investors with real-time assessments of how much risk that fund is currently taking. The technology is available to implement such a system and would be enormously more useful to investors."

How Did Your Prospective Funds Perform in a Down Market?

KEY TERM

So how's your prospect list coming along? You've now whittled your list down to a number of funds that meet your objectives *and* that do pretty well in the Morningstar rating system. Now ask a really mean, nasty question: Just how well did these funds do in a *bear market*. In a bear market, stocks go into a long-term price downtrend, sometimes lasting for several years. The downturn affects not just one or a few industry sectors, but just about the whole market. It also gets to investors. Investor confidence is low, and trading volume declines markedly.

It's something to think about. Many young investors (not to mention fund managers and brokers) were in diapers, or just a gleam in their parents' eyes, when the last really nasty bear market hit (January to December, 1974, when the Dow 30 lost 45 percent of its value). These young investors don't really know what a bear market is like. Many investment experts fear that the market's overall bullish performance during the past 20 years has led to investor overconfidence, even among those old enough to remember the last bear that had any teeth in it. Recent down markets have been mild in comparison to the rest of the century, in which the average downturn (since 1901) brought stock prices down 29.71 percent.

Here's a list of recent market downturns, based on the Dow 30 index:

◆ January 1973 — December 1974:   -45.1 percent

◆ September 1976 — February 1976:   -26.9 percent

◆ September 1978 — April 1980:   -16.4 percent

◆ April 1981 — August 1982:   -24.1 percent

◆ November 1983 — July 1984:   -15.6 percent

◆ August 1987 — October 1987:   -31.8 percent

Don't let these figures scare you away from the advantages of investing in stocks over the long haul. It's true that market downturns occur fairly regularly — and, when they do, stocks can lose up to half their value. However, over long periods of time, stocks are still the best investment you can make. A $10,000 investment in the S&P 500 at the end of 1973 became $110,000 by the end of 1993, despite having to weather four down markets.

What if your fund was created since the last downturn? Many new funds have been created since 1994, and many of them are worth investigating, but you won't be able to benchmark their performance using historical data from the 70s and 80s. More recently, and up to this book's writing, there have been no real bearish periods, but the market has been flat — or volatile — during the following periods (based on the Dow-Jones Industrial Average): September 15 — November 1, 1995, and February 15 — May 10, 1996, so you might try plugging these dates into a fund performance calculator to see how new funds did. You also can try 1994, a poor year for stocks generally, and July 1996, when the Dow dropped 8 percent and the NASDAQ dropped about 20 percent.

Here's where to find a fund performance calculator. Thanks to a nifty calculator offered on the Web by *Mutual Funds Magazine* , you can find out how a prospective fund performed during a market downswing. Currently, this calculator — called the *Fund Performance Calculator* — is available for free (but requires registration). Figure 11-3 shows the Fund Performance Calculator, ready to go.

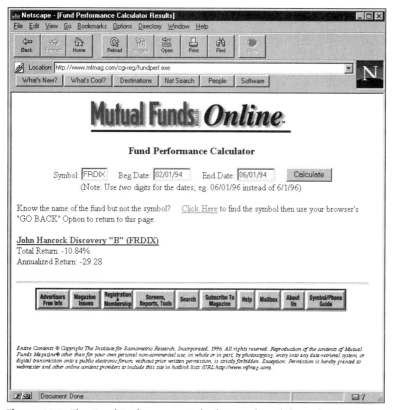

Figure 11-3: The Fund Performance Calculator is found through Mutual Funds Magazine Online.

To access the Fund Performance Calculator, go to the *Mutual Funds Magazine Online* home page (http://www.mfmag.com/) and register (if you haven't done so). After registering, you can click on Registered Users, supply your user name and password, and access the free services. Click on Screens, Reports, Tools to access the Fund Performance Calculator.

Suppose, for example, that the period from February to April, 1994, was a down market. Take a look at the total annualized return performance of the following small-cap funds that are pretty hot right now:

◆ Fidelity Low-Priced Stock (FLPSX):   -11.86 percent

◆ Dean Witter TCW Small Cap Growth (TCSCX):   -38.10 percent

◆ John Hancock Discovery "B" (FRDIX):   -29.28 percent

Currently, the Fidelity Low-Priced Stock fund isn't the hottest performer on the market, but it performed much better in declining markets than the other two funds.

> ## Interest rate hikes: signs of a down market?
>
> An interest rate hike isn't a foolproof predictor of a down market, but it's not bad.
>
> According to market analyst Edson Gould, when the Federal Reserve raises interest rates (specifically, the discount rate) three times in a row, the market may be headed for a downward spiral. One reason: Bonds, CDs, Treasury bills, and other low- to moderate-risk investments start paying more interest. As investors transfer their money to these less-risky investments, demand for stocks drops — and so do the prices.

Assessing Costs

You've selected funds that appear to meet your objectives, you've looked at past performance, and you've assessed the risk of investing in these funds. What's left? Fees, introduced in Chapter 9. A fund charging too much can dramatically reduce your gains over the long haul. Let's take a closer look at these fees — and, in particular, how they can negatively impact your return. You'll learn how to use Web-based calculators to compare the fees of the several mutual funds you're investigating.

To find out which fees a given fund charges, there's only one source to look at: the prospectus. Many mutual fund prospectuses can be obtained from the Internet. For more information on obtaining prospectuses, see Chapter 12.

Loads

Some of the fees mutual funds charge have nothing to do with managers' talents. One fee of this kind is *loads* or sales commissions. They are nothing but a hit to your investment for making a transaction. A four or five percent load on a $5,000 investment brings it down to $4,750 or $4,800. You're starting with less money, which means there's less money to compound.

Loads are front- or back-ended. *Front-end loads* are paid on entering and *back-end loads* on exiting a fund. Loads are based on the amount in the fund account at those times. If the fund is a good investment, back-end loads should be a higher charge. However, sometimes back-end loads decline on a sliding scale over time and may eventually be reduced to zero.

If a fund you like is loaded, try to figure out if the fund is one you want to stay in for a while. Then consider what effect the fees will have over a longer period of time.

To avoid sales loads, you may prefer to concentrate on *no-load funds.* No-load funds aren't inferior to funds with sales loads — in fact, most of the best funds are no-load funds. Note that no-load funds aren't free of other expenses, however, so read the fees section carefully.

12b-1 fees

At the start — before you make any investment — you may pay a marketing fee called a 12b-1. This charge is supposed to be for the fund's cost of promoting itself to shareholders and prospects. You won't know you're paying this fee unless you read the fund prospectus's fine print; it will be deducted from dividends.

In general, try to avoid funds with 12b-1 fees. In some cases, these fees are used to try to sneak the sales load in through the back door. A *true* no-load fund has neither sales loads nor 12b-1 fees.

What do loads and 12b-1 fees do to your return?

Bad things, as you discover by checking out a convenient online calculator: the Mutual Funds Online Load Performance Calculator. This calculator, available at `http://www.mfmag.com/reg_usr/loadcalc.htm`, is currently available for free (but requires registration). The calculator is shown in Figure 11-4.

To use the calculator, type in an initial investment amount and, with the prospectus to guide you, fill in the fees for each of the funds you're looking at. When you click on the Calculate button, you see a new Web page that shows the impact of the loads on your investment compared to a no-load fund. The result is pretty depressing. A $100 investment in a no-load fund, for example, grows to $161 in 5 years, assuming a 10 percent annual return, but the same investment in a load fund nets you only $140. Multiply those numbers by two or more factors of 10, and you see what loads are costing you. Ouch!

Management fees

Management fees are usually quoted as a percentage of the fund's assets (shareholders' money being managed). High fees are not necessarily related to high returns. They reflect, if anything, the costs of operating the fund, and some funds are much more costly to run than others. Buying, selling, and researching stocks and bonds in foreign countries can run up expenses, as can trading a lot. All these activities will cost you but may not mean a better return for you.

Some of the best-performing funds in 1995, for example, were index funds, which sought to match the performance of leading market indexes (such as the S & P 500). These funds have low management expenses because their managers trade much less.

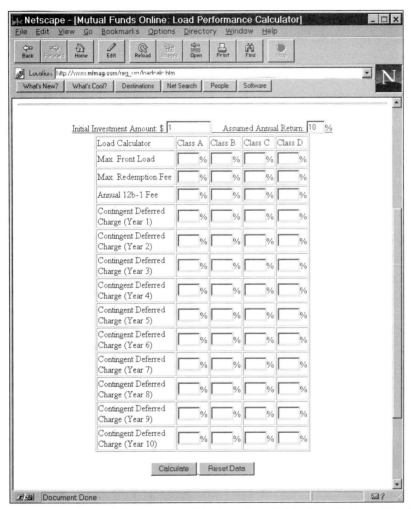

Figure 11-4: The Load Performance Calculator is available through Mutual Funds Online.

Looking for Low-Cost Funds

If you're not thrilled with the loads, fees, and costs that you discover you have to pay, you may wish to re-do your fund search with costs in mind. Once again, a great tool is NETworth's Comprehensive Search, which enables you to set maximums for costs while you're searching for funds.

To access NETworth's Comprehensive Search, you need to subscribe (it's free). After you do this, access NETworth's Fund Atlas page (`http://networth.galt.com/www/home/mutual/fund_atlas/fund_atlas.html`) and click on the Comprehensive Fund Search link.

Select an investment objective and try setting the maximum sales load and 12b-1 fees to $0. You might also try setting the minimum Morningstar rating to 4. The result is a list of funds that have performed well but have relatively low costs. In growth funds, some winners are the Janus Enterprise and the Lindner Growth fund — which, incidentally, are two of the several dozen darlings of mutual fund commentators at this writing (but please note, this favorability could change by the time you read this).

NETworth Comprehensive Fund Search tips and tricks

This chapter has explored two ways you can use NETworth's Comprehensive Fund Search — but we've just scratched the surface. Here are some additional ways you can use this service to hone your list of prospective funds:

◆ **Net assets.** To see how the size of a fund affects performance in the investment objective category you're researching, try several searches with a number of differing maximums. Enter net assets in millions (2000.0 equals $2 billion). Some researchers have found that relatively large, stable funds perform the best over long stretches of time.

◆ **Percent yield.** This refers mainly to yield from fixed-income securities, such as bonds. In an unsettled market, having some yield income can offset losses due to downturns in stock prices. To find funds with more focus on yield, perform a search that sets a minimum yield of five percent. (In a search for balanced funds, this search does an impressive job of bringing forth true balanced funds, which stress income and capital preservation, over funds that in fact put a large amount of money in growth and aggressive growth stocks.)

◆ **Minimum initial purchase and minimum initial IRA purchase.** If you have only a limited amount of money to invest, such as $1,000, you'd better type this number in the Minimum column so that you don't waste your time with funds that have higher minimums.

◆ **Minimum subsequent purchase and minimum subsequent IRA purchase.** This may be an important figure if you're planning to invest regularly but don't have that much money to do it with.

◆ **% returns.** The longer the time horizon, the better — after all, you're looking for consistent performance. However, many good new funds may be excluded by a three-, five-, or ten-year search, so perform a one-year and a three-month search, too, any newcomers will stand out.

A really useful checklist for evaluating funds' performance is in Vanguard Funds' Vanguard University site (`http://www.vanguard.com/educ/module3/ m3_4_6.html`). Vanguard is second only to Fidelity in the number of retirement funds it manages, and it has always been a booster of low-cost funds.

Summary

◆ Before investing in a mutual fund, you should try to determine how its returns balance off against the risks it takes. The Internet can help here by giving you access to Morningstar's risk-adjusted ratings.

◆ When you're looking at risk figures, bear in mind that like all other indexes of fund performance, they're about the past. The fund may have changed managers, investment styles, or investment philosophy that may mean higher or lower risk in the future than the past figures indicate.

◆ How did your fund perform in the last down market? You can find out by using Internet tools, and you'll be glad you did, especially if your tolerance for risk is low.

◆ The lower a fund's costs, the less it has to go up to meet your investment objectives. You can search for low-cost funds using NETworth and other tools.

From Here

◆ Get hold of that fund prospectus right now: Find it on the Web! Chapter 12 shows you how.

◆ Manage your mutual fund portfolio using Web- and PC-based resources. Get the lowdown in Chapter 13.

Finding and Reading Fund Prospectuses

In This Chapter

- ◆ Finding prospectuses with EDGAR
- ◆ More sources for prospectuses on the Internet
- ◆ Is this fund right for you?

No mutual fund will sell you shares until you say you've read the prospectus. However, most people don't read it.

That's not too surprising. On the surface, a prospectus is a dry and boring legal document that's a pain to read. Approached from the proper perspective, however, it's a gold mine of information.

Only the prospectus can help you determine whether a fund's objective is really right for you and whether the fund's performance justifies the risks its managers propose to take with your money. You also find all the information you need to determine the fund's costs, which may not be spelled out so coherently anywhere else.

The worst prospectus to read is the first. After you read the second and third, you begin to realize that they're written according to an SEC-defined format — the same type of information is always in the same place. With some experience, you learn how to zero in on the information that matters most to you, the prospective investor.

In this chapter, you learn how to obtain mutual fund prospectuses from the Internet using EDGAR, the

Securities and Exchange Commission (SEC) server, as well as other sources. As you quickly discover, EDGAR is a priceless tool to individual investors. Armed with the information you get from EDGAR, you can go back to the Web to find out which of the funds you selected has the lowest costs — and what those costs are going to do to your gains and your capital over time.

Finding Prospectuses with EDGAR

The U.S. Securities and Exchange Commission (SEC) offers a service called *EDGAR* (Electronic Data Gathering and Retrieval). The EDGAR database makes available the lion's share of reports (dating from January, 1994) that publicly owned companies and investment firms must submit to the SEC. (As of May, 1996, all of the country's approximately 15,000 publicly owned companies were required to submit information in EDGAR-readable form, except those exempted due to hardship.) A free public service, EDGAR is accessed more than 16,000 times every day; more than 3.1 million public documents have been distributed through EDGAR. More than 60 gigabytes of information are downloaded from EDGAR each month.

Mutual fund companies are required to file amended prospectuses and annual and semiannual reports through EDGAR, so this is a great place to start your prospectus hunt. The EDGAR database doesn't require you to use fund ticker symbols or anything fancy to pull up reports you need. In fact, you don't even need to know the full name of the fund. Often, its *family name* — the kind of brand name its management uses for funds run by the same company — will suffice to bring up a list of entries from which you can find the one (or ones) you want.

The concept of free public access to EDGAR is under attack from some firms that would love to make you pay for publicly available information. Their argument is that the government shouldn't be involved in areas that the private sector can provide. What they conveniently forget is that taxpayers have already invested more than $100 million in the EDGAR system, and it's extremely unlikely that the SEC would ever receive full compensation for this investment. It's unlikely that free access to EDGAR will ever go away, now that so many people and organizations rely on it. But the SEC is looking to give more day-to-day functions to firms such as Lexis-Nexis.

To access the EDGAR prospectus search, use `http://www.sec.gov/cgi-bin/srch-edgar`. See the EDGAR Prospectus Report form, shown in Figure 12-1.

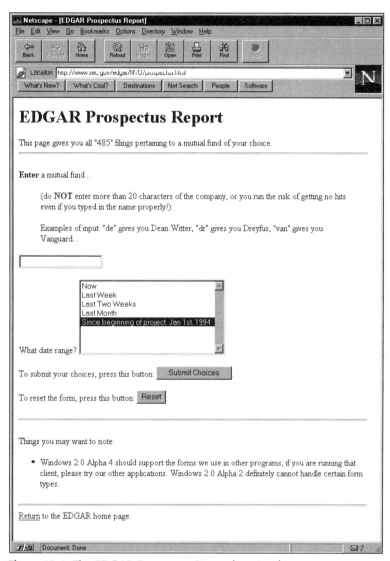

Figure 12-1: The EDGAR Prospectus Report form is where you can start a prospectus search.

Thousands of mutual fund prospectuses are available in EDGAR, but don't count on finding prospectuses for every mutual fund in existence. If you can't find the prospectus you're looking for using EDGAR, try a search using AltaVista: Search for the name of the fund and include the word *prospectus*.

Searching EDGAR

EDGAR is easy to search; just click within the text box, and type as few characters as possible of the ***beginning*** of the fund's name. For example, if you want to see the prospectus for the Fidelity Magellan fund, you can type **Magellan** — you get 84 documents. You can type **Fidelity** or **Fidelity Magellan** and get results too. What's confusing is the retrieval list, which contains many numbered documents. Remember that Form 497s are prospectuses, 485s are registration statements (prospectus updates), and 24Fs are notices of securities sold. (It's fun to see which stocks the funds are unloading!)

To perform a search in the EDGAR Prospectus Report, type the beginning of the fund's name in the text box. Then pick a time frame (since the list's inception) and click on the Submit button. You see a list of retrieved documents, as shown in Figure 12-2. (If nothing is shown, then there's nothing in EDGAR's database.) Click on the most recently dated document.

Notice in the Form column a *485* document. That's what you're after. Actually, a 485 isn't only a prospectus — it's also an annual or semiannual report in which the fund's management has to explain the fund's performance to shareholders. It may make for interesting reading, particularly if the fund manager has to explain to shareholders why the fund didn't do so well lately.

When the prospectus appears, as shown in Figure 12-3, you see what looks like garbage at the top of the document. Don't worry, this is just an encryption code that can be used to determine whether the document is genuine. But this document won't win any prizes for formatting; it's strictly government issue. Just check your aesthetic sensibilities at the door and start pressing Page Down.

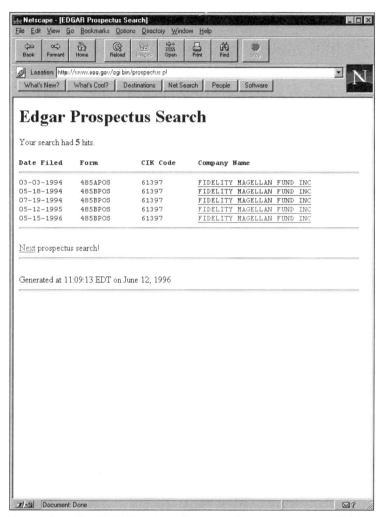

Figure 12-2: The EDGAR retrieval list shows the prospectuses available.

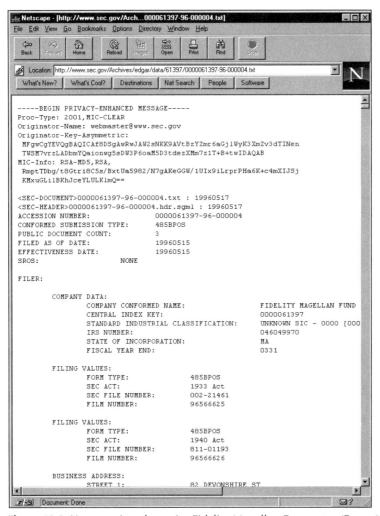

Figure 12-3: You can view the entire Fidelity Magellan Prospectus (Form 485).

Don't you wish you'd read the prospectus?

Some things you may discover about that "hot" fund you bought:

◆ There's a fee every time you reinvest your dividends, which cuts significantly into your investment's long-term appreciation.

◆ Your fund's management fees are substantially higher than comparable funds in the same category.

◆ The fund is ostensibly an "aggressive growth fund" but turns out to have substantial holdings in more conservative, dividend-paying stocks.

◆ You thought you were buying a no-load fund, but there's a hefty fee for something called "12b-1" sales expenses.

◆ If you don't keep your money in the fund for five years, there are sales fees when you redeem your shares. Too bad! You need the money for an emergency.

◆ The fund's charter places practically no limit on the ability of managers to invest in derivatives, use leverage and hedges, and to sell shares short. And you thought you were getting into a conservative balanced fund!

◆ You think you're buying a stock fund, but, in fact, the managers have the right to keep up to 33 percent of the fund in money market reserves (largely because they can't figure out what to do with all the assets they have). But you already have one-third of your money in money market funds. As a result, your entire portfolio is unintentionally skewed towards cash, which underperforms the stock market.

More Sources for Fund Prospectuses on the Internet

If you don't find the prospectus on EDGAR, don't despair — it may be on the Web in downloadable form. Check out NETworth's Fund Atlas (`http://networth.galt.com/`) for the home pages of many mutual fund families. Most of these funds enable you to download prospectuses from their sites.

Often, the prospectus is formatted for reading with Adobe Acrobat, a program that works with browsers to display non-Web data correctly. Adobe Acrobat docu-

ments have nicer formatting than your typical Web page; in fact, they're dupli-
cates, mainly, of what you would see if you ordered a printed prospectus by mail.
Figure 12-4 shows the downloaded Acrobat version of the Gabelli Asset Fund
prospectus.

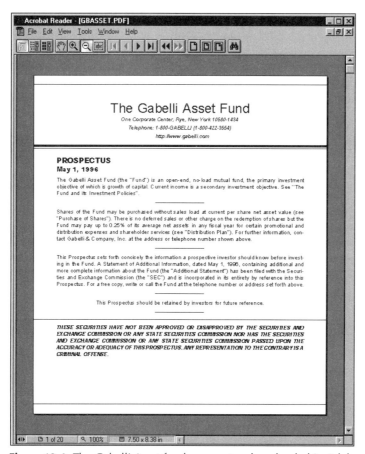

Figure 12-4: The Gabelli Asset fund prospectus downloaded in Adobe
Acrobat format.

If you don't have Acrobat, look for a link to download Acrobat on the same page
that provides links to the prospectus. Downloading the Acrobat reader takes only
a few minutes, and it's free. The reader works with Netscape, Internet Explorer,
and most other Web browsers.

If you can't find a home page for a fund or fund family, try searching AltaVista, the search service with the largest database, with key word combinations such as the following:

> +prospectus "Gabelli Asset Fund"
>
> +prospectus "Worldwide Growth Portfolio"

In AltaVista, the plus sign raises the retrieval importance of the following word, and the quotation marks set off a phrase.

If this search doesn't work, the prospectus may not be available on the Net. Shame! You'll have to order it by snail mail. But the Internet can help you here, naturally.

Do you want to order a prospectus and an application form by mail? Check out this site: `http://www.fundmaster.com/`

Accessible from this site are prospectuses from more than 75 fund families, including AIM, Calvert Group, Dreyfus Funds, Evergreen Funds, First Investors, Gabelli, John Hancock, IDEX, Invesco, Kemper, Pacifica, Templeton, and many more.

If you *still* can't find the prospectus, consider calling the fund. You find a great fund phone guide at `http://www.mfmag.com/guest/fundlist.htm` (It's the Mutual Funds Online Fund Symbols and Phone Numbers page.)

Is This Fund Right for You?

The annual (or semiannual) reports and prospectuses give most of the fundamentals of what's in the fund and how the fund works. The prospectus is what you're

Fidelity's Online Investor Center: a class act

Offering more than 2,900 pages of free information, Fidelity's Web offering (`http://www.fid-inv.com/`) sets the standard for mutual fund families. You find news about Fidelity funds; a mutual fund library, including downloadable prospectuses for all of Fidelity's funds; help with investment and retirement planning; information about Fidelity's brokerage services; tips for making the most of your company's retirement plan package; and even some investing games.

By the end of 1996, Fidelity expects to enable users to view their accounts and switch funds.

required to read before buying shares in a fund. No one will test you on it. But if you want to know what you're buying, this is where you find out.

Prospectuses from different funds vary in their organization, although they all have common elements. But the important stuff in all the prospectuses is right in the front. Here you can find statements of objectives and investment policies and fees, along with a summary of how the fund has performed over time.

Investment objectives

This section tells you what the fund managers hope to accomplish for fund investors. It also gives you a general idea of what kind of fund it is. Growth stock funds — such as Magellan — describe their objectives in terms such as *seeks significant long-term capital appreciation.* This means that they have bought stocks that they hope will increase in price.

Growth and income funds may talk about *capital appreciation and current income,* meaning they have put together a collection with some growth stocks and stocks and bonds that pay dividends and interest, too.

Value funds may speak *of capital growth from investments that are currently undervalued in the market.* These investments are usually stocks that many investors have overlooked for one reason or another — the company has recently improved from a poor performance or is small and not well-followed, for instance. These stocks may not be as fast-moving or risky as growth stocks, but they may not pay dividends, either.

Matching your objectives

Whatever the fund's objectives, they should match what you need now in your portfolio. This is not the place for impulse shopping.

Many people own Fidelity Magellan. In fact, for many, it's the only fund they own. But should this be? In the fund's 1995 prospectus, here's what Magellan has to say about its objectives:

"Magellan is in the GROWTH category . . . . The goal is to increase the value of the fund's shares over the long term by investing in stocks with growth potential . . . . Over the past six months, the fund's net assets have increased from approximately $40 billion to $53 billion, an increase of about 33 percent . . . due to a combination of appreciation of the fund's investments and money coming into the fund."

Digging deeper

Magellan is a growth fund, apparently. In the prospectus, read on to confirm this. You'll find the following in the annual report section: This fund "may be appropriate for investors willing to ride out stock market fluctuations in pursuit of potentially high long term returns."

The last statement seems to put Magellan solidly in the growth category, if you were confused before. But to get to this information, you had to read through (or skip over) a lot of other stuff.

But go back and check over what's in between, too. Near the start of Magellan's prospectus is a letter from Fidelity's chairman, Ed Johnson, who has this to say:

"Although the markets have been fairly positive this year (1995), no one can predict what lies ahead for investors. Last year, stocks posted below-average returns, and bonds had one of the worst years in history . . . . This downturn followed a period in which the investing environment was generally very positive."

In other words, you better think long and hard before committing all your savings to this fund. Although Magellan is not as risky as an aggressive growth fund, it's going to have its downs as well as its ups. Do you have time to ride out the downturns before cashing in your shares?

Why is the head of Fidelity telling you this fairly simple but gloomy stuff right up front? How did this fund do last year, after all?

The fund's performance is found further back in the prospectus. This section gives a picture — often literally, in a chart — of how the fund has performed over the years that it's been around. In Magellan's case, since 1963.

Most prospectuses, this one included, also put in a picture of how some index, such as the Standard & Poor's 500, has performed over the same time. The index is supposed to be an unmanaged yardstick for the fund. What it shows, in a rough sense, is how good a job the fund's management has done with investors' money.

Assessing total return

Look at the fund's total return. This is the increase or decrease in your investment's value after taking out the fund's costs.

Note how steady or inconsistent the fund has been over time, and compare it with the index. Has the fund had many pretty good years in a row, or have just a few good years pulled up its average return?

The goal: minimize risk, maximize gain

Here's an investment strategy that isn't too sexy, but according to thousands of investors who follow it religiously, it works.

At the start of each year, pick the ten highest-yielding stocks in the Dow Jones Industrial Average, and hold them for a year. The next year, repeat this dull exercise. Guess what? On average, you're making about 19 percent per year. The Hennessey Fund follows this system, with the added risk-aversive measure of investing half the fund's assets in low-risk Treasury bills.

According to Hennessy, this brings the fund's gains down, but it also brings down the risk. Back-tested over 23 years, which includes some down markets, this system produces average annual returns of 13 percent. Of course, there's no guarantee that even this conservative system is going to work in the future.

The total return figures are short on details. They show you where the fund and the index were at the end of each year. In reality, the funds are priced at the end of each business day, and the index is priced every time a stock in it trades.

The year-end performance snapshots in the prospectus are useful, however, because most fund investors hold their shares for long periods without trading them actively. Like the stocks and bonds in them, the funds have their ups and downs through the year, although these ups and downs are smoothed out over the longer term.

Examining investment policies

With total return in mind, what do you think about Magellan's performance? Does this seem to mesh with the objectives? Read on, this time in the investment policies section. Here you should find the rules by which the fund's manager is supposed to operate. This section also tells you what can and can't be included in the fund.

Magellan's prospectus gives you a flavor of this. Under "Investment Principles and Risks," you find:

"The fund seeks capital appreciation by investing in securities of domestic, foreign, and multinational issuers. The fund normally invests primarily in common stocks and securities convertible into common stock."

No surprises here. This is supposed to be a stock fund, after all. But read on.

"The fund may invest a portion of its assets in debt securities of all types, qualities, and maturities . . . if FMR (Fidelity) believes that doing so will result in capital appreciation . . . . The fund may buy securities, including domestic and foreign debt securities, that pay dividends."

Some of these policy sections are helpfully concise. Others, such as Magellan's, seem to give their managers great leeway and are as clear as mud to investors. If the policies seem unclear, you can be pretty sure that fund managers are taking advantage of that. In Magellan's case, it's apparent that the fund's managers could decide that it's in the best interests of the fund to transform it from a growth fund into a growth and income fund.

In 1995, the managers did just that. Apparently fearing a downturn in technology stocks, Magellan's managers cut the fund's stock holdings dramatically and moved the money into cash and bonds. By the end of 1995, 68 percent of Magellan's money was in stocks — quite a bit, to be sure, but lower than what you'd think you were getting from a stock fund. As a result, Magellan got hammered when bonds sunk and stocks took off.

Why do fund managers want this kind of latitude? To preserve capital when market conditions change. Magellan's strategy would have worked if it had been implemented just a few months later — in July, 1996, when stocks suffered big declines. In that month, Magellan significantly outperformed its peers.

While examining investment policies, you may find that a fund can use *derivatives* for various reasons. Derivatives are financial instruments that derive their performance, at least in part, from the performance of underlying securities or indexes — sometimes with a disproportionately large effect compared to the underlying instrument. Contrary to popular belief, derivatives may not necessarily increase risk. They could actually reduce it. But if you don't understand how they figure into the fund, it may be best to leave the fund alone.

So what the heck kind of fund is this?

Funds that are lumped together in the same general category have quite different objectives, policies, and overall risk. For example, here's how three *growth* funds, all of which manage over $1 billion, describe what they're trying to do:

◆ **Brandywine Fund.** This fund says it wants to produce long-term stock capital appreciation by investing in common stocks. Current income — dividends — are a secondary consideration. Its management wants to keep a major portion of investors' money invested in stocks. They concentrate on well-financed issuers with a proven record of profitability and strong earnings momentum. These issuers are likely to be lesser-known, rather than larger and better-known, companies moving from a lower to higher marketshare position in their industry groups. Brandywine says it may invest in those bigger names, too, although it plans to go lighter on *unseasoned companies,* putting less than five percent of funds in firms with less than a three-year operating history.

◆ **Strong Opportunity Fund.** This fund seems to have a similar capital growth focus. It's formula for stocks is more set — around 70 percent of holdings in stocks and in instruments convertible into stocks. Opportunity also can buy debt: Up to 30 percent of holdings can be government or corporate debt if management thinks it's advisable. This fund also can buy up to 25 percent foreign securities.

◆ **Sequoia Fund.** This fund also comes under the growth tag. This fund also can invest in stock that's often distributed when companies are acquired or merged, which is not as marketable as most stocks because it doesn't have to be registered with the SEC. Sequoia also can consider *special situations* — unique developments such as reorganizations, new products, or management changes that can provide special chances for companies to profit. Sequoia says it doesn't pay much, if any, attention to technical market factors. It can become pretty concentrated in certain areas, however, with a limit on holdings in particular industries to 25 percent of its total funds. Last year, 31 percent of its holdings were in Warren Buffett's Berkshire Hathaway.

TIP

If you want to have any hope of allocating your investments rationally, buy funds with fairly clear investment objectives. Ask: How much leeway does the manager have to move money around among stocks, cash, and bonds? If you want to control your overall allocation picture, choose funds that don't give managers much latitude to move money around. Or, you can let the fund do your asset allocation for you. That's the philosophy behind balanced funds, which move money among cash, stocks, and bonds as changing markets dictate. Just be aware when you invest in such a fund if you've already got a lot of your money in cash and bonds — be careful not to exceed the allocation that you've established for these investments.

Why buy an index fund?

Hot-performing mutual funds get lots of press, but here's the sad truth: Most mutual funds fail to top market averages, such as the Standard & Poor's 500-stock index. That's why people are increasingly giving up on pursuing "genius" fund managers and buying index funds.

In any given year, nearly three-quarters of mutual funds fail to best the indexes. During the past 10 years, only 17 percent of diversified stock funds have beaten the

S&P 500. The 357 diversified U.S. stock funds that have been around for 10 years appreciated an average 235.8 percent, but the S & P 500 increased 282.7 percent. Why? Think of how much money is going into mutual funds. Mutual funds can't beat the market because they practically *are* the market! To put this point another way, there's no possible way that all mutual funds are going to be above average, the way school superintendents would like you to think the county schools are. Somebody's got to be below it.

This is why many investors are choosing *index funds*, which attempt to match all the stocks in standard market indexes. (Not too sexy, huh?) Index funds have much going for them. If they succeed in their goal — approximating the performance of a major market index, such as the S & P 500 — they outperform roughly three-quarters of all funds. What's more, they have extremely low management expenses, because there's precious little research involved. The Vanguard Index 500 has an expense ratio of only 0.19 percent, one of the lowest in the industry. Low expenses mean higher total returns. The only way you could match this performance would be to buy a bunch of S&P 500 stocks yourself, but you'll pay much higher fees in the form of broker's commissions.

Another argument for index funds: You know your money is in stocks. You then can take care of deciding for yourself how much of your portfolio belongs in bonds and cash.

Watch out for fees

Don't forget to check out the various costs and fees the fund charges. You find this information in a section called something similar to "Summary of Fees and Expenses" or "Table of Fees and Expenses," which is located near the beginning of the prospectus. See Chapter 11 for a more detailed discussion of fees. The fees are divided into two categories:

- ◆ **Investor Transaction Fees.** Generally, these fees are bad news. Look for sales loads, deferred sales charges upon redemption, sales loads on reinvested dividends, exchange fees, wire redemption fees, and other sales charges.

- ◆ **Annual Fund Operating Expenses.** Every fund charges some management fees. However, note that 12b-1 fees may be listed in this section, confusingly. The "Other Expenses" category may sneak in some additional charges.

Are your fund's fees out of line? The more than 3,000 funds formed since 1982 have average expense ratios ranging from 1.01 percent (for fixed-income funds) to 1.53 percent (for equity funds).

Summary

◆ Don't invest in a mutual fund without reading the prospectus carefully. A good place to find mutual fund prospectuses is in the Securities and Exchange Commission's EDGAR database.

◆ You also can find downloadable prospectuses by linking to the home pages of fund families or by searching with a Web search service (such as AltaVista).

◆ To determine whether a fund is right for you, you need to review the fund's investment objectives, total return, and investment policies.

◆ You also need to look at costs and fees. Sales loads, whether they're charged up front or snuck in the back door in the form of 12b-1 fees, can significantly reduce your total return.

From Here

◆ In Chapter 13, learn how to manage your mutual fund portfolio using the Web as well as PC-based programs.

◆ Thinking about investing in individual stocks? Get started in Chapter 13, "Managing Your Mutual Fund Portfolio."

Managing Your Mutual Fund Portfolio

For many long-term investors, the best method for managing their mutual fund portfolio is to reevaluate each fund once or twice a year. Why? Some of the most successful investors are those who are blissfully unperturbed by market fluctuations — they don't buy at the top of the market when enthusiasm prevails and, by the same token, they don't sell when the market is falling. If anything, these investors see market declines as an opportunity to purchase more shares at a bargain cost.

Still, you may find that one of the funds you purchased consistently underperforms. If that's true, you may consider selling the fund or switching to another fund. If you purchased shares in a fund that belongs to a mutual fund family, switching is often quite easy — with most fund families, you can switch to another fund by phone.

As you get older, too, there are occasions when switching or selling is fully justified. You will need to make changes in the types of investments you hold as your investment plans change — as you retire and need more income or as your kids go off to school. You'll need to increase the part of your portfolio that produces income and reduce the portion allocated to long-term capital growth, perhaps, or you may want to raise the cash portion.

In This Chapter

◆ Defining acceptable performance

◆ Tracking your portfolio on the Web

◆ Tracking your portfolio with Fund Manager

This chapter discusses ways in which you can use the Internet to track your mutual fund portfolio, beginning with a handy formula that can tell you whether your funds are performing up to their expectations. You learn about fantastic Web sites that enable you to set up a custom mutual fund portfolio, with share prices updated automatically. You also learn how to get started with *Fund Manager*, the excellent shareware fund and stock portfolio manager that's included on this book's CD-ROM. Remember, however, that most investors should think in long-range terms: five to ten years, not five to ten weeks. Please don't overreact when your portfolio management software shows a short-term decline.

Defining Acceptable Performance

Formulas exist for figuring out how much return you should expect for a given level of risk, and whether a fund is delivering this return. The required return is a sum that is made up of

- ◆ the return you get for taking no risk at all (as with buying U.S. Treasury bills), plus
- ◆ the added return for investing in the fund (this is the added return on its benchmark, say the S&P 500, adjusted for the fund's beta).

If the Treasury rate is five percent, the S&P return rate is 20 percent, and the fund's beta is 1.1, you figure the required rate using the following formula:

Treasury rate + beta(S&P return rate - Treasury rate) = required rate

Please note that this formula provides only a useful rule of thumb. It's really just a shorthand method that serves as a beginning point for thinking about your investments.

Here's an example. If the Treasury rate is five percent, the S&P return rate is 20 percent, and the fund's beta is 1.1, the required rate works out like this:

5 percent + 1.1(20 percent - 5 percent) = 21.5 percent

If your fund actually returns 30 percent, then you're in great shape. If your fund is pulling down ten percent, you're still earning money on it, but it's not measuring up, considering the amount of risk you're taking in owning it.

Finding listings of betas for funds on the Web isn't easy. For a well-diversified stock fund, you can roughly figure the beta by dividing the fund's return by that of the S&P 500 for the same time period. The S&P index is assumed to have a beta of 1 when compared to these funds. For funds that aren't as diverse — such as those that focus on certain industry sectors — the S&P isn't as good a basis for comparison.

For more information on assessing your mutual funds' performance, see the American Association of Individual Investors' How Well Should Your Mutual Funds Have Performed Web page at `http://networth.galt.com/www/home/planning/aaii/mutfunds/performc.html`.

Keep current with information the fund sends you on its holdings and changes in them, fund management changes, and how the fund is performing in relation to its benchmark index. Keeping current goes a long way in helping you anticipate changes in how the fund performs — or in its objectives, in some cases.

Tracking Your Portfolio on the Web

Picture this: You log on to a free Web site and click on a few links. You're looking at a page that lists your mutual fund holdings. Automatic software examines the current net asset value (NAV) of each fund and computes the total current value of each fund as well as your entire portfolio.

Worried about privacy? Don't be. Your Web-based portfolio takes advantage of a little-known (and little-understood) feature of advanced browsers called *cookies*. In brief, a cookie is a code that a server writes to a text file stored on your hard drive. When you access the page again, your browser uploads this file. The information in this file reminds the server of the options you chose during your last visit. Among the options stored in this way are the funds in your portfolio as well as the number of shares in each fund. This information isn't seen by anybody but you, and it's stored only on your computer.

The Wall Street Journal Interactive Edition

This fee- and subscription-based online newspaper (`http://interactive.wsj.com`) is an indispensable tool for investors, even without its portfolio-tracking capabilities. Your Personal Journal Portfolio can track up to 30 issues (U.S. stocks and mutual funds). Of the two Web-based portfolio managers discussed in this chapter, this one is easier to use, but it lacks some of the features that you find in NETworth's Customized Personal Portfolio (discussed in the next section).

Before starting, you need a list of your current mutual fund holdings, complete with ticker symbols and the number of shares you own.

To set up your portfolio, follow the links to the Personal Journal Portfolio page, where you find a link to Personal Portfolio Setup. This page, shown in Figure 13-1, enables you to enter your stock or fund ticker symbols or names. The easiest way to use this page is to enter the ticker symbol; otherwise, the software has to search for the symbol, and several searches may be required to get the symbols entered correctly. You see a page showing you the preliminary results of the entry.

If you need to correct anything, click on Back and make your changes. When the list is correct, clicking on Update Portfolio displays a page showing your current holdings and their total value (see Figure 13-2).

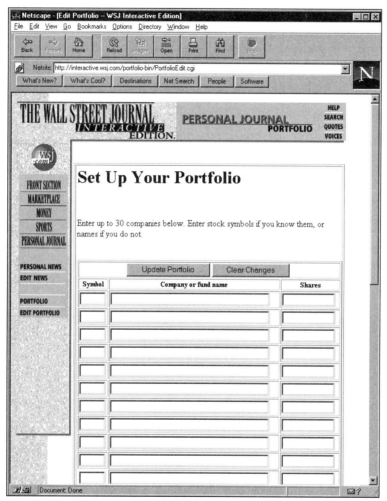

Figure 13-1: The Personal Portfolio Setup page, part of The Wall Street Journal Interactive Edition.

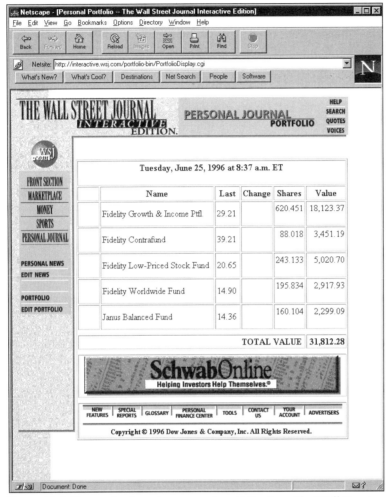

Figure 13-2: The total value of a personal portfolio, from The Wall Street Journal Interactive Edition, is calculated.

If you buy or sell shares, you need to edit your portfolio. This is easily done by clicking on the Edit Portfolio link, which again displays the Personal Portfolio Setup page. You can edit the existing entries or add new ones, up to a maximum of 30. When you click on Update Portfolio, you see the latest values.

NETworth Customized Personal Portfolio

NETworth also offers a Web-based portfolio manager. Although it's somewhat more cumbersome to use than The Wall Street Journal Interactive Edition, it has some advanced features, such as a Java-based ticker symbol scroller. In addition, this portfolio manager enables you to type in the amount you paid for your shares; after you do this, it automatically computes the amount and percentage of gain or loss for each fund and for your total portfolio.

Before you create your portfolio, call your fund companies and find out how many shares you own (and their total value) for each fund you hold. You also need the ticker symbol for each fund.

To create your portfolio, click on the links within the Mutual Fund Market Manager (discussed in Chapter 10) that lead to the NETworth Personal Portfolio system. (To access the Mutual Fund Market Manager, use the following URL: `http://networth.galt.com/www/home/mutual/`). You see a page that enables you to enter the data that you've gathered: ticker symbol, total investment/cost basis (what you paid for your holdings in the fund), and number of shares. When you click on Submit, you see a page showing the results, which are pretty impressive (see Figure 13-3).

Notice that the column and row headings are hyperlinks, which you can click on to see more information. Clicking on one of the column headings gives you a definition of the term used in the column heading, while clicking on one of the ticker symbols displays Morningstar data for the fund, including a NAV chart for the past several weeks.

After you create your portfolio, you easily can add new entries, up to a maximum of 50 items, as well as edit or delete existing ones. You also can set up a Java ticker symbol that scrolls across the screen, but there's not much point in doing this for mutual fund NAVs: They're updated every trading day only once, in the late afternoon.

For mutual fund portfolio management, one of the nicest features of NETworth's Fund Manager is the capability to track the Standard & Poor's 500 index. The standard technique for measuring mutual fund performance is to compare your funds' performance against the S&P 500, and this tracking feature enables you to do so at a glance. Simply make a new entry with the S&P 500 ticker symbol, SPX.X, and leave the rest of the fields blank. When you click on the Submit button, you see the last trading value of the index. As time goes on and the values of the index and share prices fluctuate, you can compare how well your funds are doing to the performance of the index.

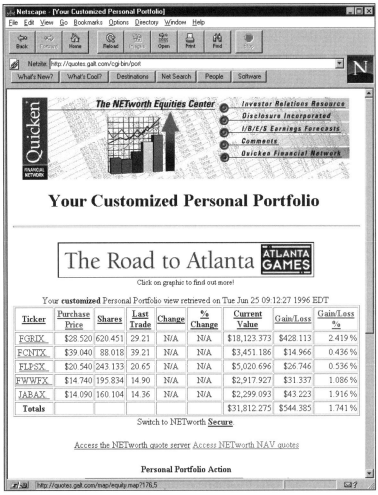

Figure 13-3: The NETworth Customized Personal Portfolio gives you a great deal of information.

Tracking Your Portfolio with Fund Manager

On the CD-ROM packaged with this book, you find Windows 3.1 and Windows 95 versions of Fund Manager, an excellent shareware program authored by Mark Beiley. If you try Fund Manager and like it — and I think you will — please register your copy of the program by sending a check for $29 to Mark Beiley at P.O. Box

51641, Phoenix, AZ 85076-1641. Remember that shareware authors are able to offer fantastic programs such as this one at a bargain price because they do not have to pay marketing and distribution costs — but the shareware concept works only if people pay registration fees.

What's so great about Fund Manager?

Although Web-based portfolio managers offer virtually effortless portfolio tracking, Fund Manager enables you perform tasks that no Web-based manager currently offers. With Fund Manager, you can do everything the Web-based managers can do, and you can also do the following:

◆ **Take time periods into account.** As you may have noticed, the two Web-based portfolio managers discussed earlier in this chapter don't provide any way to note the timing of your investment. With NETworth's portfolio manager, for example, you need to make a manual note of the date you entered the baseline total investment and number of shares held; if you don't, you won't know what time period the gain/loss percentages cover, and you'll have no way of annualizing them.

◆ **Calculate return on investment (ROI).** Calculate ROI using an accepted financial management formula. This figure represents the capital gains, capital appreciation, and yield of your investment, based on the performance of the fund since you purchased it. This figure is automatically annualized.

◆ **Calculate fund performance minus dividend distributions.** If you take your distributions in cash, this calculation gives you an annualized benchmark yield figure that you can use to compare the fund's performance to other funds.

◆ **Calculate fund performance with reinvested distributions.** Automatically annualized, this is the yield figure that's most often cited in mutual fund ads, so this calculation enables you to compare your funds' performance over any given time period to other funds.

◆ **Calculate capital gains for reporting on IRS Schedule D.** This is one of Fund Manager's greatest time-savers. These calculations are complicated and time-consuming if you have to do them by manual methods.

◆ **Track historical performance.** You can obtain historical performance figures for your funds directly from Mark Beiley — three sets of figures are included with your registration fee, and additional sets are available for a modest fee.

◆ **Create graphs that visually display your funds' performance.** You create line, bar, and pie graphs that visually track your funds' performance in comparison to markets and other funds.

For more information on Fund Manager, check out `http://users.aol.com/ Beiley/fundman.html`.

Please note that it is not the intention of this chapter to document everything that Fund Manager can do; that would require a book in itself. What you find in this chapter is a step-by-step guideline for setting up your portfolio — enough to get you started with Fund Manager portfolio management.

Installing Fund Manager

Fund Manager is available in two versions, one for Windows 3.1 (Fund Manager 8.6 for Windows) and one for Windows 95 (Fund Manager 1.3 for Win95).

To install the Windows 3.1 version of Fund Manager, use File Manager to open the FM-WIN3.1 folder, and double-click on INSTALL.EXE. Follow the on-screen instructions.

To install the Windows 95 version of Fund Manager, use Windows Explorer to open the FM-WIN95 folder, and double-click on INSTALL.EXE. Follow the on-screen instructions.

Creating a portfolio

Fund Manager enables you to create unlimited numbers of *portfolios*, which enable you to group up to 100 investments (stocks or funds). The benefit of grouping individual funds into a portfolio comes when you update prices. As you see later in this chapter, you can update prices semi automatically by downloading current share prices from the Internet.

To create a portfolio, open the File menu and choose New Portfolio. In the Save Portfolio As dialog box, type a name for your portfolio (Fund Manager automatically supplies the *.mm4 extension), and click on Save.

In the next section, you create *investments*, which track individual funds. Keep open the portfolio you just created so that Fund Manager will automatically add each investment to your portfolio.

Creating a new investment

Now it's time to create an investment file for each fund you own. From the File menu, choose New Investment. You see the dialog box shown in Figure 13-4. Here, you enter the beginning data for each of the mutual funds in your portfolio, one by one. If you've already invested in funds, use data from the last statement or call the funds for today's data. Be sure to enter the correct fund ticker symbol; this must be entered correctly or you won't be able to download current share prices from the Internet.

Figure 13-4: This dialog box lets you create a new investment.

Viewing your portfolio

After you create your investments, you can view your portfolio, but be forewarned: It won't look too exciting — just a bunch of flat-line charts — because you entered only share prices for one date. But don't worry about that right now; you add more share prices later, and you learn how to update them automatically from the Internet.

Here are some tips for viewing your investments:

◆ You can view one, four, or nine investments at a time. To choose the display, open the View menu, choose Number of Displays, and click on the number you want.

◆ The flat-line charts that you're looking at right now are share price charts (the default). To view each investment by fund value, open the Graphs menu and choose Fund Value.

◆ You can choose more display options from the Investments menu. From this menu, you can control the order in which investments appear on-screen, select which investments to display, and sort in several ways (value, percent yield, percent gain, inception date, and alphabetical). At the bottom of this menu, you find a list of the open investments. You can use this list to go quickly to the chart for one of your investments, if it's off-screen.

Updating share prices

To get beyond the flat-line look in your Fund Manager charts, you need to add data. You can add data in several ways:

◆ **By manually updating a single price for a single fund.** Open the Edit menu, choose Update Price, and choose Single Fund (or just use the Ctrl + I keyboard shortcut). Fund Manager automatically enters today's date (as shown in Figure 13-5). You can change the date if you want. Type the current NAV (share price) and click on OK.

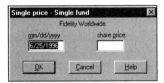

Figure 13-5: Updating a single fund's share price.

◆ **By manually updating a single price for multiple funds.** Open the Edit menu, choose Update Price, and choose Multiple Funds (or just use the Ctrl + M keyboard shortcut). Fund Manager automatically enters today's date, as shown in Figure 13-6. You can change the date if you want. Type the current NAV (share price) for each fund in your portfolio and click on OK.

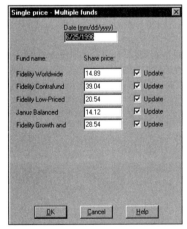

Figure 13-6: Updating multiple funds' share prices.

◆ **By manually updating prices for single or multiple funds for two or more trading days.** This option works much like the ones just mentioned — you see a dialog box that enables you to enter a date and NAVs for single or multiple funds — but there's a twist. When you click on Update, Fund Manager posts the data, increments the date by one day, and re-displays the dialog box. This option enables you to enter funds for two or more days in an assembly-line fashion. To manually update share prices for two or more days, open the Edit menu, choose Update Price, and choose Multiple - Single Fund or Multiple -

Multiple Funds. Click on Update to update one day's prices and increment the date counter by one day. Click on Stop when you finish updating.

◆ **Ordering historical data from the author.** When you register Fund Manager, you can get three sets of historical prices for free, and you can order additional sets for as little as 40 cents each. From the Help menu, choose Order Historical Prices. You see a list of index, stocks, and mutual funds, each of which lists the earliest data that is tracked. You also find a link to the Price Order Form.

◆ **Importing share price data from the World Wide Web.** This technique is initially a bit more difficult because you have to "massage" (edit) the data a little to import it, but this massaging is well worth the initial trouble. Importing data from the Web is fully covered in a later section of this chapter.

After you add some share price data to your investments, your charts take on some life. Figure 13-7 shows the performance of the Fidelity Worldwide fund (FWWFX) for a six-week period. At the top left corner of the chart area, you see the share price and total value of the fund on the chart's final day.

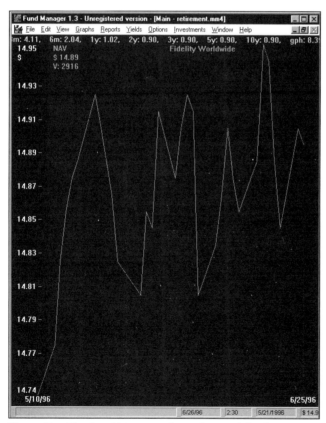

Figure 13-7: The Fund Manager chart of mutual fund performance for a six-week period.

Please note that Fund Manager's default scaling may exaggerate the volatility of an investment. The program automatically sets the lower range of the scale at the share's minimum price, while the maximum scale is set to the maximum price. The effect is to blow small price changes out of proportion, as seen in Figure 13-8. Despite the seemingly wild ups and downs of the fund over this period, its performance actually has been rather flat, as shown in Figure 13-8. In this figure, the scale has been manually set with a minimum of $10 and a maximum of $20. To set a chart's scale, open the View menu and choose Scale, or use the Ctrl + U shortcut.

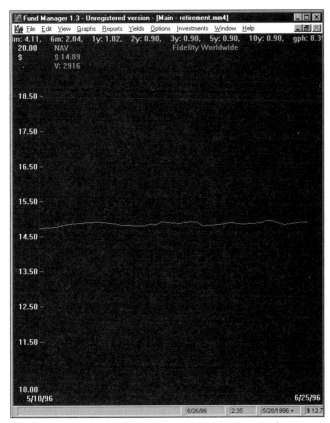

Figure 13-8: Small fund price variations blown out of proportion by scaling.

Understanding return calculations

At the top of the share price graph, you see a list of annualized return figures. Figure 13-9 graphs the Janus Twenty Fund from 8/30/91 to 4/14/93. One of Fund Manager's sample files, this graph displays some meaningful annualized return figures. You see the return for the last three months, the last six months, and the last year; the two-year figure (the next bar over) represents the annualized figure over the two-year period covered by the data. Note that the bars for three-, five-, and ten-year performance aren't meaningful because the data doesn't span that much time.

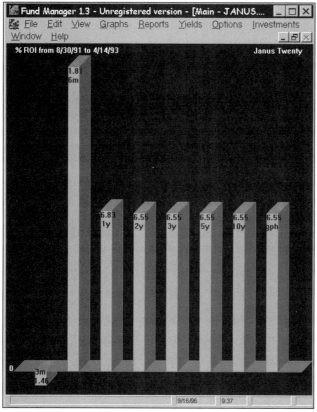

Figure 13-9: Annualized return figures for the Janus Twenty fund.

TIP

To view a graph of the yield, open the Graphs menu and choose Bar- Yields. You see a bar graph of the figures shown on top of the share price chart (see Figure 13-10).

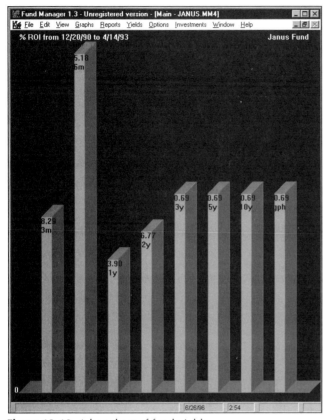

Figure 13-10: A bar chart of fund yields.

Importing data from the Web

After you figure out how to deal with the import process, the easiest way to update share prices is to download them from NETworth, discussed earlier in this chapter. Set up a NETworth portfolio for your funds, as explained in an earlier section of this chapter, and you then can download today's share prices and historical prices with ease. The following procedure enables you to download the current share prices of all the funds in your NETWorth portfolio. It's a little tricky to learn this procedure, but once you do, you will be able to import the data in two or three minutes, whenever you wish.

Downloading today's share prices

You can download today's mutual fund NAV prices into Fund Manager from NETworth. Follow these directions:

1. In NETworth, display your Personal Portfolio. (See "Tracking Your Portfolio on the Web," earlier in this chapter.) If you haven't already done so, set up your portfolio to match the funds in your Fund Manager portfolio. Make sure that the ticker symbols used in your Fund Manager portfolio match those used by NETworth. If you find a discrepancy, change the ticker symbol in Fund Manager by choosing Fund Name/Symbol from the Edit menu.

2. From the Personal Portfolio Action list box, choose Download Prices to Quicken for Windows. You see a new page listing the share prices in a text format (see Figure 3-11).

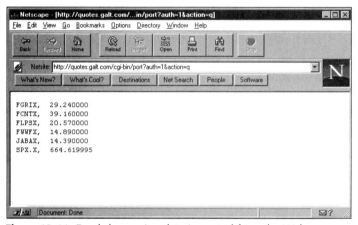

Figure 13-11: Fund share price data imported from the Web.

3. From your browser's File menu, choose Save As and save the file using the Text Only (ASCII text) option.

4. In Fund Manager, open the portfolio you want to update.

5. From the Edit menu, choose Update Price. From the pop-up menu, choose Import - Generic. You see a dialog box titled Import prices from user-defined, shown in Figure 3-12.

   This is the tricky part. To import the data successfully, you must specify the input format so that it matches the text you've downloaded. To do this, you must use some or all of the following symbols, putting them in the correct order:

   ◆ **SYMB:** The fund's ticker symbol.

   ◆ **MM/DD/YY:** The date (month/day/year).

   ◆ **NAV:** The fund's share price.

   ◆ **XX:** Any extraneous data on the rest of the line that you don't want to import.

6. When you import data using NETWorth's Quicken format, each line of data includes the following information: SYMB (the ticker symbol) followed by NAV (the fund's share price). To match this data, you need only type the following in the Input Format box: SYMB,NAV

7. Because you want this data to be recorded with today's date, select the Specify Date check box, but deselect the Specify Fund check box, which is checked by default. You don't want Fund Manager to specify the fund because this information is included in each line of the downloaded data.

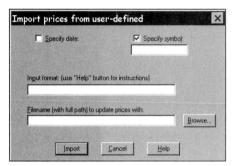

Figure 13-12: Importing share prices from NETWorth.

8. Click on the Browse button to locate the file containing the downloaded share prices, and click on Open. You see the filename in the Filename text box.

9. Click on Import to update the funds in your portfolio.

If something goes wrong, you see an error message. Likely causes of this error message include omitting the comma, misspelling one of the codes, putting the codes in the wrong order, or forgetting to click on the Specify Date option.

TIP

Update your funds' share prices at regular intervals — for example, once per week at a set time (such as 5:00 pm on Fridays).

Downloading historical quotes

Although you can obtain historical quotes from Fund Manager's author, you can get the last 120 days' worth of quotes free from NETworth.

To obtain historical data (120 days) for a mutual fund, follow these directions:

1. In NETworth, access the Mutual Fund Market Manager.

2. In the NASDAQ symbol box, type the fund's ticker symbol and click on NAV/Profile. You see a page with recent results.

3. Scroll down to the NETnavs request form and request a NAV report for the last 120 days. Click on the Request button to initiate the request. You see a

page with the last 120 NAVs.

4. Select the last 120 NAVs, omitting the header of the table (the column headings).

5. Copy the data to a text file (use the Windows Notepad or WordPad accessories for this purpose).

6. Save the file.

7. In Fund Manager, open your portfolio.

8. From the Edit menu, choose Update Price. From the pop-up menu, choose Import - Generic. You see a dialog box titled Import prices from user-defined, as shown in Figure 3-12.

9. Click on Specify Symbol, and type the ticker symbol of the fund.

10. In the Input format area, type the following to import the data (as it's currently formatted by NETworth):

    MM/DD/YY NAV XX

    Note that the *XX* part takes care of the rest of the line, which contains extraneous data.

11. Click on Browse to select the file that contains the data you're importing, and click on Open.

12. Click on Import to import the data. If something goes wrong, carefully check the import codes you used. Did you type the codes correctly? Did you leave a space between MM/DD/YY, NAV, and XX? Note that NETworth may have changed the output format by the time you read this; you may have to type the codes in a different order so that you mimic the pattern that NETworth uses.

Fund Manager horizons

You can do much more with Fund Manager, including the following:

◆ To record distribution transactions, choose Distribution from the Edit menu.

◆ To record share purchases or sales, display the fund and choose Buy/Sell from the Edit menu.

◆ To see a report of your current portfolio value, choose Portfolio Value from the Reports menu.

This chapter has only scratched Fund Manager's surface. To learn more about Fund Manager, make use of the program's good Help pages, which you can access by choosing Help from the menu bar.

Remember, you should keep your funds for the long haul, unless you're convinced that the fund just isn't keeping pace with indexes such as the S&P 500 or other funds in its category. In this sense, a fund management program such as Fund Manager can add to the psychological burden of risk-taking. It does so by exaggerating the volatility of the funds that you're tracking (please recall the scaling discussion earlier in this chapter). To be sure, some funds do turn out to be dogs, and there's no reason to hold on to them. But you can make a reliable judgment only after evaluating funds for at least six months to a year. Don't sell out when there's a minor downturn; you could miss out on big appreciation later on.

Summary

◆ The best way to invest in mutual funds is to purchase funds and reevaluate them periodically, perhaps at the end of each year. Don't react to market gyrations. Better yet, buy a few shares every month and ignore price variations.

◆ If you want to track your funds' performance, you can do so using Web-based services, or you can use a portfolio manager on your personal computer.

◆ Web-based services are very easy to use — they're virtually automatic after you set them up — but they're pretty basic. The plus here is that current share prices are updated automatically. If you use a PC-based fund manager, you can analyze your funds' performance in many ways, but you have to type in the share prices or download them from the Web.

From Here

◆ Thinking about investing in stocks as well as funds? Check out Chapter 20, "Managing Your Stock Portfolio," for Web- and PC-based programs that can handle both stocks and funds.

◆ If you're thinking about setting up a Web-based brokerage account, look for one that offers Web- or PC-based portfolio management that's integrated with the service. For a great example, see Chapter 21, "Using e.Schwab and SchwabNOW!"

V PART

Researching and Trading Stocks on the Internet

Getting Started with Stocks

When asked why he robbed banks, Willie Sutton replied, "That's where the money is." People buy stocks for the same reason. Over time, stocks give the best returns of all investments. Total returns have averaged 13 percent a year over the past 50 years. Had your grandpappy invested $100 in stocks for you in 1925, it would be worth $519,000 right now — but that same $100 would have netted you only $3,000 if invested in bonds.

If you think stocks are fun to follow, that's also fine. Having fun makes it more interesting to learn about companies, industries, the economy, and many other things that you need to know to do a good job tracking these investments.

But if you think buying stocks is like going to the racetrack and putting down a bet, reconsider! The stock market isn't the place to get your kicks. It takes the same kind of study and planning as investing in mutual funds. In fact, the stock market takes more study and planning because you're doing all the work of managing your investments. You're not leaving the work to the professional management of the mutual fund.

Stocks can reward you more than mutual funds, but you must work harder to find the right ones. Stocks are more numerous than funds, for one thing. Because a given stock gives you equity in only one company, stocks are not as diversified; they have more built-in risk.

In This Chapter

- ◆ Can you really pick your own stocks?
- ◆ What are stocks, anyway?
- ◆ Matching stocks to your investment objectives
- ◆ Consider your needs
- ◆ Selecting and buying stocks: An overview

More risk means that you need more courage to ride out the downturn. Bob Kalt, a contributor to the persfin-digest mailing list, puts it this way: "Equities always recover, panicking investors don't." The pattern is depressingly clear: When the market's going up, investors pour money in; when it's going down, they yank it out. They buy high and sell low.

Smart investors don't do this. They develop an investment plan, which involves selecting stocks that meet their investment objectives — and then they *hang on to them*. This chapter shows you how to get started with stocks, with the Internet as your research assistant.

Can You *Really* Pick Your Own Stocks?

You can pick your own stocks, but it takes a lot of work. Traditionally, that work was done by investment firms who had ready access to information that individual investors could not easily get. These firms picked stocks that looked promising — and then charged you a hefty commission when you bought or sold the stocks.

What's so exciting about the Internet, as you learn in the chapters to come, is that much of this information is now available to individual investors. What's more, most of this information is free. With the aid of your computer and the Internet, you can obtain and analyze this information in a fraction of the time it would have taken you previously.

The Internet makes it easier to obtain information, but it doesn't make stock selection automatic. You still need to exercise judgment and make choices.

You'll be wise to familiarize yourself with one or more stock-selection methods before trying to pick your own stocks. One of the best methods is the National Association of Investors Corporation's Stock Selection Guide. There's a Web-based stock selection tutorial, as explained in the sidebar "Stock selection guides and worksheets on the Net." This book shows you how to obtain the information you need to select stocks, but it doesn't attempt to teach a specific stock-selection philosophy.

What *Are* Stocks, Anyway?

When you buy a share of stock, you're actually buying a share of ownership, or equity, in a publicly owned company. That's why stocks are sometimes called *equities*.

Stock selection guides and worksheets on the Net

Stock Selection Guide Tutorial. This online version of the National Association of Investor's Corporation's Stock Selection Guide (SSG) is made available by Invest-o-Rama (http://www.investorama.com/features/ssg_00.html). The NAIC's method is strong on fundamental analysis — that is, the idea that stock price performance can be related to a company's operating performance as reflected in its public data and certain ratios derived from them.

STB Investor's SSG Combined (http://www.better-investing.org/computer/ssgcomb.html). Here's the home page for a DOS program that automates the NAIC's Stock Selection Guide computations. It's nothing to write home about, interface-wise, but it's a useful piece of software. You can download a free 30-day evaluation version.

C-A-N-S-L-I-M. (http://wahoo.netrunner.net/~kennyg/canslim.htm) Here's a good (albeit unofficial) explanation of C-A-N-S-L-I-M, a stock selection method developed by William J. O'Neil, founder of *Investor's Business Daily* and author of *How to Make Money in Stocks: A Winning System in Good Times or Bad*. In this method, you look at **current** quarterly earnings per share, **annual** earnings per share, the effect of **new** products on share prices, **supply** and demand for outstanding shares, whether the stock is a **leader** or laggard, **institutional** sponsorship, and **market** direction. This method combines fundamental and technical analysis.

This doesn't mean, of course, that you can walk into a company and haul off something that's equal to your stock's value, such as a fax machine. All you get is a piece of ownership of a company that you can buy and sell in a market.

Some stocks pay *dividends*, a per-share slice of a company's earnings, but companies aren't obliged to pay dividends — they can choose to spend the earnings on research and development, acquiring other companies, or fancy new equipment.

Most people aren't too interested in dividends when they buy stocks. What interests them is the prospect that the share price will rise over time. Why do stock prices go up? Stocks are traded on an open market, in which share prices are determined by the fundamental laws of supply and demand. Ideally, stock prices reflect the true worth of the company and its earnings — if the earnings rise, so should the stock price. In reality, market sentiment and overall market conditions can raise or lower the price of a given stock.

Stocks are either traded on a major exchange (such as the New York Stock Exchange) or traded *over the counter* (OTC), that is, in broker-managed markets.

If it's on NASDAQ, is it OTC?

Over-the-counter trading and trading in Nasdaq stocks are often confused.

Over-the-counter trading is the buying and selling of stocks by brokerage firms by phone or by computer — outside stock exchanges. The stocks traded here may be stocks that are listed on exchanges such as the New York or American Stock Exchanges.

They may also be stocks that are listed on the Nasdaq Stock Market. (NASDAQ stands for the National Assocation of Securities Dealers Automated Quotation System.) This is a major national and international stock market that uses computers and telecommunications networks for trading and surveillance of thousands of issues. It uses a network of advanced computer terminals to provide traders with a centralized price quotation system, automatic trade execution, trade reporting, and trade negotiation.

The Nasdaq Stock Market is a subsidiary of the National Association of Securities Dealers Inc. This is a self-governing body of securities professionals set up by an amendment to the Securities Exchange Act of 1934. The NASD is charged with preventing fraud and abuse in over-the-counter trading.

Companies that trade mainly or solely over the counter must file registration statements with the Securities and Exchange Commission if they are a certain size — over $1 million in assets — and have more than 500 shareholders. They also must file financial statements with the SEC and send them to shareholders.

In addition, the Nasdaq Stock Market has its own listing requirements. To be traded on the Nasdaq National Market, companies must have a national or international shareholder base (not just one state), apply for listing, meet strict financial requirements, and agree to specific corporate governance rules. They have to have significant tangible assets or operating income, a minimum public trading share float of 500,000 shares, at least 400 shareholders, and a minimum bid price of $5.

To be traded on the Nasdaq Small Cap Market, companies must apply for Nasdaq listing for their shares, meet the requirements for Nasdaq listing, and be looking for sponsorship for their shares. This last requirement means that they must find at least two market makers — brokerage firms willing to act as a buyer and seller for the shares when there are no others.

Putting investing in perspective

Tom Horn, broker/owner of Thomas Horn Realty and a regular contributor to the persfin-digest mailing list, warns investors against being dazzled by big gains:

"Investment success is not measured in rate of return, percentage increase, gain in net assets, or higher cash flow. Investment success should be measured in terms of your personal goals. Decide what you want and then develop the tactics to get what you want. Personal satisfaction and happiness for yourself and your family should be the measure of your success."

Matching Stocks to Your Investment Objectives

Where do you start to pick stocks? Don't pay any attention to the *hot tips* you hear at the office and family gatherings, at least not without researching them thoroughly to make sure they meet your needs. Investing in stocks is like any other investment: You should start by defining your investment objectives.

You can go further by relating different types of stocks to how they fit in with what you need. Do this by getting out your investment plan and noting what kind of return you need at this point in your life. In this section, you learn about the various categories of stocks. As you see, some stocks are more suitable for certain investment objectives than others.

Don't even think about buying stocks until you think through your investment objectives, as explained in Chapter 4. Figure out, too, how much risk you feel comfortable with. Does losing as much as five percent of your investment per year make you antsy? If so, you're probably in the low-risk tolerance camp. Being able to put up with a loss of 6 percent to 15 percent puts you in the medium-risk tolerant group. Being able to swallow even more loss — 15 percent to 25 percent — sets you among high-risk takers.

Consider Your Needs

Maybe you're in your mid-20s. You're still single and have a decent job. You've paid off much of your school loan, and your car's running all right. You have some shares in a stock index fund. About a year and a half ago, you bought a two-year

Treasury note, and it is maturing soon. Treasury rates seem pretty low to you now, and you want to check out some stocks to buy with the money you'll get from the T-note.

What's the best *kind* of stock to start with? For starters, what does *kind* mean? The following categories are by no means hard and fast, but they give you some idea of how you can line up groups of stocks' risk and reward profiles with your own. Some stocks follow industry lines. Others cut across them.

Let's look at these categories more closely and see how they fit with various investment objectives.

Blue chip stocks: buy and hold

These are the stocks of well-established, respected companies such as DuPont, General Electric, and Procter & Gamble. They have long and unbroken records of dividend payments, even during economic downturns. They tend to be expensive, but the promise of steady dividends and good share price appreciation attracts long-haul investors.

Blue chip stocks pay dividends and offer investors growth from gains in their stock price. They have typically been posed as *buy and hold* stocks, producing solid gains over the long haul. Compared to other companies in their industries, they're better managed, invest more in research and development, and do better in the all-important global market. But they often cost a lot. If you're thinking of buying a blue-chip stock, you can usually count on holding for a long time — as many as fifteen years or more.

Income stocks: steady as she goes

Income stocks often hold their market value well because they pay sizable dividends, which is referred to as the stock price being supported by the dividend. In addition to holding on to what you pay for these stocks, or most of it, you also get income from the dividend. These stocks are preferred by investors with shorter time horizons, especially retired people who are risk-averse and need current income.

The down side of income stocks is that they sometimes don't retain as much of their earnings as stocks that don't pay a dividend. With less money available to the company to reinvest, its growth and that of its stock price may be slower than for firms that don't pay as much out. Another minus: Income stock prices may be more sensitive to changes in interest rates in general. As rates for bonds and other fixed-income investments rise, these debt securities seem more appealing to investors than income stocks.

Growth stocks: betting on the future

A growth stock company's earnings are expanding faster than those of the average company or the economy in general, and it shows strong potential for future growth. Typically, such firms plow profits into research and development rather than paying dividends.

Growth stocks' prices may rise fast because their underlying earnings are growing faster than average or faster than the economy in general. Many technology stocks fall in this area because they're in industries that may be expanding several times faster than the overall economy. They may have varying degrees of risk — sometimes quite high — and usually do not pay dividends. Instead, these stocks plow back their earnings into their operations, which they hope will produce more growth for them. But this isn't guaranteed.

Value stocks: hunting for bargains

These companies seem to have sound fundamentals, such as sales and earnings growth, but they are not priced as high in relation to these fundamentals as other companies in the same industry or with similar growth rates. They are said to be undervalued.

Speculative stocks: taking a chance

A speculative stock is one for which it's hard to predict what will happen to its stock market performance; although some aspects of the firm might look promising, its finances may be poor, or its industry may be new and unproven. These stocks may be priced low due to factors such as unpredictable earnings, past disappointments, or lack of profit. A positive change in these factors can result in a big upswing in price for these stocks. But this may be only for a short time, or it may not happen at all.

Cyclical stocks: ups and downs

Cyclical stocks are more dependent than the average stock on changes in the economy to raise and lower their prices. These companies have peaks and valleys in their sales, profits, and stock prices (sometimes these are predictable, sometimes not). For example, when the economy's strong, people buy houses and all the things that go in houses (such as furniture and appliances). When the economy's weak, people put off these purchases.

The trick with cyclical stocks is buying at or near the low point in their cycle and selling at or near the top. Cyclicals' sales and profits may vary a great deal over their cycles, which makes it harder to value them without taking a pretty long view.

High fliers can crash

One of the hottest stocks in the opening months of 1996 was Diana Corporation (DNA), which rose from a low of $5⅜ in August, 1995, to a spectacular peak of $120 on May 24. This Milwaukee-based firm focuses on the hot telecommunications market, including cellular telephones, call controllers and ISDN hardware, switching and transmission systems, and network installation services.

Many high-flying small cap stocks hit a wall in June, 1996, thanks to a series of unspectacular earnings reports and negative comments from investment newsletters. At this writing, DNA was trading around $35.

Note that Diana is the sort of stock that you may wish to avoid: It had no earnings for the previous two years. Much of its price rise in early 1996 came after reports of planned new products and a corporate restructuring planned for later this year.

Defensive stocks: hunkering down

A defensive stock is one that is less dependent than most stocks on the overall economy, making it a good refuge in a down market. Even in a declining economy, people still buy food, medicine, soda pop, and electricity. A classic defensive stock is a utility, which usually pays dividends (which helps to support the stock price).

Defensive stocks provide a good refuge when cyclicals are performing badly (or when the whole stock market is performing poorly, for that matter). The other side is that they also don't perform as well when things are on the up and up for cyclicals and the economy. In the longer term, defensive stocks may have a slower growth rate, too.

Foreign stocks: multiplying risks

These firms operate from headquarters outside the U.S. Within this category are all the kinds of stocks just mentioned, including growth, value, income, cyclical, and defensive, only they're based and usually operate abroad rather than in the U.S.

Foreign stocks can offer better growth than U.S. stocks at certain times. Not all economies are closely linked to the U.S., although many are. Foreign stocks come with their own set of risks. These risks include trading in another currency, being dependent on a different (and often harder to follow) economy, and being subject to different governments and rules. These factors add cost as well as risk when dealing with foreign stocks.

Small-cap stocks: not necessarily small risk

Small-cap stocks are the shares of small companies, typically those with less than $100 million in capitalization (and sometimes much less).

Small companies and their small-capitalization stocks often are the pets of small investors, who love their low prices. These stocks can produce big gains, but they are often a gamble. Small companies can be riskier when they don't have the finances to ride out a slump, for one thing. For another, small company stocks often are more costly to trade and harder to sell than larger company stocks.

Initial Public Offerings (not for individual investors)

Initial public offerings, or IPOs, are stocks offered to the public for the first time. Unless you're in on the deal from the beginning, it's hard to cash in. Anyone who tells you differently is either wishing or lying. Buying these stocks at the offering price is like opening night at a show. If it's a hit, it's sold out, and if you can get in close to the offering price, you probably don't want to. You do better waiting for the opening night crowds to break up.

If you want to know more about IPOs, the site of choice is IPO Data Systems (http://www.ipodata.com/), which provides comprehensive data on IPOs in the U.S. It's a subscription-based service, but you can check out samples and take a tour of the service's offerings. Figure 14-1 shows the site's welcome page.

Stock indexes

Stocks in all the above categories change over time. Some, such as IPOs, speculative stocks, and small-cap stocks, change a lot. To help you keep track of trends in these changes, you can use *indexes*, which are lists of stocks. Indexes are out there for just about all these categories. They not only tell you which stocks are in them, but where they stack up in size, market capitalization, earnings growth, price-to-earnings ratios, and several other measures that can rank stocks in a given category.

Figure 14-1: IPO Data Systems provides information about IPOs.

Some of the more popular indexes are the following:

◆ **Dow Jones Industrial Average (DJIA).** If you want a list of the top blue chip stocks, this is a good place to start. It's probably the most visible list of popular stocks to find and follow. You find DJIA quotations at most of the stock-related sites on the Web, as well as in the *Wall Street Journal Interactive Edition* (http://interactive.wsj.com). A nice ten-day chart of the DJIA's recent performance can be found at Kuber's Trading Desk (http://www.best.com/~mwahal/invest/charts/stocks/html/n_ZRA_intraday.html) (see Figure 14-2).

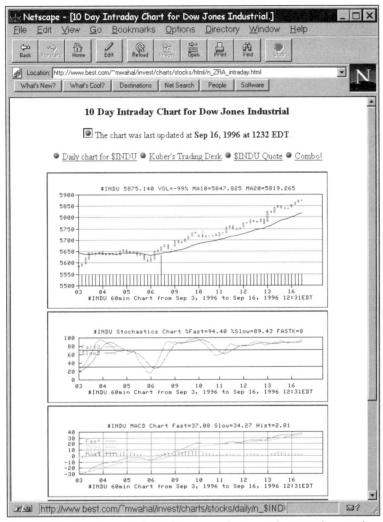

Figure 14-2: Dow Jones Industrial Average chart at Kuber's Trading Desk.

◆ **Standard & Poor's Indexes.** The three S&P indexes (S&P 400, 500, and 600) contain a good helping of growth stocks. Standard & Poor's has designed them to be a kind of proxy for the whole economy, so they cover a wide range of industries. The S&P 500 comprises the 500 biggest stocks in this mix. Next in size is the S&P 400 — a well-known grouping of mid-cap stocks. The S&P 600 is a fairly new selection of small-cap stocks. The S&P 500 covers about two-thirds of the U.S. stock market's total market capitalization. With the mid-caps added in, more than three quarters are covered, and with the small caps, over four-fifths. Check out Kuber's Trading Desk (http://www.best.com/~mwahal/invest/) for recent S&P indexes.

Or, go to the source: Standard & Poor's Equity Investor Services (`http://www.stockinfo.standardpoor.com/idxinfo.htm`) gives you links to all the S&P indexes (see Figure 14-3).

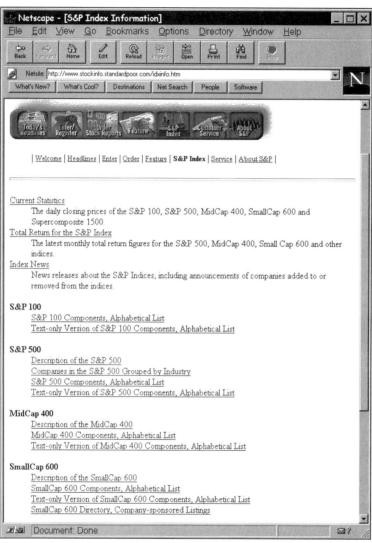

Figure 14-3: Look up all the S&P indexes at S&P's Equity Investor Services.

◆ **NASDAQ indexes.** If you would like to check on groupings of stocks that fall into the speculative area or are in cyclical industries such as transportation, or sector stocks such as computers or insurance, go to NASDAQ's home page (`http://www.nasdaq.com`), shown in Figure 14-4. Here you find descriptions of all the NASDAQ indexes for these and other sectors of the economy — bank, biotech, computer, insurance, other financial, transportation, telecommunications, and industrial companies. Also, you find the NASDAQ 100, a group of fairly big growth stocks. For many of these kinds of companies — especially the technology-related ones — the NASDAQ indexes are quite a complete index. For other industries, such as industrial or natural resource firms, the NASDAQ lists cover a much smaller portion of the total stocks listed, and usually have the smaller ones. Still, because the New York Stock Exchange doesn't have this kind of listing on the Internet yet, the NASDAQ is a good place to start searching.

Like to track the Dow Jones Industrial Average back to its inception, in 1910? You can download a text file containing the weekly price from `http://investorweb.com/djia.htm`.

Selecting and Buying Stocks: An Overview

After you determine a preliminary match between your investment objectives and one or more stock categories, then it's time to start selecting individual stocks for further study. Here's an overview of the process you should follow for each and every stock you buy:

◆ **Finding a few promising stocks for further research.** There are many ways to get started: recommendations from reasonably reliable sources (such as established investing newspapers or magazines), computer-based stock screening and, yes, tips from friends. Don't forget about personal experience with firms that you feel are doing a really good job. You don't run out and buy a stock at this point; you simply put together a list of stocks for further, intensive study.

◆ **Getting current stock quotes.** After you have a few hot stock prospects, it's time to find out what they're selling for — and how their prices have behaved recently. You find out how to do this in Chapter 15.

◆ **Learning how to evaluate a share's price.** Is the price right? In Chapter 16, you learn the basics of evaluating share prices.

◆ **Getting the information you need.** To evaluate share prices, you need facts and figures — lots of them. One good source for financial information about companies is annual and quarterly reports, which you can obtain on the Internet, as Chapter 17 explains.

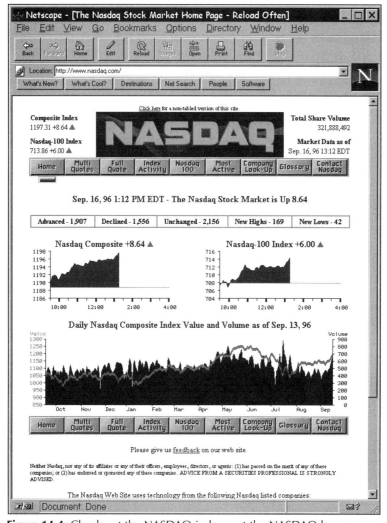

Figure 14-4: Check out the NASDAQ indexes at the NASDAQ home page.

◆ **Putting the firm into context.** If the price and financial fundamentals look good, spend some time putting the firm into its broader context. What's happening with the industry that it's in? What products are hot? What's the competition up to? What's the regulatory picture? Are any big challenges shaping up for the future? In Chapter 18, you learn how to use the Internet's powerful tools to put a firm into context.

◆ **Making your investment.** Satisfied that you have a hot prospect? It's now time to buy. One of the hottest developments in investing is the explosive growth of online brokerages, which enable you to buy and sell stocks via the Internet at low cost. Find out how to use online brokerages in Chapter 19

◆ **Tracking your portfolio.** As with mutual funds, you can track your stock portfolio using online sites or software running on your own computer. Chapter 20 surveys your portfolio-management options.

Stock recommendations on the Internet

You find plenty of stock recommendations on the Internet. They range from the uninformed musings of college students to teasers tossed out by professional analysts who are hoping to get you to sign up for an expensive newsletter. Other recommendations are put up by people who have, in one way or another, something to gain from recommending the stock — or from trashing it. Are these stocks worth examining? You be the judge, but if you look at any of these pages, please bear in mind that these picks should be seen as nothing more than a starting point for your research.

Here's a list of some stock pick pages that may be worth a look:

◆ **Growth Stock of the Month** (http://www.investorama.com/). Invest-o-rama's editor, Douglas Gerlach, picks a growth stock of interest to long-term investors. Mr. Gerlach includes previous picks, so you can see his track record.

◆ **EQUIS Hot Picks** (http://www.equis.com/). These stocks are selected using EQUIS' technical analysis program, called MetaStock.

◆ **Financial World** (http://www.financialworld.com). This independent magazine assigns a letter grade to stocks selected from a database of 1,000 companies. It's a good place to start; check out the A and A+ ranks. You find much useful information, including industry, ticker symbol, and fundamentals (including the P/E ratio).

◆ **GreatStocks Project** (http://www.geocities/com/WallStreet/3811/index.html). This is a virtual investment group: A group of individual investors who pool their knowledge rather than money. At the heart of the project is a moderated mailing list.

◆ *Money Magazine* (http://www.pathfinder.com/money). You find articles with up-to-date stock picks from investment professionals in this online version of the popular magazine.

(continued)

(continued)

◆ **Money Talks** (http://pawws.com/Mtalk_phtml/moneytalk.html). This site contains articles of general interest on investing, including stock picks from Robert Metz, formerly of the *New York Times*.

◆ **OLDE Discount Corporation** (http://www.oldediscount.com/stocks/). This discount brokerage maintains a list of 200 stocks that it currently recommends. The stocks are organized by industry grouping. A neat feature: Some of the stocks have links to the company's home pages.

◆ **STREETNET** (http://www.streetnet.com). Featured here are in-depth industry profiles for a variety of industries (currently, telecommunications, motorsports, automotive, telecommunications, and health care) as well as top stock picks in each of these industries.

Summary

◆ If you have the time to research stocks and pick them yourself, you may do better than a mutual fund — but then again, you may not. Picking individual stocks is riskier than buying a mutual fund because there's less diversification.

◆ Investors buy stocks in the hope that they'll see big capital gains from share price appreciation.

◆ To get started with stocks, look at the different types of stocks and pick one or more categories that meet your investment objectives. Go on from there to develop a list of promising candidates for investment, but don't buy unless you've done your homework, as Chapters 15 through 18 explain.

From Here

◆ Get free 15- to 20-minute-delayed stock quotes from the Internet, as Chapter 15 explains.

◆ Found a good candidate? Chapter 16 shows you how to determine whether the price is right.

◆ Like to know more about a company? Chapter 17 shows you how to use the Internet's amazing resources to do background research on a stock that you're thinking about buying — and Chapter 18 shows you how to put the company into a deeper and broader context.

Getting Stock Quotes and Charts

Y ou have a list of stocks to study, gathered from published reports, newsgroup discussions, personal experience, or explorations with a search engine. What are the current share prices?

You can get stock quotes by looking them up in the newspaper, but there's a real advantage to obtaining share price quotes from the Internet: Many of the services described in this chapter offer free charts as well as quotes. These charts show the stock's performance over time periods that you specify (such as the past 12 months).

Finding Free Quotes on the Internet

As one brokerage executive put it, charging for stock prices seems a little like expecting people to pay for department store price tags. Traditionally, real-time stock quotes — with prices updated throughout the day — were available only via pricey, proprietary services. These services used dedicated terminals and modems to display current business news and share prices from the major exchanges.

In This Chapter

◆ Finding free quotes on the Internet

◆ More than just quotes

◆ Going for the graphs

Thanks to the Internet, you now can obtain reasonably up-to-date share price quotes (with a 15- to 20-minute delay) for free. Figure 15-1 shows one of the most popular quote servers, PC Quote (`http://www.pcquote.com/`). You can obtain five quotes at a time, or receive one quote with additional details, as shown in Figure 15-2.

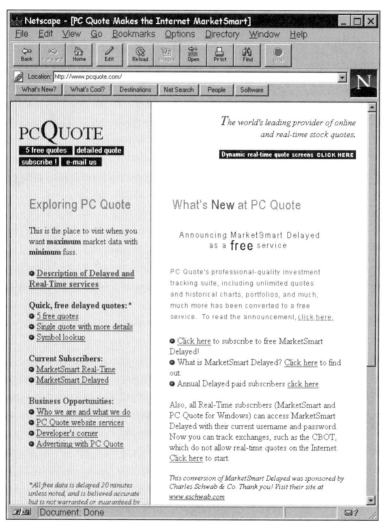

Figure 15-1: PCQuote's welcome page.

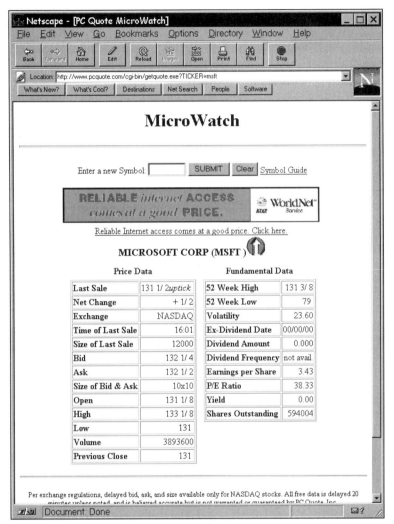

Figure 15-2: PCQuote data on Microsoft (MSFT).

Free quotes

Most of the services that provide free stock quotes on the Internet see the quotes as a loss leader. In marketing, a *loss leader* is a heavily advertised product that you sell at a slight loss. You're hoping to attract many customers, who will buy additional products or services and enable you to make a profit. At the sites offering free quotes (see the sidebar, "Quote servers on the Web"), you find that you can subscribe to additional, fee-based services, including stock research reports and real-time stock quotes. These services may prove of interest to you, but if not, you can still make use of the delayed quotes. Some of these sites also make money from advertising or links to pages of brokerage services.

Quote servers on the Web

Briefing.com (http://www.briefing.com). Briefing.com features a gateway to the DBC stock quote server (see DBC Online). Briefing also runs its own bond quote server, providing Treasury, corporate, agency, and mortgage bond quotes that are updated every 10 to 15 minutes.

Canada Net (http://www.visions.com/stocksbonds/symbol.html). Although many quote servers in the United States can give quotes on Canadian stocks, most of them are not yet able to supply historical price data. Canada Net can provide data since July 4, 1995, and the server also has some charting capability.

DBC Online (http://www.dbc.com/). DBC is an excellent source of free delayed quotes and current market information. The site also features business news capsules and a personal portfolio manager. Real time quotes and other services are available by subscription. As you quickly learn, many of the quote servers on the Web actually use DBC's data.

NETworth Quote Server (http://quotes.galt.com). NETworth provides stock quotes for both American and Canadian stocks and mutual funds traded on the major exchanges. Graphing functions and personal portfolio tracking are also available. In addition to quotes, you get current price and trading data, with some fundamental information, such as earnings per share, price-earnings ratios, dividends, and yield.

PC Quote (http://www.pcquote.com). PC Quote provides free delayed market quotes for up to five equities at a time, including stocks traded on the OTC market. More in-depth price and fundamental data, such as daily highs and lows, dividend payout dates and amounts, and P/E ratios are also available upon request through the free MicroWatch service.

Quote.com (http://fast.quote.com/fq/quotecom/quote). For a quick fix on the markets, check out the Quote.com page. This site provides delayed quotes for stocks, funds, and commodities, as well as stock market data, daily charts, major indices, exchange rates, and some sector data. A plus is that you receive earnings data as well as fundamentals, such as the P/E ratio.

Security APL Quote Server (`http://www.secapl.com/cgi-bin/qs`). This is probably the best quote server on the Internet. You get 52 week lows and highs, P/E ratio, market capitalization, beta, annual dividend, and earnings data.

StockMaster (`http://www.stockmaster.com/`). StockMaster (formerly located at the MIT Artificial Intelligence Laboratory) offers free delayed stock and mutual fund quotes and graphs.

What about real-time quotes?

At many Internet quote servers, you find information about fee-based services that enable you to get real-time quotes — you see the share price changes as they occur throughout the day.

The real question here is: If you have data this good, how can you put it to use? Unless you're a licensed trader yourself, when you buy or sell a stock, your order gets in line with a bunch of other orders, either at your broker's or with a trader later on.

If your order is to buy or sell at the market price, then it's carried out at the market price at that exact time, not at the time when you first placed the order. For this reason, it really doesn't matter if the quoted price you're using is delayed 15 or 20 minutes. As an individual investor, you can't really expect to get that close on order executions.

In short, for most readers of this book, real-time quote services aren't worth the money.

You also shouldn't get too hung up on real-time quotes right at the start of stock investing because there are other, more important things to think about. You should be thinking about how your stock will be doing fifteen years from now, not fifteen minutes from now.

More Than Just Quotes

The best Web quote services offer not only free (delayed) quotes, but much more free information — some of which will prove very valuable indeed for your research purposes.

Quote.com

One of the best things about the free parts of Quote.com (`http://www.quote.com`) is the way it gives you important information, including the stock's price/earnings ratio (P/E ratio) and the 52-week price range. (You learn more about how you can use this information in Chapter 16.) Quote.com has nearly all the elements of enhanced financial price tables that you get in publications such as Barron's, except that Quote.com has daily instead of weekly tallies. In Figure 15-3, you see Quote.com's quick quotes page for Microsoft; links take you to Microsoft-related news, a chart of today's price movements for Microsoft's stock, insider trades of Microsoft stock, and a company profile.

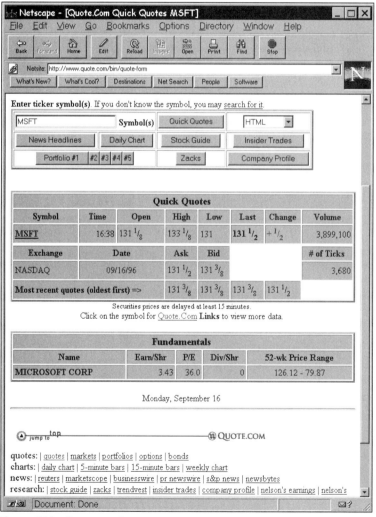

Figure 15-3: Quote.com's quote server.

As you've just seen, Quote.com enables you to research stocks, not just get quotes. Plus, it gives you daily, weekly, monthly, and intraday price charts; charts for major market indexes such as the Dow and S&P 500; and pullouts of the stocks that were the most active, were the biggest price movers, had new highs and lows, and were the biggest volume gainers for the day. If you're searching for foreign exchange or money market rates, they're also free on Quote.com, as is an annual report mailing service.

NETworth

NETworth's free stock quote service (`http://quotes.galt.com`) is not quite as neat as the Quote.com service. It has no earnings data (see Figure 15-4), but it's still excellent for a free service. NETworth's slant is more toward individual investor education. NETworth brings in copious information and references from the American Association of Individual Investors, and this alone makes it worthwhile to check back to this site often.

If you feel like doing some practice *paper trading* — tracking stocks in a hypothetical portfolio — NETworth has an easy-to-use Personal Portfolio Manager in which you can put your tests. This tool is also fine if you want to track an actual portfolio of securities that you've bought in more than one place, such as Treasury notes from the local Federal Reserve Bank, mutual funds from a fund manager, and stocks from a discount broker.

Security APL quote server

Security APL (`http://qs.secapl.com`) works as part of a larger network of services called *PAWWS*, Portfolio Accounting Worldwide, which includes fundamental securities data, portfolio accounting, news, advisory, company profile, and brokerage services — some for fees, others for free. You get three deep-discount brokers to choose from here, all of them large and reputable — Net Investor, National Discount Brokers, and Jack White & Co.

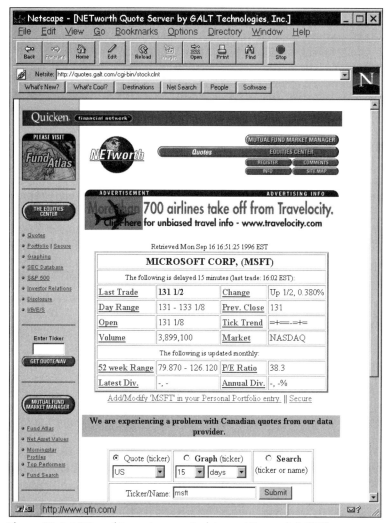

Figure 15-4: NETworth's quote server's data on Microsoft (MSFT).

Security APL also probably has more data in its stock quotes than any other server. It includes elements such as betas and five-year earnings growth rates that you just don't see anywhere else. As shown in Figure 15-5, it also gives you the last 12 months' earnings; market capitalization amounts; daily, weekly, and 52-week high and low prices; daily volume; and number of trades in a day.

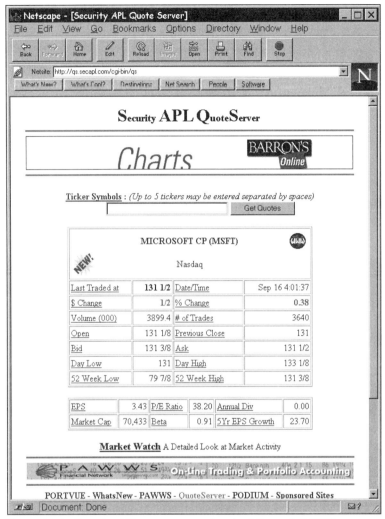

Figure 15-5: Security APL quote server data for Microsoft (MSFT).

Going for the Graphs

The best-known stock graphing service on the Web is Stockmaster (http://www. stockmaster.com/). When you ask for a quote with Stockmaster, you get pretty much the same information that NETworth gives you, plus a chart of the stock's performance for the past 12 months (including volume), as shown in Figure 15-6.

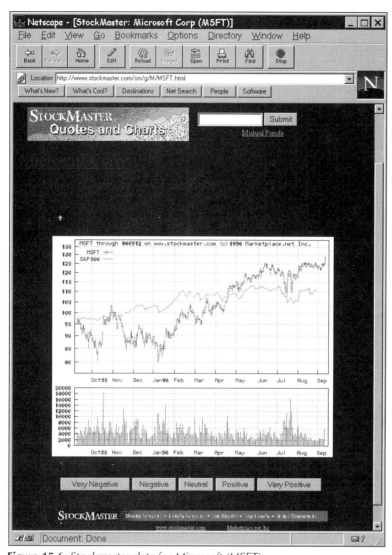

Figure 15-6: Stockmaster data for Microsoft (MSFT).

KEY TERM

But Stockmaster is not the only game in town. NETworth offers more sophisticated graphing options, including *moving averages* and the capability to plot comparative graphs with up to five stocks displayed (see Figure 15-7), which compares the share price performance of two firms. A moving average is an average of a stock's price that is spread over a certain period, such as 20 or 50 days. Moving averages are plotted against the stock price (as Figure 15-7 shows) to indicate if the current price is above or below the averages. In addition, a moving average makes it easy to see the overall trend — which may not be so readily apparent if the stock is gyrating up and down.

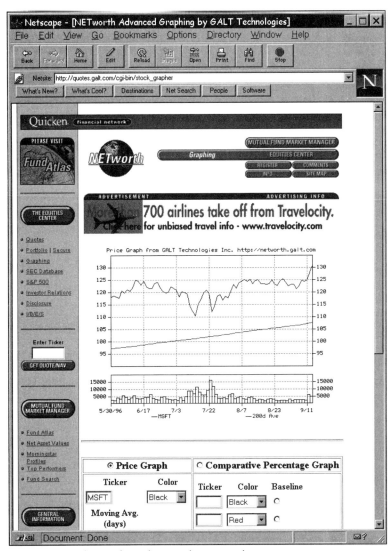

Figure 15-7: Advanced graphing with NETworth.

Summary

◆ You can obtain free, delayed stock price quotes on the Internet from services that hope to sell you additional, fee-based services.

◆ Most individual investors don't need real-time stock quotes.

◆ The best quote servers give you additional information that comes in handy when you're analyzing stock prices.

◆ Most quote servers enable you to generate graphs of the stock's performance over the past 12 months.

From Here

◆ You know the stock's price. The question is, is the price right? Find out how to use the Internet to make this determination. It's explained in Chapter 16.

◆ Learn more about the company you're thinking about investing in, with the Internet's help. Find out how in Chapter 17.

◆ Put the firm into its context, using the tools and tips in Chapter 18.

Deciding Whether the Price is Right

Is the price right? Ideally, you want to buy low and sell high. But what do *low* and *high* really mean? In this chapter, you learn some of the fundamentals of evaluating stock prices, and you also learn how to put the Internet to work for you to gather the needed information for evaluating stock prices.

Looking for Bargains

You've heard the old saying "Buy low, sell high." It seems simple enough, yet it's a good trick if you do pull it off.

In this section, you find an introduction to the *value investing strategy*, in which you try to find a stock that's underpriced in relation to the true value of the company that issued it. To try your hand at value investing, you need to learn how companies are valued.

Value investing is only one of several established investment strategies, and it isn't universally loved. And though undervalued stocks sometimes outperform the S&P 500, sometimes they haven't. For example, from 1987 to 1990, recession fears battered the prices of downtrodden cyclical and industrial stocks — and these are only the stocks most likely to pop

In This Chapter

- ◆ Looking for bargains
- ◆ Understanding the contrarian way
- ◆ Investing in growth stocks
- ◆ Introducing technical analysis
- ◆ Screening stocks on the Internet

up in a search for undervalued securities. Before you invest using this strategy, make sure that it's in line with your overall investment goals.

What's the company worth?

The company's value is one of the main bases of the stock's value. This value can be measured in several ways. First, the company has *assets*: physical, human, and intangible holdings that enable it to produce products or services of value. These products and services all have prices.

The company also has *earnings power*. Generally speaking, this is the profits a company is capable of producing in the future. Future earnings have at least an estimated value.

In a pinch, a company also has *liquidation value* or *takeout value*. This measure can vary. This value can be what the company would sell for in a fire sale, if its creditors foreclosed on it. *Liquidation value* is usually close to the lowest possible value. *Takeout value* is more related to what the highest bidder would pay for a firm if it had something many bidders wanted badly. This would be closer to a maximum value.

It's all these values

The value of a company's stock can be linked to any or all of the preceding values.

A company that was about to go under may have its stock valued closer to the liquidation value. A company with a long and profitable operating history probably would have its shares valued more on its earnings power. A company with valuable assets — maybe a metal company with big mines or a real estate firm with many buildings — may have its stock valued better in relation to its asset value. Some companies' stocks could be valued more than one way if several of these conditions fit at the same time.

Stocks' market prices reflect these valuations — but with differing degrees of precision. An *undervalued* stock is one whose market price is judged to be below what it should be, based on its earnings, assets, or other valuations.

How are stock prices judged against these values? A company that hasn't earned any profits can't be valued well on earnings. If the company has cash flow (earnings before depreciation charges), then its stock price may be a certain number of times larger than that figure. The faster the cash flow is growing, usually the higher this multiple is. If the company doesn't have cash flow, then the stock price can be compared to a multiple of the company's assets.

Earnings first

You probably don't want to buy stocks of companies that are about to go out of business just yet. Instead, for starters, check out what a stock's *price-earnings ratio* tells you about it.

Strictly speaking, the price-earnings ratio (often abbreviated P/E ratio or just P/E) is how many times the company's earnings per outstanding share you have to pay for the stock when you buy it on the stock market. For example, if a company earned $2 per share in the most recent year, and its stock costs $25 per share, the stock's P/E ratio is 12.5. In other words, the stock is selling for 12.5 times its earnings per share.

But which earnings are you buying? When you look at stock listings in the daily newspaper, you have price-earnings ratios that are based on the company's last 12 months of earnings. These data are readily available, but, like so many other pieces of financial information, they're backward-, not forward-looking. For this reason, the P/E ratio alone really doesn't tell you what you need to know. It tells you where the company has been, but not necessarily where it's going.

Tomorrow's earnings, not yesterday's

To get some idea of where a company's earnings are going, go to one of the three big earnings estimate data services.

These services are I/B/E/S (`http://networth.galt.com/www/home/equity/ibes/aboutesr.html`), Nelson's (`http://www.nelnet.com`), and Zacks (`http://www.quote.com/cgi-bin/zacks-form`). They compile and update earnings estimates from hundreds of analysts at investment companies, and they perform a number of data sorts on these figures.

Two of these services — I/B/E/S and Zacks — list price-earnings ratios based on the average estimates (also called consensus estimates) they tally for each stock. These services also compare these forecasted P/Es to those of a composite for the company's index and to the average P/E forecast for all stocks in the Standard & Poor's 500.

Quote.com, one of the leading Internet stock quote services discussed in the last chapter, offers access to Zacks's earnings reports as part of its subscription-based service. Figure 16-1 shows a portion of Zacks's earnings estimates for Microsoft. If you're not a subscriber, you can buy individual reports for $2.50 each. A plus: You get a summary of investment firms' buy and sell recommendations for the stock.

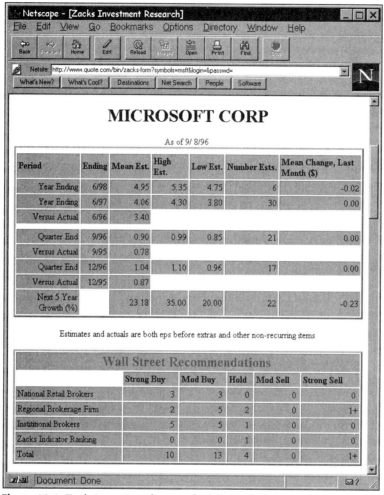

Figure 16-1: Zacks's earnings forecast for Microsoft Corporation (MSFT).

This information is the kind you want. Knowing how one company's stock price relates to its earnings doesn't really help you much. But relating these values to those of other companies, an industry, or the whole market tells you how the one company is priced compared to these others.

You have to pay a few bucks for these earnings forecasts, and the whole transaction can be handled online, thanks to secure servers. If you're thinking of plunking down some significant money into your investment, these forecasts are worth it.

The estimate services also give you other pieces of vital information that you need in figuring out the significance of a company's price/earnings. These services tell you how fast the company's earnings are growing and are expected to grow.

Does all this information put you any further ahead? You now can tell if the stock you're interested in costs more than others in its group for the same earnings, and you can compare either of these values to that of the whole market. You also can note how fast your company's earnings are growing in relation to other companies in its industry and in the market overall.

Looking at growth rates and P/E ratios

Many stock analysts have a rule of thumb about earnings growth rates and P/Es: They should be nearly the same.

If, for instance, a stock has a P/E of five (low on the overall scale of P/Es), it still may not be a cheap or undervalued stock. It may be from a company whose earnings are growing only three percent a year. In that case, the stock seems overvalued, even though its P/E is low.

Is it really undervalued?

When are stocks really undervalued? At times, individual stocks are undervalued versus their estimated value, versus the outlook for their industries, and versus the market in general.

Sometimes, certain industries may be *out of favor* with stock market buyers, because either their earnings prospects are not that favorable or other industries have better prospects than they do.

At other times, the entire stock market may be depressed versus other kinds of investment market opportunities. A long spell of this depression is called a *bear market.*

Each of these situations — a falloff in price for individual stocks, stock sectors, or the world market — can create chances for the investor to buy undervalued stocks.

Valuing stocks; Key financial ratios

As you search for undervalued stocks on the Internet, you'll find it helpful to know what some of the following terms mean.

◆ **Activity ratios.** These ratios measure how well the firm is using its current resources. They include the Average Collection Period (average receivables divided by average daily sales), Inventory Turnover (cost of goods sold divided by average inventory), Total Asset Turnover (sales divided by total assets), and Fixed Asset Turnover (sales divided by fixed assets).

◆ **Book value.** The shareholders' equity, divided by the number of shares outstanding.

◆ **Cash flow per share.** This is a company's net income plus deductions not paid in cash (such as amortization and depreciation), divided by the number of shares outstanding. For some firms with a lot of depreciation and no earnings, such as certain cable TV companies, this figure can be a better indication of a firm's strength than earnings per share (EPS).

◆ **Debt/equity ratio.** This is the firm's long-term liabilities divided by the total value of its net worth. A low ratio indicates that the firm is relatively free from debt. A high ratio indicates that the firm usually has to pay a large part of its earnings in interest payments.

◆ **Dividend yield.** This is the dividend divided by the market price per share of stock. A fairly high dividend yield (five percent or more) may indicate an undervalued stock; however, it may also be a sign that the stock price has dropped, and that the dividend may have to be lowered, too.

◆ **Earnings per share (EPS).** The firm's income after taxes, dividends, and all deductions, divided by the number of shares outstanding.

◆ **Liquidation value.** This is the price at which a company's business could actually be sold, if the firm had to be sold to pay off creditors. This value could be lower than the book value.

◆ **Liquidity ratios.** These ratios measure the firm's cash reserves, which may be needed to pull out of an unexpected crisis or to take advantage of an unexpected opportunity. Included are the Current Ratio (current assets divided by current liabilities) and the Quick Ratio (current assets minus inventory, divided by current liabilities).

- ◆ **Price/book ratio.** A company's book value is its net worth divided by the total number of outstanding common stock shares. If the price is below the book value, the stock *may be a value stock* — a bargain. But then again, some reason — such as actual or impending unprofitability — may explain the low price.

- ◆ **Price/earnings ratio (P/E ratio).** This is the ratio of the price per share of stock divided by the earnings per share for a one-year period. If a stock sells for $100 and has earnings of $10 per share, its P/E ratio is 10. Compared to typical firms in the same industry, a high P/E ratio may indicate that a stock is overpriced; you'll have a tough time making money unless earnings grow rapidly. However, it could also mean that the firm is growing faster than others in the same industry. Conversely, a low ratio may indicate that the stock is underpriced, offering the potential that you'll gain both from increased earnings and the appreciation of the stock's price.

- ◆ **Profitability ratios.** Essentially, these ratios indicate how well the company is deploying resources to turn a profit. These ratios include Net Profit Margin (net earnings before taxes), Return on Total Assets (net profit or net income), Return on Equity (common stock earnings divided by equity), Dividend Payout Ratio (dividend divided by earnings), and Plow Back Ratio (earnings divided by earnings plus dividend).

- ◆ **Transaction (acquisition) value.** If someone wanted to buy the firm, this value is what they'd have to pay. This value also is called the *private market value.*

Understanding the Contrarian Way

KEY TERM

The most obvious opportunity to buy undervalued stocks is when the whole market is depressed or *undervalued.* This is also the time when investors have a hard time bringing themselves to buy because everyone else seems to be selling. Because this strategy is contrary to what most people are doing, it's called *contrarian.* A contrarian investor does the opposite of what most investors are doing at any one time. That's often a good thing because too many investors buy at the top of the market and sell when it hits bottom! This is a good example of when to remind yourself to invest with your head, not with your heart or your gut, as many seem to think you should.

Learn more about the contrarian way by reading Calvin Wolfe's "Going it Alone" (`http://gnn.com/gnn/meta/finance/feat/archives.calvin/alone.html`), an interesting essay on the art of contrarian investing. Wolfe isn't a financial expert — he's a self-described computer technician and finance junkie — but his essay is well worth reading.

Truly, madly, deeply undervalued

But is the stock you're looking at really undervalued? For example, you determine that, based on its history and estimated future earnings, a certain stock should be trading at 20 times earnings per share. And where did the share price stand in the past, in relation to earnings per share? Has it ever traded at a P/E ratio — or higher?

You could draw a graph of this comparison that shows what the stock has traded at in the past and extend the line to what you estimate its future price should be. If the stock is priced below this level, then you could judge it to be undervalued and therefore a buy.

Have you made some sort of brilliant, solitary discovery? Not really. Thousands of institutional investors and traders that make these comparisons all day long are sitting next to computer terminals, ready to push a button to buy or sell whenever stocks get undervalued or overvalued. You'd probably be more than a bit behind them.

Where's the individual investor's advantage?

This minute-to-minute activity can give you some idea of where individual investors' strength lies, however. It's in the long-term trend. Institutional investors and traders have all the advantages in real-time and short-term markets, but their technology and money don't give them much edge in longer term market cycles. Institutional investors and traders are not much better at judging the top or the bottom of a market than you are. They, too, just hope to be close.

What does this mean for you, the individual investor? You have several possible choices, none of which seem much like what other people in the stock market may be doing at the time. You can buy when the whole market is off or when everyone else is dumping a stock. And you can look for unloved (but worthy) stocks, as the following sections explain.

When the whole market is off

You can be a buyer of undervalued stocks when the whole stock market is going down. This seems like a no-brainer, but buying undervalued stocks takes much conviction and will power.

Some people did buy stocks in the crash of 1987 — even on the first day of this decline, when the market fell 508 points. The market did rise again after that. The 1987 drop was a 22 percent correction, but it was just that. Stock markets didn't stay down. The drop seemed huge at the time, but going back over it now, after nearly a decade, it's more like a blip — and it will seem like a smaller blip after more time passes.

When everyone else is dumping a stock

You also can take a contrarian approach when individual stocks drop in price. You sometimes can find good buys after *market overreactions* — sudden one-day drops in prices of stocks that are basically sound but have visible bad news. Bad news can include airline crashes, small earnings disappointments, or management changes, for instance. These events may leave the company in the lurch temporarily. But the price reaction can be out of line with the financial or operating effect of the news on a long-term basis.

Still, these *buy opportunities* are harder to call than selloffs of the whole stock market. You need some idea of how bad the news is in relation to the market reaction. In some cases, markets do not react strongly enough to news. Because they usually focus on short-term effects, markets sometimes miss the impacts of class action lawsuits or other liabilities that may take a longer time to play out.

In search of unexcellence

To add more fuel to the notion that it's smart to look for bargains rather than to count on a greater fool to buy your expensive stocks, consider this: A number of studies have shown that over a period of several years, low P/E stocks in general tend to outperform high P/E stocks. One researcher, Michelle Clayman of the University of Oklahoma, even studied a cross-section of low P/E stocks that she called *unexcellent* companies. These low-valuation firms performed 11 percent better than a higher-value group of excellent companies over five years.

Aren't low P/E stocks riskier than blue chip stocks, you may ask? The answer: No, because part of the risk of each investment is in what you pay for it. The lower price of low-valuation stocks negates part of the risk of buying and holding them. Low-valuation stocks simply tie up less of your money.

Looking for unloved and undervalued stocks

Is it a bargain — or just a dog? The Leuthold Group, a value-oriented investment advisory firm, sets out these guidelines (`http://www.troweprice.com/mutual/insights/valuinvest.html`) for value investing:

1. The **book value** should be less than 80 percent of the average S&P 500 stock and never more than 1½ times.

2. The **price/earnings ratio** (using five-year average earnings) should be less than 70 percent of the average P/E ratio of the S&P 500. Avoid stocks with a P/E ratio higher than 12. (Incidentally, its tough to find stocks today that meet this criterion, given that the S&P 500 is trading at an average P/E ratio of 14.5. That's why many investment prognosticators think today's stock market is overvalued.)

3. The ratio of the firm's **cash per share** to the stock's **price per share** should be at least 15 percent.

4. The **dividend yield** (dividends paid for the year divided by market price) should be at least equal to that of the S&P 500, and it should never fall below four percent. Note that this criterion would rule out Microsoft and Intel, which don't pay dividends. This doesn't mean that these aren't great stocks—it just means that they aren't *value* stocks, according to Leuthold's definition.

5. The ratio of the firm's **cash flow** to its **share price** should be less than 75 percent of the S&P 500.

6. The **debt/equity ratio** should be less than 50 percent — don't forget to include unfunded pension liabilities in the debt.

7. The firm's **financial strength** (its creditworthiness) should be close to the averages for its industry.

Investing in Growth Stocks

In all the preceding sections, you've been dealing with an investment style known as *value investing*. Value investors search out securities and situations that are *undervalued* by the market or most investors. The idea is that over time the prices of these securities will rise into line with what they're *really worth*.

From the contrarian point of view, it's idiotic to buy high in the hope of selling higher — you're just falling into the trap of doing what everyone else is doing (people tend to buy stocks only after they've realized that the market is going up and up and up, but at that point, the market's probably near its peak). But are there cases when you can profit by buying high? Well, maybe not high, exactly, but higher than low.

A strategy that does not shrink from buying at a relatively high price is *growth stock investing*. In this view, it's OK to buy a stock with a high P/E ratio because the company is growing much faster than average.

Learn more about growth stock investing, courtesy of T. Rowe Price (`http://www.troweprice.com/mutual/insights/grth.html`). You learn how to find growth stocks — especially in the hot small- and mid-cap categories.

What is growth?

A *growth* company, or one in a *growth* phase, has earnings increasing significantly faster than average over a period projected to be at least several years. This projection means the growth should not be a fluke but at least somewhat sustainable.

These growth companies should be able either to expand by using their own funds or to pay back borrowed expansion money from their operations fairly easily.

Usually, both sales and profits of these companies are growing, spurred by popular new products, new technology that beats competitors, new demand, and, in some cases, from an expanding economy.

The down side of growth

But just as value investing has a few warts — such as getting you to compare poorly performing stocks with real bargains — so does growth investing. For one thing, growth stocks may not look that much better than average when the whole economy is in an up cycle. Then, in fact, cyclical stocks may put in a much better performance. It's easiest to find and invest in growth stocks at the start and end of business cycles when they're best able to outperform other sectors.

Also with growth stocks, much more is *relative*. Sure, their P/Es are higher than average. But how much higher can their prices be before investors are paying too much for them?

When growth stocks disappoint

It's not easy to pinpoint the reason for disappointing performance, especially for growth stocks that are investors' darlings. Some of these stocks that have run up much higher than they should are prone to sudden drops for little reason, except that they're probably overvalued and possibly held by a large number of short-term investors.

Because growth stocks are in the *growth phase* of their development, they usually retain earnings for expansion rather than paying them out as dividends. In this case, no dividend dates keep holders from bailing out whenever they feel like it.

Finally, companies go through growth cycles — start-up, growth, maturity, decline, and rejuvenation or reorganization — at varying speeds. It takes a fair amount of study to determine if and when a company's profit margins are growing more slowly than before, not growing, or actually declining. And one or two quarters of a change in direction may not mean a trend.

That doesn't mean some short-term investors won't *detect* a trend in such a short time and act on their perception. A growth stock only acts like a growth stock as long as growth stock investors think it is one and value it that way in the market.

Introducing Technical Analysis

You may be thinking by now that this stock selection business is not much of a science. Right. It's more of an art (or maybe a craft!). If you want more cut-and-dried decision rules, check out yet another investment style — technical analysis.

Technical analysis uses price, trading volume, and other historical patterns to detect patterns in securities trading that can be projected into the future. It doesn't assign causes and effects to trends; it merely correlates them to one another.

As an example of how many and how various the links in these trends can be, check out the Cabot Market Letter site (`http://www.cabotm.com/cabot/cabot9.html`). Editors Carlton and Timothy Lutts's list of stock buy and sell signals include the following:

◆ The power index (current Treasury bill yield divided by T-bill yield six months ago). If greater than 1, sell. If less than 1, buy.

◆ If the advance/decline line (number of stocks whose prices advance in a day divided by the number of stocks declining) goes six months without hitting a new high, it's a sign of market weakness. If the line hits a new high every two to three months, the market's strengthening.

◆ The longer a stock's price stays below its moving average (its average price for a certain number of days or weeks in the past), the less likely it is to break above the average. This is also said to be true in reverse, for rising stocks. A great variety of moving averages are used by different technical analysts. The Cabots like 20- and 39-week figures. Other analysts use 100- and 200-day averages.

What's wrong with this picture?

One problem with using technical analysis alone is that stocks can rise and fall for reasons unrelated to their advance/decline lines or moving averages. Technical analysts such as the Luttses may leave themselves open for trouble when they tout certain stocks for their wonderful charts, those stocks surge even more, and then their management suddenly sells off a major interest in the company. It makes you wonder if the Luttses knew more about this than they were letting on. It made the Securities and Exchange Commission wonder, too, which is why the commission started a probe of the Luttses.

What's the lesson for you? As you noted before, it's always good to look for confirmation from a few places when you think you're onto something worth investing in. In this case, you may want to use technical analysis to confirm a stock's seemingly strong fundamentals: If its sales and profit trends look strongly positive, its management appears solid, its products and market look good, then you may want to confirm these with a check on the stock's technical picture. But don't base your investment decisions on charts by themselves.

It would be easy to dismiss technical analysis for individual investors. However, because it's so widely used by institutional investors and traders with huge computer power, it's hard to shrug off. At the very least, be aware that technical analysis may well be the plan behind most of the trades in a stock you're looking at, especially the big-cap, heavily traded variety.

The data used in technical analysis represent the sum total of what investors of all ilks have done in the past. As you noted before, the past isn't necessarily related to what will happen in the future. Technical analysts also try to time markets and stocks. Other investment styles generally consider this a bad idea.

Technicians, however, reply by pointing to the recurring patterns they graph. If for no other reason, technical analysis seems to work because so many people with computers that can deal with it use it as their method.

Resources for technical analysis on the Net

If understanding more about technical analysis appeals to you, check out a couple of sites for beginners. One is Jason Martin's The Stock Room (`http://loft-gw.zone.org/jason/intro.html#tech`), with several pages devoted to elements of charting.

Another detailed source with references is Dan Hankins's (`deh@fir206.cray.com`) FAQ for misc.invest.technical (`http://fortress.wiwi.uni-frankfurt.de/AG/JWGI/FAQS/tech-faq.htm#1`). This site explains technical analysis parameters, what people think they mean, and why you should pay attention to this field.

Screening Stocks on the Internet

How do you look for stocks with a low P/E ratio, a high dividend yield, and the other indicators of value? With tens of thousands of stocks in existence, it's an information-processing nightmare. That's where *stock screening* comes into play. Stock screening uses the computer to comb through financial data, returning only those stocks that meet criteria you specify.

You can pay lots of money for stock screening software, but stock screening — like everything else connected with investing — is migrating to the Internet. The following sites offer free or subscription-based stock screening services:

◆ **Financial World** (http://www.financialworld.com/). Requiring registration, this site features a database of 1,000 companies ranked according to Financial World's stock selection criteria. In addition to searching by Financial World letter grades, you also can search for sales, price/earnings ratio, price/book ratio, debt/equity ratio, and dividend yield. In Figure 16-2, you see companies in the Financial World database sorted by P/E ratio. At the top of the list are a couple companies with P/E ratios of 4.

◆ **InvestLink** (http://www.investlink.com/market.hts). You can search a database of 9,000 publicly held companies by P/E ratio, 52-week price range, and stock price range. Figure 16-3 shows the results of a search for stocks with P/E ratios of less than 8. If you click on the Tell Me More button, you see a page of information about the company, including fundamental data and background information.

◆ **StockQuest** (http://www.marketguide.com/MGI/PRODUCTS/info-stq.htm). A new analytical tool from Market Guide, StockQuest requires a Windows program that accesses Market Guide's database of information on over 8,200 companies trading on the New York, American, and NASDAQ exchanges. You can search the database using over 70 predefined variables and create a variety of reports. You pay a monthly subscription fee (or a per-download charge) to use this service.

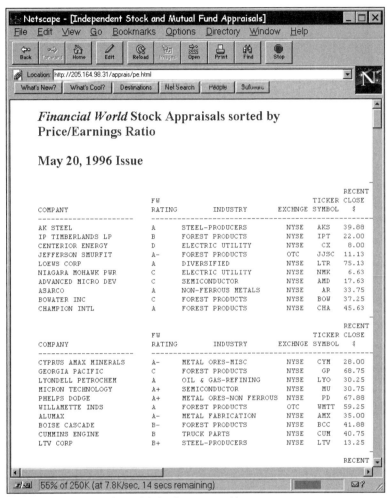

Figure 16-2: Financial World database sorted by P/E ratio.

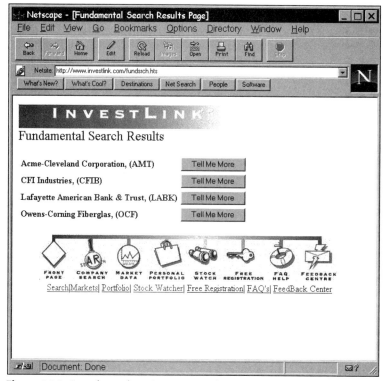

Figure 16-3: Search results using InvestLink.

◆ **NETworth** (http://networth.galt.com/cgi-bin/Disclosure_SEC). One of the best stock screening sites on the Net currently is NETworth's Disclosure SEC Database Query, which makes use of publicly available Securities and Exchange Commission (SEC) data. Containing data on more than 12,000 U.S. companies, the database is searchable in an amazing variety of ways. For example, you can search for companies with high sales growth, high percentage of shares held by employees, and low long-term debt, in addition to the standard selection criteria (P/E ratio and debt/equity ratio). You have to pay a fee for these searches, however. Shown in Figure 16-4 is the query screen, which enables you to define a wide variety of search criteria by choosing ratios as well as minimum and/or maximum values.

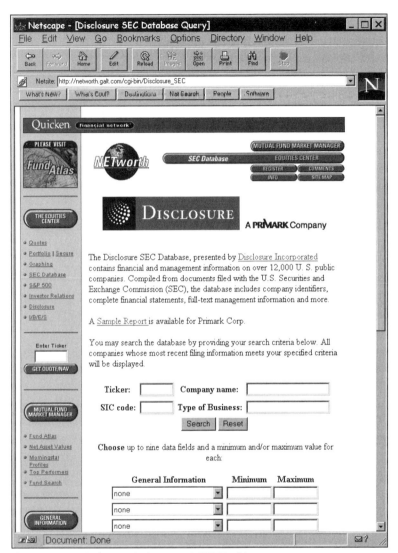

Figure 16-4: Disclosure SEC report (NETWorth).

Summary

◆ Ideally, you want to buy low and sell high. To do this, you need to figure out what the company is worth and then judge whether the share price is fair or not.

◆ A company's value isn't easy to calculate. You need to take into account the most appropriate ways to measure stock value, including past earnings and future earnings potential. For the latter, don't hesitate to fork over a few bucks for earnings forecasts.

◆ You're not alone in your search for undervalued stocks: Some of the best minds and hottest computers on Wall Street are also searching, but they're focused on the short term. For long-term gains, you can buy when the whole market is off, when everyone else is dumping a stock, or when you find a low P/E-ratio stock that's truly undervalued. This is called the contrarian strategy.

◆ Do you always look for stocks with low P/E ratios? Some growth stocks may have high P/E ratios but are still defensible buys because they'll grow far beyond their current earnings — maybe.

◆ Technical analysis bases its predictions on patterns in securities trading, but it's a controversial method. You can use it cautiously to supplement other approaches.

◆ One of the neatest things about the Internet is that you can screen huge databases of stocks for only the ones that meet criteria you specify, such as a low P/E ratio and high dividend yield. What's more, it's free.

From Here

◆ Broaden your research by consulting publicly available data, as explained in Chapter 17.

◆ Place companies in their broader context using Internet tools; it's all explained in Chapter 18.

◆ If you identify a stock that you want to buy, you need a broker. Find one on the Internet, as explained in Chapter 19.

Finding Information about Public Companies

If you're selecting individual stocks, a company's financial statements are some of the most vital pieces of data to have and understand. They're the basics on which all other information that the company releases about itself is built. As such, financial statements include important assumptions about what the company does and why it does it. These statements are a kind of handbook and history text in one. They may even be dictionaries, with lists of industry terms for shareholders.

You invest in stocks, but before buying you must learn about the companies that sell them. A big part of picking the right stock investment is understanding what's going on with the company. The stock, after all, is affected by many events involving the company's operations, financing, and products.

This chapter surveys the many ways you can get information about publicly held companies via the Internet. As you discover, you can obtain annual and quarterly reports from company home pages and from the SEC's EDGAR database, introduced in Chapter 6. Also available on the Web, often for a subscription fee, are privately maintained databases of company information, which often includes professional analyses and assessments of the company's position. As you see, the Internet has become the best possible place to hunt down information about publicly held companies.

Getting Annual Reports on the Net

The most basic of a company's financial statements is the *annual report*. In general, printed annual reports are glossy, glitzy documents designed to convey the best impression of the company to a variety of constituencies, including current and prospective shareholders. But don't equate glossiness with shallowness. Annual reports are full of information that you don't want to miss, often including frank assessments of the challenges that the company faces. You also find financial information that can help you determine if the company's finances are sound.

Searching for annual reports

Many major public companies have put their entire annual reports on the Web, linked to their home pages. The annual reports are easy to find by typing the company's name or part of it into a search engine and then going to the home page. You also can try typing the company's name followed by "annual report." Be sure to include the quotation marks.

In the AltaVista search engine (`http://altavista.digital.com/`), for example, the following line retrieves Sun Microsystems' annual report:

sun microsystems + "annual report"

Note that the plus sign forces AltaVista to place items containing "annual report" at the top of the retrieval list, while the quotation marks ensure that the search engine retrieves only those documents that contain the entire phrase "annual report."

Did you find something? Look under *financials* if the company has a category such as that listed — and they most likely do. In Figure 17-1, you see the table of contents page of the Sun Microsystem's 1995 annual report; note the link to Financial Highlights.

If your search didn't retrieve an annual report, check your spelling carefully, and try again. Still nothing? Don't give up just yet. A company directory may help you, and, if that doesn't work, you can try EDGAR. These last two options are detailed in the following sections.

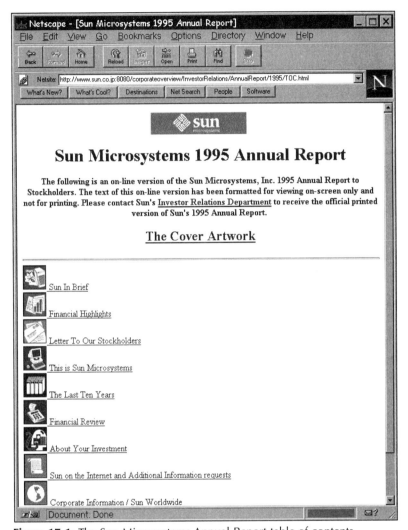

Figure 17-1: The Sun Microsystems Annual Report table of contents.

Using company directories

If your search didn't work out, try consulting one of the several Web-based annual report directories. Here's a list of the best sites to try:

◆ **Invest-o-Rama's Publicly Traded Corporations Online** (http://www. investorama.com/corp.shtml). Here you find links to more than 1,000 publicly traded corporations' Web sites, many of which include links to the companies' annual reports.

◆ **Investor Relations Information Network (IRIN)** (http://www.irin.com/colist.html). Here you find a few dozen annual reports in Adobe Acrobat format, which enables you to get a feel for the glitz of the printed product.

◆ **The Hoover's Online Company Home Page Register** (http://www.hoovers.com). Among the many wonderful things you find in this site is a searchable database of over 2,500 companies with Web presences, including public, private, and international firms. You also can search the MasterList, containing over 10,000 companies. Figure 17-2 shows Hoover's free company capsule for Sun Microsystems; for a subscription fee, you can access the full database.

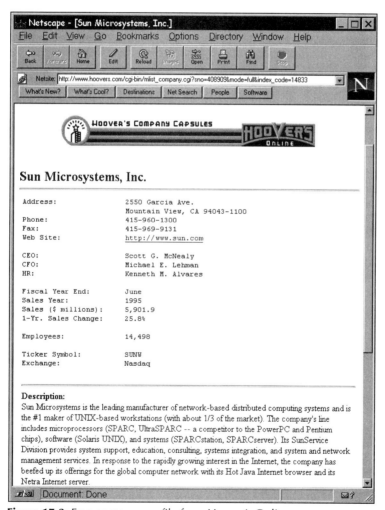

Figure 17-2: Free company profile from Hoover's Online.

◆ **Wall Street Research Net** (http://WSRN.com). In the Company Information section, you find links to information on more than 16,000 publicly held companies, including annual reports (if available). Figure 17-3 shows the cool results of a WSRN search: Look at all the information they've assembled concerning Sun Microsystems, including the firm's home page, annual reports, and scads more.

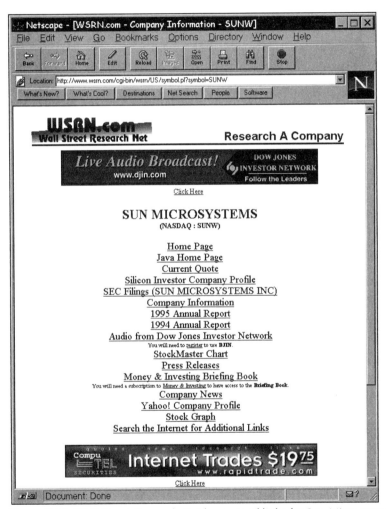

Figure 17-3: Wall Street Research Net has tons of links for Sun Microsystems.

The Web 100

How are the country's largest corporations responding to the challenges and opportunities of the World Wide Web? Find out at The Web 100 (`http://fox.nstn.ca/~at_info/w100_intro.html`), which ranks the 100 largest U.S. companies with a corporate presence on the Web. Frequently updated, the Web 100 enables you to see how some of the wealthiest companies in the world are crafting their Web strategy. Figure 17-4 shows part of the American List; you can also display a list of global corporations with a Web presence.

The big surprise (at this writing)? The third largest corporation in the U.S., Exxon, doesn't have a home page. Of the top 100 corporations in the U.S., some 16 still don't have Web presences. Some people still just don't get it, do they?

If you're a subscriber to *The Wall Street Journal*, you can request a free copy of any publicly held company's glossy printed annual report. You can place your order on the Web (`http://www.icbinc.com/cgi-bin/wsj?`) or call 1-800-654-CLUB.

Finding annual reports on EDGAR

Didn't find a company's annual report using Internet search services or company directories? You also can go to the SEC's EDGAR service (`http://www.sec.gov`), introduced in Chapter 12, for annual reports. Here the annuals may be included in a report called a *Form 10-K*. It may also be a separate report, to which the 10-K is a supplement.

EDGAR is the place to go for quarterly reports, which may contain more up-to-date information than a dated annual report. Be sure to check out the quarterly reports, too. Look for Form 10-Q.

The SEC reports are numbered. Following is a list of some of the stock-related numbers:

◆ **10-K:** annual report and/or supplement to it

◆ **10-Q:** quarterly report

◆ **8-K:** interim report of events of investor significance

◆ **S-1:** registration statement for initial public offerings (good source of data on new companies, available about a month before the offering itself)

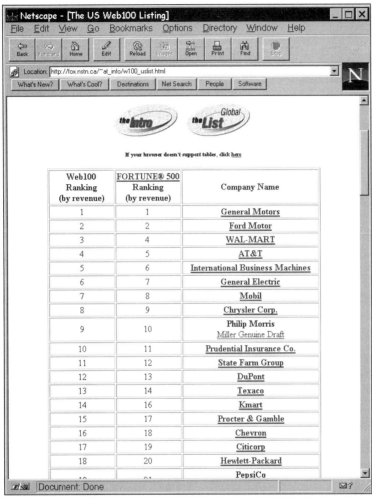

Figure 17-4: The Web 100 lists large corporations with Web presences.

◆ **S-3:** registration statement for secondary offerings by companies already public (often containing data that's more current than the last annual report, in about as much detail)

◆ **14-A:** proxy statement containing information for shareholders voting at a company's annual meeting

TIP

As you already may have noticed, the EDGAR reports on your screen are no works of art (see Figure 17-5), but they contain just as much information as the prettier versions — maybe more.

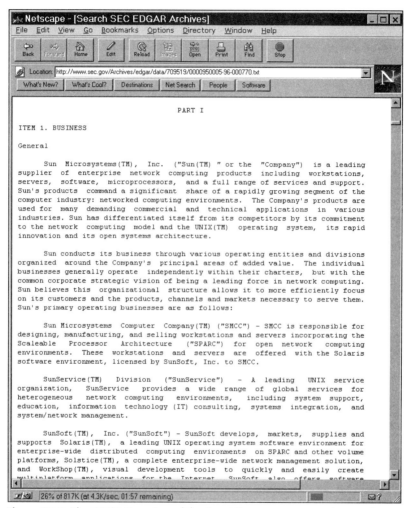

Figure 17-5: The EDGAR version of the Sun Microsystems annual report is homely but packed with information.

Reading Annual Reports

Annual reports are companies' main showcases to shareholders. But no matter how glitzy, annual reports have to contain certain things. In this sense, they're like mutual fund prospectuses, discussed in Chapter 12. The hardest one to read is the first. After you read an annual report, you find similar information, in the same place, in subsequent reports. After a bit of practice, you'll learn how to read an annual report. In this section, you learn what to look for in these reports.

TIP

If you don't have an annual report handy, grab one off the Net and take a look. Here's a neat one: First Michigan Bank's "virtual annual report" (`http://www.fmb.com/goodcompany/annual.html`), shown in Figure 17-6.

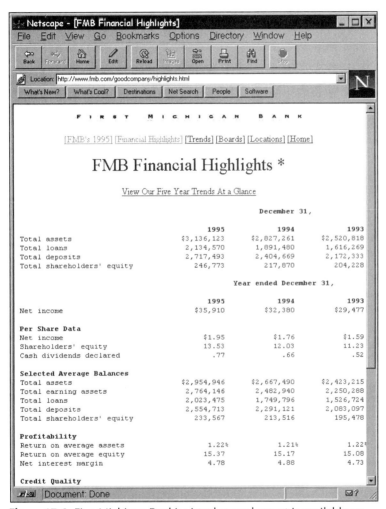

Netscape - [FMB Financial Highlights]

File Edit View Go Bookmarks Options Directory Window Help

Location: http://www.fmb.com/goodcompany/highlights.html

F I R S T   M I C H I G A N   B A N K

[FMB's 1995] [Financial Highlights] [Trends] [Boards] [Locations] [Home]

FMB Financial Highlights *

View Our Five Year Trends At a Glance

December 31,

	1995	1994	1993
Total assets	$3,136,123	$2,827,261	$2,520,818
Total loans	2,134,570	1,891,480	1,616,269
Total deposits	2,717,493	2,404,669	2,172,333
Total shareholders' equity	246,773	217,870	204,228

Year ended December 31,

	1995	1994	1993
Net income	$35,910	$32,380	$29,477

Per Share Data

	1995	1994	1993
Net income	$1.95	$1.76	$1.59
Shareholders' equity	13.53	12.03	11.23
Cash dividends declared	.77	.66	.52

Selected Average Balances

Total assets	$2,954,946	$2,667,490	$2,423,215
Total earning assets	2,764,146	2,482,940	2,250,288
Total loans	2,023,475	1,749,796	1,526,724
Total deposits	2,554,713	2,291,121	2,083,097
Total shareholders' equity	233,567	213,516	195,478

Profitability

Return on average assets	1.22%	1.21%	1.22%
Return on average equity	15.37	15.17	15.08
Net interest margin	4.78	4.88	4.73

Credit Quality

Document: Done

Figure 17-6: First Michigan Bank's virtual annual report is available on the Web.

The mission statement

Right in front, often on what would be the inside cover (if you were reading the printed copy), you find a *mission statement*. The mission statement summarizes the company's goals, basically telling you why the company is in business in the first place.

Some people tell you that the mission statement and other portions of the front sections of annual reports are nothing but fluff. Not so! These narrative sections give a good sense of how the company describes itself, what it does, and what it hopes to do. These sections also detail how important certain elements are to the company, such as its products, its management, its workers, and its history. All these elements indicate a corporate mindset that you may or may not like. Figure 17-7 shows First Michigan Bank's mission statement.

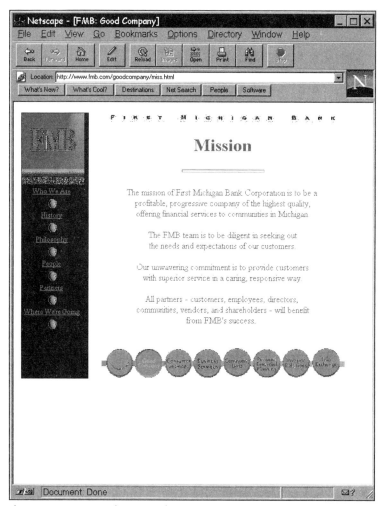

Figure 17-7: First Michigan Bank's mission statemetn is part of its virtual annual report.

Letters from the top brass

A summary or letter from the company's chairman or other top executives outlines major changes — good or bad — that occurred during the year reported. Did the company have any big disappointments in the year, as with a property-casualty insurer that faced a major hurricane? Did the company set out on a big undertaking and surpass its goals? Did it have to fend off an unwanted takeover attempt? What were the effects of events and changes? The summary is the place to find out. In Figure 17-8, you see First Michigan Bank's CEO letter — which serves, conveniently, as a kind of hypertext Grand Central Station for the entire report (nice job, FMB!).

Figure 17-8: First Michigan Banks' CEO letter is loaded with links to the rest of the annual report.

The company's line of business

Usually closely following the preceding section is a longer one that describes in some detail the company's lines of business. This part may include graphs that show you how much each of these segments contributes to the company's sales and profits. You may see some diversification in the company's revenues — or a lack of diversity. And this may or may not be related to what you see in the profits of each segment.

Some companies, especially if they're in industries that have products that are developed and obsolesced quickly — such as software — may be reluctant to talk about how dependent they are on certain products' sales or profits. The stated reason for this is that they don't want rivals to know what they're up to.

Also in this section, a company may note new lines of business that it entered into the past year; divisions it sold; acquisitions of operations, companies, or products; and discontinued lines, if any. All these new lines give you a better feel for the company's direction and plans.

Sometimes, though not always, a company, in one section of its annual report, may focus on a particular group, operation, or product — a kind of honor roll. This section may be an important piece of information, but it also may be just a big distraction if the general tone and direction of the rest of the report is neutral or negative.

On to the numbers

Around the middle of the annual report come the numbers. Don't panic. They're no more than addition, subtraction, and division — no multiplication is needed!

Get out your pocket calculator and go to the five- or 10-year summary table, if the company has one (for an example, see Figure 17-9). Use the chart that has the greatest number of years of figures in it. Look at a line near the top of the chart called *sales or revenues* or *net sales or total revenues*. At any rate, this line will be a number with a summation line above it.

Figure out the percentage rate of sales or revenue growth for each year by dividing the most recent year's sales or revenues by the prior year's and then subtracting 1. Write the result between the sales or revenue figure for each pair of years — even if you get a negative number for some. In 1995, for example, First Michigan Bank's net income was $35.9 million, up 10.8 percent from $32.4 million in 1994 (35.9/35.4-1=.108)

Rates of change

Are these numbers — which are the rates of change in sales/revenues — increasing or decreasing over time? If they're increasing, then the rate of sales growth is rising, which is a good sign, usually.

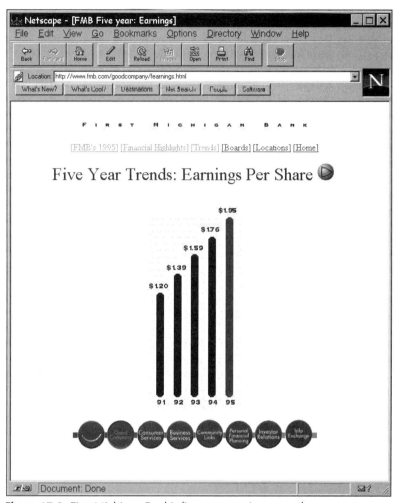

Figure 17-9: First Michigan Bank's five-year earnings growth summary.

Go down to a number labeled *net income* or *net profit.* Perform the same calculation as for sales/revenues for a year. Note how the change in earnings growth compares with the rate of sales/revenue growth. Is it larger? If earnings are growing faster than sales, the company's operations are getting more profitable over time.

If earnings are not growing faster than sales, then something is keeping the company from operating more economically as it gets bigger. This may be a problem, or it just may be that the company's spending more money on R&D to develop newer and more profitable products, for instance. You have to do the sleuthing to find out.

Looking at profits and interest expense

Go back to the financial summary and look at gross profits. Perform the same calculation as for sales and net income. Is gross profit growing faster or slower than sales? If it's growing slower, maybe the company's raw materials have increased in price. Also check operating (or sometimes pre tax) profits, further down in the chart. Again, compare the growth rates year-to-year. If these profits are growing slower than sales, maybe the company spends more on advertising or personnel — whether it needs to or not. Again, check for confirmation of whether this advertising and personnel are needed.

Another line to look at is *interest expense* or *income*, which is found right before the line for taxes. Interest expense gives you a ballpark idea of how much debt the company is paying down. Is it growing or falling? How big is it in relation to the income line right above it? Could interest expense wipe out this income line if it was slightly larger or if the income was slightly smaller? This situation is a cause for concern, especially if it hasn't happened before.

Note: Some companies, notably retailers, can be unprofitable for one or several quarters of the year, but profitable overall for the year. This is because most of their sales and profits are in the quarter around holidays at the end of the year. You won't see this in their annual reports until you get to the section on quarterly results, which is near the end of the report. This seasonality is considered quite normal in the retail industry, and there are other industries like it.

The bottom line

Finally, the bottom line of the multiyear summary is earnings per share. Is it growing faster or slower than net income/net profit? It can be growing at a different rate because the company either may have issued more shares during the year — to raise money or to buy another company with stock, for instance — or may have bought back some shares, thus reducing the number of outstanding shares.

Having more outstanding shares dilutes earnings — reduces them on a per-share basis. Each shareholder's stake in the company is made proportionately smaller compared to the total. On the other hand, buying back shares is antidilutive. It makes each shareholder's interest bigger, which makes stock buybacks popular.

The income statement

The multiyear summary is a long form of the company's income statement. This kind of financial statement is a year-end wrap up of the company's operations. The one-year form shows how the earnings or loss for the year reported came about. The one-year form follows the same formula as the multiyear form:

Sales - cost of goods sold - operating expenses + non operating income - non operating expenses - taxes = earnings.

The one-year version also usually compares the two prior years' results; in effect, you have a three-year lineup. Unlike the longer form, the one-year form is annotated, giving a line-by-line description of how the three years of results occurred. The notes may relate the *why* of trends that you may have noticed in either of the charts. Reporting rules recently were added to make it easier for companies to include more *forward looking* or predictive statements in all their financial reports. If you notice any of these statements, do they seem to indicate that the past trends you've noticed may continue? Are they positive or negative trends?

Management's discussion

One of the most important parts of the annual report is management's discussion and analysis of operations. This text follows the income statement line by line for the past three years and explains why the results are as they are.

If you're lucky, you chose a company to research that doesn't subject you to a huge dose of complex accounting language right off the bat. Some companies communicate lucidly; others don't. Some have fairly simple businesses to explain; others don't.

A financial statement that's not easy to understand is not necessarily the sign of a badly run company or one that's trying to hide something. Still, if a company seems to have a simple business and can't explain what's going on without a complicated story, you have to wonder a bit.

Stick with what you can understand. Your comprehension of financial statements will increase over time, and then you can tell better who's trying to pull the wool over your eyes.

Connecting the dots

The income statement is one of four main sets of financial figures. The other sets are the statement of cash flows, statement of changes in stockholders' equity, and the balance sheet. These sets are connected. Here's how: Look at the net income line of the income statement. Turn several pages of the annual report, and you should come to another chart — the statement of cash flows. Here, at the top of the table, you can find the net income number added in with other amounts as a source of cash from operations.

The cash flow statement

The cash flow statement details how the company has done on a cash basis for the year. Have all its funds come from its operations, or does the company have to borrow money to cover day-to-day expenses for all or part of the year? The latter is not so unusual. In fact, borrowing money is common in some industries, such as retailing. Has the company borrowed or paid down long-term debt? This is noted in the *cash flows from financing* section. Has the company made big investments in the year or received income from investments? You can find these answers in the *cash flow from investing* section.

Stockholders' equity

The net income from the income statement also gets transferred to the statement of changes in stockholders' equity. This statement shows you how much the value of stock owners' holdings in the company have changed in the year. Also carried over to this form, from the cash flow statement, are items such as the value of stock issued and dividends paid.

While the income statement fills you in on the company's activity for the year, the balance sheet takes a picture of what the company owns, what it owes, and what owns it on the last day of the year.

The balance sheet

At the top of the balance sheet are the firm's assets, its resources for doing business. Current assets, such as cash, receivables due soon, inventories that can be sold easily, and securities that can be sold for cash are listed first. These assets are followed by long-term or harder assets such as factories, equipment, and real estate. Each year, the company's accountants subtract a small part of some of these hard assets for depreciation — a reserve to replace worn-out assets. This is a bookkeeping entry, however, and not a cash loss.

The two other categories in the balance sheet *balance* against assets. That is, they always add up to the value of the assets. Liabilities are short-term (less than a year) and long-term (more than a year) debts of the company.

The book value

Stockholders' equity is the fudge factor in the balance sheet equation. It's what's left over when liabilities are subtracted from assets. When divided by the number of shares outstanding, stockholders' equity equals the company's book value.

What happens if liabilities are bigger than assets? You guessed it — the difference comes out of stockholders' interests in the company. Stockholders' equity is added into the balance sheet number each year and accumulates over time, so the gap between liabilities and assets would have to be bigger than the entire aggregated holder equity for shareholders' interest in a company to be completely wiped out.

Book versus market value

Situations in which liabilities exceed assets do happen, but again, just on paper. This situation has no *direct* bearing on how much the stock costs when traded on an exchange. Stocks that are out of favor on Wall Street may be priced at or below book value, while the darlings of the day greatly exceed book value. What's more, market conditions may affect stock prices, driving them above or below book value.

Still, when investors value stocks, they use book value as one of several benchmarks for deciding whether a stock is priced fairly. There's a discussion of book value in the previous chapter.

Getting Interim Reports

A lot can happen in a year. To find out what's been going on with a company between annual reports, look for a number of other reports. About every 90 days, companies are required to file quarterly reports. They generally don't miss these deadlines because their stock exchanges can delist them if they do.

Many firms now have put quarterly reports, as well as annuals, on the Web. Again, this is the most appealing way to view these short reports. EDGAR has the longer, text-only versions of the quarterly reports, numbered 10-Q in the SEC's scheme.

Summary

◆ You can find important financial information about a company on the Internet. In fact, the Internet is probably the best place to find such information.

◆ Many publicly owned companies make annual and quarterly reports available on the Web. You can search for them using search engines, company information directories, or EDGAR.

◆ Annual reports deserve a careful read. You find detailed assessments of the achievements and disappointments of the previous year as well as an appraisal of the prospects for the year to come. You also find valuable financial information.

◆ Interim reports, also available on the Internet, may contain more up-to-date information than annual reports.

From Here

◆ Learn more about companies using the research techniques discussed in Chapter 18.

◆ Pick an online brokerage, and buy some stock! Find out how in Chapter 19.

◆ Learn how to manage your stock portfolio with Internet and PC-based tools in Chapters 20 and 21.

Digging Deeper: Putting a Company into Context

By now, you've honed your list of promising stocks down to a manageable number. You've found some that may match your investment objectives. Perhaps they're undervalued — bargains, not dogs — or poised for rapid growth. You checked out the company's financial fundamentals and like what you see. Before logging onto your broker's site, however, you need to do a little more research. What's going on in the broader context in which the company is doing business? What about the competition? Regulation? Where's this whole industry headed?

The Internet provides excellent tools for examining a company's broader context. This chapter examines a number of Internet tools that you can use to learn more about this context, including search engines, company home pages, and company profile databases.

One of the best all-in-one jumping-off places for company and business news and data is Wall Street Research Net (http://www.wsrn.com). Its News section is one of several menu areas. News gets you to

The New York Times, The Wall Street Journal, CNN and *CCNfn,* Bloomberg's Personal service, *USA Today,* and a small selection of Knight-Ridder financial news. For more local news, it's tied to the Ecola Newsstand, with links to hundreds of U.S. and foreign papers and magazines. WSRN also links you to *APL Market Watch, PR Newswire, PC Week, Time,* and *Fortune.*

Learning More about Companies

Maybe you've been reading a lot about the weather, its effect on planting crops such as corn, short supplies of grain, and its likely effect on the future prices of food. The weather makes you think of an ad that you've seen often on Sunday morning interview shows for a company that processes food: Archer Daniels Midland (ADM). You think they're the biggest in the game.

You found ADM's ticker symbol on one of the quote servers, looked at its price, price chart, and five-year earnings trend. Then you went to EDGAR and checked out its 10-K filing, which tells you that ADM is "one of the world's largest processors of oilseeds, corn, and wheat." The stock has taken a few dips in the past year, but it's come back lately. What gives?

You continue reading the 10-K and come to a long section at the end called *Legal Proceedings.* Here you learn about several probes of and suits against ADM related to possible price fixing. ADM isn't the only company involved in these probes and suits. Several other food processors also are under investigation. However, this news is still going on, and you want to find out what's happened since the probes and suits were initiated. Is there more? How important is the planned $25 million settlement to ADM, which does $12 to $13 billion of business a year?

In search of the home page

ADM really leaves you to your own devices to find out more on the Net. Despite its enormous size and scope, ADM has no home page. However, plenty of other pages mention ADM, and these pages make one thing pretty clear: People either love or hate ADM and its audacious long-term managers.

One site, from the Horatio Alger Association (`http://www.netzone.com/ ~algers/h_algers/awardees/a9403.html`), describes the 1994 Alger award winner, ADM's chairman, Dwayne Andreas. The page details his roots in the soil — almost literally — in Kansas, his Mennonite upbringing, his climb to fortune in the grain business, and his thoughts about the world food industry. It's glowing stuff, and it jars sharply with an account from another site that AltaVista finds.

AltaVista finds *Farm & Country News,* a Canadian agricultural magazine (`http:// www.agpub.on.ca`). An article in this magazine relates Andreas' iron-handed approach to ADM's last annual meeting. According to the reporter, Andreas silenced dissident shareholders by turning off the microphone; then he told share-holders that he makes the rules, and that he makes them up as he goes along.

A little history

So where does this leave you? Reading through AltaVista's links to more newspaper accounts on ADM's latest legal forays! ADM has been muscling competitors and regulators around for decades, with pretty good success.

The company has actually done quite well for shareholders, however. Go to a long-term stock price chart, the kind you find at Quote.com (`http://www.quote.com`), for instance. Since 1985, ADM's stock has quadrupled in price, without any really big detours. That's a yearly return of 15 percent for the stock price alone — and ADM throws in another one percent in dividends. This return is probably what's in the minds of the stockholders who let Andreas run rings around dissidents at the annual meeting.

But maybe you find this stuff too offensive. If so, you're not alone in your opinion. Is this a bit different from the dry financial analysis you've been dealing with so far? Maybe, but it's another factor to think about when you invest.

Can you live with this company's stock in your portfolio for years? If not, many other investments with returns just as good are available. ADM may be trying to hog markets for their products, but they don't have a monopoly on good investments. On the other hand, maybe you find ADM's aggressiveness justified, even admirable. American business charges on to feed the world. If so, go for it.

Socially responsible investing

If you can't stomach ADM's allegedly high-handed tactics, maybe you're a candidate for socially and environmentally responsible investing. Check out the following sites:

Calvert Group: What is Responsible Investing? (`http://www calvertgroup.com/cresinv/cresp.htm`). The philosophy underlying the Calvert fund group emphasizes socially responsible investing.

GreenMoney On-Line (`http://www.greenmoney.com`). This page has links to publications, products, funds, investment planners, banks, and other socially responsible businesses.

Socially Responsible Investing: Profits and Principles (`http://www.betterworld.com/index.htm`). This is an introduction to the philosophy of socially responsible investing. Several socially responsible mutual funds are mentioned.

Using Online Newspapers

If your work with search engines digs up some interesting issues about a company, you may want to research newspaper databases to learn more about these issues. Unfortunately, there are few no-fee full-text newspapers on the Web (although several, including the *San Jose Mercury-News*, *The Washington Post,* and *The Los Angeles Times* are offering or contemplating offering fee-based search services), but there are exceptions, including the following:

◆ *San Francisco Chronicle* (`http://www.sfgate.com/chronicle/index.shtml`). You can search the full text of this newspaper back to January 1, 1995. A search for ADM netted a couple interesting columns about ADM's political ties. Note that the only articles in this database are those that originate from the *Chronicle's* reporters and columnists; still, it's worth a look.

◆ *Investor's Business Daily* (`http://www.investors.com/`). Free registration entitles you to search the rich archives of this leading business newspaper. A search for ADM netted 16 stories, including some updates on ADM's legal situation.

◆ *Deseret News* (`http://www.desnews.com/arch1.htm`). Currently free for a limited time, this Utah newspaper offers access to 1994 and 1995 databases of local, regional, national, and international stories. A search for "Archer Daniels Midland" netted 18 interesting stories.

As this book was being written, several major national newspapers, including *The Washington Post,* were contemplating making their huge databases of past news articles available to subscribers. Before subscribing, however, make sure that the search engine is a good one (you should be able to search with AND, OR, or NOT operators) and that the database is truly a full-text database that includes wire service as well as newspaper-originated articles.

Checking Out Corporate Home Pages

Maybe you're intrigued by ads you've seen in the papers for Compaq Computer Corporation. The ads invite you to visit the company's Web page to check details of its launch of a new notebook computer. The product "can transform itself in a number of ways," Compaq says.

You may be piqued by Oracle Corporation.'s ads comparing its database systems' performance to that of four big rivals'. You can check out all the companies and see what they have to say about Oracle, too. For variety, try finding their home pages with Open Market's Commercial Site Index (`http://www.directory.net`), shown in Figure 18-1. This site features a search engine, which enables you to search for companies. You can use this page to find the home pages of not only Oracle but also IBM, Microsoft, Sybase, and Informix.

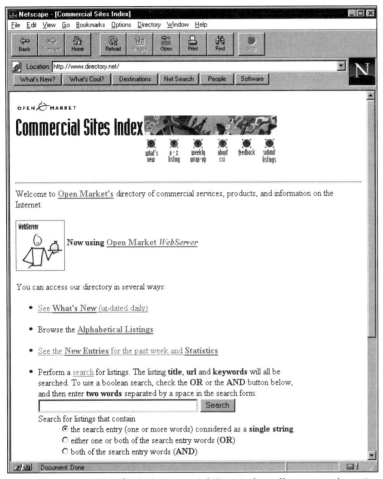

Figure 18-1: Open Market's Commercial Sites Index offers a search engine.

Software and systems companies have some of the friendliest and most-organized multi user pages on the Web. For a long time, they've served not only prospective investors but also product shoppers, equipment and systems users, independent software developers who want to work with them, and job seekers. You find good-looking annual reports and the most up-to-date news and other information on the company. You also find job postings, which, among other things, let you know which areas the company is trying to gear up.

These home pages are designed to do business, and they give you a much better idea of what these companies do. But after viewing these pages, you still may not be too clear on how these companies line up in their business. For that, you need independent market research, and increasingly, you can do your research on the Internet.

Finding Market Research Sites

If you're looking for independent research on how a company is performing in its industry, you can start with a publication aimed at the industry's customers, such as *Computerworld* magazine. Not surprisingly, *Computerworld* has a Web site (http://www.computerworld.com) with its own search engine for finding articles and surveys by topic. Plugging in "database" gives you several customer surveys, including one that Oracle mentions in its ad.

If you want to compare one company or stock with others, try some other groups that rank companies by market size. The Web is thick with market research sites, but a number of directories can help get you to the sites you want. Econsult (http://www.econsult.com) has an International Directory of Market and Opinion Research. Technometrica (http://www.technometrica.com) and Pangaea (http://www.pangaea.com) are other umbrella groups with lists of market researchers in various areas.

Industry and trade associations collect market data and do projections for their members, and they are usually pretty good about sharing with the public. NewMarket (http://www.newmarket-forum.com/assoc.html) has a lengthy listing of associations, many with links.

Looking for Informed Opinion

Okay, you're getting all this good data, but you still feel like you're missing out on something. You want to know what other people think about companies you invest in — and about companies you may want to invest in.

Try not to let concern for others' opinions get the best of you too often — even though it's perfectly normal. After all, the Web puts you in contact with unprecedented numbers of people and sites, most of which beg you to interact with them. It's like being loose in a giant candy store and being told just to look, while all your consumer buttons are being pushed.

Analysts' opinions and stock prices

You've probably noticed that certain stocks are reported to move up or down depending on what some stock analyst at an investment company has to say about them. These opinions are just that — opinions. But what makes these opinions important is that they're calculated to make the investment company's clients and brokers act a certain way. They're kind of the company's official party line on the stock. They may be prescient, or they may be the after-the-fact response to some good or bad development that's already occurred at the company whose stock is being judged.

These opinions about a stock may have less to do with what the company is doing than with what investors in it are doing. For example, a company's stock has increased from $8 to $40 in one year. A straightforward analyst who covers this stock may have forecast a 12-month target price — where he thinks the stock price will go in a year, given its company's prospects — of $40. Well, he was right. Give him some credit. But now, not wishing to push his own or his customers' luck, the analyst downgrades the stock from a *buy* to a *hold*. This is not a black mark against the company, it's just a judgment that its stock price has come up to the expected level.

But this opinion will sway at least some large institutional investors to stop buying the stock. Some of these investors may even sell it here to make a quick profit, so it probably wouldn't hurt to know if an analyst had changed his opinion of your stock — especially if he's from a major investment company or one that's been an underwriter — a public offering sponsor— for the stock in question. These investment companies usually have some inventory of the stocks they cover, and their actions in the market for these shares has an effect.

As investment companies make their way onto the Web in greater numbers now, more and more of them are making at least some of their research available. Still, with all the thousands of stocks out there, it's hard to know who covers what.

Is the company in question pretty new to public trading? Did it go public in the past year or so? If so, you can go to EDGAR (`http://www.sec.gov`) and look up its S-1 registration statement or S-4 prospectus. These documents list the stock's underwriters. Pick some of the first ones listed if there are many of them. These underwriters are the biggest investment companies and are likely to follow the stock after its initial offering. Then check if these investment companies have a Web site and if they distribute any research or news about your company there. Some brokerages' Web pages run a list of *actions of the day* — changes in stock recommendations. Big companies with many brokers and traders especially do this.

Looking for the right analyst

Are there any master lists of which analysts follow which stocks? Sort of. Both are subscriber services that provide limited free services. Nelson's (`http://www.irnet.com/pages/nelson.stm`), publisher of the original who-covers-what directory, has a $1-a-shot pay-per-view system.

A newer player in this kind of service is Zacks Investment Research (`http://www.zacks.com`, shown in Figure 18-2), with its Analyst Watch and index to brokerage research. Again, you have to pay for most of Zacks — between $11 and $30 a month. But because it competes head on with Nelson's both here and in earnings estimates, you never know what it may be giving away.

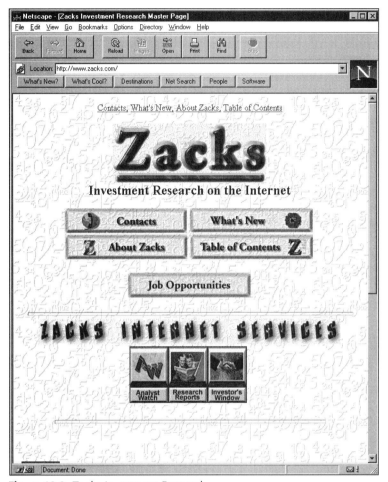

Figure 18-2: Zacks Investment Research.

Sometimes an informed guess helps you unearth research you want. Some investment companies such as Merrill Lynch (http://www.ml.com) cover thousands of stocks in a very broad *investment universe,* as they call it. Other companies specialize more. They may be particularly strong in covering heath care, technology, biotechnology, oil and gas, retail, insurance, banking, or some combinations of these. If you go to these companies' sites with one of these areas in mind, they may well have what you're looking for, or you may find other reports of interest.

Here's a short list of some brokerages with good research at their sites and some of the areas they cover best:

◆ **Hambrecht & Quist** (http://www.hamquist.com): technology and health care

◆ **Gruntal** (`http://www.gruntal.com`): technology

◆ **Piper Jaffray** (`http://www.piperjaffray.com`): technology and financial services

◆ **Robert W. Baird** (`http://www.rwbaird.com`): oil and gas

◆ **Montgomery Securities** (`http://www.montgomery.com`): technology, biotech, medical, and retail

◆ **Legg Mason** (`http://www.leggmason.com`): health care, consumer, and technology

Other brokerages are working hard on Web sites. Check back to links from members of the Securities Industry Association (`http://www.sia.com`) every so often for new sites.

Exploring Company Profile Databases

Because investing is big business, quite a few private companies compile information about other companies. This information typically includes the stuff you find in the SEC documents on EDGAR, but it's repackaged and supplemented with opinion, commentary, and analysis. Before the Internet came along, you had to pay some serious money to obtain proprietary company reports. But now many of the companies that prepare this information are prepared to give at least some of it away for free. Start with the free stuff. If you want more, you can subscribe to the fee-based service.

Hoover's Online

Hoover's Online (`http://hoovweb.hoovers.com/`) is one of the more popular sources for corporate information on the Internet. For free, you can access the MasterList Plus database, which contains information on more than 12,000 publicly held companies. An abbreviated version of Hoover's fee-based Company Profile database, the MasterList, contains the following information:

◆ **Basic information.** The company's address, phone numbers, Web site, chief executive officer (CEO), chief financial officer (CFO), latest annual sales, number of employees, ticker symbol, and exchange.

◆ **Brief description.** Describes the company's mission and line of business.

◆ **Additional sources of information.** Here's the jewel in Hoover's MasterList: A list of links to more Internet-based information about the company, including EDGAR reports, a current stock quote, a StockMaster stock chart, a Market Guide Snapshot of current financials, and a preconfigured InfoSeek Guide search.

Figure 18-3 shows a MasterList entry for Sun Microsystems. Frankly, the free offering is somewhat anemic; you find yourself wishing you could access the richer information resources of the Company Profile database.

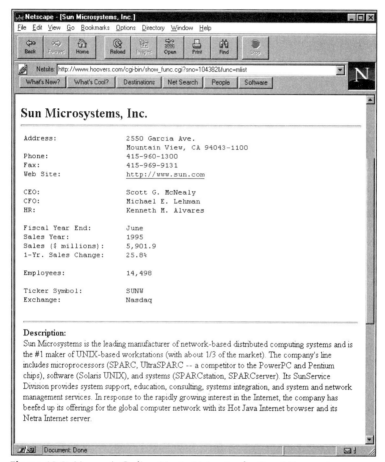

Figure 18-3: Hoover's Online MasterList entry for Sun Microsystems.

Market Guide

Founded in 1983 to publish information about unlisted small-cap companies, Market Guide has since grown into a comprehensive financial and fundamentals database on over 8,000 publicly held companies trading on the New York, American, and NASDAQ exchanges.

Like Hoover's Online, Market Guide (http://www.marketguide.com/) gives you something for free, the Market Guide Snapshots. Unlike the thin profile you find in Hoover's Online, the MarketGuide entry (see Figure 18-4) is chock full of information — specifically about every ratio ever invented, including most of those introduced in Chapter 16 (such as the P/E ratio and the debt/equity ratio). You want to spend some time exploring the Snapshot.

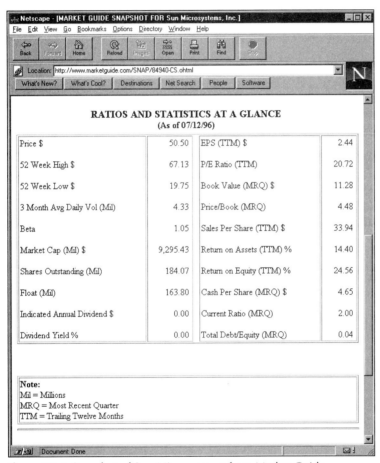

Figure 18-4: Snapshot of Sun Microsystems from Market Guide.

The Snapshot is free, but Market Guide offers fee-based services, too, including Quick Facts Report (Snapshot information plus operating results, institutional and inside ownership, and quarterly revenues/earnings data); Company Profile Report (all the Snapshot and Quick Facts information plus balance sheets and cash flow statements, capital structure, and comparisons to industry, sector, and market); a detailed Ratio Comparison Report that compares the company's ratios to industry, sector, and market averages; an Earnings Estimate Report; detailed financial reports, and more. You can obtain these reports by subscribing or by paying a fee (as little as $1) for each document retrieved. There's some great information here — particularly the reports that compare the company's ratios to industry, sector, and market averages — so you may wish to obtain some of these reports if you're really serious about investing in a stock.

Wall Street Research Net (WSRN.com)

Think of Wall Street Research Net (http://wsrn.com) as a Grand Central Station of corporate research links — some 95,000 at this writing. With so many links, you'd think that the site would be daunting, but it's well-organized. On the title page, shown in Figure 18-5, you find links to the site's eight sections, which include:

◆ **Company information entries.** Entries for over 16,000 corporations, including SEC documents, company home pages, annual reports, press releases, and other investor information.

◆ **Economic research links.** Links to economic databases containing important information about the overall investment climate.

◆ **Market news.** The latest from stock exchanges worldwide, plus currency and commodity news.

◆ **The News.** A great selection of investment-related news on the Web.

◆ **Research publications.** A directory of for-fee newsletters and market analyses.

◆ **Mutual funds.** Links to information for more than 5,000 mutual funds.

◆ **The Internet.** Links to other investment-related sites.

◆ **What's new.** News about Wall Street Research Net.

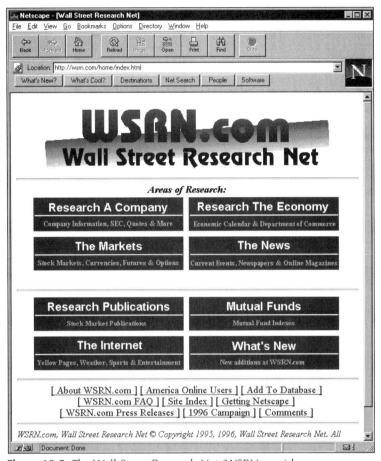

Figure 18-5: The Wall Street Research Net (WSRN.com) home page.

What's of greatest interest to you in the stock-selection process is the Company Information entry. See Figure 18-6 for the WSRN.com entry for Sun Microsystems. To find information about a company, you can search by ticker symbol or company name. What you find here varies, depending on what's available. The Sun entry, for example, has a link to Silicon Investor, which compiles information about computer companies.

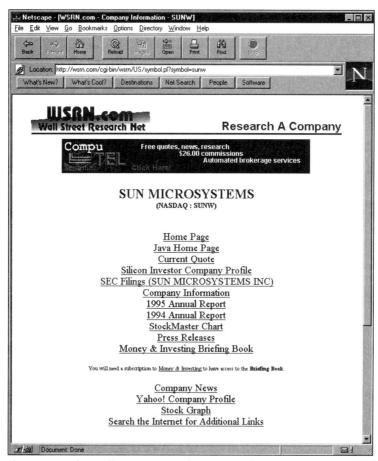

Figure 18-6: The Wall Street Research Net entry for Sun Microsystems.

Wall Street Journal Briefing Books

Venturing out of the free service area, turn now to a service that you should find close to indispensable: the *Wall Street Journal Interactive Edition* (`http://interactive.wsj.com`) with its corporate Briefing Books. Unlike the just-the-facts approach of Hoover's or Market Guide's freebie entries, the Briefing Books give you frank opinion and commentary as well as a rich dose of facts and figures. Here's what you find in a Briefing Book entry:

◆ **Company background.** A detailed, critical, and often fascinating study of the company's history and current business position.

◆ **Financial overview.** A graph of the company's recent earnings reports, with summary balance sheets for the past two years. You also find key ratios (such as P/E ratio). What's of special value here are the comparisons to industry averages for four key ratios: Price/Earnings, price/Book Value, Debt/Equity, and Return on Equity.

◆ **Stock performance.** A graphic presentation of the stock's recent (past 12 month) performance, including 52-week highs and lows, dividends, volume, institutional holdings, and much more.

◆ **Company news.** Links to full-text *Wall Street Journal* articles about the company.

◆ **Press releases.** The full text of recent corporate press releases.

◆ **Company snapshot.** A quick overview of the stock's performance and the most recent news.

One of the best things about the *Journal's* Web edition is the linkage within news articles to Briefing Book entries. As you're reading *Wall Street Journal* news reports, you see that many company names are underlined, meaning that they're hyperlinks. Click on 'em and you go straight to the Briefing Book. This is an excellent use of hypertext and shows why so many people are convinced that hypertext is the way to go for presenting complex information.

To access a Briefing Book, click on the Search link. In the Briefing Book section, you can search by ticker symbol or company name. Figure 18-7 shows the Briefing Book title page for Sun Microsystems.

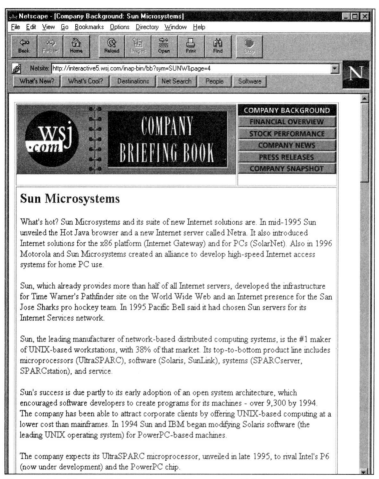

Figure 18-7: The Wall Street Journal Interactive Edition Briefing Book for Sun Microsystems.

Barron's Online

This especially useful site (see Figure 18-8), a newcomer to the Web, contains everything in the eminent weekly newspaper — except the newsprint. To access Barron's Online, use `http://www.barrons.com/`. Best feature: the Market Week data section has become Market Day (it's updated daily).

Figure 18-8: Barron's Online.

Barron's Online also includes a searchable database (called Dossier), with an amazing 15,000 stock and 5,000 mutual fund performance snapshots. Even the ads have helpful links. The magazine also plans original online content soon.

Summary

◆ You can use the Internet to get background information on a company. Tools useful for this purpose include search engines, corporate home pages, and proprietary company profile databases.

◆ A search engine can dig up all kinds of facts and opinion about companies — some pro, some con. You may pick up some important leads, which you can follow by searching the full text of Web-based newspapers.

◆ Corporate home pages contain interesting news and information about companies, but, naturally, they're slanted to give a favorable view.

◆ You can find market research reports on the Web, but you have to pay for the reports.

◆ If you're looking for informed opinion, Zacks Investment Research — a subscription-based service — offers indexes to analysts and brokerage research. You also can try accessing brokerage pages.

◆ Abbreviated versions of company profile databases are available on the Web for free. If you like what you see, you can subscribe to the full version.

From Here

◆ Done with your research and ready to buy some shares? Check out Chapter 19.

◆ Track those stocks! You can do it online or on your own PC, as explained in Chapter 20.

◆ With e.Schwab and Schwab*NOW!*, the subject of Chapter 21, you can do it all: buy stocks online and manage your portfolio.

Choosing an Internet Brokerage

If you plan to buy or sell stock, you have to have a *broker* — a licensed representative of a brokerage firm who will be your middleman with the market. You also have to have an account with the broker's firm, called a *brokerage*. For each trade, you pay a *commission*, which can really eat into your gains. Think of it this way: If you have $1000 to invest, but you have to pay a $100 commission to buy the stock, you're just breaking even when the stock goes from $1000 to $1100. The lower the commision, the less the stock will have to go up in order to produce gains for you.

If you're looking for the lowest commissions, you've come to the right place: Internet brokerages take advantage of computer automation to offer commissions as low as $12 per trade. At this writing, there were an estimated 640,000 Internet brokerage accounts, and this number is expected to increase to 1.5 million by the year 2000.

This chapter introduces all types of brokerages, including full-service brokerages, and helps you decide which type of broker is right for you. You find a full introduction to Internet discount brokerages, and you learn how to select the broker that's right for your needs.

In This Chapter

- ◆ Which type of broker is right for you?
- ◆ What to look for in a brokerage account
- ◆ Getting the facts on a prospective broker

The rise of discount and deep-discount brokerages: Good news for individual investors

Once upon a time, about 20 years ago, there were no discount brokers or deep-discount brokers who offered small investors low prices for trading shares. This was because all brokerages charged customers fixed commission rates no matter how many or how few shares they traded. Brokers had charged at this arrangement for years, saying that costs of small orders, per share, were much higher than for big orders. In 1975, the Securities and Exchange Commision (SEC) let brokers charge whatever the market would bear. This meant lower prices for big institutional customers with the clout to jawbone brokerages on price. For small investors, too, the change brought somewhat lower prices. These retail prices were not negotiable, though, unless your account was a certain size or you traded a lot and thus generated good commissions for your broker. The end of fixed commissions also brought a new breed of broker — discount brokerages. Later, the discounters were joined by deep discounters, who work with wholesale securities firms that don't work on a commission basis. It's the discounters and deep discounters that have flocked to the Internet. In fact, some of these firms work only on the Net. What does this mean for you? Lower commissions. A ballpark estimate: 100 shares of AT&T would cost you about $200 at a full-service firm, $50 at a discount house, and $25 with an Internet deep-discount brokerage.

Which Type of Broker is Right for You?

Choosing a broker is a big decision for investors. At the very least, you're choosing a firm that's going to physically handle your securities. It keeps track of when you buy and sell and how much you make and lose. It tracks how many shares you own, when your stock splits, and when dividends are paid. It also notifies you about any takeover bids for your company, any offers it may make to buy stock back from you, and other news that it has to legally disclose to you.

These services are the minimum. If you're willing to pay for additional services, you can get much more, including customized, professional investment advice that's based on recommendations from the firm's research department. It all boils down to this: Do you want to do more of the work in picking your own stocks, or do you want to pay for more help? Answering this question will help you decide whether you want a full-service broker, a discount broker, or a deep discounter.

If you're looking for a broker, the Net can help: Check out the alphabetical listings of U.S. brokers at `http://www.cs.cmu.edu/afs/cs.cmu.edu/user/jdg/www/ invest_brokers/us/index.html`. Figure 19-1 shows the beginning of the "A" listings. If a brokerage has a Web page, you can access it directly just by clicking on one of the links.

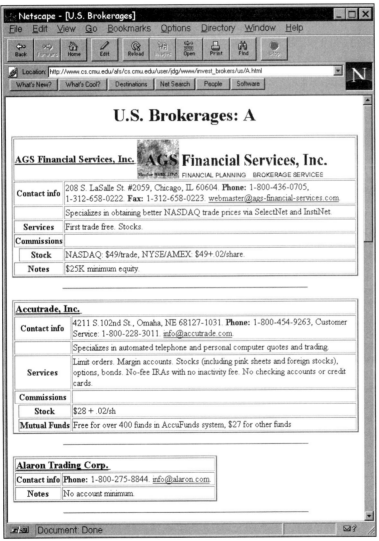

Figure 19-1: This Web guide to U.S. brokerages gives you direct links to their Web pages.

Full-service brokers

Brokers at *full-service brokerages* provide a range of services for their clients, and their services are backed by extensive research and analysis. Full-service brokers tell their clients about upcoming initial public offerings or pass on to them stock recommendations and changes in such recommendations from their research departments. They may also act as financial planners or advisors, helping clients align their investments with an organized longer-term personal plan. Again, for a fee, a full-service broker will manage your account for you.

In addition, full-service brokerages provide many services, including transfer and reregistration of securities, dividend collection and reinvestment, checking accounts, debit cards, money market accounts, detailed monthly statements, and sophisticated portfolio management.

Full-service brokers get paid well to do these things. You may not want to pay the fees for full service. At the same time, the big full-service brokerages may not want to pay much attention to your little portfolio. Your business may just fall below their radar!

If you're keen to do business online, especially on the Internet, the full-service guys won't serve you — yet. The closest you'll find to online transactions is Donaldson, Lufkin & Jenrette's PC Financial Network (`http://www.orcc.com/pershing.htm`), which maintains a presence only on America Online and Prodigy — supposedly for "security." PC Financial recently set up a retail system on the Net for its correspondents (other independent brokers who clear orders through it).

While choosing to go with a full-service broker may get you the benefits of someone else's knowledge and experience, judging the quality of the advice you're receiving may be pretty hard for you. The most important thing to keep in mind about full-service brokers is that they get paid commissions to sell financial products. A large percentage of financial advisors also get paid commissions. What's more, brokers are not legally required to give clients the best advice — only "appropriate" advice. Brokers who are interested in earning a good living for themselves may not think it unethical to sell you a product that makes them a big commission rather than a product that may bring you a bigger return and them very little commission.

A good discussion of some issues in managing "legitimate" investment advice from brokers and banks comes from the Missouri Secretary of State's office in The Five Biggest Problems "Legitimate" Investing Poses for Older Investors (`http://mosl..sos.state.mo.us/sos-sec/leginvst.html`). This advice is valuable for investors of all ages.

Full-service brokerages may have Web pages with all kinds of other useful and interesting services, such as research reports, interest rate calculators, and economic newsletters.They may give passwords to clients so that they can check their portfolios against the firm's models and advice.

However, these brokerages haven't yet figured out a way to keep their high-priced commissioned brokers busy if many of their clients — maybe even institutional ones — want to place orders for securities online. Some full-service brokerages also mention worries about security and legal compliance. Considering the huge amounts of money involved in their high-volume trading, these concerns are legitimate.

Discount brokers

KEY TERM

Discount brokerages make their money by concentrating on large volumes of retail trading, mainly for individual investors. They don't do mergers and acquisitions, or manage initial public offerings. And they don't often have big research departments, so they don't often give advice on which stocks to buy. Still, some discount brokerages resemble junior versions of their full-service counterparts; if you want personal service, you can get it, but you usually don't get a broker assigned to your account, as you would in a full-service brokerage

Individual investors have flocked to discount brokers for a simple reason: Discount brokers welcome individual investors and give them a break on commissions. Charles Schwab (`http://www.schwab.com`), the biggest discount broker, helped set the standard for no-frills, high-volume, 24-hour service with mutual funds, check writing, and asset-management features linked to accounts.

Many discount brokerages are establishing Web pages, and some offer Internet order placement. Figure 19-2 shows the Web offering of Quick & Reilly, one of the leading discount brokerage firms (`http://www.quick-reilly.com/`).

The ranks of discount and deep-discount brokers are mushrooming. Because their main customers are people like you, they have no qualms about using the Net as a sales channel. The more the merrier! Touch-tone phone orders? Orders through commercial online services? They've already set up shop there. Enabling trades via Internet? Sure, why not?

As the competition for discount accounts heats up, discount brokers offer more and more services that the big guys have. They compete on prices, too.

In its 1995 survey of discount brokerages, the American Association of Individual Investors (AAII) counted more than 80 of them. Of all those low-priced operators, a dozen were working online. Now, discounters probably number over 90, and about 20 of them are online.

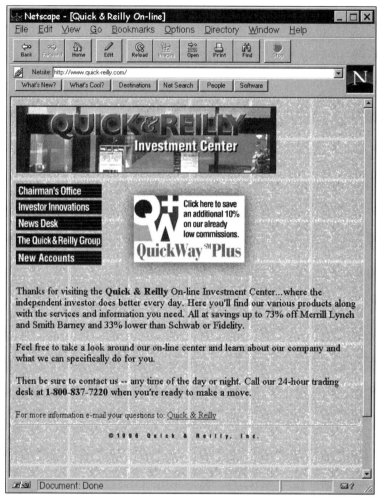

Figure 19-2: Quick & Reilly, a discount brokerage, explains its services on this Web page.

But the latest in electronic trading is buying and selling through the Internet. Thanks to improvements in the Internet's security, more discount (and deep-discount) brokerages are offering secure Web services, which enable you to initiate buy and sell orders directly from a Web page. These Web-based services aren't as full-featured as most proprietary packages that you run on your own computer, but they're very easy to use. To see how they work, see the section, "Introducing Internet Brokerages," later in this chapter.

Electronic orders: Moving from proprietary applications to the Web

Discount brokerages have been offering electronic orders for several years-but not with the Internet. They give you a proprietary PC application, which makes a modem connection directly to the firm's computer. Offering very good security, this approach has additional advantages: The PC application can include portfolio management and other capabilities (for an excellent example, see Chapter 21). After examining some of these packages, you may decide that this is the way to go.

Deep-discount brokers

The basic idea of a deep-discount brokerage is to offer one thing and one thing only: rock-bottom prices. EBroker, a deep-discount Internet brokerage (http://www.ebroker.com), offers $12 trades — but not much else (see Figure 19-3).

Many deep discounters cut their prices by working through a wholesale brokerage. Wholesalers deal with investment companies, not individuals. They don't get commissions on each buy or sell. Instead, wholesalers profit from the spread between the prices at which they buy and sell stocks themselves.

Deep-discount brokerages that charge flat fees for many transactions can do so because their costs are no higher for a larger number of shares than for a smaller number.

Like full-service brokers, most discount brokers work on commissions. However, discount brokers are mainly content to wait for your order or stuff a brochure for one of their funds in your monthly statement.

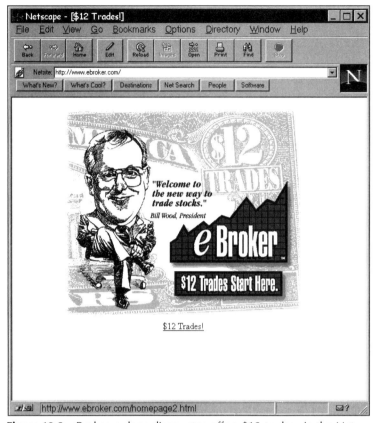

Figure 19-3: eBroker, a deep-discounter, offers $12 trades via the Net.

Comparing commissions

COOL SITE

Which brokerage really offers the best commission? It's hard to tell sometimes. Commissions aren't often expressed using a flat rate; they may vary, depending on how many shares you buy or sell. To find out where you can get the best commission rate for a given transaction, check out Robert's Online Commission Pricer (`http://www.intrepid.com/~robertl/commissions-pricer3.html`). Written in Java, this page requires a Java-capable browser, such as Microsoft Internet Explorer version 3.0, or Netscape Navigator (version 2.0 or higher). You type in the number of shares you want to buy and the current share price; the Commission Pricer finds the lowest rate, as shown in Figure 19-4.

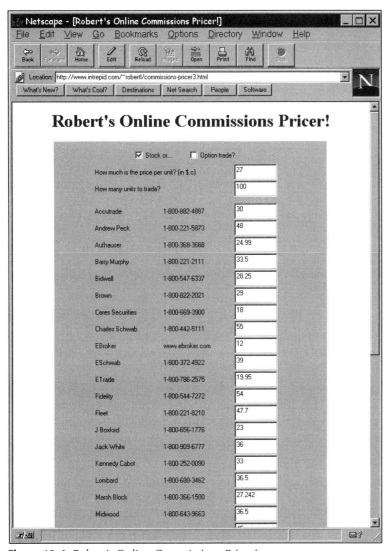

Figure 19-4: Robert's Online Commissions Pricer!

Robert's Online Commissions Pricer is part of a suite of online investment tools, written by Dr. Robert Lum. Called Robert's Online Applications (http://www.intrepid.com/~robertl/index.html), this site includes a number of very interesting Java "applets" (mini-programs), including a loan pricer, a quote sheet, stock volatility charts, and a live spreadsheet that you can load into a Web page.

So what's right for you?

Half of the broker-client match is you, of course. The kind of deal you strike with a broker — either full-service, discount, or deep-discount — depends on the kind of trading you plan to do. Just a few well-considered trades a year? A larger discount broker with some free research products may be a good choice. From this broker you want lots of materials for a long-term decision, the ability to handle a variety of stocks and other investments, and good pricing and execution. You also want a firm that you can stay with for the long haul.

If you think you want to trade many small cap stocks, you may be better off with a deep-discount broker. Your transaction costs — the expense of buying and selling many times — will be a bigger factor, but you also want to compare fee schedules for several of these brokers and find out what kinds of other services they offer, such as discounts for higher trading volume. Check with some of these brokers' current customers, if possible, to see what kind of pricing they're getting for small stocks. The brokers may vary in how much they charge, what procedures they follow, and how hard they try with *limit orders* (to buy or sell at prices not more or less than a certain limit the customer specifies) and *stop orders* (sell orders that are triggered when certain prices are reached).

Choosing a Broker

Low commissions aren't the only thing you should look for when you're choosing a broker. In this section, you learn how to avoid rogue brokers, solicit recommendations from experienced investors, compare brokerage accounts, and find reviews of brokerages on the Internet. You'll also learn what to ask when you interveiw a prospective broker.

Avoiding rogue brokers

When choosing a broker, you want to go for the good ones and avoid the bad ones. You'd think it would be easier to sift out the bad ones to narrow down your choice. In reality, working the other way is probably less trouble.

Sure, state and federal securities regulators have their *bad lists* of brokers and advisors who break laws and rules. All these disciplinary records are collected in a big database called *the Central Registration Depository* or CRD. This listing of all actions against the nation's registered brokers and dealers includes data on more than 40 years of fines, suits, and settlements. The information is compiled by the National Association of Securities Dealers, the self-regulated organization of and for brokers and dealers.

This database is about to move to the Internet. It will supplement the toll-free Public Brokers Information Hotline, which can barely handle the more than 1,700 calls a week it gets with inquiries about "rogue brokers." Until then, you can call 1-800-289-9999. Meanwhile, the New York Stock Exchange (http://www.nyse.com) releases its own disciplinary action listing each month. The Securities and Exchange Commission (http:// www.sec.gov/enforce/comctr.htm) just opened an enforcement complaint center on the Internet as well as a watch list of cyberspace frauds and abuses (http://www.sec.gov/consumer/cyberfr.htm).

A number of state securities regulators also put out cautionary lists and other advisories aimed at individual investors. The state regulators are the first line of defense investors have in dealing with suspect brokers and practices.

One of the best such state sites is from the Oklahoma Securities Commission (http://www.oklaosf.state.ok.us). This body has another bit of advice for investors: Learn as much as you can about investing so that you can spot rogues without relying only on lists.

Another helpful state site is from the Illinois Secretary of State's office (http:// www.sos.state.il.us/pubs/securities/invguide/invguide.html). Its Consumers Guide to Inve$tments (see Figure 19-5) gives you pointers on selecting someone to manage your money, types of brokers that best suit your needs, fees you should expect to pay, disclosure, your rights as an investor, and how to spot fraud and abuse.

Getting recommendations from investors

Much of the advice from these national and state regulators helps you set minimum standards for your broker, but it doesn't help you to find the right broker for you. Word of mouth is one way to find an outstanding broker, especially when the recommendations are good. People often complain about their brokers the way they complain about their plumbers: When things go wrong, it's all their fault! When you hear them being praised, it's usually for some specific good deed.

Start by asking people you know who've been investing for a while. You may find only that they are lukewarm about their brokers but have stuck with them because it was easy to keep their accounts in one place, or you may get some great testimonials. But talk to people you know before you go looking for feedback about brokers from places like newsgroups full of strangers.

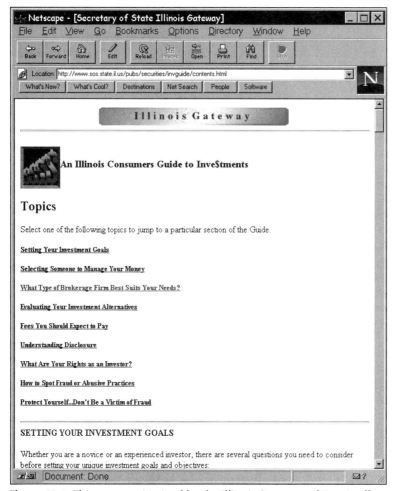

Figure 19-5: This page, maintained by the Illinois Secretary of State's office, gives sound advice for selecting a broker.

What to look for in a brokerage account

Internet brokerages require a minimum amount of money to open a *brokerage account*, generally $1,000 or $5,000. When you buy or sell stocks, funds are transferred out of (or into) your account. The commission is deducted from it, too. This is convenient — you don't have to send a check to cover your transactions and commissions — but, then again, your money's out of your hands. Your basic concerns: Is this money safe? Can you earn something on it when it's not invested?

You should check out and get, along with your brokerage account, some basic services. One is insurance in the event that the brokerage goes out of business. The Securities Investor Protection Corporation provides coverage for the first $500,000 of customers' accounts. This is required by law. Some brokerages offer you extra protection at no added cost; others charge for it. This coverage does not insure you against losses resulting from your investing activities, however. That's your responsibility.

A second service most brokerages offer is some kind of interest on cash balances in your account. These *sweep accounts* put cash in money market or tax-free mutual funds and then let you take the money out of these funds without charge to reinvest later as you want. Some brokers give you a Visa or MasterCard debit card and unlimited checkwriting with your brokerage account.

Other attractions many brokers offer account holders are no-load mutual funds and IRAs. Keeping all your accounts with one brokerage — even your mutual funds and IRAs — ensures that all your records are in one place.

Of the brokerages that emphasize the Internet, one with some of the best word-of-mouth is Lombard Brokerage (`http://www.lombard.com`). It's a flat-fee firm, although not the cheapest. Its customer service is reputed to be tops (it also handles phone order entry), and many users and customers rave about its excellent links and research services.

Should you switch from a discount to a deep-discount broker?

If you already have an account with a big discount brokerage such as Schwab, Fidelity, or Quick & Reilly, who have been through a couple generations of electronic trading services and are quite active on the Internet, then it's probably not worth your while to look for a broker all over again. This is especially true if price is the sticking point. These discount brokers may look a little high compared to the deep discounters appearing on the Internet, but the price pressure is already having its effect. E.Schwab does most of its trades at a flat $29 now.

These big players know that this is an important sales channel, and they're working hard on it. Both Quick' & Reilly's and Schwab's Internet products are vast improvements over earlier online versions in terms of user-friendliness, features, service, and price. You'll learn more about Schwab's offerings in Chapter 21.

Brokerage-selection resources on the Net

You find some interesting brokerage surveys on the Net. WebSmart Money (`http://www.dowjones.com/smart`) does a yearly customer satisfaction survey. Jack White (`http://pawws.secapl.com/jwc`) has led this list for three years running.

Another intriguing poll is the Brokerage Firm Report Card from *Registered Representative* magazine (`http://www.moneypages.com/syndicate/brokers/grading.html`). Here, brokers rate brokerage firms on features such as their over-all ethics, freedom from pressure to sell certain products, realistic sales quotas, and quality of research and sales ideas. The firms included are all full-service bro-kerages. Still another yearly ranking comes from *Institutional Investor* magazine's April issues.

Get the facts!

Your next step before choosing one broker is selecting several for closer scrutiny. Call them, e-mail them, or even write them and ask for all their account literature and a fee schedule.

Calculate a few trades that you're likely to try. Add in extra fees, if any, that apply for trading foreign stocks, orders of less than 100 shares, large orders, low-priced stocks, and whatever you think you would do. Figure these out for several brokers and compare the costs. Then look at what other services the brokers offer. Are they online? If so, how much does their software cost? Are they on the Net? If so, do they have, or are they linked to, quote services? News? Portfolio software?

You may also see some things that you don't like. For example, eBroker doesn't give you 800 line access and requires a $10,000 minimum to open accounts. Take a look, too, at Ceres Securities' site (`http://www.ceres.com`). The $18 price for order executions displayed on its home page seems pretty good. And columnist Andrew Tobias' smiling face offers you daily comments. What's not to like about this appealing service? Plenty. Ceres wants you to sign both general account and margin account applications when you open an account with Ceres. If you know what margin trading entails and you want an account to do it, fine. This is an easy place to get one. If you don't, though, you sure don't need one right away — and Ceres doesn't give you a clue as to what the margin account is for.

The biggest hackle-raising feature of this site, though, is the trading authorization forms it lets you print out and send in. One of these authorizes "the agent" — that is, Ceres — to "buy, sell, and trade in stocks, bonds, options, and other securities, commodities, or contracts for a client's account — that's *your* account. This is called "limited authorization" because it's limited to purchases and sales of securi-ties. Ceres can't go and sell your house. But it can go and trade a whole lot of other assets for you, without asking you first. Fine. Ceres is letting you have real-time quotes for $30 per month. But let them trade for you?

First impressions

What's your overall impression in dealing with the brokers so far? Did they get materials to you quickly? Did you understand it all? If you had questions, did they have someone who could explain it to you right away?

These impressions should give you some basis for drawing up a *good list* of brokers. Then, with this group in hand, run a check against the *bad lists*.

Much of the canned advice that you get from state regulators' home pages and advisories is more related to full-service brokers than to discount brokers. But with all the growth in the discount area, the regulators may well include this kind of information before long.

The account executive you deal with on the phone or in person at discount brokerages are licensed brokers, too, just like the ones that handle accounts at full-service brokerages. But instead of handling the same accounts all the time, the discounters deal with them as accountholders who want to buy and sell on a first-come, first-served basis. No one's dedicated to your account, and you don't develop a relationship with your broker.

Interview questions

Discount brokers' reps should be able to answer many of the questions you'd ask a full-service broker, such as the following:

◆ Is the firm a member of one of the national securities exchanges (such as the New York Stock Exchange)?

◆ How long have you been in business?

◆ How are investment prices and fees determined?

◆ Do any investments require fees to enter or exit them?

◆ Are there any lawsuits against the firm?

◆ How do you settle disputes with customers?

Finding the right broker is like hiring someone. In fact, that's exactly what it is. Take as much time as you need and interview as many as you have to. Ask about brokers' backgrounds, training, and specialties. Get and check references. These people will be dealing with your savings!

Introducing Internet Brokerages

Commissions vary, but Internet brokerages all work pretty much the same way:
You fill out an on-screen form indicating how many shares of a stock you want to
buy or sell (see Figure 19-6). You then see a confirmation screen (see Figure 19-7)
that summarizes your transaction (and enables you to cancel if something's not
right). After you submit your order, you receive confirmation almost immediately.

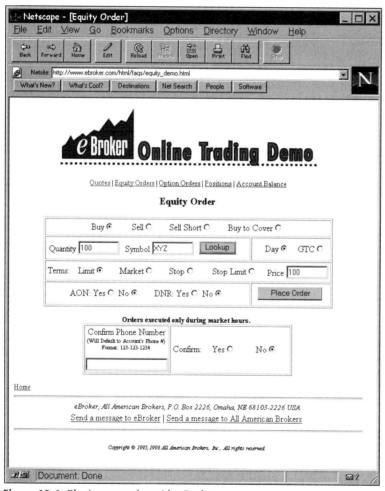

Figure 19-6: Placing an order with eBroker.

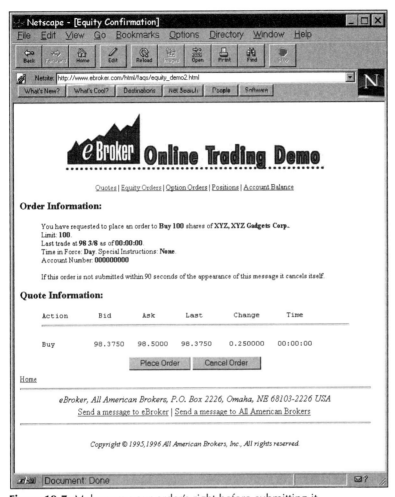

Figure 19-7: Make sure your order's right before submitting it.

E*TRADE offers a well-designed Trading Demo that's worth a look if you want to see how Internet trading works(`http://www.etrade.com/html/demo/stock. htm`). You get a mock account and you can really explore the way the system works.

Looking for convenient features

Some Internet brokerages offer little more than an order page and an account balance summary. Others offer better features. One very nice thing to look for is an automatic portfolio summary, such as the one shown in Figure 19-8. E*TRADE's portfolio summary keeps track of your transactions and shows your current account balance with active updates during trading hours.

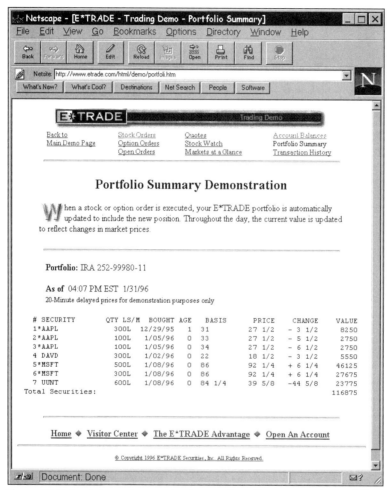

Figure 19-8: Look for an Internet brokerage that offers automatic portfolio summaries, such as E*TRADE's.

Internet brokerages at a glance

Please note that the following information was current at this book's writing. Due to the competitiveness of the online brokerage market, it is likely that several of these brokerages have since changed their commission schedules. Please contact the sites directly for more information.

Accutrade (http://www.accutrade.com/). NYSE, AMEX, and NASDAQ stocks can be traded at $28 plus two cents per share. Secured site (SSL). Minimum initial deposit: $5,000. Free delayed quotes; real-time quotes also available. Additional services: Option and mutual fund trading and simple portfolio management (account balance).

Ceres Securities (http://www.ceres com). Equities trade at $18 for any number of shares. Secured site (SSL). Minimum initial deposit: $5000. Free delayed quotes; real-time quotes also available. Additional services: Options trading, IRAs, pension trusts, simple portfolio management (account balance), portfolio management with account balance, portfolio summary, and transaction history.

E*TRADE (http://www.etrade.com). Listed equities trade for $14 plus one cent per share for listed orders over 500 shares; over-the-counter (OTC) stocks trade for $19-95 for any number of shares. Secured site (SSL). Free delayed quotes; real-time quotes are $30 per month. Additional services: options trading, margin accounts, and simple portfolio management (account balance).

eBroker (http://www.ebroker.com). Any common or preferred stock can be traded at $12 for any number of shares. Secured site (SSL). Minimum initial deposit: $10,000. Free delayed quotes; real-time quotes are $30 per month. Automatic execution of orders with real-time confirmation. Additional services: options trading and margin accounts.

The NET Investor (http://pawws.com/How_phtml/). Any stock can be traded for $29.50 plus two-and-a-half cents per share on the first 3,000 shares; one-and-a-half cents per share thereafter. Secured site (SSL). Minimum initial deposit: $5,000 ($2,000 for an IRA). Free delayed quotes; real-time quotes available based on account activity. Additional services: options, mutual funds, bonds, company research, Morningstar mutual fund reports, price forecasts, earnings analysis, IRAs, VISA debit/ATM card, money-market checking, advanced portfolio management with automatic tracking, real-time valuation, transaction history, and gains and losses. Note: Inactive accounts (defined as those generating less than $105 in commissions during the year) are subject to a $50 maintenance fee.

(continued)

(continued)

Lombard Brokerage (http://www.lombard.com). Listed stocks can be traded for $14.95 for the first 1,700 shares, plus two cents per share thereafter. Over-the-counter (OTC) stocks can be traded for $14.95 for the first 2,500 shares, plus one-and-a-half cents per share thereafter. Secured site (SSL). Minimum initial deposit: $5,000 ($2000 for an IRA). Free delayed quotes; real-time quotes available based on account activity. Additional services: bonds, mutual funds, online portfolio management, customized research services, free dividend reinvestment, and IRAs.

National Discount Brokerage (http://pawws.secapl.com/Ndb_phtml/). Any NASDAQ or over-the-counter (OTC) stock can be traded for $20; listed stocks (NYSE or AMEX) trade for $25 plus a $3 postage/handling fee for the first 5,000 shares, plus one cent per share thereafter. Secured site (SSL). Minimum initial deposit: $10,000. Additional services: Fast, automated confirmation, asset management account with MasterCard debit card and unlimited check writing, rapid research line, and touch-tone phone order system.

Charles Schwab (http://www.schwab.com). For customers who have established an e.trade account, stocks can be traded for $29.95 up to 1,000 shares, plus 3 cents per share thereafter (*e.trade* is a proprietary Windows application, but e.trade account holders can also trade using the Web). Secure site (SSL). Minimum initial investment: $5,000. Additional services: Charles Schwab is a discount brokerage that offers a full suite of services, if you want to take advantage of them. The e.schwab application offers extensive portfolio analysis and tracking, but Web orders are not automatically posted to this application.

Jack White/PATH On-Line (http://pawws.secapl.com/jwc/). PATH On-line trades receive a 10 percent discount on Jack White's discounted commissions ($33 for up to 2,000 shares, plus three cents per share thereafter). Secure site (SSL). Minimum initial investment: $5,000. Additional services: Jack White is a discount brokerage that offers a full suite of services, if you want to take advantage of them. Web ordering is pretty basic, offering only orders, order confirmation, and simple portfolio management via an account summary.

Wyse Securities (http://www.compu-trade.com/). Stocks can be traded for $19-95. Secure site (SSL). Minimum initial investment: $2,000. Additional services: options and bonds.

Can you get them on the phone?

During the stock market's wild gyrations of Summer '96, many customers of Internet brokerages found that they could not access their services. Why? The firms' servers were overloaded and customers couldn't get through.

Internet brokerages are beefing up their systems in response to this experience, but you might want to look for a brokerage that offers some kind of phone backup, such a touch-tone order system. That way you can get through if the server's overloaded.

Other features to look for

Here are more things to think about when you're choosing an Internet brokerage:

◆ **Security.** To protect your privacy and prevent someone from trading with your account, an Internet brokerage should use a secure server (such as the Netscape Commerce Server, which uses the Netscape SSL security scheme).

◆ **Minimum initial deposit.** This ranges from $1,000 to $10,000, with most services closer to the lower end of the range.

◆ **Stock quotes.** Most services offer delayed quotes, some offer real-time quotes for a stiff monthly fee, and a few waive this fee if you trade frequently.

◆ **Bonds, funds, and Retirement Accounts.** Some Internet brokerages enable you to trade bonds and funds, as well as equities. If you establish your retirement account (such as an IRA) with the brokerage, you can keep all your records in one place (that's a plus).

◆ **Portfolio management.** Some Internet brokerages offer online, real-time portfolio management, showing your current holdings and tracking your portfolio's performance. This is convenient because it requires no data entry on your part. The data is generated on the fly by the service's computers.

Summary

◆ Full service brokers provide extensive services, including research, but they charge hefty commissions. Discount brokers offer reduced versions of full-service brokerages, and deep-discount brokers employ technology (touch-tone phones and the Internet) to offer rock-bottom-low prices.

◆ Discount and deep-discount brokerages are setting up Internet services, which enable you to buy and sell stocks online. Both may offer additional services, such as check writing, Visa and MasterCard debit cards, and IRAs.

◆ You may have difficulty comparing commissions because many Internet brokerages charge a flat fee plus per-share fees if you buy more than a certain number of shares. To compare costs, use real-world examples using trades you've made in the past (or trades you're planning to make).

◆ Watch out for "rogue brokers." They're at least as easy to encounter online as anywhere else, and you should do your homework.

◆ Select two or three Internet brokerages for further study. Can you call somebody if you've got questions or need help?

◆ Make sure that your brokerage account is insured. If you're going to leave money sitting in it, you should be able to earn interest. What's the minimum to open an account?

◆ A convenient feature offered by some Internet brokerages is online portfolio management, which can save you the trouble of downloading stock information (see Chapter 20 for information on portfolio management).

From Here

◆ This book features Charles Schwab's e.Schwab service, which is described in detail in Chapter 20.

◆ Learn the basics of investing in bonds; you'll find what you need in Chapter 22.

◆ Use the Internet to investigate Treasury bills, bonds, and notes, as explained in Chapter 23.

◆ In Chapter 20, find out how to use the Internet to discover ways to manage your portfolio.

Managing Your Stock Portfolio

You've been using the Internet as a tool to learn about investing, help set your investment goals, and screen information for possible investments. As your investments grow, you'll also find that the Internet can help you keep track of your investments, thanks to portfolio management software.

If you're using a personal finance program such as Quicken or Manage Your Money, perhaps you're already taking advantage of the portfolio management features of these programs. But you may want more features from a portfolio program. After you have a certain number of investments with prices that change frequently, you'll probably want a program that can automatically link your portfolio to price updates and retally its value. Programs such as these also can help you answer certain questions, such as how much cash, stocks, and bonds you have, whether these are in line with what you want them to be, and if the returns they're giving you are in keeping with what you need. Portfolio management can help alert you to prices at which you want to buy or sell.

In this chapter, you learn about your choices for portfolio management that involve the Internet one way or another. You find free Web sites that offer online portfolio management, as well as stand-alone programs that run on your computer. The Web-based programs have the convenience advantage: Stock prices are updated automatically. Generally, stand-alone programs have more features, but you have to

In This Chapter

- ◆ Understanding your portfolio management options

- ◆ Managing your portfolio online

- ◆ PC-based portfolio managers

- ◆ Commercial portfolio managers

- ◆ Web brokerages with portfolio management

download stock prices, which (with some programs) is a tedious procedure. The best option of all, however, may be to work with a Web-based broker that gives you portfolio management software; this way, all your transactions (buy and sell orders) are entered automatically (with the other options, you have to enter transactions manually).

Understanding Your Portfolio Management Options

You can use the Internet to track and manage your stock portfolio in three ways (there are advantages and disadvantages to each approach):

◆ **Web-based portfolio management.** You sacrifice features and functionality — the Web-based portfolio managers don't have as many bells and whistles as PC-based portfolio managers, such as price alerts and tax summaries — but stock prices are updated automatically. There's no downloading to do, but you have to type in all your transactions manually.

◆ **PC-based portfolio management.** You have many more choices and functionality, including sophisticated graphs of your investments' performance. But how do you obtain the stock quotes? Downloading should be automatic, or nearly so, but all too often it isn't. Also, you still have to add new transactions manually.

◆ **Portfolio management with an Internet brokerage.** You open a brokerage account with an online broker. When you log on to the brokerage's site, you can see your current holdings and account balance. Sometimes, full-featured portfolio management software is provided. Chapter 21 features e.Schwab Online Investor, a service that gives you $29.95 trades (up to 1,000 shares) and a great portfolio manager. This is probably the most convenient choice of all because you don't have to type in your transactions — they're automatically adjusted as you buy and sell stocks.

Take a look at your choices in the following sections, starting with Web-based portfolio management.

Managing Your Portfolio Online

To track your stocks on the Web, you can use the services discussed in Chapter 12, including The Wall Street Journal Interactive Edition and NETWorth's portfolio managers. The online portfolio managers discussed in this section have special features of interest to those tracking stocks.

Is this overkill?

Do you *really* need a computer program to help you manage your stocks? As you learned in Chapter 13, you can use software to manage your mutual fund portfolio. Whether this software is housed on the Net or on your own computer, mutual fund portfolio management software can help you track the current value of your portfolio. You can tell at a glance how your funds are performing against relevant market indices, such as the S&P 500. If your funds aren't performing up to your expectations, you'll know it.

If you decide to invest in stocks, there's even more reason to track your holdings with portfolio management software. That's particularly true if you have many holdings that are traded on active markets. You'll have a tough time keeping up with changes in their value unless you have some kind of software that can link them to price updates and recalculate the value of your portfolio. Programs such as these also can help you answer questions such as how much cash, stocks, and bonds you have, whether these are in line with what you want them to be, and if the returns they're giving you are in keeping with what you need.

There's a downside to portfolio management software, however — don't let it tempt you into frantic buying and selling on the basis of daily upswings or downswings. It's interesting to see how your stocks are going up or down during a day's trading, but your investment horizon should be several years, not several minutes. Plan to check in once a week, once every couple of weeks, or once per month.

All the portfolio managers discussed here share one appealing trait: After you set up your portfolio (generally by supplying the ticker symbols of the stocks you own, and the price you initially paid for them), share prices are updated automatically using 15- or 20-minute-delayed share prices. To see how your portfolio's doing at any time, you just log on and select your personal portfolio.

Worried about security? Some of these online portfolio managers use secure servers, which means that your data can't be intercepted by somebody "listening in" on Internet data transfers. You may also be worried that somebody at one of these firms could snoop into your financial affairs. In most cases, you shouldn't worry: The information used to construct and update your portfolio is stored on your disk and dynamically uploaded every time you log on.

The NETWorth Personal Portfolio

One of the best integrated portfolio management plans around is at NETWorth's Equity Center (`http://networth.galt.com`). This is a freebie, and there's nothing to download. All you have to do is register with NETWorth. In fact, registering gives you some exposure to this system's NETWorth Secure feature, for what it's worth. If you're going to track your holdings in a public space, it makes sense to have some privacy in doing so.

Room for plenty of stocks

NETWorth's Personal Portfolio handles up to 50 U.S. and Canadian stocks, mutual funds, and stock indexes so that you can benchmark the progress of your stocks and funds, too. Personal Portfolio (see Figure 20-1) displays the stocks and funds five at a time on a page. Personal Portfolio works off NETWorth's quote server. You begin by entering into a grid the stock and fund symbols — which you can look up here, too. From there, Personal Portfolio works like a giant calculator that uses current and historical data from the quote server.

You can get a lot of information about what your portfolio's doing from the grid's default settings. This information includes last traded price, day's price changes and percent changes, current value of each holding in your portfolio, gains and losses from your purchase prices, and what percent of the purchase price the gain or loss is.

Good customizing

Some things you don't get for free, such as automatic stock splits. You have to make these adjustments by hand with Personal Portfolio — and with many other such programs. However, Personal Portfolio has some neat features that almost compensate for this. One is that you can customize the data in your portfolio for as many as 12 elements in the grid. If you're inclined to fundamental analysis, you can pick earnings per share, price-earnings multiples, dividend amounts, dates, and yields (see Figure 20-2). If you're more technical-analysis oriented, you can choose price and volume advances, declines, and percentages and up- and down-tick data.

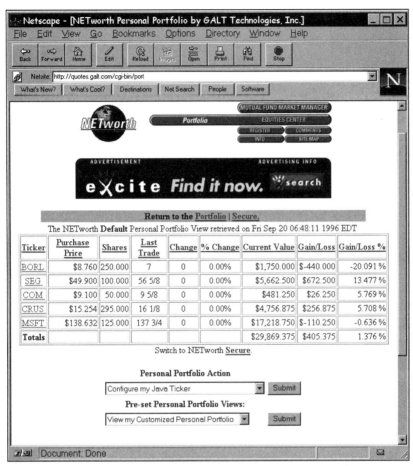

Figure 20-1: NETWorth Personal Portfolio acts like an automatic calculator, showing your portfolio's current value.

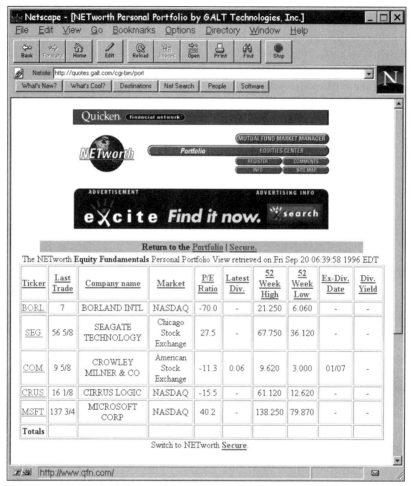

Figure 20-2: NETWorth Personal Portfolio's options include this display showing fundamentals data.

Personal Portfolio also provides some excellent charts, an unusual feature for Web-based portfolio managers. You can graph price and/or volume for the time period of your choice (see Figure 20-3) using pull-down menus. You also can add in moving price averages for a wide range of time periods. You get a choice of graphing several securities in your portfolio at once, which is useful for getting a view of their relative performances.

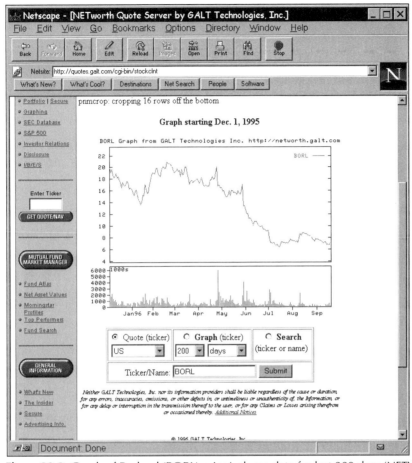

Figure 20-3: Graph of Borland (BORL) price/volume data for last 200 days (NETWorth Personal Portfolio).

If you're a Quicken user, you'll love one of NETWorth's features: You can download your portfolio's current share prices to Quicken using the Quicken for Windows format. This is one of several advanced options available on the Personal Portfolio page.

Investor's Edge Portfolio Management

Another site that offers good online portfolio management is Investor's Edge (http://www.irnet.com/). Offering the same basic features as NETWorth's

Personal Portfolio, including automatic 15-minute-delayed price updates, the Investor's Edge offering (shown in Figure 20-4) has some unique and extremely cool features:

◆ **Personal Portfolio Stock News.** Just click on the button below your portfolio to see current news about your stocks.

◆ **End-of-day e-mail portfolio update.** This is mailed to you automatically at the end of each trading day. It isn't free, though.

Like NETWorth's online portfolio manager, Investor's Edge enables you to download current share prices in the Quicken format. But don't look for other advanced NETWorth features, such as fundamental data and graphing.

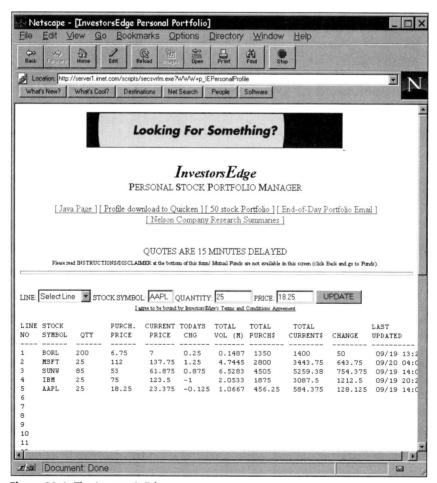

Figure 20-4: The Investor's Edge.

PC-Based Portfolio Managers

Web-based portfolio managers have a big advantage: The stock prices are updated automatically. On the down side, the Web-based offerings available thus far aren't very generous in the features department. If you want more analysis, including graphs of your investments' performance and tax figures or price/volume alerts, consider using a PC-based portfolio manager.

With a PC-based portfolio manager, your choices include online freebies and commercial packages (such as Quicken and Microsoft Money). We explore these offerings in the next sections.

If you're planning to go the PC-based route, make sure the quote downloading process is painless. Try to avoid programs that make you *import* data using a text file format, such as comma- or tab-delimited files. More often than not, you have to edit these files to get them to work properly. Better technology is available, so don't settle for less — and what's more, most of the the software is free, as described in the next section

Online freebies

Why would anyone give great software away for free? Simple — to get you to buy full-featured versions of the software, to subscribe to fee-based services, or — at the minimum — to sell advertising. This philosophy motivates the release of the following programs. You can download them from the Net by accessing the sites mentioned in the following list.

◆ **Alpha StockVue** (http://www.alphaconnect.com). Available for Windows 95 computers, this sophisticated program uses Microsoft's ActiveX technology to retrieve delayed stock quotes from the Internet automatically; you don't have to subscribe to a fee-based service or do anything manually. Alpha StockVue is not a full-featured portfolio manager by any means. For example, you can't generate custom graphs of your investments, but you can perform a portfolio valuation, set stock price and volume alerts, view an animated ticker tape display, and export data to Quicken, the best-selling commercial package.

◆ **Inside Track Lite** (http://www.microquest.com). This Windows program enables you to receive free delayed quotes throughout the day. You can track stock indexes as well as your own portfolio. For information on subscribing to real-time stock quotes ($11.95 per month, at this writing), see http://www.quote.com/info/itrack.html. With the Lite edition, you can track up to 100 securities (including bonds), receive an instant portfolio valuation at the click of a button, easily record splits and dividends, and view a wide variety of charts and graphs related to your investments' performance.

◆ **PointCast** (http://www.pointcast.com). Voted the Best Internet Application by c|net, PointCast transforms your computer into a real-time news and stock-quote reception service. PointCast pops into view like a screen saver whenever you leave your computer unattended. You see the latest news and weather as well as stock quotes for the stocks in your portfolio (it takes only a few moments to set this up). You need to be connected to the Internet to see the latest news and stock quotes. This is a large program and needs 1MB of memory.

◆ **StockTracker** (http://www.stockcenter.com/). This nice portfolio manager includes many great features, including price/volume alerts (the software alerts you if a share price falls or rises to a certain level or if volume hits a level you specify). If you subscribe to the fee-based quote service, you see active quotes all day. StockTracker is free if you use it after hours. You can produce a variety of reports and charts. The biggest stumbling block with Stock Tracker is that it's used only for stocks. Other less than optimal features include having to manually deal with dividends, stock splits, and buying and selling the same stock at more than one price.

Commercial portfolio management software

You probably already own the best-selling commercial portfolio manager: Quicken, the leading personal finance program. Quicken can track stocks, funds, and bonds and their performance, and it can produce graphs and reports based on performance. Quicken can calculate your capital gains, cash flow, income, and expenses from the portfolio and re-tally your net worth. It has links to tax calculators and reporting. Enhanced versions of Quicken feature interactive investment advice, a multimedia library, a mutual fund selector, and a tax guide.

Also available commercially is Managing Your Money, a personal finance program much like Quicken. It can track several securities portfolios and run reports and graphs on them. Managing Your Money has an asset allocation feature that can use your portfolio's risk-return data to show you the optimal mix of your assets — whether you should have relatively more or less stocks, bonds, or cash than you do. This program comes with the financial planning module attached.

How do you get current stock quotes? You can link to online data services or Internet quote servers for price updating. (You can download current stock and fund prices from NETWorth and Investor Insight, as explained earlier in this chapter.) Through an add-on package called Investor Insight (http://www.intuit.com/marketplace/investor-insight/), Quicken also enables you to track news and price information and set up watch lists and personal reports on investments in which you're interested. You also can create nearly one dozen different kinds of charts and graphs with this service, which runs between $9.95 and $19.95 a month for subscription fees.

Shareware for portfolio management and analysis

Here's an amazing resource: An online version of the Association of Shareware Professionals (http://www.formgen.com/aspcd/). The FINANCES directory contains a variety of shareware programs of interest to investors, including the following:

◆ **Capital Gainz for Windows.** This portfolio manager is ideal for dollar-cost averaging, which isn't well handled by most other programs. In addition, you can record purchases, sales, dividends, capital gains, and splits. You can calculate gain/loss and total return. You can print reports for one or more portfolios over a range of dates that you specify. This program also generates tax forms.

◆ **StockQuest.** If you feel like playing financial analyst, try the shareware program StockQuest. It's a "what-if" type program that uses earnings, growth rate, term, and yield to project what investments, mainly stocks, may do. StockQuest also explains the calculations underlying the projections made.

◆ **Total Investor.** This DOS portfolio manager includes technical analysis templates for Lotus 1-2-3 and Quattro Pro spreadsheet programs.

◆ **Wall Street Simulator.** This is cool! You can trade and manage a portfolio without actually putting your money at risk.

◆ **WINFIN-Financial Analyst for Windows.** This program takes in a huge range of investments. It has modules for bonds, options, T-bills and notes, certificates of deposit, mortgages, and car leases. It lets you perform "what-if" calculations holding some of these accounts constant and varying the results of others.

Web Brokerages with Portfolio Management — Putting It All Together

All the programs discussed so far have one or both of the following liabilities:

◆ You have to remember to get updated stock quotes.

◆ You have to type in all the data concerning every transaction, including the big ones (buying and selling) and the little ones (commissions and dividends).

Keeping up with these data-updating and data-entry tasks gets tedious fast, and you could wind up with an inaccurate valuation estimate. But there's an alternative.

Some of the Web brokers discussed in Chapter 19 include portfolio management software, either on the Web or distributed so that it runs on your PC. The advantages of portfolio management software are many. The transactions are updated automatically as you buy, sell, or receive dividends. Share prices are added automatically, too. Take a look at one of these software offerings before turning to an in-depth examination of Schwab's e.Schwab Online Investing service, the subject of Chapter 21.

One of the most comprehensive sites for investors is PAWWS (Portfolio Accounting Worldwide), located at `http://pawws.com`. A service of Security APL, PAWWS offers a mix of free and fee-based services. It also houses the pages of several deep-discount brokerages.

Housed on the Web, three discount brokers offer the PAWWS portfolio accounting software: Net Investor/Howe Barnes, National Discount Brokers, and Jack White. These brokers are readily linked to the Security APL quote server and to a number of news and research and analysis sources, some of which are subscription-based.

The PAWWS portfolio software tracks current values of your investments, open orders and transaction histories at brokerages, dividends, splits and merger transactions as they affect your portfolio, and capital gains and losses. The portfolio also breaks down your holdings on a tax lot cost basis, which is really useful if you sell only part of your holding in some stock you bought at more than one price. You also can enter holdings you happen to own that you didn't buy through the three linked discounters.

PAWWS is a pretty straightforward service for beginners, but it also has many features that you can grow into over time if you're so inclined, such as fundamental and technical analysis and stock-screening pages. PAWWS also handles the whole range of securities. In fact, if you want to try your hand at inventing your own custom derivatives, you can create and price them here first for practice.

Summary

◆ If you have more than a few stocks, a portfolio manager can help you keep track of the winners, the losers, and your portfolio's overall value.

◆ You can use Web- or PC-based portfolio management programs. Perhaps the most convenient option is to use the portfolio management software provided by Web brokerages. This software automatically enters your transactions, saving you a lot of tedious data entry.

◆ Many portfolio management programs can't handle sticky stuff such as stock splits, automatic dividend reinvestments, or tax data. The better programs generate charts and graphs so that you can judge your position visually.

◆ Web-based portfolio managers tend to be pretty simple. You soon feel the need for more features.

◆ You can download some pretty nifty PC-based portfolio managers, but be aware that the objective with many of them is to sell you something (eventually).

◆ Some pretty neat shareware is available. In particular, Capital Gainz can handle all kinds of special situations that other portfolio manager programs don't let you deal with.

From Here

◆ For a look at one of the premier online brokerages, that offers excellent portfolio management capabilities, check out Chapter 21.

◆ Maybe they're not as sexy as stocks, but there's a place for bonds in every portfolio. Learn the basics — and get Internet help — in Chapter 22.

◆ Learn how to use the Internet to explore investment opportunities in U.S. Treasury bills, notes, and bonds (see Chapter 23).

Using e.Schwab and Schwab*NOW!*

In This Chapter

◆ Introducing e.Schwab Online Investing

◆ Getting stock quotes and managing your portfolio

◆ Trading on the Web with Schwab*NOW!*

Charles Schwab is the first major brokerage to enable investors to buy and sell stocks by means of the World Wide Web. But the firm didn't jump into Internet trading overnight, unlike some of its smaller competitors. Schwab wanted to make sure that the security on the Web was adequate to protect its customers. With the arrival of Netscape and secure servers, Schwab felt that the time was right to make its discount brokerage services available on the Internet.

Making services more widely available, and using technology to do it, is nothing new at Charles Schwab. In 1984, Schwab became the first major broker to offer online trading through its DOS-based Equalizer software. In 1989, Schwab introduced TeleBroker, its touch-tone telephone trading service. Schwab communication centers offer round-the-clock order entry nationwide. In 1995, the firm introduced e.Schwab Online Investing, a proprietary application (for Windows computers) that enables you to place orders online using Telnet connections. In the summer of 1996, Schwab unveiled its Web trading site, Schwab*NOW!*.

Schwab brings a unique approach to the use of technology in investing: You should be able to contact Schwab and perform transactions through more than one electronic medium. With an e.Schwab account, which qualifies you to trade stocks for $29.95 (up to the first 1,000 shares), you can take advantage of Schwab's Web trading when you're away from your home PC. If you're away from computers of any kind, you still can buy and sell using Schwab's touch-tone TeleBroker service. From Schwab's perspective, all accesses are the same: Any point of entry goes straight to Schwab's highly secure computer systems, which keep track of your transactions no matter how they're accessed. The next time you log on with e.Schwab's Windows software, called e.Schwab Online Investing, you see correct account balances. This software is currently available for Microsoft Windows systems, and a Macintosh version is due out by the end of 1996.

e.Schwab Online Investing is an excellent portfolio manager as well as an alternative means of buying and selling stocks. It's easy to use and, best of all, data downloading — the bugbear of most proprietary portfolio managers, as explained in Chapter 20 — is virtually automatic. This chapter fully describes Schwab's online services, including e.Schwab and the firm's new Web trading site, Schwab*NOW!*.

TIP

Establishing an e.Schwab account enables you to trade for $29.95 (up to 1,000 shares), no matter how you access the system (including the touch-tone TeleBroker service, the Telnet-based e.Schwab Online Investing, or the Web trading service).

What will it cost?

Schwab currently offers two types of online trading services:

e.Schwab. Requiring a minimum $5,000 brokerage account investment, e.Schwab stock trades cost $29.95 for up to 1,000 shares (and three cents per share for trades over 1,000 shares). Investors earn this low commission rate because they agree to service their account electronically versus through a live, registered representative. You also can buy and sell mutual funds, options, and fixed-income securities, also with deeply discounted commissions. You can set up IRA and child's custodial accounts in addition to your personal investment account. The funds you haven't used to buy securities earn interest in a money market account. If you're away from your PC, you can use Schwab's Web service or the TeleBroker service for a small added fee.

Standard Schwab brokerage account. This account requires a minimum $1,000 initial investment, but it does not qualify you for $29.95 trades. When you trade on the Web, you receive a 10 percent discount on Schwab's discount commissions.

Introducing e.Schwab Online Investing

e.Schwab makes use of Telnet connections as well as a well-designed Windows application, called e.Schwab Online Investing. This easy-to-use package makes the following simple to do:

◆ Trade stocks, options, mutual funds, corporate bonds, and Treasuries

◆ Monitor your transactions as they occur

◆ Access real-time quotes

◆ Receive company research reports and the latest business news

◆ Monitor your portfolio and check your account balances

◆ Transfer your investment transactions into personal finance software, such as Quicken

◆ Create graphs of your investment performance

◆ Take advantage of free stock divident reinvestments

◆ Receive substantial savings on Schwab commissions

A standard Schwab account offers you electronic trading at a 10 percent discount and gives you unlimited access to live representatives. Through this type of account, PC customers can access Schwab through StreetSmart desktop software or through the World Wide Web.

Entering trades online

Buying or selling a stock with e.Schwab Online Investing is simple. You fill out an on-screen form and submit the order via Telnet. Your order is then checked and sent to the appropriate exchange or market. When your order is filled, Schwab's central computers make note of your trade and automatically update your records. Normally, a market order is filled within minutes, and you see a confirmation almost immediately afterward.

Getting real-time quotes and reports

With the e.Schwab Online Investing real-time quotes service, you get 50 free real-time stock quotes. You get 50 more every time you trade a stock. In addition to stock quotes, you can get real-time quotes for dozens of major market indices.

You may wish to take advantage of an advanced feature: e.Schwab alerts, which inform you when a stock has reached a particular price or volume level. Suppose, for example, that you've decided that ABC, Inc. would be a good buy if the share price declined to $25. After you set up the alert, the software keeps checking the share price. If the share price reaches the level you've specified, you see an alert.

From e.Schwab Online Investing, you also can access a wide variety of fundamental data for each stock, including 52-week highs and lows, P/E ratio, and much more. With a few keystrokes, you can display history graphs, which show stock prices and volumes for the periods you specify.

Getting news and research

When you establish an e.Schwab account, you gain access to current reports, research services, earnings estimates, and more. Some of these third-party services charge separately for accessing this information, but you pay for only what you use.

Monitoring your portfolio

One of e.Schwab's most convenient features is the ease with which you can manage your stock portfolio. When you connect with Schwab's Telnet service, e.Schwab Online Investing automatically downloads your most recent account data. You then can do the following:

◆ **Review up-to-date account balances.** You see your cash balances, security market values, margin account information, options values, current dividends and interest, and the total value of your portfolio.

◆ **Check the status of your orders.** You find out precisely when your shares are traded.

◆ **Create graphs and customized portfolio reports.** You can graphically review your asset allocation as well as your realized gain/loss — and everything's automatically computed.

Using SchwabMail and Help libraries

Even if you don't have an Internet e-mail account, you can use e.Schwab Online Investing to send and receive e-mail to the e.Schwab customer service center if you have questions about your account.

The online Help libraries provide information and support, both for your investing strategy and for Schwab Online Investing.

Trading on the Web with Schwab*NOW!*

Schwab*NOW!* is Schwab's Web trading site. It's well-secured with the latest Netscape and Internet Explorer security measures. In addition, you need to get and supply a password to gain access to the site. If you want to look at Schwab*NOW!*, you can access the demo at the following URL:
`http://www.schwab.com/Trading/demo/ html/mainmenu.html`.

Schwab*NOW!* isn't as full-featured as some Web-based trading services, but only if you look at the service in a narrow way. Considering that the Web-based service integrates smoothly with e.Schwab Online Investing, an excellent portfolio manager, and with regular Schwab accounts, this service is actually one of the most feature-packed that you find anywhere on the Internet. You should think of the Web service as just one of three ways you can access your e.Schwab account (the other two are the touch-tone TeleBroker service and the Telnet-based e.Schwab Online Investing). When you log on with e.Schwab Online Investing, Schwab's computers automatically download all your Web transactions, so you don't have to fuss with downloading and posting data manually.

Trading on the Web

With Schwab*NOW!*, you can place orders to buy and sell stocks, mutual funds, and options. You also can tell Schwab to sell stocks short, switch mutual funds, and choose additional option trading services. In Figure 21-1, you see a demonstration of Schwab*NOW!'s* trading menu.

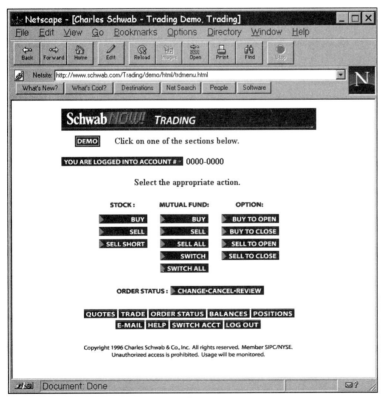

Figure 21-1: The Schwab*NOW!* trading menu.

Take a closer look at how Web trading works. To buy a stock, click on Buy on the Trading menu. You see a page such as the demo Stock:Buy page, shown in Figure 21-2. As you can see from examining the figure, Schwab*NOW!* gives you plenty of choices for controlling the purchase, including limit and stop prices. These choices allow you to specify the price range you're willing to pay or accept in a sale. (Normally, this takes just a few seconds, but trading may be delayed on exceptionally heavy days or for certain stocks or kinds of orders.)

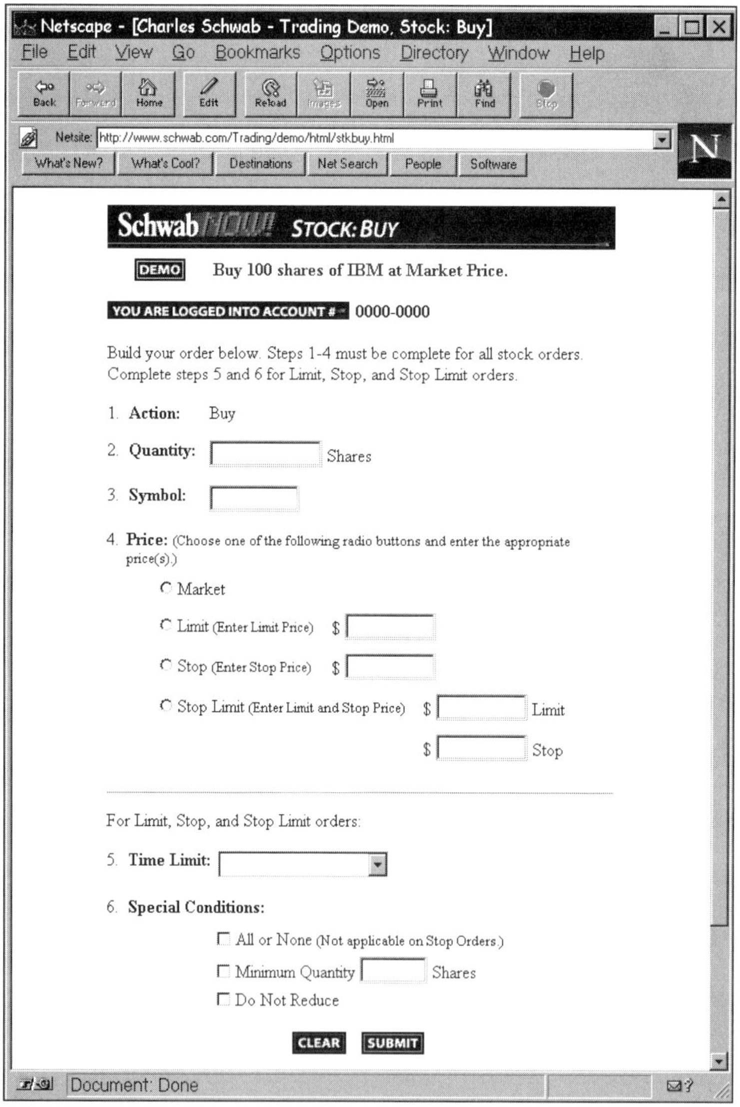

Figure 21-2: Buying a stock on the Web (Schwab*NOW!*).

After you submit your buy or sell order, you can check your order status.

Getting stock quotes

After you establish your e.Schwab account, you can get free real-time stock quotes from Schwab*NOW!*. Each quote comes with a wealth of data, including price dynamics, P/E ratio, current yield, and much more. Figure 21-3 illustrates the in-depth information you receive from Schwab*NOW!'s* real-time quotes.

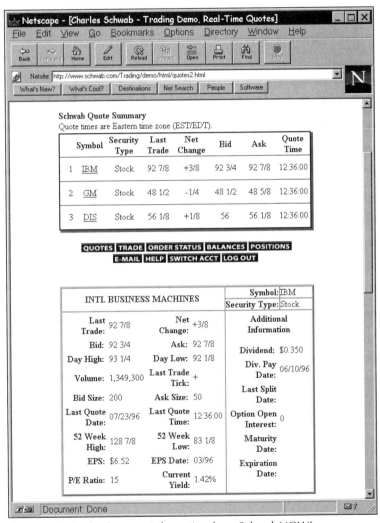

Figure 21-3: In-depth quote information from Schwab*NOW!*

Checking your account balance

You can check your account balance at any time (see Figure 21-4). You see all the data for your Schwab account, including the cash balance, margin account equity, option account, security market values, margin funds available, and dividends/interest. To see how your individual investments are doing, you can check the Positions page, shown in Figure 21-5, which shows you the latest, up-to-the-minute value of your account.

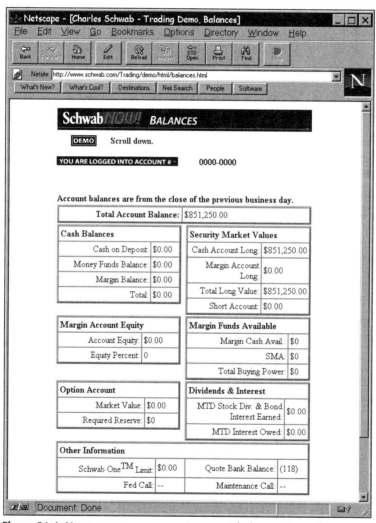

Figure 21-4: You can see your current account balance at any time.

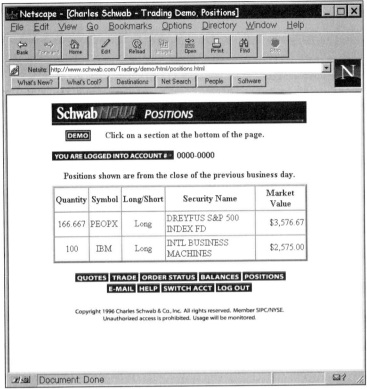

Figure 21-5: The Positions page enables you to see at a glance how your investments are doing.

Contacting Schwab

For more information concerning Schwab's online and Web trading services, you can contact Schwab as follows:

◆ Access SchwabNOW! at `http://www.schwab.com`

◆ Call 1-800-435-4000

Schwab has a strong commitment to providing increased value to customers by continuously improving the functionality and features of its brokerage offerings. Check the Schwab Web site often for new services and features.

Summary

◆ Internet trading services, e.Schwab Online Investing and Schwab*NOW!*, combine to give you the best of both worlds: An excellent, PC-based portfolio manager as well as Web trading with automatic account updating.

◆ e.Schwab Online Investing requires an initial investment of $5,000, but you can buy and sell stocks for $29.95 (up to 1,000 shares). With a Schwab brokerage account, you place only $1,000 in your brokerage account. If you trade on the Web or by phone using TeleBroker, you receive a 10 percent discount from Schwab's discount commissions.

◆ An excellent portfolio manager, e.Schwab Online Investing enables you to buy and sell stocks, options, mutual funds, and corporate bonds via highly secure Telnet connections. You can create graphs of your investment performance.

◆ With Schwab's Web trading service, Schwab*NOW!*, you can buy and sell stocks, mutual funds, and options on the Web. If you establish an e.Schwab account, your trades cost you only $29.95 (up to 1,000 shares).

◆ e.Schwab Online Investing also can be used with Schwab*NOW!*, the Web trading service. You get $29.95 trades plus excellent portfolio management. When you're away from your home PC, you can trade on the Web or use the touch-tone TeleBroker service, the latter at an additional fee. When you're back home, log on with e.Schwab Online investing to download all your latest account information, including Web and phone trades and check out your current positions.

VI
PART

Researching and Buying Bonds and Treasuries on the Internet

Introducing Bonds

In This Chapter

◆ Why invest in bonds?
◆ Bond basics
◆ Classifying bonds

Bonds — publicly traded IOUs of corporations, governments, and other organizations — conjure up images of old fuddy-duddies sitting around clipping coupons. But bonds may have a place among your other investments. What's more, the Internet has plenty to offer the would-be investor in the various types of bonds available, including corporate bonds, municipal bonds, and bond funds.

This chapter introduces bonds, pointing you to some useful information resources concerning bonds that you can find on the Net. In Chapter 23, you see how the Internet is valuable if you choose to invest in U.S. Treasury bills, notes, and bonds, as well as U.S. Savings Bonds (which have their merits, as you'll see).

Why Invest in Bonds?

Why should you want to bother with such staid investments, especially when stocks are so much more fun and, much of the time, perform much better? For one thing, bonds really have their place. At the start of 1995, the stock and bond markets both had been languishing for about a year. Interest rates on bonds were as high as they'd been for three years. Stocks weren't showing many signs of improving.

Investors then had a choice of either putting new money in stocks or buying relatively high-yielding bonds. Treasury notes — very safe government debt securities — were paying better than seven- and-a-half percent interest. For investors who were either burned by stocks the year before or needed to get all their money back plus interest in a few years for some project, these notes were a good deal.

On the other hand, maybe you get no kicks from high-flying stocks. Perhaps for you, a bigger attraction is the steady income that bonds pay out over a period of years, after which you get back your *principal* — the money you first put into the investment. To you, Treasury securities seem just fine. The federal government has always paid, after all.

Even if you think bonds are a total bore or just too expensive, it's good to know a few things about them. Reason: You probably have invested in some bonds indirectly. They may be in that balanced mutual fund you have shares in. Do you have an insurance policy or two? Insurance companies are some of the biggest holders of bonds of all kinds. Insurance companies need income to pay claims, which occur on a regular basis. Also, regulators require insurance companies to have a certain percent of their portfolios invested in fixed-income securities of a certain quality.

Educate yourself fast with the help of the American Association of Individual Investor's Bonds page (`http://wetworth.galt.com/www/home/planning/aaii/bonds/bondindex.html`). You find links here to more than a dozen in-depth articles on bonds, covering topics such as bond basics, assessing bond risk, buying Treasury bonds without a broker, and much more. Figure 22-1 lists the available articles.

Bond Basics

Unlike stocks, which give you a share in a firm's equity, bonds don't give you ownership interest in the issuer. Instead, you become a *creditor* — a debt-holder. You have a claim, but no deed. The issuer pays you interest on its debt, usually every six months, although sometimes as often as monthly. With few exceptions, you get back your invested funds — your principal — at the end of the loan term. If you need your principal back before the end of the term, you can sell the bond; it's negotiable.

Many investors buy and hold bonds for their entire *term*, or interest-paying period, but some people trade bonds, too. Most bonds pay interest at fixed rates, so when interest rates rise and fall, the rates paid on bonds may be higher or lower than those going market rates. These differences cause the bonds' prices to rise and fall in their specific markets.

Rule number one of bond trading: Bond prices move in the direction opposite that of market interest rates. When interest rates rise, bond prices fall, and vice versa.

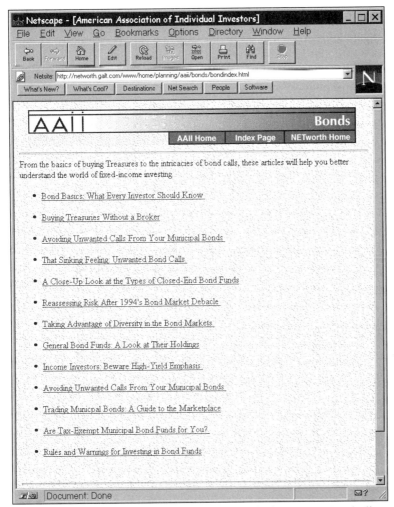

Figure 22-1: The American Association of Individual Investor's Bond offers more than a dozen useful introductory articles on bonds.

Newscasters have great fun with bond traders' views on trends such as employment, industrial production, and economic growth. High job gains, production, and growth tend to push up inflation (and then interest rates), which, in the hard-headed world of bond traders, means bond prices will fall. Good news for Main Street is bad news on Wall Street in this case.

Bond prices don't have nearly the same degree of ups and downs — volatility — that many stock prices have. Bond price fluctuations are limited because the bonds always (well, nearly always) pay back the principal in the end and interest in the meantime. However, bond prices do move enough for traders to make very good profits, and, generally, the longer the bond's term, the longer the period over which its price can change and less certainty and more risk can be connected to all events that may occur in that time. So, some bonds can and do have a big draw for aggressive and speculative investors.

Bond Sites on the Net

Bonds aren't as well represented on the Internet as mutual funds and stocks, but you'll still find some very useful information concerning bonds.

Bonds Online (http://www.bondsonline.com/). This is an excellent collection of information (links and articles) concerning bonds of all types, including municipal bonds, corporate bonds, bond funds, brokers, and Treasuries.

Bond Terms (http://lebenthal.com:80/bond_terms.html). An excellent glossary of the often-confusing terminology of bonds and related securites.

Invest-O-Rama Bonds Page (http://www.investorama.com/bonds.shtml). Links to all kinds of Web sites concerning bonds.

Making Sense Out of Bonds and Bond Funds (http://www.icmarc.org/Invest/article/bonds/bonds.html). Published by ICMA Retirement Association, this is a readable series of essays on the basics and risks of bonds.

The Syndicate's Bond Page (http://www.moneypages.com/syndicate/bonds/index.html). A few very good articles, including "The Anatomy of a Bond Swap," "Buying at a Treasury Auction," and "Moody's Bond Ratings Defined."

Public Securities Association (http://www.psa.com). PSA is the principal bond market trade association in the U.S. and represents securities firms (including banks and brokerages) that underwrite and sell fixed-income securities. Highlights of this excellent site include fast-breaking bond market news and statistical tables (including default rates in the municipal bond market).

Understanding High-Yield Junk Bonds (http://www.troweprice.com/mutual/insights/junkbond.html). A full explanation of these often-risky (but high-yielding) investments.

Classifying Bonds

Bonds are classified by type of issuer when they're bought and sold. Separate markets exist for U.S. Treasury securities, corporate bonds, municipal bonds, government agency bonds, and mortgage securities. These bonds have different risks and thus different interest rates attached to them.

Government bonds

Far and away, the biggest force in the bond market is — you guessed it — the biggest debtor, the U.S. government. With trillions of dollars of debt outstanding, the government also has a big effect on all interest rates. The government's debt is considered extremely safe because it has never defaulted. This may not quite jibe with what you read about ballooning government debt. But as it comes due, the government has always paid up, so it's entitled to pay you relatively low rates on its debt.

KEY TERM

However, sometimes, as in early 1995, the general level of interest rates is high enough to make Treasury securities (colloquially called *Treasuries*) look pretty good to investors. Treasury securities have a broad range of terms, from three months to 30 years. Treasury securities are auctioned off to the public on regular schedules that you can find on the Web pages of the Federal Reserve Bank in your area. Links to the regional Feds are in Bonds Online (`http://www.bondsonline.com`), along with research, mutual fund, and broker links.

The Treasury advantage

If you need the money, Treasury securities are easy to sell off before the end of their terms. Any brokerage will give you the market price for them for a small charge.

Treasuries come in various minimum denominations — $5,000 for two-year notes, $1,000 for five-years, $10,000 for bills (with maturities under one year). Some Treasuries are small enough for small investors; others are not. Larger Treasuries are sometimes useful for holding cash you may need for a large purchase in a few months. They're easier to cash in than bank certificates of deposit and have no penalties. Because Treasuries are considered so safe, there's not that much need to worry about risk from holding just one undiversified investment.

Interest from U.S. government securities is exempt from state and local income tax but not from federal income tax, however. *Capital gains* — profits from the sale of bonds — are subject to all taxes, and this applies to capital gains from all types of *tax-exempts*.

Agency bonds

KEY TERM

Another category of fairly safe bond investments is so-called government agency securities, called *agency bonds*. In this group are debts of federal agencies such as the Federal Housing Administration and Tennessee Valley Authority. Also included are organizations originally set up by the federal government that now are privately run and administered, such as the mortgage organizations Ginnie Mae (the Government National Mortgage Association) and Freddie Mac (the Federal Home Loan Mortgage Corp.).

Both types of agency issuers have no direct recourse to the U.S. Treasury to pay back debt they sell to investors, but they do have federal guarantees for it. The interest rates that the agencies pay on their bonds are somewhat higher than those on Treasuries, but their risk is not that much higher. Agency bonds' payment records are just as clean. Many agency bonds also are state and local tax-exempt (but they're not federal tax-exempt).

With few exceptions, agencies come in big minimum denominations: $10,000 to $25,000, in most cases. This, and the fact that a variety of agencies are available, has spurred mutual funds managers to put them in smaller packages that are easier for smaller investors to cope with.

Municipal bonds

KEY TERM

Municipal bonds — bonds issued by local and state agencies — have received much notoriety over the past two years because of a record-sized default by one issuer — Orange County, California. This default is hardly the only one on a municipal issue. Defaults are not that common, although they have increased substantially in recent years, according to statistics from the Public Securities Association trade group (`http://www.psa.com`). The municipal finance market is extremely large — over $300 billion a year — and is growing as the federal government passes more and more costs on to localities.

Some municipal issues are very safe; others are less so. Much of this safety depends on the local economy that's supporting the repayments, the size of the project being financed, whether the project will fly if its success is the key factor in supporting the payments, and what other bonds have to be repaid from the same revenue base.

Munis (as municipal bonds are often called) do have several strong points for investors, however. One is that they are federal tax-exempt, and many also have state and local tax-exemptions.

Municipal bonds on the Internet

Bloomberg Personal National Muni Bond Yields (http://www.bloomberg.com/markets/psamuni.html). Here's a quick look at current national municipal bond yields, brought to the Net by the Public Securities Association (PSA).

Municipal Resource Center (http://www.municipal.com). A service of R.R. Donnelley Financial, this site presents itself as the headquarters on the Net for information concerning municipal bonds. A key feature: A searchable Municipal Securities Disclosure Archive (MSDA), which contains official statements, annual financial information, and material event notices concerning municipal bonds, as required by the Securities and Exchange Commission (SEC). (Material events are events that investors should be told about because they may affect funds that go into bondholders' payments of interest and capital.) Adobe Acrobat is required to read the reports, but you can download this program for free from this site.

Thompson MarketEdge Municipal Bond Center (http://www.marketedge.com). This subscription service offers extensive municipal bonds news and research reports. You'll also find an introduction to municipal bonds for beginners.

Still, horror stories about munis abound. An interesting collection of these stories can be found in Muni Bond Scandals (http://www.lissack.com), compiled by Michael R. Lissack, municipal finance whistleblower and former Paine Webber investment banker (see Figure 22-2). Before buying a municipal issue, you should check if it has guarantees. *Guarantees* are insurance policies bought by the bond issuer to assure investors that the principal and interest will be paid. If the issuer defaults, the insurance pays. Guarantees take much of the risk out of these investments. Then the issuer can sell them with somewhat lower interest payments attached.

Figure 22-2: Municipal Bond Scandals: the Web site.

Understanding bond ratings

Bond insurers don't guarantee anything for money. They want the issue to have at least an *investment grade* rating, and this grade comes from financial analysts at rating agencies, which are independent firms that rate issuers' debt for fees.

The four big rating agencies — Standard & Poor's, Moody's, Fitch, and Duff & Phelps — all use similar grading schemes. Triple A is for the best quality debt. Triple

B is the lowest investment grade — the issuer is judged to have enough capacity to pay principal and interest but may not have enough resources in an economic slump. Double B and B issues are considered speculative. Triple C through single D debt is either in danger of default or actually in default and/or arrears. (Single D is as bad as it gets.) These investment grades are especially important for some institutional investors such as insurance companies, which often are limited by regulations to buying investment or better grade bonds.

These ratings are given at the time the bonds are issued. They take into account factors that determine if the issuer can pay investors. One factor is earning power and stability. Others are cash generation and management, how much debt the company owes and when it's due, and coverage — how extensive the firm's financial resources will be after servicing both existing and new debt.

Unlike stock analysis, most of which takes place after stocks start trading, most bond analysis comes before the issue. In fact, the rating plays a big part in the yield investors can get from bonds. Issuers set rates on bonds as low as possible given the rating they get. Then, as market interest rates change, the bond price may rise and fall, too.

Municipal bond funds

The municipal bond market is complex and diverse, with a wide range of risks. The big range of sizes, states, underlying projects, and terms of bonds makes one of the best cases for putting bonds in mutual funds to spread their risks and rewards around. Many bonds are packaged by state in order to give residents the triple tax-exempt edge when possible, which can be a big plus. If you're in a 30 percent tax bracket, bonds packaged by state can add the equivalent of a couple of percentage points to a four or five percent tax-free interest rate.

Munis are especially useful if you live in a state with high income taxes, such as New York or California. They're much less helpful in low tax states such as Florida, or if you pay a low federal income tax rate.

Corporate bonds

Corporate bonds — bonds issued by firms — are the biggest private-sector part of the fixed-income market. Because they have neither the government nor insurance behind them, corporate bonds are riskier. In consequence, they have to pay higher rates to get investors' money. But it's a complex picture. Corporate bonds are extremely varied, ranging from highly rated blue-chip industrial bonds to speculative high-yield or junk bonds. They're diverse not only in ratings but also in their term lengths, collateral (from unsecured to first-mortgage backed), convertibility to stock, and seniority, which is the bond's position in the company's payback schedule.

Many events and factors can make corporate bonds more challenging to follow. These circumstances can increase or reduce their payoffs to investors. For one thing, corporate issuers are more changeable than governments — companies, after all, can and do go out of business, but we hope the government doesn't. Their credit ratings change more because their circumstances change more. Corporate issuers also want and need more flexibility in their financing, so they may include in bond agreements a clause that lets them *call* a bond — redeem it before maturity for a premium. Also, corporations are more endangered than governments by periods of economic weakness or tight credit, which can hurt their ability to make payments.

Corporate bond funds

Corporate bonds are favorites of institutions rather than individual investors for several reasons. One reason is their usually long (though varied) terms. These terms are often in the 25 to 40 year range, making them not too suitable even for investors who want to buy and hold. You have to be pretty young to hold onto a 40-year issue to maturity!

Also, corporate bonds, being issues of just one company, are about as undiversified as you can get. Insurance companies and pension funds have the hundreds of millions of dollars required to have a diverse portfolio of bonds.

But for all these reasons, investors can get more bang for their buck from bond funds that include corporate bonds than they will from individual bonds. The American Association of Individual Investors has a helpful primer on Rules and Warnings for Investing in Bond Funds (`http://networth.galt.com/www/home/planning/aaii/bonds/warnfund.html`) that is well worth your while to examine before exploring bond funds further.

Corporate bond funds come in a range of risk profiles for conservative and aggressive investors and those in between. From one of the newsletters of mutual fund research company Morningstar, Inc., Bonds Online has picked up an item discussing risks and returns on different kinds of bond funds, which you can find at `http://www.bondsonline.com/page1.htm`. The article makes an interesting comparison between corporate and government bond funds. It finds that government bond funds are costlier, no less risky, and weaker performing over time.

Another reason why you want the increased diversity a fund provides is that different kinds of risk can be offset by putting bonds together in a fund. High-yield bonds have one kind of risk: the risk that you won't get paid. Low-yield bonds have another: the risk that higher market interest rates will make their prices drop.

If all else is equal, prices of bonds that pay higher and lower *coupon rates* (stated rates of interest) act differently when market interest rates change. The bonds with low coupons tend to fall more in price when rates rise, and vice versa, than the bonds with bigger coupon rates. Basically, the higher stated rates better support the bond's price.

The AAII page on bond investing gives you a table that shows this relationship (`http://networth.galt.com/www/home/planning/aaii/bonds/basics.html`).

Zero coupon bonds

Zero coupon bonds don't pay regular periodic interest. Instead, these bonds are sold at a deep discount to their face value — for example, a $300 discount to a $1,000 face value. The $1,000 is both the principal and interest that are returned at maturity.

Zeroes have their pluses and minuses. On the positive side, you don't have to worry about how to reinvest your interest payments over time: They're reinvested in the zero for you. But if market interest rates rise over this bond's term, you're locked into the stated rate on the zero. Again, if market rates rise, the price of the zero falls, unless you hold it to maturity. On the other hand, if market rates fall, you'll do well with the zero.

Another tricky thing about zeroes is taxes. You have to report interest earned on them each year, even though it's paid out only at maturity, which makes zeroes most useful for IRAs, where you won't have to worry about the taxes until years later.

Pricing Bonds

How do you find bond prices? On the Web, here are a few places to try. For Treasuries, free end-of-day prices come from the New York Federal Reserve Bank, provided either directly (`http://www.ny.frb.org/pihome/mktrates/qsheet.shtml`) or by the University of Michigan (`gopher://una.hh.lib.umich.edu/00/ebb/monetary/quotes.txt`). The GovPX pricing service (`http://www.panix.com/ ~govpx`) also gets you end-of-day prices free, as well as real-time prices by subscription.

For municipal securities, you really don't have a central source of publicly quoted prices. In fact, the quotes that are available appear as *yields* — effective interest rate quotes. The Public Securities Association trade group puts together a daily composite of prices for triple A, tax-exempt revenue bonds of various maturities. These illustrative prices are expressed as yields. This pricing service, shown in Figure 22-3, is carried by Bloomberg Business News (`http://www.bloomberg.com/markets/psamuni.html`).

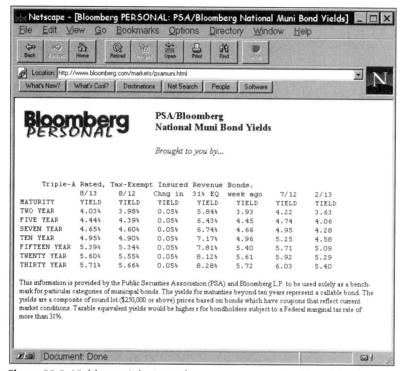

Figure 22-3: Yields on triple-A rated, tax-exempt municipal bond funds.

Corporate bonds are mostly registered securities, just as stocks are. Also like stocks, corporate bonds can be traded on exchanges or over the counter — on traders' common electronic bulletin board system. You can find a number of corporate bonds priced on some, although not all, quote servers. PC Quote (http://www.pcquote.com) and Quote.com (http://www.quote.com), for instance, give you bond quotes and help you look up ticker symbols. Delayed prices are free on both of these servers.

Buying and Selling Bonds

Buying and selling different kinds of bonds is a varied experience. Treasury securities are nearly the only kind of publicly traded securities that you can buy directly, and you can buy only when they're first auctioned off. You can buy Treasuries through the so-called Treasury Direct system, which is the subject of Chapter 23.

KEY TERM

After Treasuries are auctioned off in what's known as the *primary market* (the first-offered market), they can be bought and sold in the *secondary market* (the resale market) before they mature. Here, they're traded through brokerages for a commission, although only a small one because Treasuries are a big and liquid market.

Thin trading

Markets for other kinds of bonds are quite different. For corporates and munis, the big problem is lack of active trading. For example, if there's not much action in a corporate bond, discount brokers may not be able to give you much of a price break on commissions because their costs in doing this business will be high. If trading is so thin, getting a price is that much harder, and it's harder still for online brokers to track the price, get you a quote on the screen, and enter your order based on that quote. Many online brokers don't even provide bond price quotes.

Thin trading doesn't mean that you should never trade individual bonds. But be aware that if you or your broker have a hard time finding prices for individual bonds, they're that much harder to trade in and out of in a short time. You could be stuck with the bonds if their prices drop and you have to sell them for some reason.

Which online brokers deal with bonds? Jack White (`http://pawws.secapl.com/jwc`) handles Treasuries, corporates, and munis. National Discount Brokers (`http://pawws.secapl.com/ndb`) and Quick & Reilly deal with corporates. Lombard says it will be set up for bonds soon and also will provide some kind of bond calculator. This feature will be a great help because there doesn't seem to be a free bond calculator on the Web now.

Muni brokers

Some corporate bonds and all munis are bought and sold on a kind of brokers' and dealers' electronic bulletin board system. Munis especially are a distinct kind of market. They're not listed and regulated like corporate bonds. Dealers in munis take in a wider variety of organizations, including commercial banks. Brokers get muni prices from the banks via computer and mark them up to you based on the price they negotiate with the dealer.

Some brokers specialize in munis. They're usually much more knowledgeable than most full-service brokers about which munis are available and what they should cost. Also with munis, full-service brokers may not be any more costly to deal with than discount brokers who have little experience with these bonds. Some full-service brokers also may be able to get into bigger and better muni deals that elude smaller brokers.

If you're really bent on getting into the market for individual muni issues, check out the American Association of Individual Investors page (`http://networth.galt.com/www/home/planning/aaii/bonds/munistra.html`). Bonds Online (`http://www.bondsonline.com`) is trying to collect a national listing of muni brokers as well as a calendar of upcoming issues, both by state. This list site doesn't run smoothly yet, but check back if you're interested.

Summary

- ◆ Investors buy bonds for short-term investments, for capital preservation, or for current income.

- ◆ Unlike stocks, bonds don't give you an equity share. When you buy a bond, you become a creditor.

- ◆ Bonds pay a fixed interest rate, called the *coupon rate*. When interest rates rise and fall, the rates paid on bonds already issued may be higher or lower than the going interest rates. When this happens, bond prices rise or fall. Bond prices go up when interest rates fall, but bond prices go down when interest rates rise.

- ◆ Government bonds have little risk because they're backed by the full faith and credit of the U.S. government. (However, they're not insured.) Treasury bills, notes, and bonds pay fair rates, are easy to sell, and have certain tax advantages. Agency bonds are issued by U.S. federal government agencies and are also regarded as low-risk investments.

- ◆ Municipal bonds, issued by local, regional, and state governments, can be risky, but they are exempt from federal taxes, and some are exempt from local or state taxes. Municipal bond funds spread the risk around and enable you to take advantage of the fund company's extensive research and familiarity with the market.

- ◆ Corporate bonds are issued by private firms and vary widely in risk. For individual investors, corporate bond funds make good sense because they give you increased diversity.

- ◆ Zero coupon bonds don't pay regular periodic interest. Instead, you buy the bond at a discount rate and receive the face value at maturity.

- ◆ If you're not planning to hold a bond until maturity, you should know that many bonds — with the exception of Treasuries — aren't as easy to sell as stocks. This is another good reason to consider investing in a municipal or corporate bond fund rather than buying these securities directly.

From Here

- ◆ In the next chapter, learn about opportunities for investing in popular U.S. Treasury bills, bond, and notes, which are guaranteed by the full faith and credit of the U.S. government.

- ◆ Start exploring the rich personal finance resources of the Net in Chapter 24, "Finding Personal Finance Resources on the Net."

Investing in Treasury Bills, Notes, and Bonds

23

In the long term, stocks reward investors with the best returns. However, this may not be true in the short or medium term — one to five years. While you're waiting for the law of averages to come around to your side with stocks, it often makes sense to put some of your savings in something reliable, such as U.S. Treasury bills, notes and/or bonds.

Treasuries' yields may not seem like much compared to the double-digit rates of return that stocks average. But these yields are constant, year after year (or month after month, depending on the government security you choose).

What's more, you don't have to pay any transaction costs or commissions for Treasuries. You can buy them directly from the government.

Understanding and Buying Treasuries

KEY TERM

What are *Treasury bills, notes,* and *bonds*? Respectively, they're short-term (a year or less), mid-term (two- to 10-years) and long-term (more than 10 years) IOUs from the federal government. Their prices, and thus their rates, are set by public auctions held regularly.

The short-term bills come in $10,000 minimum denominations, with increments of $1,000 after that. Three- and six-month bills are sold weekly, 12-month bills monthly. The two- and five-year notes are auctioned at the end of each month. Three- and 10-year notes go on sale four times a year: on the 15th of February, May, August, and November. Thirty-year bonds are auctioned twice a year, on February 15 and August 15. Two- and three-year notes have $5,000 minimums with $1,000 increments. Treasuries with maturities of five years and over cost $1,000.

As you may expect, Treasuries with shorter maturities have the lowest interest rates and long-term Treasuries have the highest. There doesn't seem to be that much difference in these rates. Currently, there's around a one percentage point difference between the shortest and longest term Treasuries, but the spread is bigger than you may first think because Treasury rates are so low to begin with. The 30-year bonds currently have rates just over six percent, while the three-month bills are just above five percent. Both rates have come down somewhat in the past six months, the short-term Treasuries a bit more than the long-term ones.

Treasuries on the Net

The Economeister (http://www.economeister.com). News service with emphasis on currencies and Treasuries.

Treasury Direct: A Program For Individual Investors to Buy Treasury Securities (http://www.bonds-online.com/articles.treasur.htm). Good introduction to the Federal Reserve's Treasury Direct program.

U.S. Department of the Treasury home page (http://www.ustreas.gov/Welcome.html). Links to lots of information, including T-bill, note, and bond auction results. If your humor turns to the dark side, don't miss the Seized Property Auctions; you find links to IRS-seized properties as well as to those seized by U.S. customs, the United States Secret Service, and the Bureau of Alcohol, Tobacco, and Firearms.

Buying Treasuries

You don't really have to go to an auction to buy Treasuries. The process involves filling out a form and mailing it to the Federal Reserve Bank in your area. It's simple to do yourself.

The forms and instructions can be printed from the Web page (called Treasury Direct) of the Federal Reserve Bank of New York (`http://www.ny.frb.org/ pihome/treasdir`). Figure 23-1 shows Treasury Direct's T-bill form.

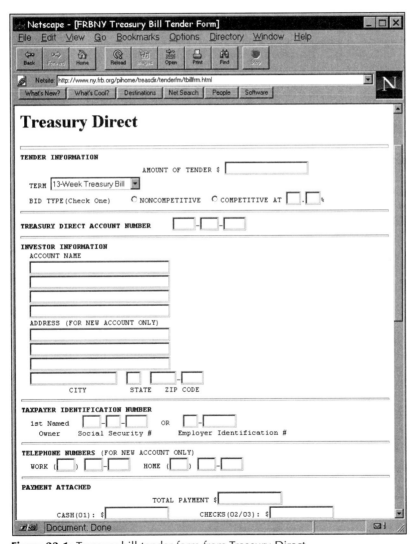

Figure 23-1: Treasury bill tender form from Treasury Direct.

For now, Treasury Direct doesn't enable you to place orders — actually bids — on the Net. You do get an updated auction calendar for various Treasury issues, forms for placing bill and longer-term issue bids, instructions for completing the forms, and the results of recent auctions, which include the rate you receive on the notes or bills you buy. The government hasn't yet worked out the security and payment systems needed for electronic bidding in the $3 trillion market.

Competitive and noncompetitive bids

As previously noted, you don't just go out and buy a Treasury bill, note, or bond: You send in a bid. Institutional investors always put in *competitive bids*. The Treasury auctions off its debt at the highest price it can get. Competitive bidders express their bid as an interest rate on their bid forms. These investors are trying for a tradeoff: They want a good yield, but they also don't want to be passed over in the bidding.

How low the yield will go in the bidding depends on a couple factors. One is how much money the government is trying to raise at once. Another is how high current market interest rates are.

As an individual investor in Treasury Direct, you have a choice. You can enter a competitive bid, specifying on your form the interest rate at which you'll buy Treasuries. In this case, you risk not getting the securities being auctioned off because the rate you specified is too high and the whole issue was bought at lower rates.

You also can enter a *noncompetitive bid*. The government usually accepts all these bids, which give you the weighted average yield of the competitive bids that were accepted in the auction. This way, you always get the Treasuries you want. If you don't specify a bid rate, the Treasury assumes that your bid is noncompetitive.

The rate is just one piece of information about the bid — or *tender*, as it's called — that the Treasury form requires. You also have to fill in the total amount of these securities that you want to buy and the term of the securities that you want — six months, one year, five years, and so on.

Creating your Treasury Direct account

You also have to fill in information about yourself because, when you bid, you'll either set up a Treasury Direct account or put more funds in an existing account. Enter the name that you want to appear as the owner of the account, as well as a mailing address for notifications. Fill in the Social Security number or tax ID number for the person or organization that appears first on the account. Minors and people whose accounts are held in trust must have Social Security numbers if they are listed first on the Treasury account.

For new accounts, you must fill in a phone number in case of a question or problem with the tender, which is quite possible the first time.

Including payment

You also have to include payment for the Treasury. Send the face amount of the security that you're trying to buy. Bills must be paid for by certified or bank checks. Notes and bonds, which cost less, can be paid for with ordinary personal checks. Make out checks to the local Federal Reserve Bank.

Looking for the nearest Fed branch? Bonds Online (`http://www.bonds-online. com/articles/treasur.htm`) has a phone directory for the 25 Fed banks and branches (`http://www.bonds-online.com/articles/treasur.htm`).

Treasuries also can be paid for with checks from the Treasury itself, such as your annual tax refund check.

Where does the interest go?

Treasury securities are issued in book-entry form through Treasury Direct, which means that you don't get any kind of certificate for them. What you do get is a Treasury Direct Statement of Account confirming that the securities you bid on were deposited in your account.

The Treasury then makes electronic payments to the account number you designate on your bid. This account can be at a bank, savings and loan, credit union, brokerage, or other investment company. The Treasury needs that bank or other institution's nine-digit routing number for electronic funds transfer.

With Treasury notes and bonds, you get paid twice a year. If you buy bills, you buy at a discount — face value less interest at the rate set at the auction. When the bills mature, the face value is paid out to your account.

When you open a Treasury Direct account, you also need to state your bank's name, its routing number, the name on the account, its number, and the kind of account (checking or savings, for example). You also have to state whether you're subject to backup withholding taxes, which you won't be, unless you've been caught for not reporting all your income in past years.

Mailing your tender

That's all there is for Treasury Direct. Simple? Sign your check and print or type **Tender for Treasury Securities** at the bottom of the envelope containing the bid.

If you mail your bid, it must be postmarked by midnight the day before the auction and must arrive at your local Federal Reserve Bank by the date on which the securities are actually issued — about three days later. If bids for three- and six-month bills miss the deadline, they're held for the next auction. Other late bids get returned to you.

You can go to the nearest Federal Reserve Bank to bid in person, too. These live bids must be in by noon on the day of the auction. The local Feds (Federal Reserve Banks) keep bankers' hours. They're open Monday through Friday, except holidays, from 9 a.m. to 3 p.m.

Getting Treasury auction results

Although the Treasury doesn't hold its auctions on the Web, the results get posted on it right away. Check for the results at the New York Federal Reserve Bank site (http://www.ny.frb.org). The San Francisco Fed (http://www.frbsf.org) will add this feature soon.

San Francisco also has plans for adding Treasury account-management software, auction graphs, and spreadsheets in the next few months. The Philadelphia Fed (http://www.libertynet.org/~fedresrv/fedpage.html) now has an auction calendar and instructions for sending direct tenders. The Chicago Fed has an auction calendar for T-bills only (http://www.frbchi.org).

When Treasuries Mature

Treasury bills, notes, and bonds stay in your account until they mature. The Federal Reserve pays interest into the bank or other account that you named. When your Treasuries mature, you can either redeem them — get cash for them — or reinvest them with the government.

If you don't instruct otherwise, the Fed pays the face amount of the Treasury into your named account at maturity.

Reinvesting your Treasuries

To reinvest your Treasury bill, you have to fill out a simple form from the Treasury. Reinvestment Request for Bills is Form PD 5181. For notes and bonds, you need Form PD 5281. You get these forms automatically from your local Federal Reserve Bank 45 to 60 days before your Treasury matures.

For bills, you not only can specify reinvestment of your proceeds for a certain term and amount of new bills but also have proceeds automatically reinvested a number of times in subsequent issues of bills as yours come due. For notes and bonds, you can request only one reinvestment — in the term and amount you want — at a time. Both reinvestment forms are simple. You just check off what you want to do and mail in the form.

Selling before maturity

If you want to sell a Treasury before maturity, and it's in a Treasury Direct account, you have to transfer the Treasury out of Treasury Direct into another account such as your brokerage account, for example.

To transfer your Treasury, either you or your broker should get Treasury Form 5179. Your broker then can sell the Treasury, for which he or she will charge you a small fee, usually about $35 at discount brokers.

Understanding and Buying U.S. Savings Bonds

Although the Treasury has a giant and well-oiled system for selling securities, it has a harder time with its old, stodgy U.S. Savings Bonds, so it's no surprise that the Treasury is making plans to sell savings bonds on the Internet. Now, the Treasury has to sell them either at the Federal Reserve Banks — of which there aren't many — or at banks, for whom there's not enough profit in selling savings bonds. For now, the Treasury plans to start using the Bureau of Public Debt's Web site for these sales.

You may not think much of U.S. Savings Bonds, but someone does. About 55 million people hold them, and around $15 million worth of savings bonds are sold each year. That's not a huge amount, but it's all from small savers. Institutions certainly don't buy them.

The rates paid on new savings bonds — those issued in the past year, at least — pay 85 percent of the past year's average six-month Treasury bill rate for the its first five years. After that, the same formula is applied to the rate on the five-year Treasury note.

What's good about savings bonds

Savings bonds don't pay high rates, but they do have a few pluses. You can invest in savings bonds with as little as $25, and you pay no transaction fees. The Treasury pays banks a small fee to handle them, but they don't charge you anything.

Savings bonds can't be resold. But if you have to, you can cash them in after six months — again, without paying anything.

Figuring out what savings bonds are worth

Savings bonds now come in two big classes — Series EE and HH. For the EEs, you pay half the face value, and, at maturity, you get back the face amount on the bond. For example, you pay $25 for a $50 EE bond. Because the rate paid on a savings bond fluctuates, you can't say exactly when the *maturity date* is. If you assume a savings bond rate of about four percent right now, the maturity date is about 18 years away. However, EEs have a 30-year term and keep earning interest after they reach the 18-year or so maturity point. They do stop earning interest after 30 years, and then you should do something else with them!

Assuming rates don't change in that time (not a safe thing to do except in an example like this), your $25 initial cost EE bond would be worth about $81 in 30 years at four percent.

If the changeable rate part of savings bonds drives you crazy, then you're not alone. This is the single biggest reason people don't like savings bonds — you don't know what they're worth without a complex calculation. The New York Federal Reserve Bank (`http://www.ny.frb.org/pihome/svg_bnds/sb_val.html`) brings you a calculator, shown in Figure 23-2, for just this purpose. It's even more useful for older bonds that you or your family may have lying around because the rules for calculating interest on them have changed several times over the years. The calculator takes care of all savings bonds.

Obtaining Series HH bonds

Series HH bonds can't be bought, but you can exchange EE bonds that are worth at least $500 in redemption value for them. You can exchange at the Federal Reserve Banks, either in person or by mail using Form PDF 3253. You don't need exactly the right amount in EEs for these exchanges as long as you have at least $500 in EEs. You can round up to the next $500 of HH bonds in cash if necessary.

Why would you want to switch? Because HHs have a few advantages over EEs. HHs pay current income every six months. Plus, their rates are fixed for 10 years. In the past few years, this fixed rate has given them an edge over EEs, whose rates have fallen.

Another plus: tax breaks

Like other Treasury investments, interest on EEs and HHs is exempt from state and local income taxes. They're not usually Federal tax exempt (although you see later that they can be for some investors), but you don't have to report interest earned on EE bonds until you either cash them in or until the end of their term. If you want, you can report the interest each year.

Figure 23-2: This savings bond calculator helps you compute your savings bonds' interest.

HHs have initial terms of ten years and are extendible for a *final maturity* in another ten years. Their rates can be reset for the second ten-year period. You exchange EEs for their face value, and they pay interest on that face amount twice a year. The Treasury sets up a direct deposit payment for the interest to an account you name — like Treasury Direct does for notes and bonds. Because you actually get interest payments, you have to report and pay federal taxes on them each year.

Redeeming savings bonds before maturity

If you need to cash in these bonds before maturity, you can take them to your bank with the proper identification. Cashing them in doesn't cost you anything, unlike bank certificates of deposit before their maturity. Because there's no cost, banks would rather sell you CDs, which pay about the same rates as savings bonds but have no tax exemptions or government backing.

You can even cash in part of a savings bond — for example, $500 worth of a bond with a $1,000 redemption value — as long as its worth more than $100 for EEs and more than $1,000 for HHs. To cash part of a savings bond, go to the nearest Federal Reserve Bank or write the Bureau of Public Debt, Savings Bank Operations Office, Parkersburg, WV 26106-1328.

Saving for education

In some cases, EE bond interest also is exempt from federal taxes. If you bought EE bonds after Dec. 31, 1989, and cashed them in during a year when you're paying tuition and fees for post-secondary education, you owe no federal income tax on the interest.

This plan has several more features and formulas, especially for higher-income families. Check IRS Publication 550 and IRS Form 8815 for more details. You can find these forms at the IRS site (`http://www.irs.ustreas.gov/cgi/websys_fmanage`).

Spring Street Goes It Alone

Wouldn't it be great if you could buy and sell more kinds of securities like you buy Treasuries and savings bonds — without the transaction costs and other penalties? Of course. But that's not how investment companies and banks make money. So don't expect much of it any time soon — even though one small company issuing stock has railed against the system with some success, using the Internet to do it.

Spring Street Brewery — a small beer company headed by a former securities lawyer — legally issued a small amount of unregistered stock in an initial public offering, and now trades it exclusively online. Spring Street took advantage of an exemption to stock registration laws that is available for companies that plan to trade less than $5 million worth of stock in a year.

The Securities and Exchange Commission gives companies like this more leeway in how they market their stock. Spring Street, for instance, set up a Web page trading system for its stock. Wit-Trade, as it was first called, was really two bulletin boards — one for buyers and one for sellers. The system let both post numbers of shares being offered and hoped-for prices, with e-mail addresses and/or phone numbers of the prospective trading partners.

Wit-Trade, now called Wit Brokerage (http://www.witcap.com), doesn't match orders. But it provides a common document — an offer and acceptance form — for any agreement the prospective buyers and sellers reach. Trades that result from the Wit system bypass underwriters, brokers, and exchanges — apparently legally.

Spring Street and Wit had to make some changes in the system to toe the line with regulators. Spring Street had to remove itself completely from the trading process, for one thing. At the same time, the company has been told by the SEC to keep historical information and records on prices and volume of all trades and to make them available to the SEC, which will end up costing it something. Spring Street has also been warned not to let its employees act as unlicensed securities brokers and dealers.

As experiments go, this is an interesting one to watch. "Going public" on the Net has raised some funds for Spring Street — although they're limited by the kind of offering done. It's hard to say how much the offering has done for investors, since the prices aren't publicly quoted. It's hardly the kind of huge and efficient market you have on an exchange. But you don't have to share your profits with anyone else.

Summary

- ◆ You don't need to pay a fee to a broker to buy U.S. Treasury bills, notes, or bonds. Thanks to Treasury Direct, you can buy directly. Although the Treasury puts numerous forms, instructions, and auction dates and results on the Web, you can't buy Treasuries there. You are limited to obtaining the tender form, which you have to submit by snail mail.

- ◆ If you've purchased Treasuries, you can hold on to them until maturity, sell them before they mature, or reinvest in additional Treasuries. To sell a Treasury before maturity, you need a broker's help and you have to pay a fee.

- ◆ U.S. savings bonds have many advantages, including low minimums, no transaction fees, and tax exemptions under certain circumstances. It's confusing to tell what they're worth, but a Web-based calculator designed for this purpose can help.

From Here

◆ The next part of this book turns to personal finance, beginning with Chapter 24, which shows you how to find personal finance resources on the Internet.

◆ Chapter 25 is the first of three chapters that detail the useful personal finance tools on the Net.

◆ In Chapter 26, you learn how you can spend all the money you've earned in internet and capital gains.

◆ In hock? The Internet is a great place to shop for loans, as Chapter 27 explains.

VII
PART

Personal Finance on the Internet

Finding Personal Finance Resources

What is personal finance? You probably have a general idea of what *finance* is, at least, after reading about why stocks and bonds are issued. Finance is about funding and its management. Narrowly, then, personal finance is about funding yourself, by means of loans, scholarships, and anything else you can do to get people to give you money. Conceived in the broadest sense, personal finance involves everything that the average person does with his or her money, including managing checks, establishing a bank savings account, looking for the best deal on credit cards, getting insurance, and planning an estate.

As you discover in this chapter, the Internet offers many resources for improving your management of personal finance. This chapter surveys the many ways the Net can help you with personal finances. You discover the biggest and best personal finance sites and move on to some specialized sites that provide valuable personal finance information. The chapters to follow delve into greater detail in the three areas in which the Internet is really picking up steam: Internet banking, bill paying, and loan-shopping.

Personal Finance Resources on the Net

You find some great places on the Net to start your exploration of personal finance. The following sections list the best personal finance resource centers on the Net, with an emphasis on their personal finance offerings.

Personal Finance Center

You can access The Wall Street Journal Interactive Edition Personal Finance Center, shown in Figure 24-1, from Interactive Edition's front page (`http://inter-active. wsj.com`). If you subscribe to the Interactive Edition (currently $29 yearly if you already subscribe to the print edition), it's a great place to start exploring personal finance on the Net. A fantastic library of personal finance resources is available from *The Wall Street Journal,* covering the following subjects (also listed are samples of the excellent *WSJ* articles you find under these headings):

- ◆ **College financing.** Loan options, saving for college, and the need for parental education.

- ◆ **Employee benefits.** Salvaging your savings from a troubled pension plan, medical savings accounts, issues with portable insurance, direct-purchase plans, dreaded-disease policies, safeguarding 401(k) plans, and making the most of employee benefits.

- ◆ **Estate planning.** Preparing for disaster with good records, the need for spouse's citizenship in estate planning, uncertainties of planning for disabled kids, and dealing with the difficulty of discussing estate planning.

- ◆ **Financial planning.** Solid money strategies, easing gasoline tabs with credit cards, dealing with credit card debt, curtailment of credit card protection, boosting your savings, finding hidden interest in credit card deals, teaching budgeting to children, and helping your spouse plan finances.

- ◆ **Home and auto.** Buying a home for the long haul, perils of fix-up costs, the good sense of mortgage paydowns, tax-return nightmares of a second home, the difference between home repairs and improvements, and why buying big may not be a good idea.

- ◆ **Retirement planning.** Protecting holdings in a timely manner, why delaying account payouts isn't always best, planning retirement while saving for a rainy day, help for the cash-poor and home-rich, why insurance won't mend the Medicaid safety net, a brief guide to investing for retirement, and boosting retirement income.

- ◆ **Taxes.** New IRS protection weapons, tax nightmares of second homes, state snoopers coming after sales-tax dodgers, and getting help from the IRS.

You also find a list of deposit and loan rates at banking institutions throughout the U.S.

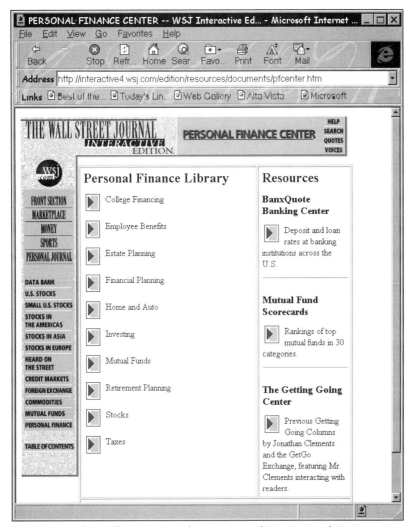

Figure 24-1: The Wall Street Journal Interactive Edition Personal Finance Center page.

Ira Krakow's Personal Finance Web Site

Don't expect glitzy graphics, Java applets, or Shockwave animations at this no-frills site; it's only a page of links. But what a page of links! These links were compiled by Ira Krakow, non-financial moderator of the Persfin-Digest mailing list.

You can access this page at `http://www.tiac.net/users/ikrakow/pagerefs.html`. In the personal finance area, you find hundreds of links in the following areas. Some are highly reputable organizations that you'll be familiar with. Others, especially those from individual professions, should be approached more skeptically — especially those from bankruptcy lawyers and estate and financial planners.

- ◆ **Banks and credit unions.** Bank deposit information, bank home pages, credit union information, Federal Deposit Insurance Corporation (FDIC) information, instructions for filing complaints against banks, and highest bank rates.

- ◆ **College planning.** Financial aid information, CollegeNet (links to all higher education Web sites), scholarship information, and financial aid software.

- ◆ **Consumer-related resources.** Better Business Bureau, debt management links, U.S. Consumer Information Center, FTC consumer brochures, Consumer Scam Alerts, Frugal Corner, consumer hardware user complaints, salary survey, Social Security information, and used car buying information.

- ◆ **Credit cards, bankruptcy, and debt management.** Center for Debt Management, personal bankruptcy FAQ, debt counseling services, credit repair kits, lowest credit card rates, and mortgage application tips.

- ◆ **Education.** A few links, including one to a Web-based personal finance course.

- ◆ **Financial planning.** Links to financial planning journals and pages specializing in estate planning.

- ◆ **Government agencies and resources.** Links to useful resources at dozens of government agencies, including Consumer Information Center, Consumer Product Safety Commission, Internal Revenue Service, Social Security Information, and Veterans Administration.

- ◆ **Insurance.** Insurance ratings, insurance terms, and links to insurance-related sites.

- ◆ **Legal issues.** Links to sites specializing in investor legal issues, class-action suits, and product recalls.

- ◆ **Personal finance-related books and magazines.** An excellent selection of links to online books and magazines, which you can read for free on the Web.

- ◆ **Real estate (buying and selling).** Internet Real Estate Directory, Mortgage Applicant's Bible, mortgage and financial calculators, and real estate listings.

- ◆ **Taxes.** Federal tax publications and forms, flat tax calculator, state tax forms, TaxTalk, Taxing Times, and the entire U.S. tax code.

Financenter's Personal Finance Calculators

Here's a for-profit site that may be worth visiting, as long as you take your consumer smarts with you. Vendors pay to place their wares here (mainly loans), and you should comparison shop before you commit yourself. The site, called Financenter (http://www.financenter.com/), was founded in 1995 by Sherri Neasham, a former real estate broker and a specialist in loans. Take a look at the loan offers — they're worth comparing with other loan possibilities — but the real gem of the site is found in the freebies: the financial calculators. Here's a quick look at what's available at this site:

◆ **Autos.** Which is better: new or used? How much will depreciation cost? Should I lease or purchase? Should I finance or pay cash? How much will my monthly payment be? How much should I put down? What term of loan should I choose? Should I use a home equity loan instead? Which is better: A rebate or a low rate? How long should I keep a car?

◆ **Credit cards.** How important is the interest rate? How will rate changes affect my balance? Is a lower rate worth the annual fee? What will it take to pay off my balance? Should I consolidate my debts? Which is better: a flight card or a low rate card? Which is better: a rebate card or a low rate card?

◆ **Homes.** How much can I borrow? How much will my payments be? How much will adjustable rate payments be? Which is better: fixed or adjustable rate? Should I pay points to lower the rate? Which is better: 15- or 30-year term? How much money should I put down? How much can I save in taxes? What will my closing costs be? Should I rent or buy? Am I better off refinancing? What will my refinancing costs be? How can I reduce mortgage insurance costs? Which lender has the better loan? Which loan is better?

These calculators are fantastic. Figure 24-2 shows the Autos Calculator. I should have financed my car with a home equity loan! Figure 24-3 shows one of the nifty credit card calculators (this one helps you determine whether a lower interest rate is worth the annual fee). Figure 24-4 shows one of the several home calculators; this one enables you to determine whether it's worth paying loan points to get a reduced interest rate.

Selected Personal Finance Sites

Of the thousands of personal finance-related sites on the Internet, the following sections list specialized sites — sites that focus on a particular topic. These sites aren't intended to be comprehensive; these are sites that you're sure to find extremely useful. If you're still not convinced that the Internet is a tremendous personal asset, this section should do the trick.

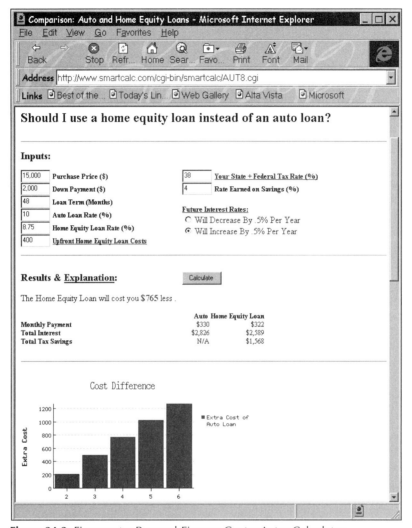

Figure 24-2: Financenter Personal Finance Center Autos Calculator.

Financing a college education

Saving and investing aren't your only options, as you find by looking at the following sites. You, or your kids, may qualify for scholarships and financial aids, but you need to do some planning!

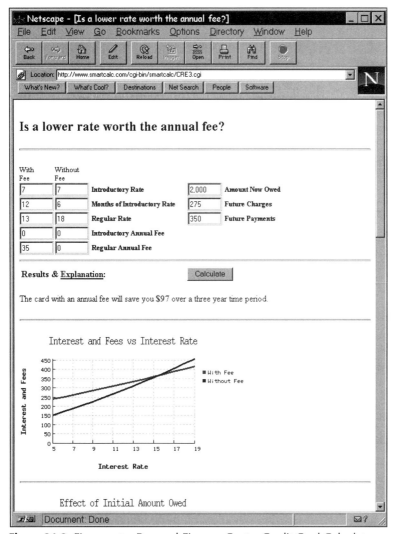

Figure 24-3: Financenter Personal Finance Center Credit Card Calculator.

◆ **Ambitious Student's Guide to Financial Aid** (http://jerome.signet.com/collegemoney/toc1.html). Here's a gem of a freebie — an entire 25-chapter book that's really worth reading! A neat twist is that the book is directed to the student rather than the parents.

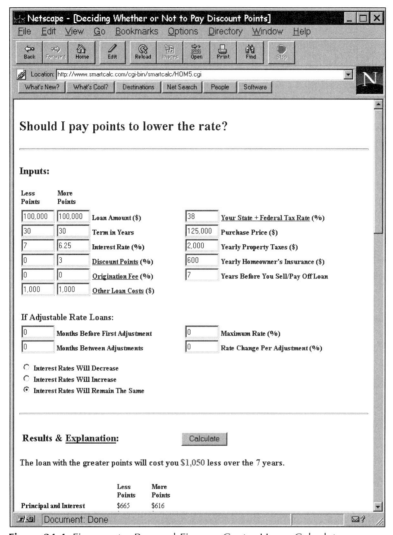

Figure 24-4: Financenter Personal Finance Center Home Calculator.

◆ **CollegeNet** (http://www.collegenet.com/). Here's an ambitious effort: A site that attempts to assemble the home pages for virtually every higher education institution that has a Net presence. This is a great place to get more information about a college that you're thinking about attending.

◆ **FastWeb** (http://www.studentservices.com/fastweb). Search for college scholarships on the Net.

COOL SITE

◆ **FinAid** (`http://www.finaid.org`). An amazingly comprehensive guide to college financial aid resources on the Net, compiled by the author of *The Prentice Hall Guide to Scholarships*. Figure 24-5 shows how comprehensive this site is.

Figure 24-5: FinAid brings together the best college financial aid resources on the Net.

◆ **The Gathering** (`http://www.takeme.com/frontdoor.html`). Described as an "online student community," The Gathering includes useful scholarship information.

◆ **The Student Guide** (`http://www.ed.gov/prog_info/SFA/StudentGuide/`). This document provides online access to Department of Education publications about U.S. government-backed grants and loans for college education.

Consumer information

You're about to get educated on a host of consumer issues — and you'll probably feel that your eyes have been opened. From the following sites, you get the lowdown on the latest scams, frauds, bogus investment schemes, and dangerous consumer products.

◆ **Better Business Bureau** (`http://www.bbb.org/`). This organization seeks to uphold business ethics, resolve disputes between consumers and businesses, and protect the public against dishonest businesses and fraud. At this site, you can locate your local BBB office and read about the latest scam alerts. A new service called BBBOnLine will soon enable you to search for reports on more than 1.3 million businesses.

◆ **Consumer Credit FAQ** (`http://www.ucsalf.ac.uk/usenet/consumer-credit-faq/`). Posted regularly to misc.consumers, this four-part FAQ contains informative answers to frequently asked questions on the newsgroup. The focus is on credit cards and credit reports.

◆ **Consumer Information Center** (`http://www.pueblo.gsa.gov`). The Consumer Information Center (see Figure 24-6), a U.S. government agency, offers online consumer information about a huge variety of subjects, including cards, children, employment, federal programs, travel and hobbies, health, food and nutrition, housing, money, small business, and the environment. You can read the publications right on your screen.

◆ **The Consumer Law Page** (`http://consumerlawpage.com`). Sponsored by the Alexander Law Firm, a San Jose, CA., consumer law legal firm, this page contains many resources concerning consumer legal issues, including articles, brochures, and links. You find much help for resolving issues with businesses, including information on filing actions in small claims courts.

◆ **Consumer World** (`http://www.consumerworld.org`). This fantastic site (see Figure 24-7)offers more than 1,100 links to consumer information on the Web. You can check airfares, find an ATM machine anywhere in the world, find the best credit card rates, look up the dealer cost of a car, and much more.

◆ **Internet Fraud Watch** (`http://www.fraud.org`). Do you want to know more about fraud on the Net? Don't miss this excellent offering from the National Fraud Information Center. You can read about the latest online scams — and report them, too, if you run across something shady.

◆ **Safety-Related Product Recalls** (gopher://cpsc/gov/11/Pre-Re/Pre-Re/
96_Pre). Have you bought something recently that's been recalled for safety
reasons? Find out from this site, which is maintained by the Consumer Product
Safety Commission, a U.S. government agency. You also can access the CPSC's
Web page (http://www.cpsc.com), where you find a search service that
enables you to search for products by typing one or more key words.

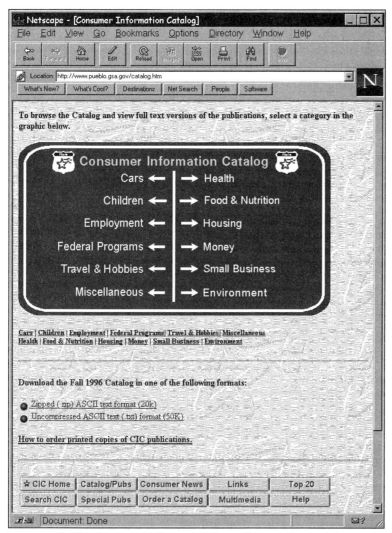

Figure 24-6: The Consumer Information Center is loaded with full-text
articles on every aspect of personal finance.

Figure 24-7: Consumer World is the best consumer-related site on the Internet.

Credit and credit cards

It's pretty interesting that these credit card links often include links to debt counseling and bankruptcy pages!

◆ **Low Rate Credit Cards** (http://www.ramresearch.com/cardweb.html). Created by an independent banking research organization called RAM Research, this page offers direct hyperlinks to some of the best credit card deals available.

◆ **Bank Rate Monitor** (http://www.bankrate.com/bankrate/rates/ccard.htm). This site contains the best credit card deals, organized for those who pay their accounts every month as well as for those who do not.

◆ **12 Credit Card Secrets Banks Don't Want You To Know** (http://www.consumer.com/consumer/CREDITC.html). Read this before you sign up for another credit card.

◆ **Federal Trade Commission (FTC) Credit Pamphlets** (http://www.ftc.gov/bcp/conline/conline.htm). This site contains tons of excellent information on many kinds of scams, brought to you by a U.S. government regulatory agency.

◆ **Debtor's Options** (http://www.berkshire.net/~mkb/). This page contains one attorney's survey of your options when faced with insurmountable debt. Read all such sites with skepticism. Bankruptcy filings are a fast-growing source of fees for attorneys in most states.

◆ **Bankcard Holders of America** (http://www.epn.com/bha/index.htm). Sponsored by an organization that defends the rights of consumers who hold bank cards, this page includes information concerning credit card consumer rights and resources for getting out of debt. You can print your own copy of BHA's Consumer Action Card, which informs merchants that they really can't do most of the things that they routinely do, such as demand a credit card for identification purposes when you write a check.

◆ **Victims of Credit Reporting (VCR)** (http://pages.prodigy.com/ID/vcr/vcr.html). This page collects information about the hundreds of thousands of people whose lives have been disrupted by flaws in the current credit report industry.

Estate planning and senior citizen issues

Unless you really want the U.S. Federal government to take just about everything you have worked all your life to achieve, you'd better start doing some estate planning — even if you're still relatively young. Check out these pages to get started:

◆ **Robert Clofine's Estate Planning Page** (http://home.ptd.net/~clofine/). Robert Clofine, an estate attorney, offers this excellent collection of in-depth articles concerning estate planning. There's some focus on Pennsylvania, where Clofine practices, but there's much to interest readers from other states.

◆ **SeniorNet** (http://www.seniornet.org/intute/index.html). Created by
an organization of computer-using seniors, this site (see Figure 26-8) is full of
information of interest to seniors and retired people.

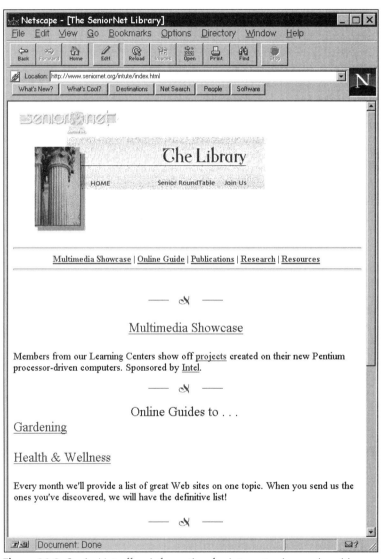

Figure 26-8: SeniorNet offers information for Internet-using senior citizens.

◆ **Senior Law Home Page** (http://www.seniorlaw.com). This page is an excellent information resource concerning Medicare, Medicaid, Elder Law, Supplemental Needs Trusts, and more.

Insurance

If you're thinking about buying insurance of any kind, including home, auto, or life, these pages can help you understand insurance policies and find a company with a good claims-paying record.

◆ **The Complete Glossary of Insurance Coverage Explanations** (http://www.lcgroup.com/explanations/). Created by the Lewis-Chester Group, a full-service insurance and financial services company, this glossary defines business insurance terms such as Actual Cash Value (ACV), Alienated Premises Exclusion, Fiduciary Liability Coverage, and many more.

◆ **Insurance News Network (INN)** (http://www.insure.com). Founded by Philip Moeller, a writer specializing in insurance, Insurance News Network (see Figure 24-9) is an excellent source of consumer-oriented news concerning auto, home, and life insurance. Among the fantastic goodies: Crash test results for cars, auto collision rates, auto theft rates, city-by-city theft losses, and much more.

◆ **Standard and Poor's Insurance Ratings** (http://www.ratings.standardpoor.com/spirs.htm). An independent firm that rates the claims-paying ability of insurance companies worldwide, Standard and Poor's ratings page enables you to access the firm's related publications, and provides a link to the Insurance News Network, where you find the ratings.

Taxes

The Internet is a great place to find information concerning state and federal taxes. The following sites provide forms, regulations, and assistance:

◆ **The Digital Daily** (http://www.irs.ustreas.gov/prod/cover.html). The IRS home page (see Figure 24-10) is a great resource. You'll find tax forms, tax help, and tax brochures, organized by means of a tree or searchable by means of a search engine. Great job, IRS!

Figure 24-9: Insurance News Network has lots of news of interest to consumers.

◆ **NetTax** (`http://www.vni.net/~nettax/`). Prepare your taxes on the Web? Yes, it's possible! This on-line tax preparation program is free. It's not as full-featured as standalone PC programs such as Turbo Tax, but it might suffice if your return is fairly simple. The site is secure so you don't have to worry about somebody reading your tax information.

Figure 24-10: The IRS home page offers tax forms, tax advice, and tax brochures.

◆ **1040.com** (http://www.1040.com/) Sponsored by Drake Software, this page offers federal and state tax forms as well as tax-related news and information.

◆ **Tax Code Online** (http://www.fourmilab.ch/ustax/ustax.html) Here it is, folks — the entire U.S. tax code with a searchable interface. It's current up to 1994. Unfortunately, the law has been changed since.

◆ **Income Tax Information on the Internet** (http://www.best.com/~ftmexpat/html/taxsites.html) An amazingly comprehensive collection of links concerning every aspect of taxation.

Summary

◆ Personal finance involves everything the average person does with his or her money, including managing checks, establishing a bank saving account, looking for the best deal on credit cards, getting insurance, and planning an estate.

◆ Start your explanation of personal finance resources by checking out resource centers, including The Wall Street Journal Personal Finance Center, Ira Krakow's Personal Finance Web Sites, and Financenter's Personal Finance Calculators.

◆ To see how rich the Internet's personal finance resources can be, check out some of the specialized pages mentioned in this chapter. You learn how to find college scholarships, how to avoid fraud, how to find the dealer cost of a new car, and much more.

From Here

◆ Reconcile your bank statement on the Net? You can. Find out how in Chapter 25.

◆ Pay your bills — and go shopping! You can do it on the Net, as Chapter 26 explains.

◆ The Internet's a great place to shop for loans, as Chapter 27 explains.

Banking on the Internet

The about the last time you balanced your checkbook. You sat down with that lengthy, incomprehensible bank statement and tried to match the data with the scribbling in your checkbook register. At the end of the lengthy ordeal, you found that you were $483 off — in the bank's favor, not yours, naturally, and you couldn't figure out why.

Unpleasant, huh? Okay, fast-forward time. You log on to the Net and access your checking account via a secure link. After a few minutes, you've paid all your bills electronically. For the checks you wrote in the past few days, you make entries in your online check register — a bit of work, to be sure, but here's the good part: As each check comes in to be cleared, the bank *automatically* reconciles your online checkbook register. Any discrepancy between the amount of the cleared check and the amount you recorded in your register triggers a warning flag.

Is Internet banking about to take off? Right now, it's just getting started, as you see in this chapter, but that's going to change. As soon as security concerns can be cleared up, Internet banking likely will grow rapidly.

In This Chapter

- ◆ Banks are already electronic

- ◆ Security First Network Bank

- ◆ More Internet banks are on the way

Banks Are Already Electronic

Here are some statistics that may surprise you.

More than 60 percent of all bank transactions now are electronic, conveyed via private data networks. That number is expected to rise to 80 percent by the year 2000. Currently, about a third of all utility bills, car loans, and mortgages in the U.S. are paid electronically.

According to data gathered by CheckFree Corp., 40 percent of U.S. households use some kind of direct deposit. This number has increased 14 percent since 1987. Of these direct deposit customers, 34 percent use some kind of phone banking service to pay bills and transfer funds. Also, 43 percent of all U.S. households use some kind of automatic bill payment service.

What does all this information mean? It's simple. Banks are already accustomed to the idea that they can move funds from place to place using bits and bytes rather than armored trucks. From there, it's a relatively small step to start doing business with their customers via the Internet.

However, don't expect Internet banking to happen overnight. Although many banks are already on the Internet with loan pricing, interest rates, and personal finance information, they're not quite ready to cross the line with more sensitive functions such as electronic payments using the Net. "Soon," they all say. Banks are still figuring out how best to serve their customers, and they're worried about security.

A Pioneer: Security First Network Bank

Despite the hesitancy most banks have about Internet banking, some pioneers are taking the plunge. Security First Network Bank (http://www.sfnb.com), an offshoot of Kentucky's Cardinal Bancshares, gives you a heavy-duty presentation of its security system — and for good reasons. Security First is making a pioneering effort to show that it can do business on the Internet — where it could find millions of potential customers.

At the same time, the bank has reassured potential customers that their money is safe and secure. It's a bank, after all, and banks have to insure customers' deposits for hundreds of thousands of dollars.

What can you do at this Internet bank? Most of its features have to do with checking, which is probably the bank's best offering. You can make electronic payments, record and reconcile transactions, look at online images of cleared checks, or export your records to Quicken. You also have 24-hour phone banking access, fund transfer, and customer service. Aside from checking, Security First also offers money market accounts and CDs. You take a closer look at SFNB's electronic bill-paying features in the next chapter.

We begin by looking more closely at the Security First Network Bank (SFNB) checking account offerings, and we start with the question that's uppermost on your mind.

Is it safe?

Security First puts several layers of public key encryption, filtering routers, and firewalls between you and itself and possible interlopers. Security First assures customers that they're communicating with the bank when a key icon on the screen becomes solid. This sign means that the customer's session with the bank is encrypted — encoded and decipherable only by the bank.

With all the military style security, Security First tries to keep some homey touches. Opening an account is kind of like walking into a bank branch and doing it (see Figure 25-1). You can go to the information desk (on your screen) or see a branch manager (also on the screen). In fact, the bank's home page is called the Virtual Branch Manager. It depicts all the personnel you see in a branch: account opening officer, customer service rep, personal banker, and tellers.

But is it safe? Security First uses your browser's security encryption, which means that the data you're sending and receiving can't be intercepted while en route. That's good, but there are other security issues. What if somebody gets hold of your password and logs into your account? Somebody could walk into your office after you've gone out for a cup of coffee and thoughtlessly left your bank account information on-screen. This person could empty your account in short order or accomplish additional mischief. To prevent this, Security First plans to implement some sort of personal authentication by means of a *smart card,* or secure identification certificate, but that's in the future.

In the meantime, using Security First is probably about as safe as using an ATM, where you have to supply a four-digit personal identification number to access your account. With ATMs, there's always a danger of *shoulder surfers,* who try to get your PIN by observing you while you enter data. The electronic banking equivalent of your PIN is your login name and password, which you should keep extremely safe.

If you're using Internet Explorer, bear in mind that the program automatically remembers login names and passwords and automatically supplies them when you contact a site that demands them. This feature is convenient for fee-based services such as online newspapers, but it's terrible for online banking. A thief could sneak into your office and use your computer to gain access to your checking account. The first time you access the bank and are asked to supply your login name and password, disable this feature by deselecting the check box that configures Internet Explorer to supply this information automatically.

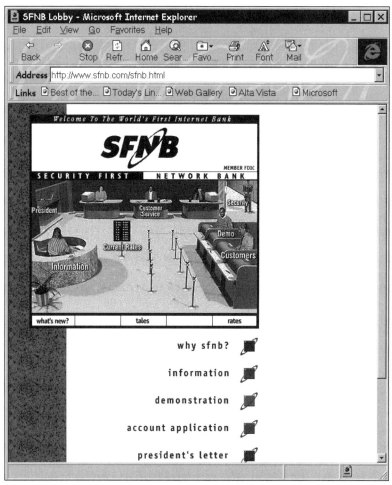

Figure 25-1: Security First's virtual bank.

You're much safer accessing an Internet banking account from home, where someone is less likely to try to use your computer to access your account. Just in case you're still worried, Security First guarantees that any money stolen from your account by a hacker will be refunded, right down to the last penny. Note that the guarantee doesn't apply if you've done something stupid, such as posting your password to Usenet or leaving your computer unattended after logging on to Security First.

The out-of-state problem

Here's the scenario: It's the end of the month, and your account balance is rapidly heading south. You just received a check, and you desperately need to get it deposited, but your Internet bank is in another state. The options here aren't that great. You can FedEx the check to the bank, but that costs serious money. If you send it by snail mail, it could take a week or more to reach the bank — and it may take another three to five days to clear.

Unless you're lucky enough to have a local bank that offers Internet banking, the deposit problem poses some real inconvenience. You can get around this problem by using direct deposit for your paycheck, if your employer offers direct deposit services.

Here's another problem: You want to write a check, but the merchant notices that your check is drawn on a bank somewhere in Pineville, Kentucky — it's an out-of-state check. "Sorry, we don't accept out-of-state checks," you're told. An alternative: Most Internet banks will give you a debit card, which you can use anywhere that credit cards are accepted.

Your account summaries

The first screen you see in the Security First in-depth demonstration is the account summary, shown in Figure 25-2. On this page, you see the current balances of all your accounts. Take a look next at an online checkbook register.

Your checkbook register

In Figure 25-3, you see a demonstration of a Security First checkbook register. To make entries into this register, you use the Record Register Transaction page, shown in Figure 25-4. To make data entry easier, you can set up payees so that you can choose them from a list box. For budgeting purposes, you can assign each check to a budget category, and you even can split a given check among as many as four categories, if you want.

If you've ever used a personal finance application such as Quicken or Microsoft Money, you're familiar with this type of computerized checkbook register. The inconvenience here lies in the reconciliation area. You have to manually "clear" each item by going through your computerized register with that old-fashioned, printed statement at hand. With Security First's register, however, there's a cool payoff: As each check clears, the bank's software updates and reconciles your register automatically. This is a major time-saver.

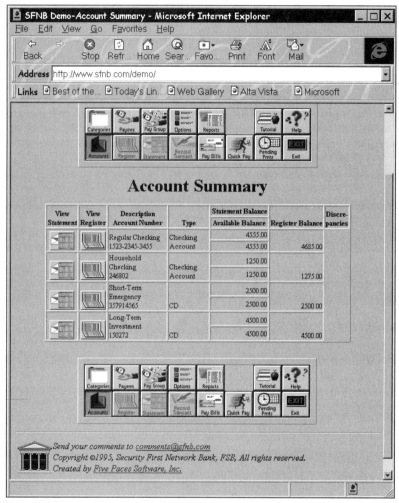

Figure 25-2: A Security First National Bank account summary.

EXCELLENT

Automatic reconciliation is one of the best reasons to consider Internet banking. Security First's system is extremely convenient and highlights errors instantly: If a discrepancy exists between the amount you recorded and the amount paid when the check cleared, you're notified with on-screen flags. By choosing the Reconciliation Report option, you can tell at a glance whether you forgot to record a debit card or other transaction. You can edit the register to bring it up-to-date. In just a few minutes, you can reconcile your checkbook register down to the penny.

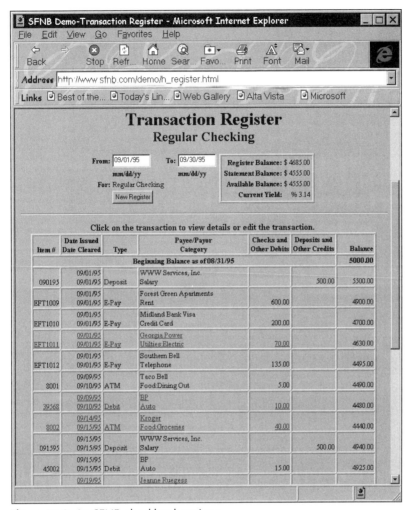

Figure 25-3: An SFNB checkbook register.

Reports and summaries

For budgeting purposes, Security First's reports and summaries are nothing short of excellent. Provided you classify each transaction using the Record Register Transaction page's budget categories, you can produce the following reports:

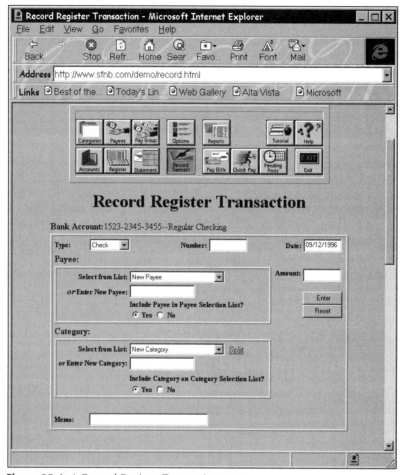

Figure 25-4: A Record Register Transaction page.

◆ **Transactions by category.** How much did you spend during the past month on entertainment? Food? Gasoline?

◆ **Cash flow.** This report displays a summary of income and expenses by category.

◆ **Tax report.** Lists tax-related transactions.

◆ **Transactions by payee.** Find out how much you've paid a given payee.

More Internet Banks on the Way

The decision by Cardinal Bancshares to split off Security First has given other banks a ramp to doing transactions on the Internet. The second bank getting in on this action is Huntington Bancshares Incorporated (`http://www.huntington.com`) in Ohio, Kentucky, Indiana, and Florida. Huntington bought a small share in Security First and is using the same software and security system.

Huntington's system is similar to Security First's — right down to the Quick Pay, payment pending, account statement, and long-term transaction register features.

Some of the heavies are jumping in on the action, too. Wells Fargo (`http://www.wellsfargo.com/`) recently introduced its Online Banking offering, with Internet banking features. But Wells Fargo would be wise to study Security First's software, which is more convenient to use: Wells Fargo's offering doesn't include the cool, online reconciliation features that make SFNB's service a very attractive option. Another debut from a heavyweight is Bank of America's HomeBanking (`http://www.bankamerica.com`).

The Dial-up Alternative

Security First National Bank's online software is very much like Quicken or Microsoft Money in terms of user features, but there are two huge differences: Reconciliation is automatic, and you're not tied down to the computer that houses your personal finance software. With online banking software such as SFNB's, you can access your Internet bank account wherever you happen to be — from your office, from your laptop in a hotel room, or from an Internet bar on Portobello Road, London.

Still, Intuit — the publisher of Quicken — is working hard to interface its best-selling software with bank data. Intel chose the dial-up route to access your bank's computer. You don't use the Internet at all. Instead, you use Quicken and a proprietary dial-up program, linking to the bank's computer via a non-Internet data network. Is there an advantage to this method? Yes — better security.

To see what's cookin' with dial-up plans, take a look at Compass Bank's CompassPC page (`http://partner.qfn.com/directory/compass_bank/compasspc.html`). If you sign up for Compass's service, you get a free copy of Quicken, the CompassPC dial-up software, and a number to dial to access the service. Note that this connection is a direct modem one that doesn't use the Internet.

With some dial-up banking services, there's a huge disadvantage: cost. In order to make the services available nationwide, the banks have to contract with commercial data networks to enable you to access their computers, which costs money that you naturally wind up paying. One Quicken participant charges a hefty $7.50 per month.

Online banking likely will migrate to the Net the same way that so many other proprietary services have, for the simple reason that Net-connected people have already paid for the Internet connection. Security First Network Bank doesn't charge for connectivity — the charge is hidden in the payments that you make to your Internet Service Provider. Of course, you get much more than Security First for your money.

The Money Page's Top Ten Banks in Cyberspace (http://www.moneypage.com/topten) is updated monthly, so it's a great place to see what's happened in online banking since this chapter was written. Another place to look is NETBanker (http://www.netbanker.com/resources/fullserv.html).

Summary

◆ Banks are already electronic. A big part of their transactions already are conveyed via private data networks.

◆ Security and other concerns are keeping most banks from offering Internet online checking accounts, but a few have taken the leap; most notably, Security First Network Bank.

◆ The Security First Network Bank software shows how Internet checking accounts are supposed to work. The software is versatile, with many of the features you find in a personal finance program such as Quicken or Microsoft Money.

◆ Encrypted data transmission helps to assure that your password and account data won't be intercepted, but you must safeguard your password carefully and make sure that you don't leave your computer unattended while logged on to your account data.

◆ Internet banking has the edge over dial-up services in that you can access the Internet service anywhere. You don't have to be using the computer that houses the dial-up program.

From Here

◆ Many of the Web-based banking services now operating, and several that are still in the planning stages, will offer Net-based bill payment. Get the lowdown on this controversial service in Chapter 26.

◆ The Web is a great place to look for loans, as Chapter 27 explains.

Bills on the Net

Here's the scenario for the Bank of the Future: no tellers, no deposit slips, no checks — no office, even. You simply sit down at your computer, access your account information, and perform all your transactions online — including writing "checks." Although you fill out something that looks like a real check, no paper is involved. After you click on the Pay button, the bank sends an instantaneous electronic payment to your payee, which is accepted and verified that very moment. You can hang on to your money until the day the payment's due, and you don't have to worry about the vagaries of snail mail (including the possibility that a mail delay may result in a lost payment).

Have we reached this point yet? Nope. Although you can pay bills electronically, as this chapter explains, few payees are set up to accept electronic payments. For this reason, electronic bill-paying services have to send paper checks to most payees, and these services send the checks via the U.S. postal service. Still, electronic bill-paying has some advantages, and the costs have come down. You may be interested in giving it a try, as long as you're aware of the potential pitfalls.

Other online payment schemes are still in the planning stages or awaiting key technological developments. Electronic cash (ecash) may play a role in the

In This Chapter

◆ Paying your bills electronically

◆ Paying bills with CheckFree

◆ Exploring bank bill-paying services

◆ Using electronic cash (ecash)

◆ Paying with credit cards—is it safe?

future. Online credit-card payments are already well-established on the Internet but growing slowly, for now. This situation is likely to change, as this chapter explains. Something similar to the Bank of the Future seems very likely indeed.

Paying Your Bills Electronically

The technology and security for paying your bills electronically have been around for decades. This technology is called *electronic funds transfer,* or EFT. Banks and big companies have long been concerned with moving money around as quickly as possible to realize the maximum benefit from having it on hand as long as possible. They have long used electronic links to *wire* money within minutes from one account to another, from customer to vendor, or from payor to payee. If you deal in huge amounts of money, it's worth having it around for even a few days longer to gain extra interest.

If you're a small consumer, the benefits are less obvious and, well, smaller. Your employer (or the government, if you receive Social Security or other government payments) may wire funds directly into your account as a direct deposit, which is cool because it gives you access to your money for a few extra days. Currently, some 30 percent of U.S. paychecks are directly deposited by electronic funds transfer.

You also can wire out money by subscribing to an online bill-paying service or opening an account with an Internet bank. To be sure, not every creditor accepts electronic payments; in fact, very few do. A Philadelphia-based bank, for example, pays customers' bills each month to more than 21,000 firms; all but 172 of them require an old-fashioned, paper check. Direct paycheck deposit has really caught on, but electronic bill-paying lags behind. However, this situation may be about to change.

What's the edge?

So, what's so great about online bill-paying? Control, for one thing. It's easier to press a few keys on your computer than to write the check, fill out the checkbook ledger, do the math, lick the stamp, and go to the mailbox. The software organizes this part of your finances for you pretty well. With it, you know who's been paid, how much has been paid (for the month, the year, or longer), how much is left, and how this amount compares to last month or year. You also know who still has to be paid and how far along you are in saving for your vacation or your child's first year of college.

You save time, too. The average consumer pays about 10 to 12 bills per month, spending as much as one and one-half hours on this dreadful ritual. Online, you can finish the job in half the time — or less.

For recurrent bills — the ones that you pay every month — online bill-paying has another advantage: convenience. You can set up recurring payments so that paying a bill that's always the same amount (and always goes to the same payee) is as simple as choosing an item from a menu.

You may even save money. Ideally, online bill-paying would cost less than the cost of a first-class postage stamp. The industry is getting close to or even passing this important point of price sensitivity. Don't forget that you pay for paper checks and envelopes as well as postage.

In combination with a checkbook program such as Quicken or Managing Your Money, online bill paying has yet another advantage: The program automatically deducts the payments and computes your balance. This is a real advantage if you'd rather not go through the bill-paying-day depression that follows adding up all the checks you've just written! It also helps prevent bounced checks — and the fees that you get charged by both the merchant and your bank.

Online bill-paying: Far from universal acclaim

Is there a downside to online bill payment? You bet.

Not all payees accept electronic funds transfer (EFT). If they don't, the online bill-paying company has to send a regular, printed check via snail mail, and that's where problems begin. To allow time for the possibility that some of your bills may go out by snail mail instead of EFT, online bill-paying firms generally request that you initiate payments as much as six or seven days in advance of the bill's due date.

If you look around on Usenet, you find that more than a few customers of online bill-paying services complain about payments arriving late, even though they say that they requested the payment a week or more in advance. Some people who quit these services say that they spent more time dealing with late payment hassles than they did writing ordinary checks and sending them by mail. Complaints are often posted, too, about inadequate customer service. For every complaint you find, however, you find other posts from customers who are quite happy with the service.

Another problem with online bill paying is that you can't enclose the payee's preprinted payment coupon with your electronic payment. For most creditors, this isn't a problem. Some, however, require as much as 10 additional days to process payments that are received without the payment coupon — and these days count as a late payment, unless the payment was received 10 days in advance. For this reason, many online bill-paying firms suggest that you pay your bills 15 days in advance — 5 days in case it's necessary to send your payment via snail mail plus another 10 days for manual processing after it's received. This is the future?

(continued)

(continued)

What happens to your money in the interim? With conventional bill paying by snail mail, your money stays in your account until the check is received and processed, which is known as *float*. If you have an interest-earning account, you make a little money during this period.

Not so with electronic bill paying. Some electronic bill-paying firms debit your account the minute you request the payment! This poses no problem if the bill gets paid by EFT — there's no float at all — but what if the bill doesn't get paid electronically? The bill-paying firm has your money during this float period, which can last as long as 15 days. If the bill-paying firm can get millions of people to subscribe to electronic bill paying with disadvantageous terms, then they're going to get rich by depositing these funds and collecting interest.

For all these reasons, if you're thinking about paying your bills electronically, you may be wise to restrict your payments to only those few payees that accept EFT.

If you're already on the Net

CheckFree, the leading online bill-paying service, relies on private data communications systems and proprietary software. But online bill-paying is migrating to the Internet, where it's available from a few online banks. If you've decided to go the electronic bill-paying route, which method is right for you, proprietary software or the Internet?

Banks are just getting into the bill-paying game, so doing much comparison shopping right now is difficult. But this picture is about to change. Online Resources and Communications (`http://www.orcc.com`), one of several providers to offer inexpensive Web site set-ups to banks, offers bill payment and other transaction services as features of its package for small banks.

Online banking is reaching critical mass. With more customers accessing banking services online, fewer tellers and offices are needed. In consequence, banks' fees for online services are coming down and, in some cases, disappearing completely. Electronic banking helps bring in customers who are farther and farther away from the bank. With more customers, these services become even more cost-effective to provide. Citibank, which used to charge hefty fees for online services, cut out charges for these services when it hit the 45,000 customer level. Now these users number more than 200,000.

The following sections compare CheckFree and bank bill-paying services; if you're thinking about getting into online bill paying, take a look at each option before you decide.

Paying Bills with CheckFree

Originating in 1981, CheckFree is the veteran of online bill paying, hands down. The company enables you to pay virtually any organization or individual with funds from a demand deposit account at any U.S. bank or financial institution. You can access CheckFree by means of a touch-tone telephone, a PC equipped with the necessary software, and — most recently — the Web. Currently, the company has more than 500,000 subscribers. After you sign up, you use the company's proprietary software to log on to a private data network. You see the CheckFree bill payments on your monthly checking account statement, just as if you'd written a check.

CheckFree assures you that your check will reach its destination, even if the payee doesn't accept electronic transfers. Payees receive a regular printed check if they haven't joined the Electronic Age. To allow sufficient time for such payments to wend their way through snail mail, CheckFree asks that you make your payments five days in advance of the bill's due date. If you're concerned about late charges, CheckFree promises to pay late charges (up to $50) if you follow their recommended procedures.

To minimize your losses due to float, CheckFree enables you to specify the date on which the payment should be made. You can set this payment dates as close as possible to the actual due date. Still, you need to leave time for the check to be mailed — at least four days — in case the vendor doesn't accept electronic payments.

You can subscribe to CheckFree in the following ways:

◆ Access CheckFree's Web site (`http://www.checkfree.com/`) and download CheckFree's software, which is available for Windows and Mac systems.

◆ Buy a copy of one of the following checkbook programs: InCharge, Simply Money, or Managing Your Money. All these programs include CheckFree.

◆ CheckFree soon will be available with AT&T's HomeCenter System, which enables your TV to function as a telephone answering system and information service.

◆ Check with your bank to find out whether CheckFree services are available.

The leading personal finance program, Quicken, offers its own online bill-paying service, which resembles CheckFree's service. There are other, smaller firms that also offer online bill paying.

What will it cost, and is it safe?

CheckFree services can now cost less than the price of a first-class stamp — and you don't need an envelope. Offering rates as low as $5.95 for 20 payments, CheckFree lets you pocket the 45 cents that you would have spent on 32-cent postage stamps. Additional payments are $2.95 for each additional group of 10 payments (or portions thereof). Quicken's online bill-paying service matches CheckFree's rates.

Because CheckFree uses private data networks, data transmission is much more secure than the Internet. In addition, the firm employs industrial-strength encryption and requires a four-digit PIN number for access. Basically, online bill paying is as safe as using an ATM — which isn't surprising, because the same technology is used. To give you some protection against unauthorized access to your account, most online bill-paying companies promise to limit your losses to $50 if you notify them within 24 hours of any pilferage.

That's precious little comfort, however, to those of us who examine our statements only once per month. Chances are that you have an ATM card and, if so, you're already taking this risk. If you examine your ATM agreement, you probably find a similar 24-hour notification clause. The moral: If you go the electronic route, watch your account carefully.

Exploring Bank Bill-Paying Services

Secure bill-paying is possible on the Internet, just as secure credit card transactions are possible. Currently, though, there are not just several but many different models for these transactions. Big players in the business want to be early with these services, but they also want to have standard technology provided by a big, well-respected supplier — when there is such a thing. Right now, all that's available are many workable but smaller emerging technologies.

So what's really available in bill paying? Security First Network Bank's Quick Pay service is available for a walk-through (`http://www.sfnb.com/demo/`). This bank's package is produced by a software and security firm called Five Paces Inc., with another software firm, SecureWare Inc.

Looking at Quick Pay

Quick Pay is a nice, easy-to-follow, complete payment system. From the first time you enter a payee's name, as shown in Figure 26-1, you can specify if you want it on a list of regular payments that you make, which saves you from entering it over and over. You also can detail if you want this payee included in your expense and reporting tracking — for taxes, for example. For the payee, you enter the name, address, phone number, amount of payment, and account number. Clicking on Pay Now sends the electronic payment. If the payee can't accept the payment in the electronic form, Quick Pay sends out a paper check for you at no cost (for the first 20 checks).

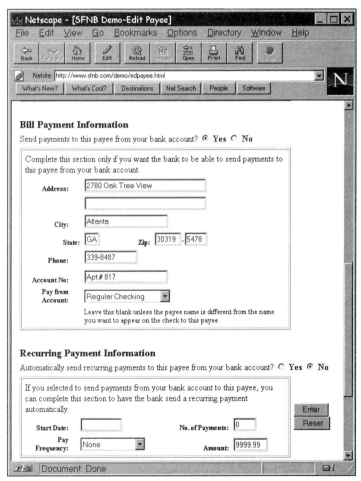

Figure 26-1: Payee information from Quick Pay.

After you make an electronic payment, Quick Pay automatically updates your checkbook register (see Figure 26-2). It's also updated and reconciled as checks, deposits, and ATM transactions take place. Items that haven't cleared are labeled as *pending*.

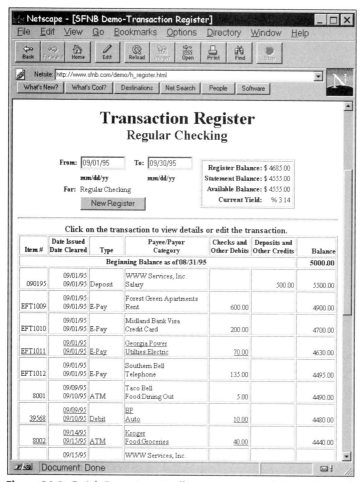

Figure 26-2: Quick Pay automatically posts payment information to the checkbook register.

You can get a complete activity record for your account for up to the past two years. Try getting that from a regular bank! You also can get expense reports and custom reports sorted by activity, such as utility bills or educational expenses, and you can download any of this data as Quicken files. Good start, Security First!

More early experiments — and plenty of uncertainty

Huntington Bancshares has picked up this same system. The other four banks that own shares in Security First obviously want to adopt the plan for themselves, too.

No doubt more banks will follow these initial banks onto the Internet. A good many are hanging back, however, because as with so many other things about the Internet, the economies aren't clear yet.

Neither are the technologies. As you learned in the last chapter, online banking can be handled in two ways: all the information can be kept on the bank's computer and made accessible through the Internet, which means that the account holder can access this information anywhere. You also can ask the account holder to use a proprietary PC package such as Microsoft Money or Quicken, which means that the full account data can be accessed only from the account holder's home PC.

Intuit, the makers of Quicken, is working with banks to set up Quicken-based home banking with bill paying. So far, about 25 banks have signed up.

It's far from clear which of these two online banking models — direct Internet access or PC-based proprietary software — will carry the day. There are advantages and disadvantages to both approaches.

However, there are many other questions. How big does a bank have to be to handle electronic banking? How many customers have PCs, use them for banking, and do enough other stuff on the Internet to move their banking activities there? Will online banking be profitable? Do customers feel secure enough on the Internet to make payments from it? Will they pay more to do this? What's the best and most cost-effective technology for this size bank? Has it been invented yet? How fast will it become obsolete? These questions are just a few that banks are grappling with.

Using Electronic Cash (ecash)

KEY TERM

What about paying cash? It's supposed to be the universal exchange medium, after all. Is cash going to disappear in the all-electronic world? Not if the proponents of ecash have their way. In brief, ecash is an Internet-based payment mechanism that uses secure, encrypted transactions to transfer small sums of money. Like cash transactions, ecash transactions don't leave a record of where you've spent your money - which is a real plus in these days of overzealous information-gathering for marketing purposes.

How does ecash work? With ecash, you make a payment to an ecash bank, which lets you download to your computer a collection of digital *coins*. Each coin is encoded with the bank's encrypted digital signature so that the vendor knows that the coins are valid. You then make payments to online vendors who don't know from whom they're receiving the money. (Like regular cash, ecash preserves your privacy.) Of course, you can reveal your identity if you want to, and you probably will if you're ordering something that has to be shipped to you.

What about nefarious uses of ecash? This is one of the major objections to the various ecash proposals — namely, that drug dealers and tax dodgers will use ecash to evade prosecution. But there's not much to worry about. Ecash preserves *buyer* anonymity but not *payee* anonymity. If somebody pays you in ecash, then you have to go back to the ecash bank to get real money. And after you do, there's a record of the transaction. You cannot conceal income when you're using ecash. In short, a drug dealer or tax dodger can't disguise income. In addition, with most ecash schemes, an ecash payer can prove that he or she made a specific payment to a specific vendor. In other words, a law enforcement agency could carry out a sting operation quite easily, making payments and then proving that they were received.

What if your hard disk crashes? Do you lose your coins? Every responsible ecash system includes the capability to recover from this and other accidental losses — or so the vendors say.

For clear explanations of ecash-related questions and issues, see DigiCash's ecash FAQ (`http://www.digicash.com/ecash/faq.html`).

DigiCash

Is there a future for cash on the Net? Products such as DigiCash (`http://www.digicash.com`) hope to let you use an electronic bank account into which you deposit "cash" to buy merchandise on the Net.

DigiCash is currently undergoing a couple trials. In the U.S., you can open a DigiCash account with Mark Twain Banks (`http://www.marktwain.com/ecash.html`). There's no minimum initial deposit — or maximum deposit, for that matter — but the trial is open to a maximum of 10,000 customers. Currently, there are no transaction charges at all, and your account is free as long as you maintain a minimum balance. Don't deposit more than you plan to spend, however, because there's a "transfer-out" fee of up to five percent.

Other trials are underway in Europe, where the ecash concept seems to be more readily accepted. (It's already used in *smart cards,* credit card-sized electronic devices that enable people to pay bridge tolls and subway fares.)

Pluses and minuses

What's good about paying with ecash? The benefits are much the same as the benefits that come from real cash: You can't lose control over your spending with ecash — you can't spend what you don't have.

Your payments aren't traceable because there's no account link from you to merchants. This means that they can't send you e-mail or other solicitations after you buy something from them. Of course, you may need to reveal your identity if you want something shipped to you, in which case the anonymity is lost.

Any takers?

Ecash isn't going to take over the world any time soon, and for a very simple reason: Few vendors accept it. In contrast to the relative ease with which somebody can set up shop to accept Visa or MasterCard orders over the telephone, it takes plenty of computer smarts — and some industrial-strength security — to accept ecash. Right now, you can subscribe to a Swedish newspaper, buy CDs, sunglasses, vitamins, and a few other odds and ends. For a list of items you can purchase, see `http://www.marktwain.com/shops/alpha.html`.

Like foreign currency

Perhaps ecash won't transform the economy, but it will become a fairly widespread way to spend small amounts on the Net. That's what the folks at NetCash seem to think. Like DigiCash, NetCash is promoting an ecash scheme that's slow to catch on.

"When we travel to a foreign country, we obtain the local currency to make purchases," NetCash's Web page explains (`http://www.netbank.com/~netcash/ncintro.html`). "When we travel the autobahn in Germany, we carry Deutsche marks; when we travel the Infobahn, we carry NetCash.

"When we return home, we usually cash in our foreign currency and we lose a little in the process due to conversion fees. With NetCash, we can avoid this problem by not immediately cashing in the NetCash when we receive it. Instead, we should keep a few NetCash coupons in our pockets to spend later. This is similar to what folks who live near borders do. If they frequently cross the border, they might always want to have some local currency in their pocket. For those of us who frequently cross the border into Cyberspace, keeping a little NetCash in our pockets makes sense."

Where does ecash go from here?

For now, as Mark Twain Bancshares says of ecash, it's only a test. Still, the original Dutch DigiCash system has potential. Testers of Mark Twain Bancshares, Deutsche Bank of Germany, and EU Bank of Finland believe that the system eventually could take in several international currencies; offer 24-hour, seven-day services; facilitate the movement of cash to smart cards; and enable payments to more "physical" stores rather than only online merchants.

But if you're new to the Net and new to its financial services, much of this stuff is pretty hard to use. Don't despair! Help is on the way from a growing group of software and media companies that are working to give the Net an easier, friendlier face. The format that some of them — Sony, Philips, and WebTV — have picked is that of a TV network. The interface that they use is the TV remote control. Their "consumer product for the Internet," coming soon, will include among its easy-to-use features a smart card slot for making payments on the Net. ecash may yet have its day!

Paying with Credit Cards — Is It Safe?

When you access a Web site that's running a secured server, ordering by credit card is possible. Because the credit card data you're sending is encrypted, the data cannot be intercepted and read while it's en route — at least not without putting a roomful of computers to work on cracking the code. And that wouldn't be worth the effort.

Does this mean that online credit card ordering is safe? Not to the satisfaction of the major credit card companies. Although encryption technology is coming along nicely, two problems remain: Vendor pilferage and authentication, as the following two sections explain.

The pilferage problem

Encryption protects credit card data only while it's en route. Credit card companies know only too well that most credit card pilferage results from credit card numbers and expiration dates lying around a vendor's office or carelessly discarded where they're accessible to thieves. This is a possibility when you order via the Web: After arriving, your credit card data must be printed out for manual verification. That's where opportunities for pilferage arise.

For this reason, the major credit card companies have not encouraged vendors to accept credit card orders online — despite the fact that online ordering is, at present, at least as safe as mail or phone ordering. Credit card companies prefer, instead, that the vendors and customers alike await the next generation of online ordering technology, which is being developed by the same company that makes those validation machines that you see almost everywhere credit cards are accepted. When this technology is in place, no one except the credit card company will ever see your credit card data. Online ordering will be far safer than any other type of ordering.

Will this advanced safety lead to an explosion of online commerce? Probably. Phone ordering with credit cards was slow to develop at first; vendors and customers alike were concerned about security issues. As people grew more accustomed to phone ordering, a huge, new mail-order industry arose, replete with glossy, junk-mail catalogs and billions of dollars of orders. Were this business to migrate to the Internet, there would be many benefits, not the least of which are environmental, because catalogs could be made available on the Web rather than printed and mailed. That means fewer dead trees and less landfill space consumed.

The authentication problem

There's one additional problem with online credit card ordering, however: How does a vendor know that you are really the person that you say you are? You could be an impostor, ordering with a stolen credit card.

The solution to this problem is to equip credit card holders with an encrypted *personal certificate*, which proves that the person ordering with the card is actually the card's rightful owner. A personal certificate is an encrypted document, one that cannot be faked by another person, that establishes your identity — in much the same way that you'd show your driver's license when buying something in a real store.

Both major browsers — Netscape Navigator and Microsoft Internet Explorer — are set up to use personal certificates. The problem is that few people understand why personal certificates are needed, what they're for, or how to get them. Worse, personal certificates cost money — currently, about $24 per year for the highest level of security (you must appear before a notary and have your application notarized). To get the online commerce market jump-started, Microsoft and Netscape have announced limited-time specials, during which they'll foot the bill (at least for the first few months).

Do you want to get your own personal certificate? Check out `http://digitalid.verisign.com`.

A potential solution comes from CheckFree, the company with the most experience in online bill paying. CheckFree Wallet, which works with most major browsers, provides a personal certificate for online credit card ordering. For more information about CheckFree Wallet, see `http://www.checkfree.com`.

Summary

◆ Electronic funds transfer (EFT) has been around for a long time. About one in three people get their paychecks by means of direct deposit, but electronic bill paying has been much slower to develop.

◆ The problem with online bill paying is that few payees accept electronic payments. If a vendor doesn't accept such payments, then the bill-paying service has to send it a paper check through snail mail.

◆ Electronic bill paying saves time and may be marginally cheaper than first-class mail.

◆ A major disadvantage of electronic bill paying is the loss of your money during the period of *float,* the time period between paying online and the payee's receiving the payment. The bill-paying company, not you, profits from this. Also, some users complain of late payments when payees do not accept electronic payments. Submission of payments without the payment coupon may result in manual processing and delays in posting your payment, with late charges accruing to you.

◆ If you decide to go the electronic bill-paying route, you can choose between a national service, such as CheckFree, and an online banking service. The latter has all the advantages because it automatically updates and reconciles your checking account information.

◆ Electronic cash (ecash) is off to a slow start in the U.S., but it has gained more acceptance in Europe. ecash protects your privacy, just as paying with cash does, but those who accept payments can't hide their income.

◆ You can pay with a credit card when you order online, but this business is growing slowly. Although your credit card data is safe while en route, thanks to encryption, it's not safe after it arrives. New technologies will make credit card ordering far safer than ordering by phone or mail, and an explosion of online commerce may be the result.

From Here

◆ Thinking about getting a loan? The Net's a great place to comparison shop, as Chapter 27 explains.

Comparing and Analyzing Loans

Thanks to some big changes in securities markets, there's a national market for home, car, and recreational equipment loans. And thanks to the Internet, you can take advantage of this competitive national market by shopping for a loan online. This chapter explains the useful resources you find for loan shopping on the Net, including some dandy calculators. These resources can help you answer key questions — for example, whether it's better to lease a car rather than buy.

What You Need — and What You Want

You acquire some kinds of assets — stocks, bonds, and more cash-like ones — with your savings. For buying other assets, however, it's somewhat different. When you buy a house or a car or get an education, you go into debt — borrow money — most of the time.

You no more think of doing without a house or a car than without the means to retire. The house and the car, at least, have potentially higher returns on your investment in them — the house might appreciate, while the car is a virtual necessity for finding and

In This Chapter

- ◆ Finding a starting point for pricing loans
- ◆ Financing a car
- ◆ Obtaining educational loans

keeping a job. But if you had to save all the money to buy them, you'd never get them when you needed them, so you borrow money.

You must make two kinds of decisions when you acquire assets such as a house or car. One decision is based on need. You need housing. You need some kind of car to transport you to your job, in most cases. You also need education to be able to get a certain kind of job that can afford you a decent living. The other decision is based on want.

Save or borrow?

You have a choice of ways to pay for these assets. You can buy them outright with your own cash, which implies that either you've saved enough to do this or they don't cost too much. You can also borrow money (rent the money and pay it back over time) for them, which implies that you don't have all the cash for them because you haven't saved it, you need these things soon, or they cost a lot.

The want factor

Aside from the need factor, a *want* factor often is just as important when deciding to buy certain kinds of assets. You may want a better education because you think that it will give you a bigger edge in your career in the long run. You may want a better car to impress bigger customers if you sell real estate or travel to visit important accounts. These factors may figure in when you decide what type of asset to purchase and how much to pay for it.

In sum, you're making important decisions when you decide to buy or lease houses, cars, schooling, and other big assets. These decisions may have a large effect on your personal net worth, even though you usually don't think of them as "investment decisions."

Speeding up the decision process

People who make and administer loans are quite familiar with loan decision processes, such as trying to figure out whether it's better to lease or to buy. They go through them with customers over and over again, so it's not surprising that they have decision software for them. Guess what? Repeating these processes over and over again is a bore and a waste of time for loan officers, too. They would be glad — and you can be relieved — if you did the processes yourself. Many of the models and interactive programs that loan officers and brokers use now are on the Web.

Maybe your computer keyboard can't quite serve as an on/off switch for all your financial transactions. However, you probably can use your monitor screen as a perfectly good menu or brochure for many financial services.

Loan pricing: well-suited to the Web

Both you and your bank may not feel secure yet doing business on the Net, but using the Net is a great way to price services. In fact, pricing certain kinds of services, such as loans, is much easier on the Net.

Mortgages, auto financing, and some other kinds of loans are priced and sold in national markets, not just in your local bank market. If you live in California, you can price your mortgage with a New York-based bank or a New Jersey-based mortgage company that's not a bank. All these lending institutions make rates available on national electronic market services.

These lenders also use computerized credit scoring services to figure out how good a risk you are and how much to charge you, which is not risky to do over the Internet. Researching on the Net is easier and faster than calling around or going to the bank and hoping for the best rate.

Finding a Starting Point for Pricing Loans

Financenter (`http://www.financenter.com`) is a good one-stop site to get you thinking about some of these decisions. It's useful to start with a site such as this — a site that brings several loan models into the mix— because it may show you some financing alternatives that you didn't know you had.

Say your old car is about to go. You need another car, whether new or used. You think going to a dealer is what you should do because you want a warranty. You may be less clear on whether to buy or lease, or what kind of terms you'll get for the size payment you can afford.

A non car loan for your car?

You can figure out your payment options using the interactive calculators that the carmaker's, car dealer's, or Financenter's sites have. What you may not think of is that if you decide to buy a car, a car loan may not be the best way to go.

For example, do you own a home? Could you take out a home equity loan at a lower rate? There's usually about a three to four percentage point difference in car and home equity loan rates. Financenter has a calculator that enables you to figure out this tradeoff, among many others. (see Figure 27-1.)

Financenter's consumer slant can be noticed in some of the hints that it gives you in using its calculators. For example, how will your repayments change, for car loans and home equity loans, as market interest rates rise or fall? You can ask "what-if" questions with these calculators, changing the purchase price, down payment, length of loan repayment term, and cost to get the loan (for the home equity loan, there may be mortgage points or other fees). You can also examine how your taxes will be affected in your income bracket. Interest on home equity loans is tax deductible, such as that for other mortgages. For making lease vs. buy decisions, Financenter's especially useful: There are calculators that let you input prices and terms, and you get a detailed cost breakdown for both alternatives.

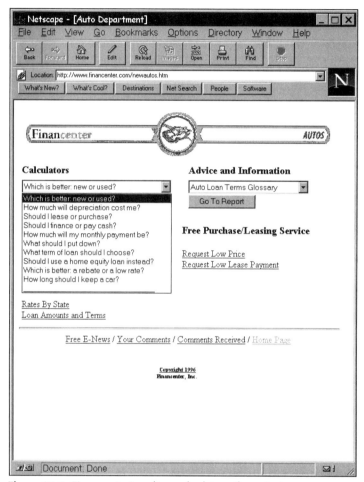

Figure 27-1: Financenter's online calculators (for autos).

Comparing lenders' prices

A number of organizations have sites on the Web where they compare interest rates on mortgage, consumer, and education loans. One old-line publisher that keeps on eye on mortgage, credit card, savings, CD rates, and many other goings-on in credit, especially from banks, is Bank Rate Monitor (`http://www.bankrate.com`). Bank Rate Monitor (see Figure 27-2) also monitors scams in banking and lending, so it's a good place to start before venturing off to commercial Web sites of actual loan providers.

Also at the Bank Rate site are articles that may help you understand some short-term "trends" in the credit markets and developments and promotions in lending, such as how to find free or low-cost debit card offers before they expire, or whether mortgage rates can be expected to stop yo-yoing around.

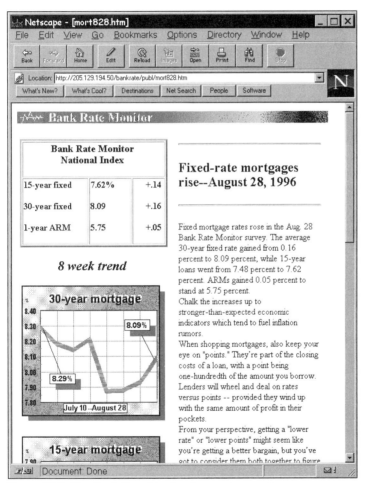

Figure 27-2: The Bank Rate Monitor for mortgage rates.

Okay, now you have a better idea of what kind of loan you want. Where can you get the best deal?

Finding lender directories

Financenter gives you some links to apply for loans online, get preapprovals for mortgages, and ask questions of lenders before proceeding further with them.

Also in the area of credit rate analysis, with some personal finance guidelines thrown in, is AAA National Mortgage Directory (`http://www.dirs.com/mortgage`). It's one of a series of directories under the AAA banner. Another directory, AAA Business Finance Directory, aids you in funding your business. The mortgage version includes a nationwide directory of mortgage firms, to which you can apply online. From this site, you can check national rate trends, read up on loan programs for which you may be eligible, or ask a question of a mortgage expert on the site's help desk.

HSH Associates (`http://www.hsh.com`) is a research firm that's one of the nation's leading authorities on loan rates. It surveys about 2,500 lenders each week. Its Web site doesn't give you a free complete listing from its big rate database, but it does give you a sizable sample that's updated weekly. HSH also has a set of calculators for finding out what your monthly (or biweekly) mortgage payments could be like, how much income you need to afford a certain monthly payment level, or how much house you can afford for a certain payment. The site also includes a paid section, called Lender Showcase. Many of these lenders, sorted by region, have loan application links here.

Prime Rate (`http://www.primerate.com`) is another service that rates and ranks financial products, primarily from banks nationwide. It finds and compares car and home loans, credit and debit cards, CDs, savings and money market rates. One problem with this database is that a number of banks are listed as being in the wrong state, which makes you wonder about the rest of the data.

More loan resources

Mortgage Mart's Mortgage Lending Resource Center (`http://www.mortgagemart.com/library.html`) tells you much more about the mortgage industry than you'll ever want or need to know if you're just starting to look for these loans. Much of this information could come in handy later, however, when you want to know if you really need mortgage insurance.

The Mortgage Mart site lets you find some lenders and brokers in about 25 states. Its resource center has interactive programs for mortgage prequalification and rent-buy decisions, as well as links to consumer protection information, instructions on how to get a mortgage, and other sites. The site also includes an online mortgage application you can walk through.

It's a national market

National loan pricing databases are possible because of changes in the past decade in the way these loans are originated. Loan officers or brokers, instead of having access to loan money from just one source, now serve more to screen loan applications and then find which lender — government, bank, or finance company — is willing to lend borrowers money given their repayment risk.

The broker does a canned credit check on the loan prospect. You find many of these forms online. They may not look like much, but they require enough information to run a complete check on you with a credit-scoring company such as TRW, Equifax, or Transmedia. You're sorted into a risk pool and, then, depending on this rank, lenders can give quotes for your loan. This process is kind of like a stock market auction in reverse.

The loan broker is the go-between for you and the lender. You may not be able to cut out the broker completely on the Web, because he or she may be running the Web site. But the Internet speeds up the process for you considerably — and you may uncover financing sources that you wouldn't find going to just one physical broker.

Financing a Car

What about car loans? A good part of car financing is handled by car dealers as brokers. They have a group of loan suppliers to whom they send — by computer — your application for financing. The dealers get a response to your loan request in a matter of hours. The main difference from home loans is that the mortgage broker usually doesn't sell you the house, too. The car dealer gets his commission from the car manufacturer and from the loan company he deals with.

A lot of business between non-bank car lenders and dealers goes on in this channel. Check the CarLoan site (`http://www.carloan.com`). This service provides leads to car loan brokers from information you fill out on the Web (see Figure 27-3).

Figure 27-3: 1-800-CARLOAN helps you find a car loan with the terms you want.

A Net for dealers

To give you some idea of how well-organized the car dealer/car maker/loan broker business is, check out DealerNet (http://www.dealernet.com). Reynolds & Reynolds, a business information networking service provider, provides this page, which is a virtual showroom (see Figure 27-4). The site is a global automotive information network for dealers, helping about 12,000 of them with their sales and marketing, loan application submissions to finance companies, parts location, and many other data needs.

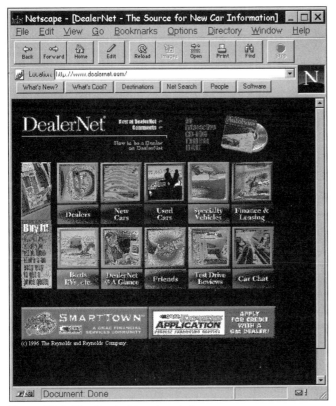

Figure 27-4: The DealerNet virtual showroom.

The Virtual Showroom takes advantage of this system to let potential customers check out online brochures, find dealers, and price cars and loans. It includes dealers for most makes of cars. You can search by car model, and then by state, for dealers. These dealers may or may not have Web pages (but DealerNet facilitates such pages for them). Linked dealers' home pages have similar menus for finding models, financing, credit scoring, and other services.

DealerNet has another set of links to auto makers' home pages. They also have yet another set of financing applications — from their own finance companies.

Just the forms, please

If you have a loan product already picked out, know just what it is, and need only a quick and easy way to apply for it, see Quantum Business Solutions' E-Apps (http://www.eapp.com).

This service give you electronic applications forms for car loans, commercial leases and financing, consumer loans, credit cards, mortgages, magazine subscriptions, university enrollment, and, soon, employment, membership in organizations, and utility services.

Obtaining Educational Loans

Educational loan applications and processing have been automated in much the same ways as other kinds of loans — only even earlier. That's the effect of the big role the government plays in this market and of its huge size. The routine you go through in getting financial aid and loans is long and involved, so computerizing it and putting it on the Internet helps considerably.

Several testing and related service organizations have developed whole packages on the Web to guide students and their families through the process. One effective package is The Complete Source of Financing Education from University Support Systems Inc. (http://www.uss.org). Its section on the Federal Guaranteed Student Loan programs takes you online through the whole process of applying for subsidized and non-subsidized Stafford Loans and the Parent Loan for Students.

Also part of this site is PLATO, a private program package for loans to undergraduate, graduate, and professional students in accredited school programs. The Complete Source has a preapproval form for this program that lets you know quickly if you qualify. The USS Educational Loan is a similar plan for preparatory, military, and religious-affiliated private high schools.

Nellie Mae, the nonprofit provider of loans for these programs, also has a Web site (http://www.nelliemae.org) that describes the programs, tells you what the current rates and repayment plans are, and lets you request applications for its programs by e-mail.

Looking for scholarship money on the Net

If you'd rather not go the loan route, go to FinAid, the Financial Aid Information Page (http://www.finaid.org). This service is from Mark Kantrowitz, author of *The Prentice-Hall Guide to Scholarships and Fellowships for Math and Science Students.*

FinAid gives you financial aid calculators, school financial aid office Web page links, and related newsgroups. It also brings you free access to FastWeb — Financial Aid Search Through the Web — a searchable database of over 180,000 private sector scholarships, fellowships, grants, and loans.

Summary

◆ It pays to think through your decisions when you buy a car or home. You're wise to use the Net to search for the best loan deals.

◆ Financenter's great calculators can help you answer key questions, such as whether it's better to finance a car loan with a home equity loan.

◆ You can use the Net to shop for a car as well as a car loan, thanks to DealerNet.

◆ If you're shopping for college loans, don't miss The Complete Source of Financing Education (http://www.uss.org).

From Here

You've reached the end of *The Savvy Investor's Internet Resource.* We hope this book has helped you fully use this powerful new technology and, at the same time, avoid its pitfalls. For further exploration of Internet goodies for investors, take a look at the directory to follow.

Internet Investing Directory

The Internet is jammed with resources of interest to individual investors, but the quality of these resources varies. This directory rates hundreds of investment-related sites using a four-star system (see "The Ratings Explained").

This directory doesn't attempt to list every site on the Net. Instead, it attempts to rate, rank, and assess the more popular ones, particularly those that relate to the investing themes stressed in this book. For this reason, you won't find much coverage of options, margin accounts, and other complex or high-risk investments. The focus here is on the sites you're most likely to use when you try to allocate your resources intelligently among mutual funds, stocks, and bonds.

The Ratings Explained

Here is an explanation of this directory's ratings.

★★★★ Of interest to any investor — one of the very best investment-related sites on the Net. Don't miss this one!

★★★ An excellent site, rich in resources and well worth visiting even if the site's subject matter isn't at the center of your interests.

★★ A useful site for those interested in its subject matter. Has some unusual features or resources that may interest you.

★ Worth visiting if you're interested in the site's subject matter, but probably not worth your time otherwise. Please note that this isn't a put-down. Some sites have a narrow focus and appeal mainly to those with very specific interests.

Basics of Investing

100% No-Load Mutual Fund Council ★★★

http://networth.galt.com/www/home/mutual/100/100dirmf.htm

This site is dedicated to no-load mutual fund investing — funds that do not charge fees upon entering or exiting. The site contains useful information for the new investor looking for a good overview of the ins and outs of mutual fund investing, including discussions of fund safety, fund management, retirement planning, and the importance of expense ratios. There are also links to nearly 40 families of no-load funds.

Highlights

- ◆ Facts and fallacies about no-load mutual fund investing
- ◆ How to invest in mutual funds
- ◆ Reading a prospectus
- ◆ Basic rules for successful investing
- ◆ Choosing the first fund
- ◆ Expanding your portfolio
- ◆ Dollar-cost averaging
- ◆ Children and mutual funds

◆ Managing your fund portfolio

◆ A 401(k) plan for small businesses

◆ List of no-load funds

◆ How funds are managed

◆ Regulation of funds

◆ Discussion of mutual fund safety

◆ Importance of expense ratios

◆ How to analyze fund expenses

◆ How to read fund stock tables

◆ Where to find more information on mutual fund investing

◆ Helpful glossaries of mutual fund and general investing terms

101 Questions to Ask About Investing ★★★★

http://mosl.sos.state.mo.us/sos-sec/101que

Developed by the Missouri Division of Securities, this excellent resource lists 101 questions to ask about a wide range of investments, including the riskier ones (such as commodities, lease lotteries, and penny stocks). Don't miss this page if you're thinking about putting money into an investment that you don't fully understand.

Highlights

◆ Business ventures

◆ Oil and gas investing

◆ Lease lotteries

◆ Options

◆ Tax shelters

◆ Bank brokerage services

◆ Commodities

◆ Penny stocks

Building Your Portfolio ★★★★

http://www.vanguard.com/educ/module2/univ_m2.html

A thorough introduction to investing, this online course walks you through the basics of a sound approach, including learning the difference between saving and investing, understanding the risk/reward tradeoff, allocating your assets, building a balanced portfolio, and understanding mutual fund performance. Part of the Vanguard Online University (`http://www.vanguard.com/educ/univ.html`), this is one of many excellent tutorials at this site.

Highlights

- ◆ A look at historical investment returns
- Assessing your risk tolerance
- ◆ The right investment risk

Calvert Group: What Is Responsible Investing? ★★★

`http://www.calvertgroup.com/cresinv/cresp.htm`

The philosophy underlying the Calvert fund group emphasizes socially responsible investing.

Frequently Asked Questions About Investing ★★★

`http://www.fid-inv.com/investors/faqs/faqs.html`

Although these FAQs (frequently asked questions — with answers) focus on Fidelity investments, they're of interest to anyone who's getting into investing. You find five FAQs, focusing on general investing, Fidelity's Web site, Fidelity target timeline funds, retirement investing, and tax reporting.

Highlights

- ◆ What is dollar cost averaging?
- ◆ How can I prepare for a market correction?
- ◆ Who can contribute to an IRA?

Getting Started: Investing with Mutual Funds ★★★★

`http://www.troweprice.com/mutual/basics.html`

T. Rowe Price is one of the larger fund families. Even if you're not interested in a T. Rowe Price fund, this introduction to mutual funds is well worth reading — especially if you're a complete beginner. You learn basic investing terms and concepts.

Highlights

- ◆ Defining your financial goals
- ◆ Understanding risk and your risk tolerance
- ◆ Finding funds that match your objectives

Glossary of Investing and Trading Terms ★★

http://www.moneymentor.com/mm_gloss.html

This is an advanced glossary that focuses on terms related to technical and fundamental analysis. The definitions are extensive and illustrated with examples. You'll find this of interest only if you've learned the basics of stock analysis.

GreenMoney Online ★★★

http://www.greenmoney.com

This page has links to publications, products, funds, investment planners, banks, and other socially responsible businesses.

Guide to Investment Terms ★★★

http://wps1.fid-inv.com/fir/ime/ime-id.htm

This is a good glossary for beginners. Although it's not very extensive, you find solid explanations of basic terms such as "aggressive," "maturity," and "variable annuity."

Investor Education Glossary ★★★★

http://www.vanguard.com/educ/glos.html

Probably the best glossary for beginning investors, this dictionary is part of Vanguard's investor education course, which is highly recommended.

Invest-o-Rama Education Center ★★★

http://www.investorama.com/learn.shtml/

If you're asking, "How do I get started in investing?" this is an excellent place for answers. You find some useful resources here, as well as links to other great starting points for investor education.

Highlights

- ◆ Invest-o-Rama glossary of investing terms
- Stock selection guide tutorial
- ◆ Quick tips for balance sheet analysis

Invest-o-Rama Glossary of Stock Investing Terms ★★★★

http://www.investorama.com/gloss.shtmlhttp://www.investorama.com/gloss.html

A thorough, authoritative dictionary that focuses on stocks. It's not organized for easy or efficient access, but the content is top-notch.

InvestorNet Getting Started ★★★★

http://www.researchmag.com/iInvestor/getting.htm

An excellent series of articles on getting started in investing, emphasizing consumer issues and rights. Shouldn't be missed by anyone — including those who have some investing experience.

Highlights

- ◆ Investing 101
- What every investor should know
- ◆ Investing wisely
- ◆ Glossary of investment terms
- ◆ How's your portfolio doing?

Quotable Quotes ★★★

http://www.moneypages.com/syndicate/stocks/qquotes.html

Douglas Gerlach's fun collection of investment-related quotations from the likes of Benjamin Franklin, Peter Lynch, and Mark Twain.

Socially Responsible Investing: Profits and Principles ★★★★

http://www.betterworld.com/index.htm

This is an introduction to the philosophy of socially responsible investing.

Bonds

Bloomberg Personal National Muni Bond Yields ★★

http://www.bloomberg.com/markets/psamuni.html

Here's a quick look at current national municipal bond yields, brought to the Net by the Public Securities Association (PSA).

Bonds Online ★★★★

http://www.bonds-online.com/

Bonds Online is a service of Twenty-First Century Municipals, Inc., an online fixed income investment information company allowing individuals to buy municipal bonds over the Microsoft Network. This excellent Web site contains much information for the online investor who wishes to learn more about bonds. The site features the "Bond Professor," who answers bond questions. Other sections feature specific information about zero coupons and other forms of bond investments.

Highlights

- Frequently asked bond questions
  - ◆ Recent bond market news and offerings
- Glossary of terms
  - ◆ Ask the Bond Professor
- Bond question of the week
  - ◆ Investing game
  - ◆ Free online bond-oriented newsletter
- About zero coupons and STRIPS
  - ◆ Current savings bond rates
  - ◆ About U.S. Savings bonds, with frequently asked questions
  - ◆ Savings Bond redemption calculator
  - ◆ About the Treasury Direct program
  - ◆ Daily Treasury Quotes
  - ◆ Upcoming Treasury auctions
  - ◆ Current economic indicators
  - ◆ Corporate and municipal bond information
  - ◆ Highest yielding bond funds
  - ◆ Lists of bond brokers

Bond Terms ★★★

http://lebenthal.com:80/bond_terms.html

An excellent glossary of the often-confusing terminology of bonds and related securities.

BondTrac ★

http://www.bondtrac.com/

BondTrac is a subscription-based service that enables bond investors to search for municipal, agency, corporate, and Treasury bonds. Without a subscription, you can search for bonds that meet certain criteria, but you won't see the information concerning where and how they can be purchased.

Economeister ★★

http://www.economeister.com

News service with emphasis on currencies and Treasuries. The articles are concise and enable you to span an impressive amount of information in a few minutes. Daily updates keep the information fresh.

Highlights

- ◆ Latest economic indicators
- ◆ Daily market news
- ◆ Currency and bond news
- ◆ News of currency rates
- ◆ Labor news

Moody's Bond Ratings ★★

http://www.moneypages.com/syndicate/bonds/ratings.html

Curious what those bond ratings mean? The definitions are on this page.

Municipal Resource Center ★★★

http://www.municipal.com

A service of R.R. Donnelley Financial, this site presents itself as the headquarters on the Net for information concerning municipal bonds. A key feature: A searchable Municipal Securities Disclosure Archive (MSDA), which contains official statements, annual financial information, and material event notices concerning municipal bonds, as required by the Securities and Exchange Commission (SEC). (Material events are events investors should be told about because they may affect funds that go into payments to bondholders.) Adobe Acrobat is required to read the reports, but you can download this program for free from this site.

Highlights

👍 Searchable database of mutual fund disclosure statements

◆ Information on issuers, including data, demographics, marketing materials, and hot links to states and municipalities

◆ Library of resource materials from the SEC and various industry organizations

◆ Information from various financial services organizations that handle municipal securities

◆ Tools and utilities of interest to mutual fund investors

Treasury Direct ★★★★

`http://www.ny.frb.org/pihome/treasdir`

You can buy Treasury bonds directly from the U.S. Federal Reserve Bank, as this document explains, without paying brokers' fees. You can't order them on the Web, but this page explains how to obtain these securities by mail.

Highlights

◆ Basic information on Treasury Direct

◆ Frequently asked questions

◆ Tender forms and instructions

◆ Treasury note and bond auction results

◆ Historical auction results

◆ Treasury auction dates

Company Research Services

Disclosure/SEC ★★★

`http://networth.galt.com/cgi-bin/Disclosure_SEC`

One of the best stock screening sites on the Net is NETworth's Disclosure SEC Database Query, which makes use of publicly available SEC data. Containing data on more than 12,000 U.S. companies, the database is searchable in an amazing variety of ways. For example, you can search for companies with high sales growth, high percentage of shares held by employees, and low long-term debt, in addition to the standard selection criteria (P/E ratio and debt/equity ratio). You have to pay a fee for these searches, though. The same information is available from EDGAR for free, but you don't get the sophisticated search engine or the beautifully organized reports.

EDGAR ★★★

http://www.sec.gov/

Though a bit clunky, the Securities and Exchange Commission's EDGAR database offers a tremendous amount of information to the online investor willing to slog through to find the gems. Material includes filings on some 15,000 companies and includes one or more of the following: proxy statements, stock registration, reports on recent events, annual and quarterly reports, mutual fund prospectuses, and shareholder reports.

Highlights

- ◆ Stock registration (Form S-1)
- ◆ Proxy statements, including annual meeting notices (Form DEF14A)
- ◆ Notices of attempts to gain control of a company's board (Form DEFC14A)
- ◆ Notices of acquisitions, changes in control, resignations, and bankruptcy (Form 8-K)
- ◆ Annual reports (Form 10-K)
- ◆ Quarterly reports (Form 10-Q)
- ◆ Mutual fund prospectuses (Form 497)
- ◆ Reports to Shareholders (Forms N-30D and N-30B-2)

Financial World ★★★★

http://www.financialworld.com/

Requiring registration, this site features a database of 1,000 companies ranked according to Financial World's stock selection criteria. In addition to searching by Financial World letter grades, you also can screen stocks for declining sales, price/earnings ratio, price/book ratio, debt/equity ratio, and dividend yield. This is an indispensable research tool for any investor.

Highlights

- ◆ Forecast 500 tables predict end-of-the-year performance versus competitors in the same industry for 500 top companies
- ◆ Market Value 500 tables predict end-of-the-year stock performance for

500 top companies

Best and worst analysts rank brokerages according to performance from last year's recommendations

Hoover's Online ★★★★

`http://www.hoovers.com/`

Well-organized, information packed, and decorated with attractive art-deco image maps, Hoover's Online offers a wealth of information to the online investor. IPO Central, for example, lists the current and past week's public stock offerings; furthermore, a Beginner's Guide is provided to help new investors understand the ins and outs of the venture capital/IPO landscape.

Biz Buzz and Industry Focus sections provide capsules of top general business and aerospace/defense sector news. A corporate directory provides brief overviews of companies, along with their recent financial status and stock quotes. An admission-by-subscription-only area contains more detailed profiles of some 2,500 companies, as well as access to a database of European companies, the Biz Buzz archives, and the Industry Focus archives.

Highlights

Recent IPOs and Understanding IPOs

◆ Visible Hand (column on corporate structure and finance)

Company profile database (by subscription)

◆ Company earnings reports

Brief American company profiles, along with recent earnings information and stock quotes

Brief European company profiles (by subscription)

In-depth company profiles (by subscription)

◆ Business Web site directory

◆ Giant list of company trivia

◆ List of best-selling business books

Annotated list of links

InvestLink ★★★

`http://www.investlink.com/investlink.html`

This is an excellent site for research on stocks and companies. InvestLink offers a database of 9,000 publicly held companies, which you can screen by P/E ratio, 52-week price range, and stock price range. Use of some features requires free registration, but you have to fill out a particularly invasive questionnaire.

Highlights

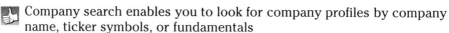 Company search enables you to look for company profiles by company name, ticker symbols, or fundamentals

◆ Market Information gives the latest results from major exchanges

◆ Personal portfolio manager

◆ Stock Watcher enables you to track all your stocks and see the results on a single page

InvestorWEB ★

http://www.investorWeb.com/default.htm

InvestorWEB is a new investment-oriented site. Perhaps the most significant feature is its large list of links to company information and home pages. There is also a list of newly offered IPOs. InvestorWEB appears to be designed to grow in the direction of being a chat site, with space near new IPOs for people to share gossip and insight about new stock offerings. Already present are chat areas for people to discuss their favorite financial magazines, books, newsletters, data services, and online brokerages.

Highlights

◆ New IPO listings

◆ IPO discussion area (coming soon)

◆ Beginning investors section

◆ Miscellaneous investing articles

◆ Members-only chat areas

Market Guide ★★

http://www.marketguide.com/

Market Guide provides free brief profiles and market statistics for over 8,000 companies; more detailed information is available by subscription. The site also contains daily lists of highest gaining sectors, along with largest gaining and biggest losing stocks.

Highlights

- ◆ About Market Guide
- 👍 Largest gaining and losing stocks ($2-$10, and $10 or more)
- ◆ Hottest sectors and industries
- 👍 Brief company profiles
- ◆ Glossary of terms
- ◆ Products and services offered

Newspage ★★★

http://www.newspage.com

This is an excellent source of industry-specific news from a huge variety of sources, including industry-specific newspapers, magazines, and PR releases. An added benefit: You can search the huge database of articles for information on a company (or any other subject).

Highlights

- 👍 Company tracking section enables you to follow the news on 1,400 companies
- ◆ Search engine enables you to search for today's stories or for stories from the entire database

Pathfinder Business ★★★★

http://pathfinder.com/pathfinder/secondmoney.html

The Pathfinder site contains Web sites for Money, Your Company, and Fortune. The section sponsored by Money includes a number of short audio clips on a variety of investment topics, loan rates sorted by region, a search page to help you choose a good city for relocation, and similar tools and information. The Progressive Farmer, and especially the Your Company and Fortune pages, offer more substantial samplings of recent content of the respective parent magazines. You can also access the full text of the Money and the Fortune Business Report from this site. This is an excellent place to research companies.

Highlights

- ◆ Full text of *Fortune* and *Money Magazine*
- ◆ Fortune 500 special reports
- ◆ *Fortune's* Investor's Guide

Wall Street Journal Company Briefing Books ★★★★

`http://interactive3.wsj.com/edition/resources/documents/search.htm`

This superbly organized service generates a company profile when you search by ticker symbol. The profile includes background information, a financial overview, stock performance charts and data, recent news, and press releases.

Wall Street Research Net ★★★★

`http://WSRN.com`

This research-focused site contains an amazing 110,000 links. It's designed to assist professional and individual investors in researching fundamental data about actively traded companies.

Highlights

 Research a Company enables you to search for companies by company name or stock ticker symbol; the result of the search is a list of links that includes the company's home page, company profiles, StockMaster charts, links to press releases and company names, and much more

◆ Research the Economy provides links to the best sources of information concerning the economy, including the latest government reports

◆ The Markets contains links to the pages of U.S. and world stock exchanges

◆ The News contains links to the best business-news sections of Web-based newspapers and magazines

Comprehensive Investing Sites

Interactive Nest Egg ★★

`http://nestegg.iddis.com`

The INE site is a conglomeration of several related investment-oriented services. Smith Barney offers commentaries and recommendations based on current market trends. Tradeline, which sells market tracking software, sponsors stock and mutual fund quote servers and online performance graphing of an equity's past performance. Nest Egg is a general interest personal finance magazine; the site contains the magazine's articles, both past and present, as well as an index. Perhaps the best feature of the site is Web Finance, an interesting and useful online financial magazine featuring both general and Internet-specific business news.

Highlights

- ◆ Smith Barney investment advice and stock picks
- ◆ Past and present Nest Egg articles, with index
- 👍 Past and present Web finance articles, with index and search engine
- ◆ Large directory of mutual funds
- 👍 Tradeline mutual fund and quote servers, with performance history graphing programs

InvestQuest ★★★

http://www.investquest.com

The InvestQuest site contains quarterly reports and proxy statementsfiled with the SEC (and in some cases, substantially more information) for the companies making up Dow indices and the S&P 500. Even more interesting, however, is the information about many commonly traded ADRs (American Depository Receipts), complete with balance sheets and income statements.

Highlights

- 👍 Large list of common ADRs, with balance sheets and income statements
- ◆ Dow Jones index companies, with quarterly and year-end reports and proxy statements
- ◆ S&P 500 index companies, with quarterly and year-end reports and proxy statements

INVESTools ★★★★

http://www.investools.com

Subtitled "On-Demand Information for Self-Reliant Investors," this excellent page features analysis, opinion, commentary, and research information. Don't miss this site. Lots of information is available for free; you can purchase additional reports and articles for fees ranging from $1 to a few dollars.

Highlights

- 👍 Press digests of business news from *The Washington Post, The Wall Street Journal,* and *The New York Times,* as well as latest changes in analyst's ratings of top stocks
- 👍 Written by John Brobst of INVESTools, *Investor's Web Watch* is a newsletter that provides an excellent introduction to the Web's resources from the point of view of an investment life cycle (getting oriented, getting started, allocating assets, and so on)

◆ Produce a variety of charts for any stock or mutual fund

◆ Hundreds of online investment newsletters; you can read sample issues for free

◆ America Online's technical analyst, Carl Swenlin, is now on the Web, offering daily and weekly stock and market reports

◆ Analysis, opinion, and commentary on growth stock investing

◆ Links, commentary, and resources for precious metals investors, including the latest Reuters quotes

◆ In-depth analysis of international investing opportunities

◆ A list of the most talked-about companies in INVESTool's publications

👍 Usenet-style newsgroups on mutual funds, stocks, newsletters, Internet resources, and general investing, but without the spamming and antisocial behavior

◆ Pick the top stock for the next month and win free usage credit

invest-o-rama! ★★★

http://www.investorama.com/

This well-organized and stimulating site contains information about the main topics of interest to an investor: bonds, brokerage firms, DRIPs, investing clubs, international investing, market information, mutual funds, quotes, technical analysis, and the list goes on. There are also featured articles, featured growth stocks, and a running "Ask Doug" question and answer forum.

Highlights

👍 Feature articles for investment club members

◆ Growth stock of the month

👍 Guide to DRIPs directory of investment clubs with home pages

◆ Links to mutual fund home pages and fund information

👍 E-mail and Internet investing discussion mailing lists

◆ Lots of links to good sites!

MarketEdge ★★★★

If you're serious about investing, perhaps you'd be willing to fork over the $7.95 per month subscription fee for this well-designed service.

Highlights

- ◆ Market Monitor provides daily earnings, surprises and forecasts, up-to-the-minute news concerning mergers and acquisitions, industry news, news concerning tech stocks, latest stories on the credit markets and economy, weekly economic calendar of events, and end-of-day market stats

- Stock Center provides stock quotes and price charts, complete coverage of the day's market activity, company reports covering over 7,000 of the month's top performers, stock screening search services with 18 search parameters, and industry reports from leading brokerage firms

- ◆ Investing Insight features daily and weekly analysis and columns

- ◆ Mutual Fund Center features expert analysis and discussion of the month's developments in the mutual fund industry, a mutual fund screening service that lets you use 12 search parameters, the month's top performers, and in-depth NAV charts

- ◆ Municipal Bond Center features daily bond buyer news and analysis, as well as regional coverage

- ◆ Portfolio tracking software enables you to create multiple portfolios that can contain unlimited securities; after entering your investments, you automatically receive news alerts that relate to your stocks

- ◆ Stock and Fund Alerts enables members to search by company name or ticker to receive updates on financial news, earnings announcements, management changes, and other fast-breaking news

MSN Investor ★★★

`http://www.msn.com/investor/content.asp`

The Microsoft Network's Investor center is freely available to Web users. It's worth a visit, especially for the interactive news features.

Highlights

- ◆ Market Summary: A concise summary of leading market indexes

- ◆ Top Ten: The top volume leaders; click on one of the ticker symbols to see fundamental data and recent price/trading trends for the listed stocks

- ◆ Personal Portfolio: An easy-to-use online portfolio manager for stocks and funds, but it's not secure

- ◆ Quote Lookup: Enter a ticker symbol to see a delayed quote

- ◆ Resources: Links to online brokerages, exchanges, market summaries, and general reference

National Association of Investors Corporation (NAIC) ★★

http://www.better-investing.org/

Founded in 1951, NAIC is a nonprofit organization composed of investment clubs and individual investors. NAIC has continued this mission to the present, offering advice on long-term investment in stocks, fact sheets on companies, guides for organizing investment clubs, and pointers on filing taxes. Members of NAIC are also able to gain low-cost entry into any of 145 DRIPs. NAIC also runs its own closed-end mutual fund. The NAIC Web site contains information about all these activities, plus lists and order forms for NAIC publications, a calendar of NAIC activities and lectures, and other information.

Highlights

- ◆ Online NAIC company information request form
- ◆ NAIC tips and resources for forming investment clubs
- ◆ Calendar of NAIC events

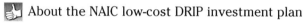 About the NAIC low-cost DRIP investment plan

- ◆ NAIC software and data files
- ◆ Top 200 stocks held by investment clubs
- ◆ About the NAIC Computer Group Online store

NETworth ★★★★

http://networth.galt.com/

NETworth is what the investor's Internet is all about: Lots of fabulous, free information on companies and funds. You search the famed Morningstar database of more than 5,000 mutual funds, looking for fund performance and Morningstar's respected fund rankings. Registration is required to access mutual fund data.

Highlights

 Morningstar database of mutual fund performance statistics and rankings

- ◆ Mutual Fund Market Manager (groups mutual fund information)

 Personal Portfolio (enables you to track your mutual fund portfolio)

- ◆ Fund Atlas (includes a customized search function that enables you to define your mutual fund interests)
- ◆ Weekly market outlook

 Prospectus links to thousands of mutual funds

- ◆ Delayed stock quotes from major exchanges
- 👍 Large list of free and subscription-based newsletters
- ◆ Commodities and derivatives
- ◆ Currency exchange rates
- ◆ Government economic data (various economic indicators and census data)
- ◆ Online mutual fund prospectuses
- ◆ Interviews with fund managers
- 👍 Top 25 performing mutual funds
- ◆ Company IPOs, secondary offerings, SEC data, and other information
- 👍 Links to a variety of glossaries

PAWWS Financial Network ★★★

http://pawws.com/

PAWWS is a comprehensive investment Web site, but with more emphasis on trading securities than some others. The site is home to several online brokers and offers free online personal portfolio tracking with optional daily e-mail updates. An online quote server provides prices for both the large exchanges and the OTC market. A variety of other news and information services are offered, though many are fee-based.

Highlights

- 👍 Delayed quote server, listing both major exchange and OTC bulletin board quotes
- ◆ Market news, indices, new issues, trade alerts, and hot stocks (by subscription)
- 👍 Free market outlook, stock reports, and microcap profiles
- ◆ How to choose a financial newsletter
- ◆ Request free sample newsletters
- 👍 Free microcap hot stock picks
- ◆ About mutual fund investing
- ◆ Online mutual fund brochures, with online form to request full prospectuses
- ◆ Gabelli Mutual Funds site
- ◆ Frequently asked questions about the various PAWWS services

Research: InvestorNet ★★

http://www.researchmag.com/investor.htm

Research: Online Magazine (described in the magazines section) sponsors a Web site for individual investors called InvestorNet. The site features delayed quotes, complete with 52-week price history and expected long-, mid-, and short-term expected results. Free write-ups and S&P reports are available for selected stocks and mutual funds.

Highlights

👍 Free quotes, with 52-week charts and other information about and reports on selected stocks and mutual funds

◆ Shareholder news and other information about selected companies and mutual funds

◆ Top-performing funds

👍 Free portfolio tracking with investor alerts

◆ Guide to basic investing

👍 Spotlighted industries, with analysts' buy recommendations

◆ Guide to retirement planning

👍 Global investing through depository receipts

Silicon Investor ★★★

http://www3.techstocks.com/

For those interested in high-tech investing, the Silicon Investor is the place to be. The site contains hundreds of user-created chat forums, most of which focus on individual computer, software, communications, and semiconductor companies, though a few exist for other miscellaneous subjects (biomedical investing, mutual funds, and so on).

Highlights

👍 Technology company profiles (derived from SEC 10-K reports)

◆ Spotlight (articles on featured companies, daily "big movers" and "hot stocks" tables)

👍 Charts (individual or group stock performance graphed from 10 days up to 100 months; may be printed out)

◆ Sector performance tables

◆ Ongoing bear/bull weekly market sentiment survey

👍 Stock talk (forums with chat threads)

◆ Interactive tour Silicon Valley Business (description of upcoming content of business-oriented TV news show)

◆ Delayed quotes

◆ Online calendar of events

◆ Online demo of the CompuTEL Internet brokerage system

◆ Guru corner (humorous stock trading advice)

◆ Links to other news sources

Starting Point — Investing ★★★

http://stpt.com/invest.html

Starting Point is a Net directory service that maintains a well-organized, straightforward page dedicated to investing. The site features delayed stock, bond, and fund quotes and daily charts of stock market activity and various sector indices. Links are available to a number of sources of financial news and trading houses.

Highlights

◆ Daily charts, market activity, and indices

◆ Delayed quotes

◆ Bonds and futures

◆ Online stock trading companies

◆ Links to free investors' newsletters

◆ Financial news sources

The Syndicate ★★★

http://www.moneypages.com/syndicate/

The Syndicate site contains a good bit of information about investing, including material on IPOs, DRIPS, bonds, and mutual funds. There is also a huge list of links to some 1,600 financial sites.

Highlights

◆ Investment headlines (updated daily)

◆ What is the Dow Jones Industrial Average?

◆ About DRIP investing

- About IPOs
- Investment management styles
- 👍 SEC investment guide
- Market performance by president
- Index options
- Foreign stocks
- About bond/tax swaps
- Buying bonds at the Treasury auction
- Historical graph of the 3-month T-bill rate (1934 to 1994)
- Definitions of Moody's bond ratings
- Municipal bond terms
- Broker's Corner
- 👍 Frequently asked questions about mutual funds
- Stock, commodity, mutual fund, and index quotes
- Fraction to decimal converter
- 👍 Large list of links, sorted by subject

Wall Street City ★★

http://www.wallstreetcity.com/

Subtitled "The Investor's Supersite on the Web," this feature-packed place offers market news, stock quotes, commentary, and a mutual-fund screening service. A lot of unmoderated discussion groups at this site — beware.

Highlights

- Current quotes with ticker symbol lookup
- Market averages
- Market commentary (three times daily)
- Hot stocks with price leaders, volume leaders, and stocks making news
- Stocks in industry groups (lists stocks by industry)
- Mutual fund quotes with symbol lookup
- 👍 Best-performing mutual funds over seven time periods
- Funds with best yields
- Individual broker listings

- ◆ Brokerage links on the Web
- 👍 Stock screening by P/E ratio, highest dividend yield, and more
- ◆ Company snapshots and corporate overviews of thousands of companies
- ◆ Discussion forums on a variety of topics
- ◆ Top investment news stories

Dividend Reinvestment Programs (DRIPS)

Dividend Re-Investment Program (DRIP) Guide ★★★

http://www.cs.cmu.edu/%7Ejdg/drip.html

Shareholder reinvesting (using dividends from owned stock to buy more shares of the same stock) has been around for some time, and interest in this form of investment has recently mushroomed. Many companies have instituted DRIP programs of various types, with some allowing direct stock purchases through the company, thus avoiding broker's fees.

Others are allowing shareholders to purchase small amounts of stock on a monthly basis, again avoiding brokerage fees. The DRIP Guide contains a large list of companies offering DRIPs, along with contact information, lists of books and newsletters about DRIPs, and other useful information.

Highlights

- ◆ DRIP basics
- 👍 List of companies with DRIPs
- ◆ How to join a DRIP
- ◆ List of books and newsletters
- ◆ Other DRIP information sources

NetStock ★★

http://www.netstockdirect.com/

This is the best DRIP-related site on the Net. It's well designed and packed with useful information, including a complete list of current DRIP plans and online enrollment forms.

Highlights

 Complete list of direct purchase stock plans

◆ Order DRIP prospectus and enrollment forms for mail delivery

◆ Access DRIP enrollment forms online

◆ Search for DRIPs

◆ DRIP investor newsletter

FAQs (Frequently Asked Questions)

misc.invest FAQ ★★★

`http://www.smartpages.com/faqs/investment-faq/general/top.html`

This FAQ covers general investment topics, and it's organized like a glossary (for the most part). Although the coverage is uneven, some gems can be found here, and it's well worth reading. Divided into seven parts, this is a fairly weighty work, as FAQs go.

Highlights

◆ Advice for beginning investors

◆ One-line wisdom (quotations concerning money and investing)

◆ Warning concerning advertisements in the misc.invest.* newsgroups

misc.invest.funds FAQ ★★

`http://www.cis.ohio-state.edu/hypertext/faq/usenet/investment-faq/mutual-funds/faq.html`

This FAQ discusses some of the basic concepts of mutual funds. Unlike the seven-part misc.invest FAQ, this one is much more concise; there's only one file to read. Actually, this FAQ is pretty sparse. It's worth reading, but it doesn't discuss many key points concerning mutual funds.

Initial Public Offerings (IPOs)

Alert-IPO ★

`http://www.ostman.com/alert-ipo/`

This subscription-only service scans EDGAR reports for news of upcoming initial public offerings and sends notifications to you via e-mail.

Going Public ★

http://www.rrdfin.com/goingpub/goingpub.htm

Ever wondered what's involved — and what's at risk — when a company seeks capital by means of a public stock offering? This fascinating document explains the whole process. Prepared by a group of attorneys, this document is of interest to anyone thinking about going public or just investing in an IPO.

Investor's Edge IPO Calendar ★

http://www.irnet.com/scripts/ethos.exe?WWW+p_IEIPOCalendar

If you'd like to know about upcoming IPOs, this page lists them in a month-by-month calendar format.

IPO Data Systems ★★

http://www.ipodata.com/

If you want to know more about IPOs, this is the site of choice. It provides comprehensive data on IPOs in the U.S. It's a subscription-based service, but you can check out samples and take a tour of the service's offerings.

IPO Source ★★

http://www.ipo-source.com/

This service offers several freebies of interest to investors, including commentaries and news on IPOs.

Highlights

- ◆ Weekly commentary on IPO market
- ◆ Today's hottest IPO filing announcement
- ◆ Today's newest IPO starts trading
- ◆ IPO glossary

ProspectusNet ★★

http://www.netresource.com/pn/home.html

This page offers a searchable interface to companies who are preparing public stock offerings. You can search by company, industry, or investment bank.

Investor Associations

American Association of Individual Investors ★★★★

http://www.aaii.org/

AAII's Web site is packed with information every investor should carefully study.

Highlights

 Investing basics

◆ Glossary of investment terms

◆ Financial and retirement planning information

◆ Understanding and investing in mutual funds

◆ Regulatory agencies and investor complaints

◆ Screening and analyzing stocks

◆ Basics of portfolio management

◆ Avoiding problems with brokerage accounts and brokers

◆ Computerized investing: Reviews of online brokers

National Association of Investors Corporation ★★★

http://www.better-investing.org/

This site doesn't offer as much information as the AAII offering, but it does include a jewel: the Stock Selection Guide (SSG). You also find information on investment clubs.

National Council of Individual Investors ★★★

http://com.primenet.com/ncii/

Like AAII and NAIC, this organization provides investor education, but it also has a strong focus on advocacy. NCII represents the interests of individual investors in state and federal regulatory agencies and legislatures.

Highlights

◆ Latest information on the lack of small-investor access to IPOs

 Washington Watch

◆ Information for self-reliant investors

◆ What's "inside information"?

◆ Links to state securities agencies

 ScamWatch

◆ Learn how to make investment decisions the Warren Buffet way

Magazines

Asia, Inc. Online ★★★

http://www.asia-inc.com/

The AIO Web site contains selections from *Asia, Inc.*, one of the premier magazines dedicated to business and investing in Asia. The site features selections from the hard copy magazine, as well as moderated discussion forums, Asian financial information, and excerpts from Asia, Inc.'s radio show. There are also daily news summaries, as well as an archive of recent back issues, complete with an online key word search engine.

Highlights

◆ About Asia, Inc., Online Today's financial news

◆ New this week

◆ Guest features (articles appearing in Asia, Inc., which originally appeared elsewhere)

◆ Current and past issues

◆ Asia Internet directory

◆ Conference rooms

◆ Hong Kong stock recommendations (for registered users)

◆ Subscribe to the hard copy publication

◆ Index of advertisers

Business Week ★★★

http://www.businessweek.com

The Business Week Web site features the lead articles from the most recent print edition, as well as audio clips from the publication's radio broadcasts. The site also contains ads for the journal's site on America Online.

Highlights

- ◆ Excerpts from current issue
- ◆ Business Week Radio Reports
- ◆ Business Week editorial awards
- ◆ Business Week news offices

The Economist ★★★

http://www.economist.com/

The Economist is a leading international British weekly magazine that covers world news, especially events affecting business. This site contains selections from the current issue, plus an online edition of the journal's monthly supplement, Review of Books and Multimedia. More features are slated to be added in coming months.

Forbes Magazine ★★

http://www.forbes.com/

This site features selected articles from the current hard-copy edition of *Forbes*. Selections from Forbes FYI and Forbes ASAP are also present. The magazine promises that the full text of all three publications, along with additional content and services, will be available in the near future.

Highlights

- ◆ Selections from current magazines
- ◆ Tables of contents
- ◆ Subscribe to the hard copy edition

Mutual Funds Online Weekly ★★★★

http://www.mfmag.com/

This site may represent the future of Web publishing. It features the entire content of both present and recent past editions of the magazine's printed publication. Magazine covers and contents pages are reproduced at roughly life size; these double as clickable image maps, allowing for easy navigation.

The advertisements are conspicuous but are also hypertext links to information and services of real potential interest. Several online databases and tools are of interest to the online investor, such as a load performance calculator to help you decide which class of shares of a load-bearing fund will have the lowest load burden for you. This virtual edition virtuosity comes with a price, however — page loading rates can be frustratingly slow at times.

Highlights

- ◆ Entire contents of print editions
- ◆ Request advertiser information via online forms
- 👍 Large list of fund families, with phone numbers
- 👍 Daily list of top-performing funds
  - ◆ Top and bottom fund performance rankings for the past 4, 13, and 52 weeks
  - ◆ Fund performance calculator (type a fund and two dates and the calculator figures performance)
- 👍 Load performance calculator
  - ◆ Recent fund NAV histories
  - ◆ Personal portfolio performance screens (under construction)
  - ◆ Database of 7,000 funds

Research: Online Magazine ★★

http://www.researchmag.com

Research: Online Magazine is a Web-based magazine for "investment professionals;" that is, professional brokers. However, the journal also has material that is of interest for regular investors, too, including present thinking among brokers on which industrial sectors are about to heat up. The site also contains broker gossip and interesting write-ups of influential companies.

Highlights

- 👍 Analyst-recommended buys
  - ◆ Broker profiles
  - ◆ Exchange gossip
  - ◆ Feature articles and regular columns
- 👍 Company and industry write-ups and fact sheets
  - ◆ Monthly ranking of top mutual funds

Mutual Funds: Companies and Families

Alger Fund ★

http://networth.galt.com/www/home/mutual/alger/alger.htm

A modest but effectively laid-out page describing the Alger family of six no-load funds. The site includes an overview of the Alger investment strategy and an online prospectus.

Ameristock Mutual Fund ★

http://www.ameristock.com/

Ameristock is a new mutual fund focusing on blue chip companies. This site contains several interesting features, such as a risk tolerance test to help investors determine the investing strategy best suited to their needs and temperament.

Highlights

- ◆ The fund at a glance
- ◆ Financial planning and you
- ◆ Ameristock's investment philosophy
- ◆ Daily and historical performance of the fund
- Risk tolerance test
- ◆ Biography of the fund manager
- ◆ View a prospectus
- ◆ Links to other sites

Baxter Financial Corporation ★

http://www.netrunner.net/~philfund/

A basic site featuring online prospectuses for the Philadelphia Fund, a growth and income fund, and Eagle Growth Shares, a small capital growth fund.

Highlights

- ◆ Download prospectuses
- ◆ Investment strategies
- ◆ Money management services offered

Benham Group ★

http://www.twentieth-century.com

A page dedicated to the Benham Group, a subfamily of nearly 40 funds within the Twentieth Century fund family. Benham funds tend to oriented toward conservative investment strategies, primarily dealing in index funds, money markets, bonds, and treasury securities. Funds are sold without a load.

Calvert Group ★★

http://www.calvertgroup.com/

Calvert Group is a sizable mutual fund family that emphasizes socially responsible investing. The Calvert site includes online prospectuses of several of the Calvert Group funds; prospectuses not online can be requested to be sent by mail using an online form. Investors in Calvert securities are able to view their current account information online (though they are not yet able to conduct online investment transactions).

Highlights

- ◆ Information about Calvert Group and socially responsible investing
- ◆ Online prospectuses
- ◆ Online account balances
- ◆ Current newsletters

Citizens Trust ★★

http://www.efund.com

Citizen's Trust (formerly known as Working Assets) is a management company that seeks to avoid investing in industries such as tobacco, heavy equipment, oil, chemicals, and weapons, concentrating instead on industries such as health care, food products, high technology, and finance. The company maintains a family of some seven mutual funds, ranging from money market and fixed-income portfolios to an aggressive growth fund.

Highlights

- ◆ Weekly update on the performance of selected future-oriented companies
- ◆ Biographies of company trustees
- ◆ Performance of Citizen funds
- ◆ Banks that invest in communities
- ◆ Companies with sexual orientation nondiscrimination policies
- ◆ Press release of Citizen's Trust company profile

Colonial Mutual Funds ★

http://www.lib.com/colonial/colonial.html

Colonial Mutual Funds are a family of 38 funds administered by the Liberty Financial Companies. At present, the site appears to be unfinished and is somewhat buggy.

Highlights

- ◆ List of Colonial Mutual Funds
- ◆ Young investors parent's guide
- ◆ Links to other investment sites

Compass Capital Funds ★

http://www.compassfunds.com/

Compass is a family of 28 funds. This site contains online brochures and an online prospectus that covers all Compass funds. At the time of this writing, fund performances are not included on Web site, though they are expected to be added in the near future. Their Web site is still under construction.

Crabbe Huson Funds ★★

http://www.contrarian.com/

Crabbe Huson is a family of contrarian funds that seek to utilize market buying and selling cycles to increase financial gain. The company has a well-laid-out Web site which explains this philosophy more fully. You can also subscribe to a free monthly e-mail newsletter.

Highlights

- ◆ The Crabbe Huson investment philosophy
- ◆ Online fund brochures, fund yields, and prospectuses
- ◆ Fund manager biographies
- ◆ Register online to receive daily NAV prices and a monthly newsletter via e-mail
- ◆ CHAP, a service for professional advisors and brokers only (under construction)

DEVCAP ★

http://www.greenmoney.com/devcap

DEVCAP is a socially responsible no-load mutual fund that seeks to earn solid returns on investments while creating new economic opportunities in the developing world. Shareholders in this fund have the opportunity of contributing a portion of their returns to microenterprise development programs such as Appropriate Technology International, Catholic Relief Services, Save the Children, and Seen Capital Development Fund. A Microsoft-Word readable prospectus may be downloaded from the site.

Highlights

- ◆ Introduction to the DEVCAP shared return fund
- ◆ Fund performance
- ◆ How your investment can make a difference
- ◆ A success story of a person helped by DEVCAP
- ◆ How you can invest in DEVCAP
- ◆ List and descriptions of DEVCAP member organizations
- ◆ Download a brochure and prospectus

Dreyfus ★★

http://www.dreyfus.com

Providing information about the numerous funds making up the Dreyfus fund family, this page features a weekly commentary written by Richard Hoey, Dreyfus's chief economist. Another feature is a handy online investment calculator, which enables the investor to calculate total return from a monthly investment program. Full fund prospectuses are not available online, but investors can fill out an online form and then receive a prospectus via U.S. mail.

Highlights

- ◆ Descriptions of Dreyfus funds
- ◆ Automatic investment calculator
- ◆ Strategies for creating a personal portfolio
- ◆ Ten investment principles
- ◆ Weekly market commentary by Richard Hoey
- ◆ Online prospectus request form

Eclipse Financial Asset Trust ★

http://networth.galt.com/www/home/mutual/eclipse/

Provides information about the four funds in the Eclipse family of no-load mutual funds. This site includes an easy to read introduction to the funds, an online prospectus, an online newsletter, and a study on the dangers and rewards of trying to time the market.

Evergreen Funds ★

http://www.evergreenfunds.com/

The Evergreen fund family consists of some 35 funds ranging from the conservative to the aggressive.

Highlights

- ◆ Overviews of the most popular Evergreen funds
- ◆ Comparing risk levels and objectives of the various fund types
- ◆ Online prospectuses
- ◆ Request hard copy information via e-mail

Federated Investors ★

http://networth.galt.com/www/home/mutual/federated/

This page provides online prospectuses for the large family of Federated Funds. Tools are available to help you determine which Federated Fund may be best suited to your investment needs. There is also a helpful section dedicated to investing basics.

Highlights

- ◆ Review of basic investing
- ◆ Profile of your investing needs
- ◆ Fund specifics
- ◆ Online quarterly newsletter
- ◆ Request prospectuses either online or via U.S. mail

Fidelity Investments ★★★★

http://www.fid-inv.com/

The largest mutual fund house in existence, Fidelity Investments has a home page to match! This site has a large number of features, including online prospectuses for many of its funds. In addition, the site has an impressive online handbook providing information about various Fidelity funds, including past and present annual growth rates, cumulative returns for 1, 3, 5, and 10-year periods, Lipper rankings, top asset holdings, and even records of dividend payouts. Fidelity has recently expanded its services to include brokerage services, enabling investors to purchase non-Fidelity mutual funds through Fidelity Investments; stocks may be purchased as well.

Highlights

- News about Fidelity Investments
- Mutual fund library and online prospectuses
- Investment and retirement planning
- Brokerage services
- Games and contests

Franklin Properties ★

http://www.frk.com/properties

A subsidiary of the Franklin Templeton fund family, this group of funds focuses on the California metropolitan real estate market. The site contains online brochures, financial statements, proxy statements, current market information, and press releases concerning these funds.

Highlights

- List of the funds with descriptions
- Financial statements
- Proxy statements
- Press releases
- Market information

Gabelli Funds ★★

http://www.gabelli.com/

These sites are dedicated to the Gabelli mutual funds. This fund family includes the Gabelli Global Interactive Couch Potato Fund, a fund which invests primarily in computer multimedia and entertainment industries. Online prospectuses for the various Gabelli funds are available. Other features of the sites include tips for investing toward retirement, a list of news articles about the Gabelli funds, daily closing prices, a list of frequently asked questions about IRAs, and recent company announcements. You will soon be able to purchase Gabelli funds direct from the company online.

Highlights

- ◆ The Gabelli fund family
- ◆ Investing for a comfortable retirement
- ◆ The Gabelli 401(k) plan
- ◆ News clippings
- ◆ Mutual fund quarterly reports
- ◆ Dividend information
- 👍 Daily closing prices
- ◆ Recent company announcements
- 👍 IRA frequently asked questions

Galaxy Funds ★★

`http://www.fleet.com/persbank/invstmnt/mutfun/galfun/index.html`

Galaxy funds are a family of mutual funds sold by Fleet Financial Group, which also owns Fleet Bank. The Galaxy fund site includes online brochures for the mutual fund, as well helpful tools such as a glossary of mutual fund terms and a list of frequently asked investment questions.

Highlights

- ◆ List of Galaxy funds with descriptions
- ◆ Online test to help you determine your investment needs
- ◆ Commonly asked questions about investing
- ◆ Glossary of mutual fund terms
- ◆ Galaxy annuities
- ◆ The Galaxy Automatic Investment Program

GAM Funds ★

`http://www.usinfo.gam.com/`

Global Asset Management (GAM) funds are load-bearing funds that generally require a $10,000 minimum initial investment per fund. The GAM site contains online brochures and prospectuses for the various funds. There is also a subscription-based information service for professional financial advisors.

Highlights

- ◆ Online fund brochures and prospectuses
- ◆ Biographies of fund managers

◆ Frequently asked questions about GAM funds

◆ GAM fund information for professional financial advisors

GIT Investment Funds ★★

http://www.gitfunds.com/

GIT offers a family of 13 no-load mutual funds. This site features online brochures, portfolio listings, and prospectuses, as well as helpful investing information such as daily market barometers and tax suggestions.

Highlights

◆ Latest news from GIT

◆ Summaries of information about GIT mutual fund portfolios

◆ Online GIT Update newsletter

◆ Online prospectuses

◆ Current NAV prices for GIT funds

◆ Daily market barometers

◆ Nine tax tips for mutual fund investors

Guinness Flight ★★

http://networth.galt.com/www/home/mutual/guinness/

Guinness Flight is a London-based financial firm managing a number of mutual funds oriented toward international investment. Only recently, however, have a small number of these funds become available to U.S. investors. This site contains online brochures for the funds and an e-mail form for investors to request hard copies of the prospectuses. The site also contains a couple of reports on international investing.

Highlights

◆ China and Hong Kong fund brochure

◆ Global Government Bond fund brochure

◆ Current portfolio holdings

◆ Shareholder benefits

◆ Research report on investment opportunities in China

◆ Research report on global currency risk

◆ Request hard-copy prospectuses

Hudson Investors Fund ★

http://www.greenmoney.com/hudson/index.htm

HI is a no-load capital accumulation fund that practices socially responsible investing. Their rather basic Web site contains a very brief overview of the fund and an online prospectus.

Highlights

- ◆ Ten largest share holdings
- ◆ Online prospectus
- ◆ Downloadable application
- ◆ Form to contact the fund via e-mail

INVESCO ★★

http://www.invesco.com

This informative and well-laid-out site provides information about INVESCO's extensive family of no-load funds. If you are a beginning investor, you'll find useful advice on how to determine your investment goals and how to build a basic portfolio. More advanced investors will be interested in the online prospectuses, the charts comparing the return rates on various INVESCO funds, and the list of financial services provided by the company.

Highlights

- ◆ List of INVESCO funds and services provided by the company
- ◆ Relative performance of INVESCO funds
- ◆ How to build your portfolio

Janus Funds ★★

http://networth.galt.com/www/home/mutual/janus/

Dedicated to the Janus family of no-load funds, this site contains brief overviews and performance data on the various funds, as well as profiles of the fund managers. There is also a helpful section discussing the pros and cons of dollar-cost averaging as a means of smoothing out market fluctuations and as a means to disciplined investing. While the site does not yet contain an online prospectus, interested investors can fill out an online form to receive a prospectus by mail.

Kaufmann Fund ★★

`http://networth.galt.com/www/home/mutual/kaufmann`

A page dedicated to the Kaufmann Fund, a no-load small company growth fund that has historically posted above-average returns. Includes profiles of the fund managers, information about fund performance, an online prospectus, and a downloadable investment application.

Kemper Funds ★★★

`http://www.kemper.com/`

Kemper Funds began in 1948 with the Television Fund, a sector fund devoted to investing in the then-new television industry. Today Kemper has grown to include some 61 open and 7 closed-end funds. The rambling Kemper Web site contains the online brochures and prospectuses common to large mutual fund companies. However, the Web-savvy investor with the patience to search all of the various links to their conclusion will be rewarded with interesting information and tools.

One if these is a device that compares market indicators for the past ten years — say, for example, the Standard and Poor's 500 with the Dow Jones Industrial Average or the Russell 2000 Growth Index. One can also compare the historical growth of each Kemper fund to the same indexes. A section called "The Curious Investor" contains a number of interesting essays and economic forecasts for both beginning and advanced investors.

Highlights

- ◆ Kemper fund summaries and online prospectuses
- 👍 Compare market indices with Kemper fund performance
- ◆ Services offered to Kemper investors
- 👍 Compare market indices for the past 10 years
- ◆ The Weekly Money Report
- 👍 Understanding mutual funds
- ◆ You and your financial advisor
- 👍 The economy
- ◆ Planning for your child's future
- 👍 About market indices
- ◆ How to plan for retirement
- ◆ Information for financial professionals (closed to nonprofessionals)

Lebenthal and Company ★★

http://www.lebenthal.com

Lebenthal is an investment firm specializing in bonds. Their chatty site provides information about buying individual bonds, unit investment trusts, Lebenthal bond-oriented mutual funds, zero coupon bonds, or shares from other mutual fund families. A glossary of bond-related terms is provided, and there is a brief tutorial explaining tax-free bond yields. Prospectuses are not available online, but can be requested via e-mail.

Highlights

- ◆ Offerings of bonds
- 👍 Bond terms
- ◆ Online brochure about services offered
- ◆ Online test to determine your investment IQ
- 👍 Calculating tax-free bond yields
- ◆ Webware (under construction)
- ◆ Set up a Lebenthal account, request prospectus, or ask questions via e-mail

Legg Mason Funds ★★

http://www.leggmason.com/

A investment company, Legg Mason also administers a family of 15 mutual funds. The firm's Web site is basic but well constructed, with online fund brochures and daily updated NAV tables. E-mail forms are provided to request hard copy prospectuses.

Highlights

- ◆ Overview of Legg Mason funds
- 👍 Learning center with explanations of investing concepts
- ◆ Daily fund net asset values
- 👍 Stock market daily news and market research
- ◆ Historical fund performances
- ◆ Profiles of fund managers
- ◆ Request a prospectus via e-mail or send questions to the fund mangers

Liberty Asset Management Company ★

http://www.lamco.com

LAMCO, a part of the Liberty Financial Group, administers two closed-end mutual funds: the Liberty ALL-STAR Equity Fund and the Liberty ALL-STAR Growth Fund. The Web site for these funds contains archives of monthly press releases about the fund, including net asset values, trading prices, and results of shareholder meetings.

Highlights

- ◆ Very brief overview of the funds
- ◆ Recent press releases
- ◆ E-mail form for more information

Lutheran Brotherhood ★

http://www.luthbro.com/

Lutheran Brothers began in 1917 as a church-oriented mutual aid society. Today it is an independent financial institution that offers financial services to Lutherans, including mutual funds, life and health insurance, retirement plans, and church loans. The LB site features online mutual fund brochures and prospectuses, along with tips on disciplined investing. The site also contains a Lutheran humor page, as well as links to Lutheran Church oriented sites!

Highlights

- ◆ Company history
- ◆ Services offered Lutheran Brothers' mutual fund information and prospectuses
- ◆ Five tips for successful investing
- ◆ Twelve common financial mistakes
- ◆ LB's fraternal outreaches
- ◆ Career opportunities with LB

Midwest Group ★

http://www.midwestgroup.com/index.html

The Midwest Groups is a Cincinnati-based financial institution that has its own family of mutual funds. It also administers and services funds sponsored by others. The site is basically an online brochure of services offered, though hard copy prospectuses of Midwest Group funds can be requested via e-mail.

Highlights

- ◆ Shareholder services
- ◆ Synopses of mutual funds offered
- ◆ Mutual fund administrative and accounting services offered
- ◆ Organizational retirement plan services
- ◆ Private portfolio management (under construction)

Montgomery Funds ★★

http://networth.galt.com/www/home/mutual/montgomery/

The Montgomery Funds are a diversified group of no-load mutual funds. At this site the online investor finds and overviews of the funds as well as online prospectuses and performance histories. Another feature is a "Meet the Experts" page, where Montgomery Fund managers discuss recent market trends.

Highlights

- ◆ Message from the Montgomery Funds president
- ◆ How to invest in the funds
- ◆ View fund brochures and prospectuses online
- ◆ Recent fund NAVs
- Meet the Experts/fund manager biographies

Munder Funds ★

http://www.munder.com/funds.html

This site contains information about the sizable family of Munder Funds. This site includes good information about the funds.

Highlights

- ◆ Munder Funds investment philosophy
- ◆ Online fund overviews and prospectuses
- ◆ Snapshots of portfolio holdings and recent stock transactions
- ◆ Fund manager biographies

Nations Fund ★★

http://www.nationsbank.com/mutual_funds/

The Nations Fund mutual fund family is sold by Nations Bank. The Web site for these fund is rather basic, consisting mainly of an online brochure containing a brief overview of the funds, along with recent press releases. Some investors' tools are present, however, including interactive worksheets for estimating college costs and retirement planning.

Highlights

◆ Summary of the Nations Fund family, with indicators of relative risk and return

◆ Investors tools

◆ Understanding different types of mutual funds

◆ Reasons to consider investing abroad

◆ Interview with a fund manager

◆ How to contact Nations Fund

New England Funds ★

http://www.mutualfunds.com

New England Funds is a family of 22 mutual funds. The funds are managed jointly by ten specialized management firms, with each firm contributing expertise from the professionals best equipped to pursue fund objectives. The chatty NEF Web site is basically an online brochure providing an overview of the funds and investor services offered. An e-mail form is provided with which one may request a hard copy prospectus.

Highlights

◆ Virtual tour of the New England Funds' offices

◆ Overview of the contributing fund management firms

◆ Fund profiles and performance tables

◆ Investor services offered

◆ Recent issues of the newsletters

◆ Retirement Update and Fund Letter

◆ Tips on college funding and retirement planning

◆ Request literature and contact a financial representative by e-mail

Newport Pacific Management ★

http://www.lib.com/newport/newport.html

Newport Pacific is a San Francisco-based investment firm specializing in Asian markets. The company manages the Colonial Newport Tiger Fund. This Web site is basically a sign post; for more information on the fund, see the Colonial site described earlier.

Nicholas Applegate Mutual Funds ★★

http://www.secapl.com/applegate/nac.html

This basic but well-organized site contains online prospectuses.

Norwest ★★

http://www.norwest.com/

Norwest is a bank holding company and financial services institution. This site contains information on international banking and foreign trade.

 International banking articles

 Economic indicators, including biannual reports for the Midwest and Rocky Mountain regions

◆ Company information and recent press releases

Pax World Fund Inc. ★

http://www.greenmoney.com/pax/

The Pax World Fund is a no-load fund investing in industries involved in pollution control, health care, food, housing, education, and other "green" and life-supportive enterprises. Well-organized and well-written, the Pax Web site provides an overview of the fund and an online form to request a hard copy of the prospectus.

Highlights

◆ Fund overview and investment objectives

◆ Commonly asked questions

◆ Recent fund performance

◆ Order a prospectus

PBHG Funds ★

http://www.pbhgfunds.com/

PBHG is a no-load family of seven growth stock funds and one money market fund. The stock funds have generally posted above-average returns for much of their existence. The PBHG Web sites contain, in addition to online prospectuses and synopses of the funds' performances, information about the PBHG investment strategies, and biographies of the fund managers.

Highlights

- ◆ Fund summaries and prospectuses
- ◆ Fund manager profiles
- ◆ PBHG investment approach
- ◆ Recent company news
- ◆ Online form to request more information

Piper Capital Management ★★

http://www.piperjaffray.com/money_management/

Piper Capital Management administers a family of 17 open-end and 16 closed-end mutual funds. The firm's Web site provides a list of the funds with little detail, plus an online form with which to request a hard copy of the prospectus. The site contains a handy interactive form for calculating retirement income needs.

Highlights

- ◆ Lists of open- and closed-end funds
- ◆ Investment services offered
- 👍 Monthly economic commentary
- ◆ News releases about the company
- ◆ Calculate retirement financial needs
- ◆ Contact a financial advisor/request prospectus via e-mail

T. Rowe Price ★★★

http://www.troweprice.com/

T. Rowe Price is a brokerage firm that administers over 65 mutual funds. Large, well-organized, and fact laden, the T. Rowe Price site on the world wide Web has much to offer to the online investor. The beginning investor will benefit from numerous tutorials (some of which change monthly) explaining basic investing concepts and terminology. More advanced subjects, such as sector investing and high yield bonds, are covered as well.

Daily market updates and a variety of weekly market summaries are present. A substantial amount if space is dedicated to retirement planning. The T. Rowe Price site offers free delayed stock and fund quotes, in addition to clearly presented overviews of Price funds and fund performances. However, online prospectuses are not present and hard copies must be ordered via e-mail.

Highlights

- ◆ Overview of company
- 👍 Library of investing tutorials
- 👍 Retirement planning guide
- 👍 Free delayed stock quotes
- ◆ Online investment planner/building a portfolio to fit your needs
- ◆ Price mutual fund overviews and performance information
- 👍 Market outlook
- ◆ Price Report (the T. Rowe Price quarterly newsletter) (under construction)
- 👍 Daily market updates of major economic indicators
- ◆ Weekly updates of fixed income, equity income, and credit markets
- ◆ Overview of discount brokerage services and broker commission calculator

Princor Funds ★

http://www.principal.com/about/know9.html

The sizable Princor and Principal mutual fund families are sponsored by the Principal Mutual Life Insurance Company. The funds' Web site presents only a few details about the funds, however. Online investors desiring more information must submit a request for hard copies of prospectuses through an online request form.

Highlights

- ◆ List of the funds
- ◆ Fund profiles
- ◆ Online form to request hard copy information

Prudent Bear Fund ★

http://www.tice.com/PRUDBEAR.HTM

The Prudent Bear fund is an "alternative" mutual fund for pessimistic investors who feel that the 13-year long bull market is an anomaly that must end with a sharp market decline in the near future. The PB site includes a downloadable prospectus, along with an exposition of bear philosophy and analysis of current economic conditions.

Highlights

- ◆ Overview of the fund
- ◆ Downloadable prospectus
- 👍 Market commentary
- ◆ Common objections to the bearish forecast, with rebuttals
- ◆ List of recent articles supporting the PB outlook
- ◆ Sample PB company research reports

Prudential Mutual Funds ★

http://www.prusec.com/Prudential/purmutfd.htm

Prudential administers a variety of load-carrying mutual funds. The Web site for the funds is basically an online brochure listing the performance of the various funds, a list of services offered, and an e-mail form to request more information.

Highlights

- ◆ List of funds, with fund performances
- ◆ Services offered to investors
- ◆ Biographical sketch of the fund manager

Reynolds Funds ★

http://networth.galt.com/www/home/mutual/100/reynolds/

This site provides basic information about the Reynolds Funds, a small family of no-load funds operated by Reynolds Capital Management.

Highlights

- ◆ Fund profile
- ◆ NAV history

Robertson Stevens & Company ★

http://www.rsim.com/

Robertson Stevens offers a variety of mutual funds, including the Robertson Stevens Contrarian Fund. The company's Web site is under construction. When finished it will provide information about the various funds, audio updates from the fund managers, and other features.

Schwab Funds ★★

http://www.schwab.com/SchwabOnline/CSNav3/CS-SFunds.html

In addition to its other services, Schwab offers a line of no-load mutual funds. This site contains a brief overview of the funds and online fund prospectuses.

Highlights

- ◆ Fund overviews
- ◆ Request hard copies
- ◆ Go to the main Schwab page

Scudder Funds ★

http://networth.galt.com/www/home/mutual/scudder/

Scudder Funds are no-load funds dedicated primarily to international investing. The Scudder site contains online brochures and prospectuses for their family of funds.

Highlights

- ◆ Fund overviews
- ◆ Online prospectuses
- ◆ Request more information via an online form

Seligman Mutual Funds ★

http://www.cts.com/browse/poirier/seligman.html

Seligman offers several load-bearing mutual funds, some of which post very good returns. This Web site contains online brochures about the funds, as well as an online form that you can use to request hard copies of the prospectuses.

Stein Roe Mutual Funds ★★

http://www.steinroe.com/

Stein Roe is a family of 18 no-load mutual funds. In 1995 several of these funds, namely the Capital Opportunities Fund and the Young Investors Fund, achieved substantially higher than average rates of return. Visitors to the Stein Roe online sites will find it both informative and well laid out. In addition to online prospectuses, summaries of fund performances, and lists of services, the Web-literate investor finds lists of fund holdings, brief but thoughtfully written monthly market updates, and a helpful glossary of mutual fund terms. A section featuring investor tools will be added soon.

Highlights

- ◆ Directory of Stein Roe mutual funds
- ◆ Recent Stein Roe company announcements
- ◆ Services offered
- ◆ Investor tools (forthcoming)
- ◆ Monthly market analysis
- ◆ Glossary of mutual fund terms

Stratton Funds ★

`http://networth.galt.com/www/home/mutual/100/stratton`

This Web site contains basic information about Stratton Management's small group of no-load mutual funds.

Highlights

- ◆ Fund overview
- ◆ NAV information

Strong Funds ★★

`http://www.strong-funds.com/strong/java/welcome.htm`

Strong administers a sizable family of funds, and each fund is 100 percent no-load. Visitors to the Strong site can see fund overviews and download prospectuses. You also find investing tips and an online quiz.

Highlights

- ◆ Fund profiles, with downloadable prospectuses
- ◆ Daily fund NAVs and cumulative return histories
- ◆ Recent fund news
- ◆ Investor tips
- ◆ SEP-IRA information
- ◆ Investing for retirement
- ◆ Online issue of The Strong Investor newsletter
- ◆ How to request more information or contact the fund

SunAmerica Mutual Funds ★

`http://www.sunamerica.com/b05.html`

This site is an online flyer for the 12-fund SunAmerica group.

Thornburg Funds ★★

http://www.thornburg.com

Thornburg Funds tries to increase its shareholders wealth after accounting for inflation, taxes, and investment expenses. The firm's Web site contains overviews of the group's funds, as well as online prospectuses, fund returns, and daily NAV prices. The site contains an interesting section, A Study of REAL Real Returns, discussing the effects of inflation, the budget deficit, and taxes (including the proposed flat tax system) upon long-term investments.

Highlights

- ◆ Thornburg fund overviews and online prospectuses
- ◆ Fund returns and daily NAVs
- 👍 Research report: A Study of REAL Real Returns
- ◆ Thornburg annual report
- ◆ Biographies of the portfolio managers

Transamerica Online ★

http://www.transamerica.com

Transamerica is a large financial company offering a variety of services, including mutual funds, loans and finance, insurance, and real estate. The company's Web site is mostly devoted to describing the corporation's history, financial performance, and annual reports, rather than describing specific services in detail.

- ◆ Company announcements and upcoming events
- ◆ Products and services
- ◆ The history and construction of the Transamerica Pyramid
- ◆ Directory of division headquarters

Twentieth Century Mutual Funds ★

http://www.twentieth-century.com

Twentieth Century is a well-known family of no-load mutual funds. The Giftrust Fund, designed to be given as a gift to minors or to charities, has traditionally enjoyed a high rate of return. The Twentieth Century Web site contains online prospectuses and tables describing performance of the various funds.

Highlights

- ◆ Descriptions of Twentieth Century funds
- ◆ Fund performance
- ◆ Asset allocation funds
- ◆ Retirement plan options for the self-employed
- ◆ Online prospectuses and applications

United Group ★

http://www.waddell.com/ugmf.htm

The United Group of mutual funds is a family of 17 mutual funds administered by Waddell and Reed, who also manages the Waddell and Reed fund family. This site presents a brief overview of the United funds, along with their NAV prices and 10-year performance histories.

Highlights

- ◆ Brief fund descriptions
- ◆ Performance histories
- ◆ Current NAV price
- ◆ Online form to request more information

United Services Funds ★★

http://www.usfunds.com/

United Services operates diversified family of 13 no-load mutual funds. At the firm's Web site the online investor finds fund overviews and online prospectuses, along with daily NAVs and selected market indicators. Online editions of the United Services newsletter and special fund reports are also available.

Highlights

- ◆ Fund information and online prospectuses
- 👍 Investor Alert (weekly market update)
- ◆ Daily fund NAV prices with selected market indexes
- ◆ Shareholder Report (online editions of the quarterly newsletter)
- ◆ Special report on Far Eastern emerging markets
- ◆ E-mail form to request more information or to contact the United Services

Van Kampen ★

http://www.vkac.com/

Van Kampen mutual funds are a load-bearing family of open-ended mutual funds sold exclusively through investment brokers. The Van Kampen Web site includes overviews of the funds, along with performance histories and lists of largest fund stock holdings. The firm also offers other types of investments, such as closed-end funds and unit investment trusts; however, details about these are not yet on the Web page. Perhaps due to its brokered sales, Van Kampen does not furnish a way to secure online prospectuses. Instead, tips are provided on how to find and select a professional investment representative.

Highlights

- ◆ The Van Kampen investment philosophy
- ◆ Fund overviews, with historic performance data and largest holdings
- ◆ Biographies of fund managers
- ◆ How to find an investment representative
- ◆ What a professional representative can do for you
- ◆ Closed section for investing professionals
- ◆ Send e-mail to be contacted by an investment representative

Vanguard Group ★★★★

http://www.vanguard.com

With over 80 member funds, the Vanguard Group is one of the largest mutual fund families. In addition to online fund overviews, downloadable prospectuses, and past and present fund return rates, the Vanguard Web site houses a remarkable Investor Education Center offering a series of investor education "courses." Unlike tutorials found in many other Web sites, the Vanguard courses cover a number of advanced topics, such as mutual fund taxation, in considerable depth. A library of articles on investing is also present. Other interesting site features include an online retirement savings calculator and a portfolio planner.

Highlights

- ◆ Overview of the Vanguard Group
- ◆ News and announcements
- ◆ Overview of the funds and downloadable prospectuses
- 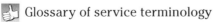 Glossary of service terminology

- ◆ Directory of investor services
- 👍 Information for the informed investor (articles)
- ◆ Current and back issues of MoneyWhys and Market View
- 👍 University
- ◆ Your investor personality profile
- 👍 Online library
- ◆ Retirement savings calculator
- 👍 Glossary of investing terms
- ◆ Portfolio planner
- ◆ Employment opportunities at Vanguard
- ◆ E-mail form to order hard copies of prospectuses or educational literature

Vista Investment Services ★

http://www.vista-funds.com/index.html

Managed by Chase Manhattan, Vista Investment Services offers mutual funds, variable annuities, and other financial services. The Vista Web site contains overviews of the group's various funds, including historic financial performance and stock holdings.

Highlights

- ◆ Fund overviews with past performance and stock holdings
- ◆ Shareholder services
- ◆ Retirement services

Waddell and Reed Funds ★

http://www.waddell.com/wrf.htm

Managed by the same group that administers the United Funds, this fund sub-family includes three stock, two bond, and one mixed fund. The online site includes fund profiles and performance histories.

Highlights

- ◆ Overview of the funds
- ◆ Fund performance histories
- ◆ Online form to request a hard copy prospectus

Weiss, Peck, and Greer ★

http://www.mediasource.com/WeissPeckGreer/index.html

Weiss, Peck, and Greer offers a family of 11 no-load mutual funds, including three long-, medium-, and short-term "Tomorrow" retirement funds. The mutual fund site is basically an online flyer for the firm's services.

Highlights

- ◆ WPG mutual find profiles
- ◆ Company information
- ◆ Products and services (under construction)
- ◆ Investor tips
- ◆ Manager and analyst biographies

Jack White and Company ★★★

http://pawws.com/Jwc_phtml/jwmain.html

Jack White and Company is a discount brokerage firm that allows the computer-literate investor to execute trades of stocks or mutual funds online. This Web site contains handy tables of information about mutual funds that Jack White trades. Another service offered is CONNECT, which helps persons buy loaded mutual funds at a reduced rate by matching up load fund buyers and sellers. See also the Jack White listing in the "Online Brokerages" section.

Highlights

- ◆ Letter from Jack White
- ◆ Brokerage services
- ◆ Mutual fund services
- ◆ Links to sources of market news
- ◆ How to open and account and place a trade
- ◆ CONNECT — buy loaded funds without paying a load

Zaske, Sarafa, & Associates ★

http://www.zsa.com/

ZSA offers three no-load mutual funds, including the ZSA Social Conscience Fund. The ZSA Web site presents brief profiles of the funds, along with earnings histories.

Highlights

- ◆ Investment philosophy
- ◆ Biographies of the managers and analysts
- ◆ E-mail form to request more information

Zweig Mutual Funds ★

http://networth.galt.com/www/home/mutual/zweig

Zweig administers a family of five funds. The Zweig Web page contains a synopsis of Zweig's investment philosophy, fund descriptions, and an online fund prospectus.

Highlights

- ◆ The Zweig difference
- ◆ Profiles of the funds
- ◆ Online prospectus

Mutual Funds: Information Services

Financial World ★★★★

http://www.financialworld.com/

Financial World magazine's Web site offers some excellent goodies for mutual fund investors. After you've learned the basics of mutual funds, check out *Financial World's* risk-adjusted grades for 600 top mutual funds. You can also screen mutual funds for one-year total return, yield, assets, *Financial World's* proprietary manager ratings and portfolio ratings. In addition, you can screen for funds with excellent short-term and long-term track records that do not have a sales charge, funds with below-average expense ratios and proven track records, hot funds best positioned for further gains, and poorly performing funds with big loads. Not to be missed!

Internet Closed-End Fund Investor ★

http://www.icefi.com/

Closed-end funds (CEFs) combine some of the characteristics of mutual funds (in both cases you are buying shares in a professionally managed diversified portfolio) with those of stocks (CEFs are traded through a broker). Unlike open end mutuals, however, the funds are "closed," meaning that only a limited number of shares are available. As a result, shares can trade at a premium (that is, at a rate greater than their straight net asset value, or NAV) or at a discount (at rates lower than their NAV).

Confused? Then check out the Internet Closed-End Fund Investor site, which explains the ins and outs of this sometimes neglected investment opportunity. The site includes a brief but helpful tutorial, quarterly fund performance results, basic information, and analyses of market sentiment for the overall CEF market. Daily synopses, weekly charts, and monthly tables and profiles for particular funds are also available by subscription. The site neglects to mention that many closed-end funds are market underperformers, though.

Highlights

- Tutorial on closed-end funds
  - ◆ Basic information on each fund
- Quarterly performance tables of closed end funds
  - ◆ Market sentiment analysis based on market discount rates
- List of hot CEFs to watch
  - ◆ Daily reports (by subscription)
  - ◆ Profiles, tables, and relative and overall performance charts (by subscription)

Mutual Fund Company Directory ★★★★

http://www.cs.cmu.edu/~jdg/funds.html

Set up by John Griener, a PhD candidate at Carnegie Mellon and project designer for Galt Technologies, this site contains a sizable list of mutual funds, fund telephone numbers, and Web site addresses (if the fund has one). Funds are listed by location, including the U.S., Bermuda, Canada, Germany, Great Britain, Hong Kong, Hungary, and Luxembourg. This page also contains links to useful information about Dividend Reinvestment Programs (DRIPS) and a guide to brokerage houses both in the U.S. and abroad.

Highlights

- Mutual fund company directory
  - ◆ Dividend Reinvestment Program Guide
  - ◆ Guide to brokerage houses, with comparisons

Mutual Funds Interactive (The Mutual Funds Home Page)
★★★★

http://www.brill.com/

Mutual Funds Interactive is an excellent site offering something to both beginning and advanced mutual fund investors. Those new to mutual funds will wish to look at the "Funds 101" section, which explains the basics of how mutual funds work and provides tips on basic investing.

Fund investors with more experience will be interested in the "Profiles" section, where managers of top funds are interviewed and their strategies described. "Experts Corner," which features mutual fund market analysis and opinions, is also noteworthy. Other site features include articles on mutual fund investing, a growing list of links to mutual fund home pages, and links to financial news sources and quote servers.

Highlights

- Profiles of top fund managers
  - ◆ Link to Internet mutual fund newsgroup
- Funds 101
  - ◆ Links to mutual fund group home pages
- Mutual fund news and features
  - ◆ Links to financial news and a mutual fund quote server
- Expert's corner

Mutual Fund Investor's Resource Center ★★

http://www.fundmaster.com

This site is a sort of central repository for mutual fund family home pages on the Net. You can obtain prospectuses and account applications here.

NETWorth Mutual Fund Market Manager ★★★★

http://networth.galt.com/www/home/mutual/

One of the best investment-related sites on the Internet, this page is indispensable for anyone contemplating an investment in mutual funds. Networth's Mutual Fund Atlas (http://networth.galt.com/www/home/mutual/fund_atlas/fa.html) describes more than 30 mutual fund families and their investment styles.

The Atlas lets you retrieve fact sheets, net asset values, Morningstar profiles and prospectuses for the following big fund families: Alger, Burnham, Calvert Group, Dreyfus, Eclipse, Federated Investors, Gabelli, INVESCO, Janus, Jones & Babson, Kaufmann, Kemper Money Funds, Muhlenkamp, Neuberger & Berman, PBHG, Royce, Scudder, Stein Roe, T. Rowe Price, Transamerica Premier, Twentieth Century-Benham, Van Kampen American Capital, Van Wagoner, Wright Investors Service and Zweig Mutual Funds

Highlights

- ◆ Fund Atlas: A directory to all the funds and fund family pages available at NETworth
- ◆ Net Asset Values: Recent and historical fund prices
- 👍 Morningstar risk-adjusted fund ratings
- ◆ Top performers by category
- 👍 Search for funds by fund objective, description, fees, or fund performance

Wall Street City Mutual Fund Search ★★★★

`http://host.telescan.com/Stocks/Mutual_Fund_Search.html`

Just made available as this book was being completed, this excellent mutual fund screening service is the first to enable you to screen funds by beta. You can also screen funds using a variety of other indexes of fund performance, including performance in down markets! It's free and not to be missed!

News Services

Bloomberg Personal ★★★★

`http://www.bloomberg.com/`

The Bloomberg Personal site is a large, well laid-out news digest, with great breadth. The Web site offers an amazing amount of market information, plus capsules of major news stories and business news, quick stories about markets and hot U.S., British, and Japanese stocks, a large number of headlines from domestic and foreign newspapers, and synopses of major market indices and indicators. A variety of columns are featured, as well as miscellaneous section with sports, weather, reviews, and even horoscopes. This site rewards patience; though it is well organized, there is so much material that it takes a while to learn to navigate around it!

Highlights

 World markets

◆ Money and credit markets

◆ Financial and general news capsules

◆ Columns on markets, companies, stocks, bonds, currencies, and other topics

◆ Sports, weather, reviews, holidays, horoscopes, lottery, trivia

◆ List of Bloomberg products

briefing.com ★★★

http://www.briefing.com

Briefing, founded by Richard C. Green, former president of Standard & Poor's MMS International division, provides a variety of services, including stock, bond, and dollar "tickers." Briefing also provides political and economic forecasts, accompanied by pithy, insightful, and occasionally dryly humorous commentaries. This carries a small monthly subscription charge.

Highlights

◆ Stock, bond, and dollar tickers

◆ Economic data

◆ Market brief (constantly updated)

◆ Market, political, and economic forecasts

◆ Market calendar

◆ Delayed stock and bond quotes

Business Update ★★

http://www.fyionline.com/infoMCI/update/BUSINESS-MCI.html

The Business Update, sponsored by Reuters and MCI, provides a daily synopsis of financial and business news. Political, entertainment, sports, and general news capsules are also available.

CNN*fn* ★★★

http://cnnfn.com/

The CNN Financial Network Web site provides the sort information that we would expect from CNN — thorough, but organized for rapid and easy browsing. The CNN site provides a list of top stories, as well as a list of continuously updated business news. A number of columns are also present, such as "Managing your Money" and a racier, sarcastic one called "Grapevine." Delayed stock quotes are also available.

Highlights

- ◆ Recent business and financial news
- ◆ Delayed stock, bond, and fund quotes
- ◆ Delayed commodities quotes
- 👍 Large list of WWW financial resources
- ◆ World market indexes
- ◆ Interest rates
- 👍 Links to world stock exchanges
- ◆ CNN special reports on a variety of topics
- ◆ Glossary of business terms
- 👍 CNN Financial Network programming schedules, profiles, and transcripts

electronic enews newsstand ★★★

http://www.enews.com

The electronic enews newsstand publishes selections from the current issues of a number of periodicals. Journals available include *Barron's, Business Week, Forbes, Fortune,* and Kiplinger's *Personal Finance* magazine.

The Holt Report ★★★★

http://207.67.198.21/holt/index.html

A daily market summary of 29 market indexes and averages; included are the most actively traded stocks, high-momentum stocks, and stocks with new highs and lows.

Highlights

- 👍 E-mail notification service (free) sends daily summary of market indexes to your electronic mailbox
- ◆ Currency and gold quotes
- ◆ Interest rates

The Investors Internet Journal ★★

http://www.discover.co.uk/~iij/

The IIJ is an online British periodical. While portions of the journal are of interest only to British investors, substantial portions are dedicated to providing information about both the U.S. and world markets.

Highlights

- ◆ U.K., U.S., European, Japanese, Far East, and emerging market reports
- ◆ Performance of major world stock exchanges for the year to date
- ◆ Typical journal contents
- ◆ Biography of the editor
- ◆ How to get the best results while spreading the risk

Kiplinger Online News of the Day ★★★

http://kiplinger.com/dailynews/dailyn.html

Updated each business day, this newsletter features an in-depth article as well as brief business updates. You can access the voluminous and valuable archives from this site. You also find a link to the online version of the popular *Kiplinger's Personal Finance Magazine,* with selected articles from the current issue. You can use a search engine — a good one — to search back issues of the magazine.

Highlights

- 👍 Personal finance Highlights from Kiplinger's Personal Finance Magazine
- ◆ Business, tax, and agriculture forecasts
- 👍 The top mutual funds

Money Daily ★★★

http://pathfinder.com/pathfinder/secondmoney.html

A part of *Money* magazine, the Money Daily is a nice daily publication containing one or two short articles of broad general interest. Subjects may be either breaking news, such as the sudden closure of a large mutual fund, or more thematic, as is the case of widespread differences of opinion about the meaning of various economic indicators. Back issues of the publication are available online. You can also subscribe to the newsletter via the Web site, in which case you receive the Money Daily each day by e-mail.

Highlights

- ◆ Business travel tips
- ◆ Currency converter
- ◆ Daily money rates
- ◆ Global market indexes
- ◆ Major market indexes
- ◆ Market scoreboard
- ◆ Stock quotes
- ◆ Top savings accounts rates
- ◆ Wall Street summary

moneynet.com ★★★

http://www.moneynet.com/homepage.htm

Sponsored by Reuters Money Network, the moneynet.com site features delayed quotes, current financial news headlines, and a regularly updated list of economic indicators. Also featured is a free personal portfolio tracker capable of tracking up to 10 portfolios, each containing up to 30 quotes.

Highlights

- ◆ Delayed quotes
- ◆ Capsules of current market indexes (such as the DJIA, NASDAQ composite, and S&P 500)
- 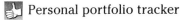 Personal portfolio tracker
- ◆ Online newsletter
- ◆ Press releases about Reuters Money Network
- ◆ Subscription-based reports and products

Nando Business Network ★★★

http://www2.nando.net/newsroom/nbn

A division of the Raleigh, N.C., *News and Observer*, the Nando Business Network offers the equivalent of a printed newspaper. A headline story is offered, along with business headlines that serve as hyperlinks to full-length stories. Extensive market data is presented, with continually updated market news and stock quotes, as well as reports on world markets and indexes. Daily stock, commodity, currency, and credit summaries are given for the American, European, and Asian/Japanese markets. Online business tools and a large number of online financial columns are also present.

Highlights

- ◆ Headline story, latest business stories, and market synopsis
- ◆ Stock and mutual fund quotes
- 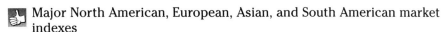 Major North American, European, Asian, and South American market indexes
- ◆ End-of-day American, European, and Asian business highlights
- ◆ Market, commodity, exchange, and credit summaries for the U.S., Europe, and Asia/Japan
- ◆ Numerous weekly business columns on saving, investing, housing markets, working women, and more
- ◆ Currency exchange rates
- Online currency converter
- ◆ Dictionary of financial terms
- ◆ Access SEC/EDGAR database
- ◆ Large list of links

Pathfinder News Now ★★★★

http://pathfinder.com/News/news.html

This is an excellent place to get a quick overview of today's top news stories. A plus: If you find something that interests you, perform a search of Pathfinder's huge database (including current and past issues of *Time, Money, People Tech, Fortune*, and other Time-Warner magazines) using a search engine.

Time Daily ★★★★

http://pathfinder.com/Time/daily/

Make this page a part of your daily Internet usage. You find intelligent summaries of top news stories, coupled with insightful analysis by Time's reporting staff. If you find a story that interests you, a search box at the end of the story is already configured to search Pathfinder's huge database for more stories pertinent to this topic. Links take you to the full text of the current edition of *Time,* which is fully searchable using Pathfinder's excellent search engine.

Highlights

- ◆ Each article concludes with a predefined search, enabling you to find additional Pathfinder articles relevant to the article's subject.
- ◆ Links to full text of *Time* print edition

Yahoo! Business Summary ★★

http://www.yahoo.com/headlines/current/business/summary.html

This is today's top Reuters business news stories, formatted in an easy-to-read Web page. It's not searchable, however.

Newsletters

Newsletter Library ★★

http://pub.savvy.com

This site includes links to over 11,000 free sample newsletters covering all subjects, including dozens of investment-related topics. You fill out an online form, select the newsletters you'd like to receive, and you get a free sample copy in the mail.

On Choosing a Financial Newsletter ★

http://pawws,secap1.com/mfis_phtm/m106.shtml

This site features Mark Hulbert, editor of the newsletter of financial newsletters, Hulbert Financial Digest, telling newcomers to this medium what to look for and avoid. It contains links to some samples as well.

Newspapers

Barron's Online ★★★★

http://www.barrons.com/

The premier investing news weekly offers a fantastic Web site, with the full text of leading stories, columns, and analysis.

Highlights

◆ Index enables you to search for information related to a specific company

👍 Barron's Archives provides key-word searching to current and past issues of Barron's

👍 Barron's Dossiers provide stock performance charts, news, and links to 15,000 stocks and 5,000 funds

Financial Times (FT.com) ★★★

http://www.ft.com/

The Financial Times is a British-based international online business daily; ft.com is its online counterpart. Each edition is divided into three "sections." News and Comment covers the main international business and news stories of the day, provides end-of-day equity and fund prices, and contains a bulletin that is updated several times during the day. Themes and Topics covers more less time-sensitive subjects, such as economic and technological trends, or sports and leisure topics, in a more thematic manner. Connect and Respond is a forum where readers can talk to the journal and to each other.

Investor's Business Daily ★★★★

http://ibd.ensemble.com/

IBD is an online edition of the printed paper of the same name. The paper covers national business news and tracks current economic and business trends. An online searchable archive is available. Market synopses and selected stock quotes and stock performance histories are also present. IBD editorials and economic analysis tend to have a somewhat conservative cast.

Highlights

- ◆ What's new at the Web site
- ◆ Front Page
- ◆ Executive Update
- ◆ Computers and Tech
- ◆ The New America (current trends)
- ◆ The Economy
- ◆ The Markets (market news and indices)
- ◆ Vital Signs (international trade synopsis)
- ◆ Volume Tables (selected NYSE, AMEX, and NASDAQ quotations)
- ◆ IBD archives
- ◆ Contact IBD

New York Times Business Section ★★★

http://www.nytimes.com/yr/mo/day/news/financial/

The latest national and international business news from *The New York Times*.

USA Today Money ★★★★

http://www.usatoday.com/money/mfront.htm

Here's the "Money" section from the popular national newspaper, done up in a well-conceived Web version. You can see everything at a glance. You find stock quotes, the latest news, commentary and opinion, and market analyses. A plus is a search page that enables you to search for keywords. A search for *steakhouse* retrieved a story about Outback's advertising agency

The Wall Street Journal Interactive Edition ★★★★

http://www.wsj.com/

The WSJIE presents nearly every story from *The Wall Street Journal* print editions, plus selections from the Asia and European editions. The WSJIE also provides its own unique features, including continuous news updates 24 hours a day, hypertext links for stock quotes and information about companies in the news, a searchable archive for the past two weeks worth of news from the WSJ and the Dow Jones news wires, and constant sports and weather updates. The WSJIE is a subscription-based service.

Highlights

- ◆ Front page news
- ◆ Special reports
- ◆ Washington news update
- ◆ Delayed stock quotes
- ◆ Marketplace
- ◆ Money and investing
- ◆ Regional financial news
- ◆ Synopses of markets (U.S., Americas, Asian, European), credit markets, foreign exchange, commodities
- ◆ Mutual fund scorecards for 30 categories
- ◆ Economic indicator archives
- ◆ Banking journal (loan and deposit rates)
- ◆ Editorials and responses
- Large glossary of financial terms

Online Brokerages

Accutrade ★★

http://www.accutrade.com/

Accutrade allows the online investor to trade any NYSE, AMEX, or NASDAQ stock for $28 plus 2 cents per share. Options and bonds may be traded, and some 5,700 mutual funds are available for purchase. Trading can be carried out through the World Wide Web, by direct modem connections, by touch-tone telephone, by fax, by personal digital assistant, or through a registered representative. Accutrade clients receive check writing and debit card privileges.

Highlights

◆ Getting started with Accutrade

◆ Ways to place transactions

◆ Accutrade software updates

◆ Log on Accutrade (account holders only)

◆ Contacting the company

Aufhauser/WealthWEB ★

http://www.aufhauser.com

Aufhauser is a full-service discount brokerage firm. Using the company's WealthWEB, Aufhauser clients can trade stocks and options. Confirmation of order executions via telephone is possible. WealthWEB also features online company research reports, free 20-minute delayed quotes on stocks, options, funds, bonds, and indices; account balances, stock tracking, and portfolio management can also be performed online.

Highlights

◆ List of services

◆ WealthWEB demonstration

◆ Commission rates

◆ Request free market research reports

◆ How to open an Aufhauser account

◆ Enter WealthWEB (current clients only)

eBroker ★

http://www.ebroker.com

eBroker is an Internet-only brokerage house offering any number of shares of any common or preferred stock for a flat $12 commission. Options may also be purchased at low prices. For some traders, however, these low prices may come with an unacceptably low level of service; to keep expenses low, there is no "800" telephone service, no free stock quotes, no research or sales staff, no local offices. In addition, a $10,000 initial deposit is required to open an account. For the high-volume trader who does his or her own research, however, eBroker may offer no-frills trading at a good price.

Highlights

- ◆ About eBroker
- ◆ Commission rates
- ◆ Getting started with eBroker
- ◆ Access eBroker accounts (account holders only)

E*TRADE ★★★

http://www.etrade.com/

E*TRADE is an online brokerage firm that charges a $14.95 to $19.95 flat rate for online stock purchases of under 5000 shares. Options may also be purchased online. The E*TRADE Web site furnishes the online investor with delayed stock quotes (or real-time quotes, for a fee), a "Stock Watch" custom stock ticker monitoring a selected number of stocks, a market index overview, and online viewing of account balances and transactions histories. A variety of account and retirement account options are available.

The E*TRADE site offers a well-laid-out online demonstration of services available, and an online game is coming soon. In addition to Web-bases transactions, E*TRADE transactions may also be placed via Internet/Telnet, touch-tone telephone, and direct modem access.

Highlights

- ◆ Welcome to E*TRADE
- ◆ Commission schedule
- E*TRADE demo
- ◆ Stock market game (under construction)
- ◆ Open an account online
- ◆ Log on to E*TRADE

Fidelity Online Xpress ★

http://www.fid-inv.com/brokerage/brokerage.html

Fidelity Online Express (FOX) is not Web-based at the present time; rather, it is an integrated PC-based dial-up system using proprietary software running in an MS-DOS environment. FOX allows users to trade stocks and options, as well as buying, selling, and exchanging mutual funds that are either Fidelity funds or are a part of Fidelity's 2,000-member FundsNetwork. The FOX system also provides account balances and transaction histories. Other features include real-time security quotes and a 10 percent discount off of Fidelity stock commissions. Touch-tone trading is available.

Highlights

◆ About FOX

◆ How to download the FOX demonstration program

Lombard Brokerage, Inc. ★★★

http://www.lombard.com/

Lombard allows online buying, selling, buying to cover, and selling short, all online. Option trading is also available, and mutual fund and bond trading is coming soon. Delayed and real-time stock and option quotes are available, along with a quote server allowing up to ten securities to be monitored every two minutes. An online demonstration of Lombard services and links to a variety of financial information sources are provided.

Highlights

◆ About Lombard/services offered

Demonstration of services offered

◆ Enter account transactions (account holders only)

◆ Links to sources of financial information

National Discount Brokers ★★

http://pawws.secapl.com/Ndb_phtml/top.shtml

National Discount Brokers allows the online investor to purchase any number of NASDAQ or OTC shares for $20, or $28 for up to 5000 shares of NYSE or AMEX stock. Other services offered (not online) include options, mutual funds, money market funds, IRAs, treasuries, zero coupon bonds, and certificates of deposit.

Highlights

- ◆ What's new at NDB
- ◆ Frequently asked questions
- ◆ Commission schedule and price comparison calculator
- ◆ Opening a new account
- ◆ How to place a transaction
- ◆ How to access your existing NDB account online
- ◆ Go to the order entry page (account holders only)

Net Investor ★★

http://pawws.secapl.com/invest.html

The Net Investor is a discount brokerage firm that offers online many services that you would expect from a regular brokerage firm. NI offers services enabling the investor to place orders for a variety of securities — including stocks, bonds, CDs, and over 3,000 load and no-load mutual funds — online. NI clients receive free delayed stock quotes, historical prices graphs, a personal "hot list" automatically tracking up to 150 securities, free online financial news, company profiles, mutual fund reports, discounts on many other types of financial information, free checking and a free Visa debit card. Frequent traders also receive free real-time quotes.

Highlights

- ◆ Net Investor news
- ◆ Services offered
- ◆ Reasons to use Net Investor
- ◆ Commission schedule
- ◆ How to sign up
- ◆ Client log-in (account holders only)

Pacific Brokerage Services ★★

http://www.tradepbs.com/

Pacific Brokerage Services' proprietary "Remote Access" system can place orders online. The system also provides market indices and statistics, delayed stock quotes, portfolio management, and real-time pricing of your portfolio value. Stock prices may be imported into spreadsheets. By the time you read this, PBS is expected to provide these services through the World Wide Web as well.

Highlights

- ◆ Commission rates
- 👍 Updated market statistics for the Dow indexes, Internet stocks, NYSE, AMEX, and NASDAQ
- ◆ Online market watch ticker
- ◆ Stock performance graphs
- ◆ Links to various financial and general news sources

Quick and Reilly ★★

http://www.quick-reilly.com/

Soon to launch Internet brokerage services, Quick and Reilly's QuickWay Plus is a proprietary dial-up brokerage interface system that enables you to trade stocks, bonds, options, and mutual funds. Online investors using QuickWay Plus subscribe to one of four subscription programs offering varying levels of service. Options available include stock quote services, various news services, portfolio updates, mutual fund scorecards, e-mail support, a news clipping service, alerts, mutual fund, CD, and money market updates, and stock and bond databases. QuickWay requires an IBM-compatible 486 computer running Windows 3.1 or higher and a 9600 baud modem.

Highlights

- ◆ Chairman's office
- ◆ About Quick and Reilly
- ◆ About QuickWay Plus
- ◆ Links to financial news sources
- ◆ How to set up a new account

Schwab Online ★★★★

http://www.schwab.com/

Schwab offers several online trading options. One may trade securities through the Schwab Web page, or one may choose to use one of Schwab's PC-based dial-up systems. For more information on both of these services, see Chapter 21.

Jack White/PATH Online ★★

http://pawws.secapl.com/jwc/

Jack White and Company's PATH Online system enables the online investor to place both stock and mutual fund orders online. Purchases made via PATH also receive a 10 percent discount off of JWC's regular commission fee. Other non-online services include trading of equities, options, and warrants; corporate, municipal, and government bonds; unit investment trusts and limited partnerships; and precious metals.

Highlights

- ◆ Message from Jack White
- ◆ News at JWC
- ◆ Brokerage and mutual fund services offered
- ◆ How to open an account and place trades
- ◆ Links to quote sources and financial news

Quote Servers

DBC Online ★★★★

http://www.dbc.com/

DBC is an excellent source of free delayed quotes and market information, all of which is regularly updated. The site also features business news capsules and a personal portfolio manager. Real-time quotes and other services are available by subscription.

Highlights

- ◆ Delayed quotes and charts from major exchanges
- ◆ Personal portfolio tracking
- ◆ Major market indices
- ◆ Dow Jones industrials, transportation, and utilities tracking
- ◆ NYSE, AMEX, and NASDAQ leaders and losers
- ◆ News summaries (constantly updated)
- ◆ Bank rates monitor
- ◆ Market summaries by industry
- ◆ Largest mutual and money market funds

- International stocks traded in the U.S.
- Closed-end funds traded as stocks
- Financial products available

Mercury Mail Closing Bell ★★★

http://www.merc.com/cb/cgi/cb.cgi

Closing Bell, a free service from Mercury Mail, is an automatic e-mail notification service that sends you closing prices and news for a personalized portfolio of market indices, mutual funds, and securities from the three major U.S. exchanges. The stories are condensed for brevity.

NETworth Quote Server ★★★

http://quotes.galt.com

(stock quotes and graphs, basic mutual fund quotes)

http://www.networth.galt.com/www/home/mutual/mfmm.html

(mutual fund quotes and graphs)

NETworth provides stock quotes for both American and Canadian stocks and mutual funds traded on the major exchanges. Graphing functions and personal portfolio tracking are also available.

PC Quote ★★★

http://www.pcquote.com

PC Quote provides free delayed market quotes for up to five equities at a time, including stocks traded on the OTC bulletin board. More in-depth price and fundamental data, such as daily highs and lows, dividend payout dates and amounts, and P/E ratios are also available upon request through the free MicroWatch service.

Highlights

- Free delayed quotes for stocks, commodities, and options traded on the major exchanges
- Delayed quotes for stocks traded on the OTC bulletin board
- MicroWatch
- Real-time Dow Jones industrials composite
- Descriptions of fee-based services

Quote.com ★★★

`http://fast.quote.com/fq/quotecom/quote`

For a quick fix on the markets, check out the Quote.com page. This site provides delayed quotes for stocks, funds, and commodities, as well as stock market data, daily charts, major indices, exchange rates, and some sector data.

Highlights

 Delayed quotes from both major exchanges

◆ Major market indices

◆ Charts for the Dow Jones Industrial, S&P 500 Index, NASDAQ Composite

◆ Stock market synopsis

◆ Daily performance data for industry groups (including Internet, computer, electronics, biotech stocks)

◆ Personal portfolio charting

StockMaster ★★★

`http://www.stockmaster.com/`

StockMaster (formerly located at the MIT Artificial Intelligence Laboratory) offers free delayed stock and mutual fund quotes and graphs.

Highlights

Delayed stock quotes and graphs of recent price history for stocks traded on major American exchanges

◆ Delayed mutual fund quotes and graphs of recent NAV histories

Stock Exchanges

American Stock Exchange (AMEX) ★★★

`http://www.amex.com/`

The AMEX Web site is quite impressive, featuring complete listings of companies and options traded, extensive and regularly updated lists of economic indicators, and even interviews with leaders in government, business, and finance.

Highlights

- ◆ Welcome message, with description of the Exchange most active stocks (updated daily)
- ◆ Percent gainers and decliners (updated daily)
- ◆ Most active option statistics (updated daily)
- ◆ Archive of past market summaries
- 👍 Listed companies, with links to business summaries, market data, and (in some cases) links to company home pages
- ◆ Options and descriptions of sector indices
- ◆ Recent AMEX news, with archive
- ◆ Gallery of AMEX movies and pictures
- 👍 Trendline (daily list of equity prices, treasury yields, and currency exchange rates)
- ◆ AMEX Newsmaker (interviews with business and financial leaders)
- ◆ List of links to financial information

NASDAQ ★★★

http://www.nasdaq.com

NASDAQ is a vast computerized trading network listing over 5,100 American and foreign companies. The exchange's Web site offers a substantial amount of financial data, including delayed quotes, recent composite histories, activity of sector indexes, and lists of most active stocks.

Highlights

- ◆ NASDAQ composite index with intraday history graph
- ◆ NASDAQ 100 index with intraday history graph
- ◆ NASDAQ composite index value and volume graph for the past year
- 👍 Regularly updated sector indexes
- ◆ Most active stocks (by dollar volume, advance, decline, and volume share)
- ◆ Company symbol look-up table
- 👍 Glossary of trading terms
- ◆ Links to listed companies' home pages

New York Stock Exchange (NYSE) ★★

http://www.nyse.com

The New York Stock Exchange is the largest exchange in the world, listing over 2,500 companies. The site contains recent news releases and trading-related memos, descriptions and histories of the exchange, recent publications and newsletters, and some historic data. Unfortunately for the online investor, there is relatively little recent hard market data.

Highlights

- ◆ What's New (weekly update of NYSE news, memos, and position statements)
- ◆ Recent financial highlights
- ◆ NYSE history
- ◆ Downloadable list of stock symbols with company names
- ◆ Historical statistical trading summaries
- ◆ List of products and publications offered for sale
- ◆ How to visit the Exchange as a tourist
- Glossary of financial and investing terms
- ◆ Online abstracts of NYSE working papers

Philadelphia Stock Exchange ★

http://www.libertynet.org/~PHLX/

Founded in 1790, the Philadelphia Stock Exchange is the oldest stock exchange in the United States. This exchange currently trades over 2,700 stocks, plus stock, sector, and currency options.

Highlights

- ◆ Recent Philadelphia Stock Exchange news
- ◆ Stock, sector, currency, and LEAPS options carried by the exchange
- ◆ Foreign currency options — the week in review
- ◆ Daily settlement values for currency options
- ◆ Weekly sector index charts
- ◆ Video clip of the trading floor
- ◆ Links to other financial sites and business schools

Stock-Picking Strategies

Once you've decided to put money into stocks and funds, how do you pick the good ones and avoid the bad? The people running the following sites have all developed systems to help investors with just that choice. Not surprisingly, methods vary widely — from the traditional methods of analyzing markets and company balance sheets, to computer programs, to social impact, to astrology.

Astrologer's Fund ★★

http://www.ids.net/starbridge/afund/

If you are an investor who is also into astrology, this site may of interest. Sections of this page are devoted to questions such as the relationship of gold prices and market fluctuations to eclipses. There are also links to other financial astrology sites, as well. While the Astrologer's Fund is primarily a financial consulting firm, the group expects to open two astrologically oriented mutual funds by early 1997.

Highlights

- ◆ Market alert (notice of an expected market correction)
- ◆ How to join the Astrologer's Fund mailing list
- ◆ Stock pick of the month
- ◆ Gold and eclipses
- ◆ Advice about investing in Mexico
- ◆ Astrology and socially responsible investing
- ◆ Frequently asked questions about astrological investing
- ◆ Links to other sites of interest

Avid Trading Company ★

http://avidinfo.com/

The Avid site is a largely subscription based site for persons interested in momentum investing. A free daily market commentary is provided, though its jargon-laden and occasionally obscure style may limit its appeal for some readers. An online conference room is available.

Highlights

- ◆ Daily market predictions
- ◆ Weekly advisory

◆ Strategy and tactics

◆ Delayed quote server

◆ Chat room

◆ Tables comparing momentum investing to the S&P 500

C-A-N-S-L-I-M ★★★

http://wahoo.netrunner.net/~kennyg/canslim.htm

Here's a good (albeit unofficial) explanation of C-A-N-S-L-I-M a stock selection method developed by William J. O'Neil, founder of *Investor's Business Daily* and author of *How to Make Money in Stocks: A Winning System in Good Times or Bad*. In this method, you look at current quarterly earnings per share, annual earnings per share, the effect of new products on share prices, supply and demand for outstanding shares, whether the stock is a Leader or laggard, institutional sponsorship, and market direction. This method combines fundamental and technical analysis.

Good Money Home Page ★★

http://www.goodmoney.com/index.htm

Good Money is dedicated to socially responsible investing. Though lacking snazzy graphics, the Good Money site contains some excellent material for the socially conscious investor. These include articles on how to screen investments for social and environmental impact, directories of and links to socially conscious businesses and activist groups, and a large list of socially and environmentally oriented mutual funds.

Highlights

◆ About Good Money

◆ Recent news for socially aware investors

◆ Selections from the Good Money Quarterly Reports newsletter

◆ How to screen investments

👍 Over 100 socially and environmentally screened funds

◆ List of socially screened stocks

👍 1996 directory of activist companies and groups online

GreenMoney ★★★

http://www.greenmoney.com

If you are interested in socially responsible investing, the GreenMoney Web site is for you. Features include guides to banks, mutual funds, and businesses committed to improving, rather than simply exploiting, the world in which we live.

Highlights

- ◆ Socially responsible business guide
- ◆ Selections from The Green Money Journal Guide to the World Wide Web Guide to publications
- ◆ Socially responsible financial planning, banks, and mutual funds

Motley Fool ★★★

http://fool.Web.aol.com

The Motley Fool brothers, Dave and Tom Gardner, have developed something of a cult following, first with their newsletter and then with their America Online forum. Love them or hate them, they have — so far at least — shown themselves to be remarkably adept at making their unorthodox, populist, "foolish" investment strategies pay off.

The Fools now maintain a presence on the World Wide Web, complete with an excellent (if opinionated) tutorial for beginning investors, charts of the Fools' portfolio's growth and upcoming and recent trades, investment strategies, investment news, and a game. It appears that online Web-based discussion forums are coming soon.

Highlights

- ◆ 13 steps for "Foolish" investing
- 👍 Fools and Their Money (basic investing)
- ◆ Fool Wire (special reports)
- 👍 IPO Central (about investing in IPOs, with recent offerings)
- ◆ Fool portfolio (updated daily)
- ◆ Dow dividend investing
- ◆ Investing for growth
- 👍 Daily News (markets and economic analysis)
- ◆ Stock research forums (coming soon)
- ◆ Frequently asked questions, with opinionated answers

STB Investor's Stock Selection Guide Combined ★★

http://www.better-investing.org/computer/ssgcomb.html

Here's the home page for a DOS program that automates the NAIC's Stock Selection Guide computations. It's nothing to write home about, interface-wise, but it's a useful piece of software. You can download a free 30-day evaluation version.

Stock Selection Guide Tutorial ★★★★

http://www.investorama.com/features/ssg_00.html

This online version of the National Association of Investor's Corporation's Stock Selection Guide (SSG) is made available by Invest-o-Rama. The NAIC's method is strong on fundamental analysis — that is. the idea that stock price performance can be related to a company's operating performance as reflected in its public data and certain ratios derived from them.

The Companion CD-ROM

What's on the CD-ROM?

The CD-ROM packaged with this book contains a
selection of the finest Internet-savvy software available for investors. In addition, you find a free copy of
Microsoft Internet Explorer 3.0, recently hailed by *PC
Magazine* as the best browser available. For your
convenience, you also find a complete Web version
of the "Internet Investing Directory." Instead of typing the URLs (Web addresses) of the sites you'd like
to visit, just access this disc with Internet Explorer
or Netscape, connect to the Internet, and click on a
site's name.

How to Use the CD-ROM

The CD-ROM included with this book contains an
extensive Web presentation. This presentation features the information you need to install the software
contained on the disc.

If you already have a browser and an Internet connection

To get started, do the following:

1. Place the disc in your computer's CD-ROM
   drive.

2. Log on to the Internet and start your browser.

3. Use your browser's File Open command to locate and open the file `welcome.htm`. This is a Web page that contains links to all the resources on the disc.

If you don't have an Internet connection yet

This disc contains a free, fully functional copy of Microsoft Internet Explorer 3.0. If you have a modem and Windows 95 or Windows NT, you have everything you need to get on the Net. After you install Internet Explorer, click Start→Program→Accessories→Internet Tools→Get on the Internet. You get a wizard that enables you to make contact with the Internet.

To install Internet Explorer, do the following:

1. Place the disc in your computer's CD-ROM drive.

2. Click Start Run, and use the Browse button to open the folder on the CD-ROM disc called msie30.

3. Locate and select the file `msie30m.exe`.

4. Click Open.

5. Double-click OK.

6. Follow the on-screen instructions.

Then refer to preceding instructions, "If you already have a browser and an Internet connection."

The Best Software for Internet-Savvy Investors

Here's a quick introduction to the software on the CD-ROM.

AlphaCONNECT StockVue

Designed for Windows 95 and Windows NT, this sophisticated program uses Microsoft's ActiveX technology to retrieve delayed stock quotes from the Internet automatically — you don't have to subscribe to a fee-based service or do anything manually. For a selected company, you can view news reports, access SEC records, and track recent share price performance. In addition, you can perform a portfolio valuation, set stock price and volume alerts, view an animated ticker tape display, and export data to Quicken. AlphaCONNECT StockVue is a fully functional, 30-day evaluation copy; after the expiration of the 30-day trial period, you can register and receive a key to the full program's features for $39.95.

Capital Gainz for Windows

This stock and fund portfolio manager is especially well suited for investors who use dollar-cost averaging, which isn't well handled by most other programs. In addition, you can record purchases, sales, dividends, capital gains, and splits. You can calculate gain/loss and total return. You can print reports for one or more securities/portfolios over a range of dates that you specify and generate tax forms. This program also generates tax forms. Capital Gainz is shareware and requires a $69 registration fee if you decide to keep using the program after an evaluation period.

Fund Manager

This shareware program can handle stocks as well as funds, but it's especially well suited to managing your mutual funds portfolio. You can generate a variety of reports and graphs, including IRS Schedules B and D. The program can import data from any Web site that generates share prices in Quicken format (such as NETworth). Should you decide to keep using the program after an evaluation period, you must pay the registration fee. The Windows 3.1 version requires a $23 registration fee, while the Windows 95 version requires a $29 registration fee.

Inside Track Lite Internet Edition

Like AlphaCONNECT StockVue, this Windows program enables you to receive stock quotes throughout the day. You are able to track stock indexes as well as your own portfolio. With the Lite edition, you can track up to 100 securities (including bonds), receive an instant portfolio valuation at the click of a button, record splits and dividends easily, and view a wide variety of charts and graphs related to your investments' performance. The program is free, but you need to subscribe to Quote.com's basic subscription service (currently $9.95 per month). The program runs on Windows 3.1 as well as Windows 95 and Windows NT systems.

StockQuest

StockQuest is a full-featured stock screening program that puts professional investment analysis tools at your fingertips. You need a subscription to Market Guide's data sets ($7.95 per download or $19.95 per month). StockQuest is free, and a sample data set is included on the disc.

Please note: Neither the authors nor IDG Books Worldwide possess the resources to provide technical support for the programs included on this CD-ROM. If you are experiencing problems, please contact the companies that publish this software.

Index

Special Characters

* (asterisk) in Usenet newsgroups addresses, 40, 102, 132
+ (plus sign) as inclusion operator, 103
- (minus sign) as exclusion operator, 103
@ (at sign) in e-mail addresses, 32

A

AAII (American Association of Individual Investors), 376, 377, 474
acquisition (transaction) value, 271
Acrobat (Adobe), 205–206
activity ratios for stocks, 270
Address Book feature of e-mail programs, 35
addresses
    for e-mail, 32
    for Usenet newsgroups, 39–40
    of Web sites, 24–25
ADM (Archer Daniels Midland), 302–303
Adobe Acrobat, 205–206
advertising (spamming) on Usenet newsgroups, 40
age considerations for investing, 70, 71
agency bonds, 56, 372
AlphaCONNECT StockVue, on CD accompanying this book, 349, 530
.alt (Usenet newsgroup category), 39
AltaVista (Web search engine), 103, 104, 105–106, 113, 143–144, 201, 284
America Online (AOL)
    costs of, 23
    See also online services
American Association of Individual Investors (AAII), 376, 377, 474

annual reports of publicly held companies (*entries in sequential order*)
    advantages of studying, 283, 284
    finding on Internet, 284–290
    mission statement, 291–292
    CEO letter, 293
    business description, 294
    revenues, profits and bottom line, 294–296
    income statement, 296–297
    management's analysis of operations, 297
    cash flow statement, 297–298
    stockholder's equity, 298
    balance sheet, 298
    book value versus market value, 298–299
anonymity of Internet site visits, 27, 28
anonymous FTP, 42
anti-virus protection, 27
Archie, 42
ARPANET, 16
articles on Usenet newsgroups, 39, 40–41, 136
assets
    allocating, 73–74
    described, 64
    of public companies, 266, 298
    purchasing through loans, 437–438
asterisk (*) in Usenet newsgroup addresses, 40, 102, 132
AT&T Interchange, 18–19
at sign (@) in e-mail addresses, 32
authentication of Internet users, 27
auto purchases
    borrowing for, 237–238, 443–446
    Internet information sources, 399, 400

B

back-end loads on mutual funds, 193
balance sheet in annual reports, 298

(continued)

(continued)

AUTOMATIC STOCK AND FUND TRACKING WITH NO MONTHLY FEES.

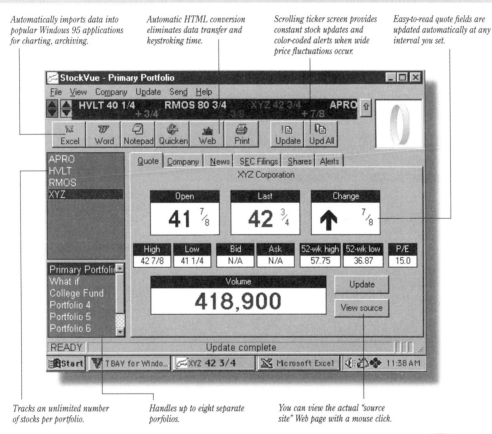

Automatically imports data into popular Windows 95 applications for charting, archiving.

Automatic HTML conversion eliminates data transfer and keystroking time.

Scrolling ticker screen provides constant stock updates and color-coded alerts when wide price fluctuations occur.

Easy-to-read quote fields are updated automatically at any interval you set.

Tracks an unlimited number of stocks per portfolio.

Handles up to eight separate porfolios.

You can view the actual "source site" Web page with a mouse click.

Now your PC can track your stocks and funds all by itself with AlphaCONNECT StockVue™ software. Get quotes, news and SEC filings for multiple portfolios with no monthly service fees to pay. You can also auto-import data into Quicken, Word and Excel to chart performance and better manage your investments.

Reg. Retail Price
$39.95

SAVVY INVESTORS SAVE $5.00

CALL TODAY TOLL FREE 888-226-6398. USE CODE IDG 101.
FOR MORE INFORMATION, CONTACT OUR WEB SITE AT WWW.ALPHACONNECT.COM

ALPHACONNECT STOCKVUE. SOFTWARE THAT AUTOMATICALLY TRACKS STOCKS AND MUTUAL FUNDS VIA THE INTERNET. WITH NO SUBSCRIPTION FEES.

Now get the latest quotes, news and SEC filings on stocks and mutual funds automatically with AlphaCONNECT StockVue.™ StockVue brings you portfolio updates as often as you want — from every 15 minutes to once a day. It automatically calculates your current portfolio value. And you can import quotes, news and filings directly into Quicken, Microsoft Word and Excel so you can chart performance and better manage your investments.

What's more, you pay no monthly subscription fees for access to the financial data unlike many online stock services.

You don't need to be market savvy either. StockVue is a perfect way for both investors and would-be investors to track portfolios and "what if" scenarios. And it's so easy to use, you'll be up and running in no time.

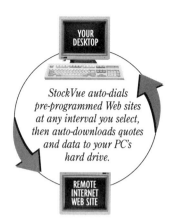

StockVue auto-dials pre-programmed Web sites at any interval you select, then auto-downloads quotes and data to your PC's hard drive.

Track news and SEC filings.
Click on displayed headlines and retrieve company news from the Web, including SEC filings from the EDGAR database.

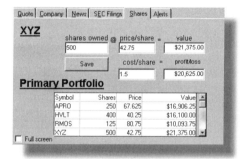

Auto-calculate your own portfolio values.
Automatically calculate the current value and profit or loss for each stock. Track values of personally programmed portfolios.

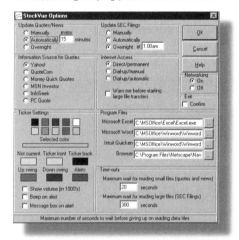

Choose your own update intervals.
You can select any update interval you want—from 15 minutes to overnight. Also choose alert color codes and source sites for your data.

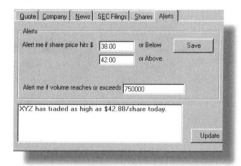

Receive buy and sell alerts.
Set price and volume fluctuation alerts for each stock. Get instant readout of highest or lowest trade.

SYSTEM REQUIREMENTS:

Hardware: *PC with 486/66 or higher microprocessor At least 8MB (16MB recommended) Connection to Internet**

Software: *StockVue is a 32-bit Windows application that runs under commercially-released versions of Windows 95 and Windows NT 3.51 or higher.*

ALPHA MICROSYSTEMS™
2722 South Fairview Street, Santa Ana, California 92704
Phone: (714) 957-8500 • Sales Line: (888) 226-6398 • Fax: (714) 957-8705
E-mail: alphaconnect@alphamicro.com • URL: http://www.alphaconnect.com

IDG Books Worldwide, Inc. End-user License Agreement

3. <u>**Restrictions on Use and Transfer**</u>.

(a) You may only (i) make one copy of the Software for backup or archival purposes, or (ii) transfer the Software to a single hard disk, provided that you keep the original for backup or archival purposes. You may not (i) rent or lease the Software, (ii) copy or reproduce the Software through a LAN or other network system or through any computer subscriber system or bulletin-board system, or (iii) modify, adapt, or create derivative works based on the Software.

(b) You may not reverse engineer, decompile, or disassemble the Software. You may transfer the Software and user documentation on a permanent basis, provided that the transferee agrees to accept the terms and conditions of this Agreement and you retain no copies. If the Software is an update or has been updated, any transfer must include the most recent update and all prior versions.

4. <u>**Restrictions on Use of Individual Programs**</u>. You must follow the individual requirements and restrictions detailed for each individual program in "The Companion CD-ROM" section of this Book. These limitations are contained in the individual license agreements recorded on the disk(s)/CD-ROM. These restrictions may include a requirement that after using the program for the period of time specified in its text, the user must pay a registration fee or discontinue use. By opening the Software packet(s), you will be agreeing to abide by the licenses and restrictions for these individual programs. None of the material on this disk(s) or listed in this Book may ever be distributed, in original or modified form, for commercial purposes.

5. <u>**Limited Warranty**</u>.

(a) IDGB warrants that the Software and disk(s)/CD-ROM are free from defects in materials and workmanship under normal use for a period of sixty (60) days from the date of purchase of this Book. If IDGB receives notification within the warranty period of defects in materials or workmanship, IDGB will replace the defective disk(s)/CD-ROM.

(b) IDGB AND THE AUTHOR OF THE BOOK DISCLAIM ALL OTHER WARRANTIES, EXPRESS OR IMPLIED, INCLUDING WITHOUT LIMITATION IMPLIED WARRANTIES OF MERCHANTABILITY AND FITNESS FOR A PARTICULAR PURPOSE, WITH RESPECT TO THE SOFTWARE, THE PROGRAMS, THE SOURCE CODE CONTAINED THEREIN, AND/OR THE TECHNIQUES DESCRIBED IN THIS BOOK. IDGB DOES NOT WARRANT THAT THE FUNCTIONS CONTAINED IN THE SOFTWARE WILL MEET YOUR REQUIREMENTS OR THAT THE OPERATION OF THE SOFTWARE WILL BE ERROR FREE.

(c) This limited warranty gives you specific legal rights, and you may have other rights which vary from jurisdiction to jurisdiction.

6. <u>Remedies</u>.

(a) IDGB's entire liability and your exclusive remedy for defects in materials and workmanship shall be limited to replacement of the Software, which may be returned to IDGB with a copy of your receipt at the following address: Disk Fulfillment Department, Attn: The Savvy Investor's Internet Resource, IDG Books Worldwide, Inc., 7260 Shadeland Station, Ste. 100, Indianapolis, IN 46256, or call 1-800-762-2974. Please allow 3-4 weeks for delivery. This Limited Warranty is void if failure of the Software has resulted from accident, abuse, or misapplication. Any replacement Software will be warranted for the remainder of the original warranty period or thirty (30) days, whichever is longer.

(b) In no event shall IDGB or the author be liable for any damages whatsoever (including without limitation damages for loss of business profits, business interruption, loss of business information, or any other pecuniary loss) arising from the use of or inability to use the Book or the Software, even if IDGB has been advised of the possibility of such damages.

(c) Because some jurisdictions do not allow the exclusion or limitation of liability for consequential or incidental damages, the above limitation or exclusion may not apply to you.

7. <u>U.S. Government Restricted Rights</u>. Use, duplication, or disclosure of the Software by the U.S. Government is subject to restrictions stated in paragraph (c) (1) (ii) of the Rights in Technical Data and Computer Software clause of DFARS 252.227-7013, and in subparagraphs (a) through (d) of the Commercial Computer—Restricted Rights clause at FAR 52.227-19, and in similar clauses in the NASA FAR supplement, when applicable.

8. <u>General</u>. This Agreement constitutes the entire understanding of the parties and revokes and supersedes all prior agreements, oral or written, between them and may not be modified or amended except in a writing signed by both parties hereto which specifically refers to this Agreement. This Agreement shall take precedence over any other documents that may be in conflict herewith. If any one or more provisions contained in this Agreement are held by any court or tribunal to be invalid, illegal, or otherwise unenforceable, each and every other provision shall remain in full force and effect.

CD-ROM Installation Instructions

To access the disc's resources and learn more about installing and using the software included on the disc, place the disc in your CD-ROM drive, start your browser, and use your browser's File Open command to open `welcome.htm`. That's the opening page of a Web presentation that fully explores the disc's resources.

If you don't have a browser or Internet connection, see "The Companion CD-ROM" appendix for more information. The appendix also introduces the software on the CD-ROM.

IDG BOOKS WORLDWIDE REGISTRATION CARD

RETURN THIS REGISTRATION CARD FOR FREE CATALOG

Title of this book: The Savvy Investor's Internet Resource

My overall rating of this book: ❑ Very good [1] ❑ Good [2] ❑ Satisfactory [3] ❑ Fair [4] ❑ Poor [5]

How I first heard about this book:

❑ Found in bookstore; name: [6] _____

❑ Advertisement: [8] _____

❑ Word of mouth; heard about book from friend, co-worker, etc.: [10]

❑ Book review: [7] _____

❑ Catalog: [9]

❑ Other: [11]

What I liked most about this book:

_____

_____

What I would change, add, delete, etc., in future editions of this book:

_____

_____

Other comments: _____

_____

Number of computer books I purchase in a year: ❑ 1 [12] ❑ 2-5 [13] ❑ 6-10 [14] ❑ More than 10 [15]

I would characterize my computer skills as: ❑ Beginner [16] ❑ Intermediate [17] ❑ Advanced [18] ❑ Professional [19]

I use ❑ DOS [20] ❑ Windows [21] ❑ OS/2 [22] ❑ Unix [23] ❑ Macintosh [24] ❑ Other: [25]_____
(please specify)

I would be interested in new books on the following subjects:
(please check all that apply, and use the spaces provided to identify specific software)

❑ Word processing: [26] _____

❑ Data bases: [28] _____

❑ File Utilities: [30] _____

❑ Networking: [32] _____

❑ Other: [34]

❑ Spreadsheets: [27] _____

❑ Desktop publishing: [29] _____

❑ Money management: [31] _____

❑ Programming languages: [33] _____

I use a PC at (please check all that apply): ❑ home [35] ❑ work [36] ❑ school [37] ❑ other: [38] _____

The disks I prefer to use are ❑ 5.25 [39] ❑ 3.5 [40] ❑ other: [41]_____

I have a CD ROM: ❑ yes [42] ❑ no [43]

I plan to buy or upgrade computer hardware this year: ❑ yes [44] ❑ no [45]

I plan to buy or upgrade computer software this year: ❑ yes [46] ❑ no [47]

Name: _____ Business title: [48] _____ Type of Business: [49] _____

Address (❑ home [50] ❑ work [51]/Company name: _____)

Street/Suite# _____

City [52]/State [53]/Zipcode [54]: _____ Country [55] _____

❑ **I liked this book!** You may quote me by name in future
IDG Books Worldwide promotional materials.

My daytime phone number is _____

IDG BOOKS

THE WORLD OF
COMPUTER
KNOWLEDGE

 ## YES!

Please keep me informed about IDG's World of Computer Knowledge.
Send me the latest IDG Books catalog.